Linux Kernel Development

Third Edition

Developer's Library

ESSENTIAL REFERENCES FOR PROGRAMMING PROFESSIONALS

Developer's Library books are designed to provide practicing programmers with unique, high-quality references and tutorials on the programming languages and technologies they use in their daily work.

All books in the *Developer's Library* are written by expert technology practitioners who are especially skilled at organizing and presenting information in a way that's useful for other programmers.

Key titles include some of the best, most widely acclaimed books within their topic areas:

PHP & MySQL Web Development
Luke Welling & Laura Thomson
ISBN 978-0-672-32916-6

MySQL
Paul DuBois
ISBN-13: 978-0-672-32938-8

Linux Kernel Development
Robert Love
ISBN-13: 978-0-672-32946-3

Python Essential Reference
David Beazley
ISBN-13: 978-0-672-32978-6

Programming in Objective-C 2.0
Stephen G. Kochan
ISBN-13: 978-0-321-56615-7

PostgreSQL
Korry Douglas
ISBN-13: 978-0-672-33015-5

Developer's Library books are available at most retail and online bookstores, as well as by subscription from Safari Books Online at **safari.informit.com**

**Developer's
Library**
informit.com/devlibrary

Linux Kernel Development

Third Edition

Robert Love

♦♦Addison-Wesley

Upper Saddle River, NJ • Boston • Indianapolis • San Francisco
New York • Toronto • Montreal • London • Munich • Paris • Madrid
Cape Town • Sydney • Tokyo • Singapore • Mexico City

Linux Kernel Development

Third Edition

Copyright © 2010 Pearson Education, Inc.

ISBN-13: 978-0-672-32946-3
ISBN-10: 0-672-32946-8

Library of Congress Cataloging-in-Publication Data:

Love, Robert.

Linux kernel development / Robert Love. — 3rd ed.

p. cm.

Includes bibliographical references and index.

ISBN 978-0-672-32946-3 (pbk. : alk. paper) 1. Linux. 2. Operating systems (Computers) I. Title.

QA76.76.O63L674 2010

005.4'32—dc22

2010018961

Text printed in the United States on recycled paper at RR Donnelley, Crawfordsville, Indiana. Third Printing: June 2011

The publisher offers excellent discounts on this book when ordered in quantity for bulk purchases or special sales, which may include electronic versions and/or custom covers and content particular to your business, training goals, marketing focus, and branding interests. For more information, please contact:

U.S. Corporate and Government Sales
(800) 382-3419
corpsales@pearsontechgroup.com

For sales outside the United States please contact:

International Sales
international@pearson.com

Visit us on the Web: informit.com/aw

Acquisitions Editor
Mark Taber

Development Editor
Michael Thurston

Technical Editor
Robert P. J. Day

Managing Editor
Sandra Schroeder

Senior Project Editor
Tonya Simpson

Copy Editor
Apostrophe Editing Services

Indexer
Brad Herriman

Proofreader
Debbie Williams

Publishing Coordinator
Vanessa Evans

Book Designer
Gary Adair

Compositor
Mark Shirar

❖

For Doris and Helen.

❖

Contents at a Glance

Table of Contents

xiv   Contents

Foreword

As the Linux kernel and the applications that use it become more widely used, we are seeing an increasing number of system software developers who wish to become involved in the development and maintenance of Linux. Some of these engineers are motivated purely by personal interest, some work for Linux companies, some work for hardware manufacturers, and some are involved with in-house development projects.

But all face a common problem: The learning curve for the kernel is getting longer and steeper. The system is becoming increasingly complex, and it is very large. And as the years pass, the current members of the kernel development team gain deeper and broader knowledge of the kernel's internals, which widens the gap between them and newcomers.

I believe that this declining accessibility of the Linux source base is already a problem for the quality of the kernel, and it will become more serious over time. Those who care for Linux clearly have an interest in increasing the number of developers who can contribute to the kernel.

One approach to this problem is to keep the code clean: sensible interfaces, consistent layout, "do one thing, do it well," and so on. This is Linus Torvalds' solution.

The approach that I counsel is to liberally apply commentary to the code: words that the reader can use to understand what the coder intended to achieve at the time. (The process of identifying divergences between the intent and the implementation is known as debugging. It is hard to do this if the intent is not known.)

But even code commentary does not provide the broad-sweep view of what a major subsystem is intended to do, and of how its developers set about doing it. This, the starting point of understanding, is what the written word serves best.

Robert Love's contribution provides a means by which experienced developers can gain that essential view of what services the kernel subsystems are supposed to provide, and of how they set about providing them. This will be sufficient knowledge for many people: the curious, the application developers, those who wish to evaluate the kernel's design, and others.

But the book is also a stepping stone to take aspiring kernel developers to the next stage, which is making alterations to the kernel to achieve some defined objective. I would encourage aspiring developers to get their hands dirty: The best way to understand a part of the kernel is to make changes to it. Making a change forces the developer to a level of understanding which merely reading the code does not provide. The serious kernel developer will join the development mailing lists and will interact with other developers. This interaction is the primary means by which kernel contributors learn and stay abreast. Robert covers the mechanics and culture of this important part of kernel life well.

Please enjoy and learn from Robert's book. And should you decide to take the next step and become a member of the kernel development community, consider yourself welcomed in advance. We value and measure people by the usefulness of their contributions, and when you contribute to Linux, you do so in the knowledge that your work is of small but immediate benefit to tens or even hundreds of millions of human beings. This is a most enjoyable privilege and responsibility.

Andrew Morton

Preface

When I was first approached about converting my experiences with the Linux kernel into a book, I proceeded with trepidation. What would place my book at the top of its subject? I was not interested unless I could do something special, a best-in-class work.

I realized that I could offer a unique approach to the topic. My job is hacking the kernel. My hobby is hacking the kernel. My love is hacking the kernel. Over the years, I have accumulated interesting anecdotes and insider tips. With my experiences, I could write a book on how to hack the kernel and—just as important—how *not* to hack the kernel. First and foremost, this is a book about the design and implementation of the Linux kernel. This book's approach differs from would-be competitors, however, in that the information is given with a slant to learning enough to actually get work done—and getting it done right. I am a pragmatic engineer and this is a practical book. It should be fun, easy to read, and useful.

I hope that readers can walk away from this work with a better understanding of the rules (written and unwritten) of the Linux kernel. I intend that you, fresh from reading this book and the kernel source code, can jump in and start writing useful, correct, clean kernel code. Of course, you can read this book just for fun, too.

That was the first edition. Time has passed, and now we return once more to the fray. This third edition offers quite a bit over the first and second: intense polish and revision, updates, and many fresh sections and all new chapters. This edition incorporates changes in the kernel since the second edition. More important, however, is the decision made by the Linux kernel community to not proceed with a 2.7 development kernel in the near to mid-term.[1] Instead, kernel developers plan to continue developing and stabilizing the 2.6 series. This decision has many implications, but the item of relevance to this book is that there is quite a bit of staying power in a contemporary book on the 2.6 Linux kernel. As the Linux kernel matures, there is a greater chance of a snapshot of the kernel remaining representative long into the future. This book functions as the canonical documentation for the kernel, documenting it with both an understanding of its history and an eye to the future.

Using This Book

Developing code in the kernel does not require genius, magic, or a bushy Unix-hacker beard. The kernel, although having some interesting rules of its own, is not much different from any other large software endeavor. You need to master many details—as with any big project—but the differences are quantitative, not qualitative.

---

[1] *This decision was made in the summer of 2004 at the annual Linux Kernel Developers Summit in Ottawa, Canada. Your author was an invited attendee.*

It is imperative that you utilize the source. The open availability of the source code for the Linux system is a rare gift that you must not take for granted. It is not sufficient *only* to read the source, however. You need to dig in and change some code. Find a bug and fix it. Improve the drivers for your hardware. Add some new functionality, even if it is trivial. Find an itch and scratch it! Only when you *write* code will it all come together.

Kernel Version

This book is based on the 2.6 Linux kernel series. It does not cover older kernels, except for historical relevance. We discuss, for example, how certain subsystems are implemented in the 2.4 Linux kernel series, as their simpler implementations are helpful teaching aids. Specifically, this book is up to date as of Linux kernel version 2.6.34. Although the kernel is a moving target and no effort can hope to capture such a dynamic beast in a timeless manner, my intention is that this book is relevant for developers and users of both older and newer kernels.

Although this book discusses the 2.6.34 kernel, I have made an effort to ensure the material is factually correct with respect to the 2.6.32 kernel as well. That latter version is sanctioned as the "enterprise" kernel by the various Linux distributions, ensuring we will continue to see it in production systems and under active development for many years. (2.6.9, 2.6.18, and 2.6.27 were similar "long-term" releases.)

Audience

This book targets Linux developers and users who are interested in understanding the Linux kernel. It is *not* a line-by-line commentary of the kernel source. Nor is it a guide to developing drivers or a reference on the kernel API. Instead, the goal of this book is to provide enough information on the design and implementation of the Linux kernel that a sufficiently accomplished programmer can begin developing code in the kernel. Kernel development can be fun and rewarding, and I want to introduce the reader to that world as readily as possible. This book, however, in discussing both theory and application, should appeal to readers of both academic and practical persuasions. I have always been of the mind that one needs to understand the theory to understand the application, but I try to balance the two in this work. I hope that whatever your motivations for understanding the Linux kernel, this book explains the design and implementation sufficiently for your needs.

Thus, this book covers both the usage of core kernel systems and their design and implementation. I think this is important and deserves a moment's discussion. A good example is Chapter 8, "Bottom Halves and Deferring Work," which covers a component of device drivers called bottom halves. In that chapter, I discuss both the design and implementation of the kernel's bottom-half mechanisms (which a core kernel developer or academic might find interesting) and how to actually use the exported interfaces to implement your own bottom half (which a device driver developer or casual hacker can find pertinent). I believe all groups can find both discussions relevant. The core kernel developer, who certainly needs to understand the inner workings of the kernel, should have a good understanding of how the interfaces are actually used. At the same time, a device driver writer can benefit from a good understanding of the implementation behind the interface.

This is akin to learning some library's API versus studying the actual implementation of the library. At first glance, an application programmer needs to understand only the API—it is often taught to treat interfaces as a black box. Likewise, a library developer is concerned only with the library's design and implementation. I believe, however, both parties should invest time in learning the other half. An application programmer who better understands the underlying operating system can make much greater use of it. Similarly, the library developer should not grow out of touch with the reality and practicality of the applications that use the library. Consequently, I discuss both the design and usage of kernel subsystems, not only in hopes that this book will be useful to either party, but also in hopes that the *whole* book is useful to both parties.

I assume that the reader knows the C programming language and is familiar with Linux systems. Some experience with operating system design and related computer science topics is beneficial, but I try to explain concepts as much as possible—if not, the Bibliography includes some excellent books on operating system design.

This book is appropriate for an undergraduate course introducing operating system design as the *applied* text if accompanied by an introductory book on theory. This book should fare well either in an advanced undergraduate course or in a graduate-level course without ancillary material.

Third Edition Acknowledgments

Like most authors, I did not write this book in a cave, which is a good thing, because there are bears in caves. Consequently many hearts and minds contributed to the completion of this manuscript. Although no list could be complete, it is my sincere pleasure to acknowledge the assistance of many friends and colleagues who provided encouragement, knowledge, and constructive criticism.

First, I would like to thank my team at Addison–Wesley and Pearson who worked long and hard to make this a better book, particularly Mark Taber for spearheading this third edition from conception to final product; Michael Thurston, development editor; and Tonya Simpson, project editor.

A special thanks to my technical editor on this edition, Robert P. J. Day. His insight, experience, and corrections improved this book immeasurably. Despite his sterling effort, however, any remaining mistakes remain my own. I have the same gratitude to Adam Belay, Zack Brown, Martin Pool, and Chris Rivera, whose excellent technical editing efforts on the first and second editions still shine through.

Many fellow kernel developers answered questions, provided support, or simply wrote code interesting enough on which to write a book. They include Andrea Arcangeli, Alan Cox, Greg Kroah-Hartman, Dave Miller, Patrick Mochel, Andrew Morton, Nick Piggin, and Linus Torvalds.

A big thank you to my colleagues at Google, the most creative and intelligent group with which I have ever had the pleasure to work. Too many names would fill these pages if I listed them all, but I will single out Alan Blount, Jay Crim, Chris Danis, Chris DiBona, Eric Flatt, Mike Lockwood, San Mehat, Brian Rogan, Brian Swetland, Jon Trowbridge, and Steve Vinter for their friendship, knowledge, and support.

Respect and love to Paul Amici, Mikey Babbitt, Keith Barbag, Jacob Berkman, Nat Friedman, Dustin Hall, Joyce Hawkins, Miguel de Icaza, Jimmy Krehl, Doris Love, Linda Love, Brette Luck, Randy O'Dowd, Sal Ribaudo and mother, Chris Rivera, Carolyn Rodon, Joey Shaw, Sarah Stewart, Jeremy VanDoren and family, Luis Villa, Steve Weisberg and family, and Helen Whisnant.

Finally, thank you to my parents for so much, particularly my well-proportioned ears. Happy Hacking!

Robert Love
Boston

About the Author

Robert Love is an open source programmer, speaker, and author who has been using and contributing to Linux for more than 15 years. Robert is currently senior software engineer at Google, where he was a member of the team that developed the Android mobile platform's kernel. Prior to Google, he was Chief Architect, Linux Desktop, at Novell. Before Novell, he was a kernel engineer at MontaVista Software and Ximian.

Robert's kernel projects include the preemptive kernel, the process scheduler, the kernel events layer, inotify, VM enhancements, and several device drivers.

Robert has given numerous talks on and has written multiple articles about the Linux kernel. He is a contributing editor for *Linux Journal*. His other books include *Linux System Programming* and *Linux in a Nutshell*.

Robert received a B.A. degree in mathematics and a B.S. degree in computer science from the University of Florida. He lives in Boston.

1

Introduction to
the Linux Kernel

This chapter introduces the Linux kernel and Linux operating system, placing them in the historical context of Unix. Today, Unix is a family of operating systems implementing a similar application programming interface (API) and built around shared design decisions. But Unix is also a specific operating system, first built more than 40 years ago. To understand Linux, we must first discuss the first Unix system.

History of Unix

After four decades of use, computer scientists continue to regard the Unix operating system as one of the most powerful and elegant systems in existence. Since the creation of Unix in 1969, the brainchild of Dennis Ritchie and Ken Thompson has become a creature of legends, a system whose design has withstood the test of time with few bruises to its name.

Unix grew out of Multics, a failed multiuser operating system project in which Bell Laboratories was involved. With the Multics project terminated, members of Bell Laboratories' Computer Sciences Research Center found themselves without a capable interactive operating system. In the summer of 1969, Bell Lab programmers sketched out a filesystem design that ultimately evolved into Unix. Testing its design, Thompson implemented the new system on an otherwise-idle PDP-7. In 1971, Unix was ported to the PDP-11, and in 1973, the operating system was rewritten in C—an unprecedented step at the time, but one that paved the way for future portability. The first Unix widely used outside Bell Labs was Unix System, Sixth Edition, more commonly called V6.

Other companies ported Unix to new machines. Accompanying these ports were enhancements that resulted in several variants of the operating system. In 1977, Bell Labs released a combination of these variants into a single system, Unix System III; in 1982, AT&T released System V.[1]

---

[1] What about System IV? It was an internal development version.

The simplicity of Unix's design, coupled with the fact that it was distributed with source code, led to further development at external organizations. The most influential of these contributors was the University of California at Berkeley. Variants of Unix from Berkeley are known as Berkeley Software Distributions, or *BSD*. Berkeley's first release, 1BSD in 1977, was a collection of patches and additional software on top of Bell Labs' Unix. 2BSD in 1978 continued this trend, adding the csh and vi utilities, which persist on Unix systems to this day. The first standalone Berkeley Unix was 3BSD in 1979. It added virtual memory (VM) to an already impressive list of features. A series of 4BSD releases, 4.0BSD, 4.1BSD, 4.2BSD, 4.3BSD, followed 3BSD. These versions of Unix added job control, demand paging, and TCP/IP. In 1994, the university released the final official Berkeley Unix, featuring a rewritten VM subsystem, as 4.4BSD. Today, thanks to BSD's permissive license, development of BSD continues with the Darwin, FreeBSD, NetBSD, and OpenBSD systems.

In the 1980s and 1990s, multiple workstation and server companies introduced their own commercial versions of Unix. These systems were based on either an AT&T or a Berkeley release and supported high-end features developed for their particular hardware architecture. Among these systems were Digital's Tru64, Hewlett Packard's HP-UX, IBM's AIX, Sequent's DYNIX/ptx, SGI's IRIX, and Sun's Solaris & SunOS.

The original elegant design of the Unix system, along with the years of innovation and evolutionary improvement that followed, has resulted in a powerful, robust, and stable operating system. A handful of characteristics of Unix are at the core of its strength. First, Unix is simple: Whereas some operating systems implement thousands of system calls and have unclear design goals, Unix systems implement only hundreds of system calls and have a straightforward, even basic, design. Second, in Unix, *everything is a file*.[2] This simplifies the manipulation of data and devices into a set of core system calls: open(), read(), write(), lseek(), and close(). Third, the Unix kernel and related system utilities are written in C—a property that gives Unix its amazing portability to diverse hardware architectures and accessibility to a wide range of developers. Fourth, Unix has fast process creation time and the unique fork() system call. Finally, Unix provides simple yet robust interprocess communication (IPC) primitives that, when coupled with the fast process creation time, enable the creation of simple programs that *do one thing and do it well*. These single-purpose programs can be strung together to accomplish tasks of increasing complexity. Unix systems thus exhibit clean layering, with a strong separation between policy and mechanism.

Today, Unix is a modern operating system supporting preemptive multitasking, multi-threading, virtual memory, demand paging, shared libraries with demand loading, and

---

[2] *Well, okay, not everything—but much is represented as a file. Sockets are a notable exception. Some recent efforts, such as Unix's successor at Bell Labs, Plan9, implement nearly all aspects of the system as a file.*

TCP/IP networking. Many Unix variants scale to hundreds of processors, whereas other Unix systems run on small, embedded devices. Although Unix is no longer a research project, Unix systems continue to benefit from advances in operating system design while remaining a practical and general-purpose operating system.

Unix owes its success to the simplicity and elegance of its design. Its strength today derives from the inaugural decisions that Dennis Ritchie, Ken Thompson, and other early developers made: choices that have endowed Unix with the capability to evolve without compromising itself.

Along Came Linus: Introduction to Linux

Linus Torvalds developed the first version of Linux in 1991 as an operating system for computers powered by the Intel 80386 microprocessor, which at the time was a new and advanced processor. Linus, then a student at the University of Helsinki, was perturbed by the lack of a powerful yet free Unix system. The reigning personal computer OS of the day, Microsoft's DOS, was useful to Torvalds for little other than playing *Prince of Persia*. Linus did use Minix, a low-cost Unix created as a teaching aid, but he was discouraged by the inability to easily make and distribute changes to the system's source code (because of Minix's license) and by design decisions made by Minix's author.

In response to his predicament, Linus did what any normal college student would do: He decided to write his own operating system. Linus began by writing a simple terminal emulator, which he used to connect to larger Unix systems at his school. Over the course of the academic year, his terminal emulator evolved and improved. Before long, Linus had an immature but full-fledged Unix on his hands. He posted an early release to the Internet in late 1991.

Use of Linux took off, with early Linux distributions quickly gaining many users. More important to its initial success, however, is that Linux quickly attracted many developers—hackers adding, changing, improving code. Because of the terms of its license, Linux swiftly evolved into a collaborative project developed by many.

Fast forward to the present. Today, Linux is a full-fledged operating system also running on Alpha, ARM, PowerPC, SPARC, x86-64 and many other architectures. It runs on systems as small as a watch to machines as large as room-filling super-computer clusters. Linux powers the smallest consumer electronics and the largest Datacenters. Today, commercial interest in Linux is strong. Both new Linux-specific corporations, such as Red Hat, and existing powerhouses, such as IBM, are providing Linux-based solutions for embedded, mobile, desktop, and server needs.

Linux is a Unix-like system, but it is not Unix. That is, although Linux borrows many ideas from Unix and implements the Unix API (as defined by POSIX and the Single Unix Specification), it is not a direct descendant of the Unix source code like other Unix systems. Where desired, it has deviated from the path taken by other implementations, but it has not forsaken the general design goals of Unix or broken standardized application interfaces.

One of Linux's most interesting features is that it is not a commercial product; instead, it is a collaborative project developed over the Internet. Although Linus remains the creator of Linux and the *maintainer* of the kernel, progress continues through a loose-knit group of developers. Anyone can contribute to Linux. The Linux kernel, as with much of the system, is *free* or *open source* software.[3] Specifically, the Linux kernel is licensed under the GNU General Public License (GPL) version 2.0. Consequently, you are free to download the source code and make any modifications you want. The only caveat is that if you distribute your changes, you must continue to provide the recipients with the same rights you enjoyed, including the availability of the source code.[4]

Linux is many things to many people. The basics of a Linux system are the kernel, C library, toolchain, and basic system utilities, such as a login process and shell. A Linux system can also include a modern X Window System implementation including a full-featured desktop environment, such as GNOME. Thousands of free and commercial applications exist for Linux. In this book, when I say *Linux* I typically mean the *Linux kernel*. Where it is ambiguous, I try explicitly to point out whether I am referring to *Linux* as a full system or just the kernel proper. Strictly speaking, the term *Linux* refers only to the kernel.

Overview of Operating Systems and Kernels

Because of the ever-growing feature set and ill design of some modern commercial operating systems, the notion of what precisely defines an operating system is not universal. Many users consider whatever they see on the screen to be the operating system. Technically speaking, and in this book, the *operating system* is considered the parts of the system responsible for basic use and administration. This includes the kernel and device drivers, boot loader, command shell or other user interface, and basic file and system utilities. It is the stuff you *need*—not a web browser or music players. The term *system*, in turn, refers to the operating system and all the applications running on top of it.

Of course, the topic of this book is the *kernel*. Whereas the user interface is the outermost portion of the operating system, the kernel is the innermost. It is the core internals; the software that provides basic services for all other parts of the system, manages hardware, and distributes system resources. The kernel is sometimes referred to as the *supervisor*, *core*, or *internals* of the operating system. Typical components of a kernel are interrupt handlers to service interrupt requests, a scheduler to share processor time among multiple processes, a memory management system to manage process address spaces, and system services such as networking and interprocess communication. On

---

[3] I will leave the free versus open debate to you. See http://www.fsf.org and http://www.opensource. org.

[4] You should read the GNU GPL version 2.0. There is a copy in the file COPYING in your kernel source tree. You can also find it online at http://www.fsf.org. Note that the latest version of the GNU GPL is version 3.0; the kernel developers have decided to remain with version 2.0.

modern systems with protected memory management units, the kernel typically resides in an elevated system state compared to normal user applications. This includes a protected memory space and full access to the hardware. This system state and memory space is collectively referred to as *kernel-space*. Conversely, user applications execute in *user-space*. They see a subset of the machine's available resources and can perform certain system functions, directly access hardware, access memory outside of that allotted them by the kernel, or otherwise misbehave. When executing kernel code, the system is in kernel-space executing in kernel mode. When running a regular process, the system is in user-space executing in user mode.

Applications running on the system communicate with the kernel via *system calls* (see Figure 1.1). An application typically calls functions in a library—for example, the *C library*—that in turn rely on the system call interface to instruct the kernel to carry out tasks on the application's behalf. Some library calls provide many features not found in the system call, and thus, calling into the kernel is just one step in an otherwise large function. For example, consider the familiar `printf()` function. It provides formatting and buffering of the data; only one step in its work is invoking `write()` to write the data to the console. Conversely, some library calls have a one-to-one relationship with the kernel. For example, the `open()` library function does little except call the `open()` system call. Still other C library functions, such as `strcpy()`, should (one hopes) make no direct use of the kernel at all. When an application executes a system call, we say that the *kernel is executing on behalf of the application*. Furthermore, the application is said to be *executing a system call in kernel-space,* and the kernel is running in *process context*. This relationship— that applications *call into* the kernel via the system call interface—is the fundamental manner in which applications get work done.

The kernel also manages the system's hardware. Nearly all architectures, including all systems that Linux supports, provide the concept of *interrupts*. When hardware wants to communicate with the system, it issues an interrupt that literally interrupts the processor, which in turn interrupts the kernel. A number identifies interrupts and the kernel uses this number to execute a specific *interrupt handler* to process and respond to the interrupt. For example, as you type, the keyboard controller issues an interrupt to let the system know that there is new data in the keyboard buffer. The kernel notes the interrupt number of the incoming interrupt and executes the correct interrupt handler. The interrupt handler processes the keyboard data and lets the keyboard controller know it is ready for more data. To provide synchronization, the kernel can disable interrupts—either all interrupts or just one specific interrupt number. In many operating systems, including Linux, the interrupt handlers do not run in a process context. Instead, they run in a special *interrupt context* that is not associated with any process. This special context exists solely to let an interrupt handler quickly respond to an interrupt, and then exit.

These contexts represent the breadth of the kernel's activities. In fact, in Linux, we can generalize that each processor is doing exactly one of three things at any given moment:

- In user-space, executing user code in a process
- In kernel-space, in process context, executing on behalf of a specific process

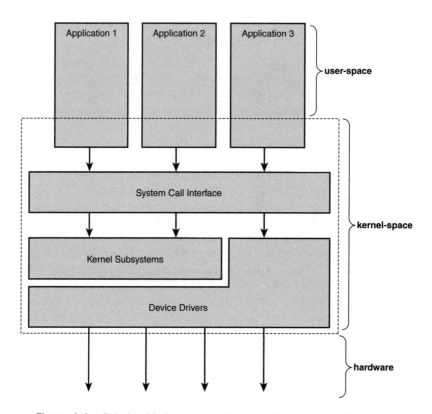

Figure 1.1   Relationship between applications, the kernel, and hardware.

- In kernel–space, in interrupt context, not associated with a process, handling an interrupt

This list is inclusive. Even corner cases fit into one of these three activities: For example, when idle, it turns out that the kernel is executing an *idle process* in process context in the kernel.

Linux Versus Classic Unix Kernels

Owing to their common ancestry and same API, modern Unix kernels share various design traits. (See the Bibliography for my favorite books on the design of the classic Unix kernels.) With few exceptions, a Unix kernel is typically a monolithic static binary. That is, it exists as a single, large, executable image that runs in a single address space. Unix systems typically require a system with a paged memory-management unit (MMU); this hardware enables the system to enforce memory protection and to provide a unique virtual address space to each process. Linux historically has required an MMU, but special versions can actually run without one. This is a neat feature, enabling Linux to run on very small MMU-less embedded systems, but otherwise more academic than practical—even simple embedded systems nowadays tend to have advanced features such as memory-management units. In this book, we focus on MMU-based systems.

Monolithic Kernel Versus Microkernel Designs

We can divide kernels into two main schools of design: the monolithic kernel and the microkernel. (A third camp, exokernel, is found primarily in research systems.)

Monolithic kernels are the simpler design of the two, and all kernels were designed in this manner until the 1980s. Monolithic kernels are implemented entirely as a single process running in a single address space. Consequently, such kernels typically exist on disk as single static binaries. All kernel services exist and execute in the large kernel address space. Communication within the kernel is trivial because everything runs in kernel mode in the same address space: The kernel can invoke functions directly, as a user-space application might. Proponents of this model cite the simplicity and performance of the monolithic approach. Most Unix systems are monolithic in design.

Microkernels, on the other hand, are not implemented as a single large process. Instead, the functionality of the kernel is broken down into separate processes, usually called *servers*. Ideally, only the servers *absolutely* requiring such capabilities run in a privileged execution mode. The rest of the servers run in user-space. All the servers, though, are separated into different address spaces. Therefore, direct function invocation as in monolithic kernels is not possible. Instead, microkernels communicate via *message passing*: An interprocess communication (IPC) mechanism is built into the system, and the various servers communicate with and invoke "services" from each other by sending messages over the IPC mechanism. The separation of the various servers prevents a failure in one server from bringing down another. Likewise, the modularity of the system enables one server to be swapped out for another.

Because the IPC mechanism involves quite a bit more overhead than a trivial function call, however, and because a context switch from kernel-space to user-space or vice versa is often involved, message passing includes a latency and throughput hit not seen on monolithic kernels with simple function invocation. Consequently, all practical microkernel-based systems now place most or all the servers in kernel-space, to remove the overhead of frequent context switches and potentially enable direct function invocation. The Windows NT kernel (on which Windows XP, Vista, and 7 are based) and Mach (on which part of Mac OS X is based) are examples of microkernels. Neither Windows NT nor Mac OS X run any microkernel servers in user-space in their latest iteration, defeating the primary purpose of microkernel design altogether.

Linux is a monolithic kernel; that is, the Linux kernel executes in a single address space entirely in kernel mode. Linux, however, borrows much of the good from microkernels: Linux boasts a modular design, the capability to preempt itself (called *kernel preemption*), support for kernel threads, and the capability to dynamically load separate binaries (kernel modules) into the kernel image. Conversely, Linux has none of the performance-sapping features that curse microkernel design: Everything runs in kernel mode, with direct function invocation—not message passing—the modus of communication. Nonetheless, Linux is modular, threaded, and the kernel itself is schedulable. Pragmatism wins again.

As Linus and other kernel developers contribute to the Linux kernel, they decide how best to advance Linux without neglecting its Unix roots (and, more important, the Unix API). Consequently, because Linux is not based on any specific Unix variant, Linus and company can pick and choose the best solution to any given problem—or at times, invent new solutions! A handful of notable differences exist between the Linux kernel and classic Unix systems:

- Linux supports the dynamic loading of kernel modules. Although the Linux kernel is monolithic, it can dynamically load and unload kernel code on demand.
- Linux has symmetrical multiprocessor (SMP) support. Although most commercial variants of Unix now support SMP, most traditional Unix implementations did not.
- The Linux kernel is preemptive. Unlike traditional Unix variants, the Linux kernel can preempt a task even as it executes in the kernel. Of the other commercial Unix implementations, Solaris and IRIX have preemptive kernels, but most Unix kernels are not preemptive.
- Linux takes an interesting approach to thread support: It does not differentiate between threads and normal processes. To the kernel, all processes are the same— some just happen to share resources.
- Linux provides an object-oriented device model with device classes, hot-pluggable events, and a user-space device filesystem (sysfs).
- Linux ignores some common Unix features that the kernel developers consider poorly designed, such as STREAMS, or standards that are impossible to cleanly implement.
- Linux is free in every sense of the word. The feature set Linux implements is the result of the freedom of Linux's open development model. If a feature is without merit or poorly thought out, Linux developers are under no obligation to imple- ment it. To the contrary, Linux has adopted an elitist attitude toward changes: Mod- ifications must solve a specific real-world problem, derive from a clean design, and have a solid implementation. Consequently, features of some other modern Unix variants that are more marketing bullet or one-off requests, such as pageable kernel memory, have received no consideration.

Despite these differences, however, Linux remains an operating system with a strong Unix heritage.

Linux Kernel Versions

Linux kernels come in two flavors: stable and development. Stable kernels are production- level releases suitable for widespread deployment. New stable kernel versions are released typically only to provide bug fixes or new drivers. Development kernels, on the other hand, undergo rapid change where (almost) anything goes. As developers experiment with new solutions, the kernel code base changes in often drastic ways.

Linux kernels distinguish between stable and development kernels with a simple naming scheme (see Figure 1.2). Three or four numbers, delineated with a dot, represent Linux kernel versions. The first value is the major release, the second is the minor release, and the third is the revision. An optional fourth value is the stable version. The minor release also determines whether the kernel is a stable or development kernel; an even number is stable, whereas an odd number is development. For example, the kernel version 2.6.30.1 designates a stable kernel. This kernel has a major version of two, a minor version of six, a revision of 30, and a stable version of one. The first two values describe the "kernel series"—in this case, the 2.6 kernel series.

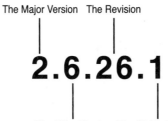

Figure 1.2   Kernel version naming convention.

Development kernels have a series of phases. Initially, the kernel developers work on new features and chaos ensues. Over time, the kernel matures and eventually a feature freeze is declared. At that point, Linus will not accept new features. Work on existing features, however, can continue. After Linus considers the kernel nearly stabilized, a code freeze is put into effect. When that occurs, only bug fixes are accepted. Shortly thereafter (hopefully), Linus releases the first version of a new stable series. For example, the development series 1.3 stabilized into 2.0 and 2.5 stabilized into 2.6.

Within a given series, Linus releases new kernels regularly, with each version earning a new revision. For example, the first version of the 2.6 kernel series was 2.6.0. The next was 2.6.1. These revisions contain bug fixes, new drivers, and new features, but the difference between two revisions—say, 2.6.3 and 2.6.4—is minor.

This is how development progressed until 2004, when at the invite-only Kernel Developers Summit, the assembled kernel developers decided to prolong the 2.6 kernel series and postpone the introduction of a 2.7 development series. The rationale was that the 2.6 kernel was well received, stable, and sufficiently mature such that new destabilizing features were unneeded. This course has proven wise, as the ensuing years have shown 2.6 is a mature and capable beast. As of this writing, a 2.7 development series is not on the table and seems unlikely. Instead, the development cycle of each 2.6 revision has grown longer, each release incorporating a mini-development series. Andrew Morton, Linus's second-in-command, has repurposed his 2.6-mm tree—once a testing ground for memory management-related changes—into a general-purpose test bed. Destabilizing changes thus flow into 2.6-mm and, when mature, into one of the 2.6 mini-development series. Thus, over the last few years, each 2.6 release—for example, 2.6.29—has taken several months, boasting significant changes over its predecessor. This "development series in miniature" has proven rather successful, maintaining high levels of stability while still introducing new features and appears unlikely to change in the near future. Indeed, the consensus among kernel developers is that this new release process will continue indefinitely.

To compensate for the reduced frequency of releases, the kernel developers have introduced the aforementioned *stable release*. This release (the *8* in 2.6.32.8) contains crucial bug fixes, often back-ported from the under-development kernel (in this example, 2.6.33). In this manner, the previous release continues to receive attention focused on stabilization.

The Linux Kernel Development Community

When you begin developing code for the Linux kernel, you become a part of the global kernel development community. The main forum for this community is the *Linux Kernel Mailing List* (oft-shortened to *lkml*). Subscription information is available at http://vger.kernel.org. Note that this is a high-traffic list with hundreds of messages a day and that the other readers—who include all the core kernel developers, including Linus—are not open to dealing with nonsense. The list is, however, a priceless aid during development because it is where you can find testers, receive peer review, and ask questions.

Later chapters provide an overview of the kernel development process and a more complete description of participating successfully in the kernel development community. In the meantime, however, lurking on (silently reading) the Linux Kernel Mailing List is as good a supplement to this book as you can find.

Before We Begin

This book is about the Linux kernel: its goals, the design that fulfills those goals, and the implementation that realizes that design. The approach is practical, taking a middle road between theory and practice when explaining how everything works. My objective is to give you an insider's appreciation and understanding for the design and implementation of the Linux kernel. This approach, coupled with some personal anecdotes and tips on kernel hacking, should ensure that this book gets you off the ground running, whether you are looking to develop core kernel code, a new device driver, or simply better understand the Linux operating system.

While reading this book, you should have access to a Linux system and the kernel source. Ideally, by this point, you are a Linux user and have poked and prodded at the source, but require some help making it all come together. Conversely, you might never have used Linux but just want to learn the design of the kernel out of curiosity. However, if your desire is to write some code of your own, there is no substitute for the source. The source code is *freely* available; use it!

Oh, and above all else, *have fun!*

2

Getting Started with the Kernel

In this chapter, we introduce some of the basics of the Linux kernel: where to get its source, how to compile it, and how to install the new kernel. We then go over the differences between the kernel and user-space programs and common programming constructs used in the kernel. Although the kernel certainly is unique in many ways, at the end of the day it is little different from any other large software project.

Obtaining the Kernel Source

The current Linux source code is always available in both a complete *tarball* (an archive created with the *tar* command) and an incremental patch from the official home of the Linux kernel, http://www.kernel.org.

Unless you have a specific reason to work with an older version of the Linux source, you *always* want the latest code. The repository at kernel.org is the place to get it, along with additional patches from a number of leading kernel developers.

Using Git

Over the last couple of years, the kernel hackers, led by Linus himself, have begun using a new version control system to manage the Linux kernel source. Linus created this system, called *Git*, with speed in mind. Unlike traditional systems such as *CVS*, Git is distributed, and its usage and workflow is consequently unfamiliar to many developers. I strongly recommend using Git to download and manage the Linux kernel source.

You can use Git to obtain a copy of the latest "pushed" version of Linus's tree:

```
$ git clone git://git.kernel.org/pub/scm/linux/kernel/git/torvalds/linux-2.6.git
```

When checked out, you can update your tree to Linus's latest:

```
$ git pull
```

With these two commands, you can obtain and subsequently keep up to date with the official kernel tree. To commit and manage your own changes, see Chapter 20, "Patches,

Hacking, and the Community." A complete discussion of Git is outside the scope of this book; many online resources provide excellent guides.

Installing the Kernel Source

The kernel tarball is distributed in both GNU zip (gzip) and bzip2 format. Bzip2 is the default and preferred format because it generally compresses quite a bit better than gzip. The Linux kernel tarball in bzip2 format is named linux-$x.y.z$.tar.bz2, where $x.y.z$ is the version of that particular release of the kernel source. After downloading the source, uncompressing and untarring it is simple. If your tarball is compressed with bzip2, run

```
$ tar xvjf linux-x.y.z.tar.bz2
```

If it is compressed with GNU zip, run

```
$ tar xvzf linux-x.y.z.tar.gz
```

This uncompresses and untars the source to the directory linux-x.y.z. If you use git to obtain and manage the kernel source, you do not need to download the tarball. Just run the *git clone* command as described and git downloads and unpacks the latest source.

> ### Where to Install and Hack on the Source
>
> The kernel source is typically installed in /usr/src/linux. You should not use this source tree for development because the kernel version against which your C library is compiled is often linked to this tree. Moreover, you should not require root in order to make changes to the kernel—instead, work out of your home directory and use root only to install new kernels. Even when installing a new kernel, /usr/src/linux should remain untouched.

Using Patches

Throughout the Linux kernel community, patches are the *lingua franca* of communication. You will distribute your code changes in patches and receive code from others as patches. *Incremental patches* provide an easy way to move from one kernel tree to the next. Instead of downloading each large tarball of the kernel source, you can simply apply an incremental patch to go from one version to the next. This saves everyone bandwidth and you time. To apply an incremental patch, from *inside* your kernel source tree, simply run

```
$ patch -p1 < ../patch-x.y.z
```

Generally, a patch to a given version of the kernel is applied against the previous version. Generating and applying patches is discussed in much more depth in later chapters.

The Kernel Source Tree

The kernel source tree is divided into a number of directories, most of which contain many more subdirectories. The directories in the root of the source tree, along with their descriptions, are listed in Table 2.1.

Table 2.1 **Directories in the Root of the Kernel Source Tree**

Directory	Description
arch	Architecture-specific source
block	Block I/O layer
crypto	Crypto API
Documentation	Kernel source documentation
drivers	Device drivers
firmware	Device firmware needed to use certain drivers
fs	The VFS and the individual filesystems
include	Kernel headers
init	Kernel boot and initialization
ipc	Interprocess communication code
kernel	Core subsystems, such as the scheduler
lib	Helper routines
mm	Memory management subsystem and the VM
net	Networking subsystem
samples	Sample, demonstrative code
scripts	Scripts used to build the kernel
security	Linux Security Module
sound	Sound subsystem
usr	Early user-space code (called initramfs)
tools	Tools helpful for developing Linux
virt	Virtualization infrastructure

A number of files in the root of the source tree deserve mention. The file COPYING is the kernel license (the GNU GPL v2). CREDITS is a listing of developers with more than a trivial amount of code in the kernel. MAINTAINERS lists the names of the individuals who maintain subsystems and drivers in the kernel. Makefile is the base kernel Makefile.

Building the Kernel

Building the kernel is easy. It is surprisingly easier than compiling and installing other system-level components, such as glibc. The 2.6 kernel series introduced a new configuration and build system, which made the job even easier and is a welcome improvement over earlier releases.

Configuring the Kernel

Because the Linux source code is available, it follows that you can configure and custom tailor it before compiling. Indeed, it is possible to compile support into your kernel for only the specific features and drivers you want. Configuring the kernel is a required step before building it. Because the kernel offers myriad features and supports a varied basket of hardware, there is a *lot* to configure. Kernel configuration is controlled by configuration options, which are prefixed by CONFIG in the form CONFIG_FEATURE. For example, symmetrical multiprocessing (SMP) is controlled by the configuration option CONFIG_SMP. If this option is set, SMP is enabled; if unset, SMP is disabled. The configure options are used both to decide which files to build and to manipulate code via preprocessor directives.

Configuration options that control the build process are either *Booleans* or *tristates*. A Boolean option is either *yes* or *no*. Kernel features, such as CONFIG_PREEMPT, are usually Booleans. A tristate option is one of *yes*, *no*, or *module*. The *module* setting represents a configuration option that is set but is to be compiled as a module (that is, a separate dynamically loadable object). In the case of tristates, a *yes* option explicitly means to compile the code into the main kernel image and not as a module. Drivers are usually represented by tristates.

Configuration options can also be strings or integers. These options do not control the build process but instead specify values that kernel source can access as a preprocessor macro. For example, a configuration option can specify the size of a statically allocated array.

Vendor kernels, such as those provided by Canonical for Ubuntu or Red Hat for Fedora, are precompiled as part of the distribution. Such kernels typically enable a good cross section of the needed kernel features and compile nearly all the drivers as modules. This provides for a great base kernel with support for a wide range of hardware as separate modules. For better or worse, as a kernel hacker, you need to compile your own kernels and learn what modules to include on your own.

Thankfully, the kernel provides multiple tools to facilitate configuration. The simplest tool is a text-based command-line utility:

```
$ make config
```

This utility goes through each option, one by one, and asks the user to interactively select *yes*, *no*, or (for tristates) *module*. Because this takes a *long* time, unless you are paid by the hour, you should use an ncurses-based graphical utility:

```
$ make menuconfig
```

Or a gtk+-based graphical utility:

```
$ make gconfig
```

These three utilities divide the various configuration options into categories, such as "Processor Type and Features." You can move through the categories, view the kernel options, and of course change their values.

This command creates a configuration based on the defaults for your architecture:

```
$ make defconfig
```

Although these defaults are somewhat arbitrary (on i386, they are rumored to be Linus's configuration!), they provide a good start if you have never configured the kernel. To get off and running quickly, run this command and then go back and ensure that configuration options for your hardware are enabled.

The configuration options are stored in the root of the kernel source tree in a file named .config. You may find it easier (as most of the kernel developers do) to just edit this file directly. It is quite easy to search for and change the value of the configuration options. After making changes to your configuration file, or when using an existing configuration file on a new kernel tree, you can validate and update the configuration:

```
$ make oldconfig
```

You should always run this before building a kernel.

The configuration option CONFIG_IKCONFIG_PROC places the complete kernel configuration file, compressed, at /proc/config.gz. This makes it easy to clone your current configuration when building a new kernel. If your current kernel has this option enabled, you can copy the configuration out of /proc and use it to build a new kernel:

```
$ zcat /proc/config.gz > .config
$ make oldconfig
```

After the kernel configuration is set—however you do it—you can build it with a single command:

```
$ make
```

Unlike kernels before 2.6, you no longer need to run make dep before building the kernel—the dependency tree is maintained automatically. You also do not need to specify a specific build type, such as bzImage, or build modules separately, as you did in old versions. The default Makefile rule will handle everything.

Minimizing Build Noise

A trick to minimize build noise, but still see warnings and errors, is to redirect the output from make:

```
$ make > ../detritus
```

If you need to see the build output, you can read the file. Because the warnings and errors are output to standard error, however, you normally do not need to. In fact, I just do

```
$ make > /dev/null
```

This redirects all the worthless output to that big, ominous sink of no return, /dev/null.

Spawning Multiple Build Jobs

The `make` program provides a feature to split the build process into a number of parallel *jobs*. Each of these jobs then runs separately and concurrently, significantly speeding up the build process on multiprocessing systems. It also improves processor utilization because the time to build a large source tree includes significant time in I/O wait (time in which the process is idle waiting for an I/O request to complete).

By default, `make` spawns only a single job because Makefiles all too often have incorrect dependency information. With incorrect dependencies, multiple jobs can step on each other's toes, resulting in errors in the build process. The kernel's Makefiles have correct dependency information, so spawning multiple jobs does not result in failures. To build the kernel with multiple make jobs, use

```
$ make -jn
```

Here, *n* is the number of jobs to spawn. Usual practice is to spawn one or two jobs per processor. For example, on a 16-core machine, you might do

```
$ make -j32 > /dev/null
```

Using utilities such as the excellent `distcc` or `ccache` can also dramatically improve kernel build time.

Installing the New Kernel

After the kernel is built, you need to install it. How it is installed is architecture- and boot loader-dependent—consult the directions for your boot loader on where to copy the kernel image and how to set it up to boot. Always keep a known-safe kernel or two around in case your new kernel has problems!

As an example, on an x86 system using grub, you would copy `arch/i386/boot/bzImage` to `/boot`, name it something like `vmlinuz-version`, and edit `/boot/grub/grub.conf`, adding a new entry for the new kernel. Systems using LILO to boot would instead edit `/etc/lilo.conf` and then rerun `lilo`.

Installing modules, thankfully, is automated and architecture-independent. As root, simply run

```
% make modules_install
```

This installs all the compiled modules to their correct home under `/lib/modules`.

The build process also creates the file `System.map` in the root of the kernel source tree. It contains a symbol lookup table, mapping kernel symbols to their start addresses. This is used during debugging to translate memory addresses to function and variable names.

A Beast of a Different Nature

The Linux kernel has several unique attributes as compared to a normal user-space application. Although these differences do not necessarily make developing kernel code *harder* than developing user-space code, they certainly make doing so *different*.

These characteristics make the kernel a beast of a different nature. Some of the usual rules are bent; other rules are entirely new. Although some of the differences are obvious (we all know the kernel can do anything it wants), others are not so obvious. The most important of these differences are

- The kernel has access to neither the C library nor the standard C headers.
- The kernel is coded in GNU C.
- The kernel lacks the memory protection afforded to user-space.
- The kernel cannot easily execute floating-point operations.
- The kernel has a small per-process fixed-size stack.
- Because the kernel has asynchronous interrupts, is preemptive, and supports SMP, synchronization and concurrency are major concerns within the kernel.
- Portability is important.

Let's briefly look at each of these issues because all kernel developers must keep them in mind.

No libc or Standard Headers

Unlike a user-space application, the kernel is not linked against the standard C library—or any other library, for that matter. There are multiple reasons for this, including a chicken-and-the-egg situation, but the primary reason is speed and size. The full C library—or even a decent subset of it—is too large and too inefficient for the kernel.

Do not fret: Many of the usual libc functions are implemented inside the kernel. For example, the common string manipulation functions are in `lib/string.c`. Just include the header file `<linux/string.h>` and have at them.

Header Files

When I talk about header files in this book, I am referring to the kernel header files that are part of the kernel source tree. Kernel source files cannot include outside headers, just as they cannot use outside libraries.

The base files are located in the `include/` directory in the root of the kernel source tree. For example, the header file `<linux/inotify.h>` is located at `include/linux/inotify.h` in the kernel source tree.

A set of architecture-specific header files are located in `arch/<architecture>/include/asm` in the kernel source tree. For example, if compiling for the x86 architecture, your architecture-specific headers are in `arch/x86/include/asm`. Source code includes these headers via just the `asm/` prefix, for example `<asm/ioctl.h>`.

Of the missing functions, the most familiar is `printf()`. The kernel does not have access to `printf()`, but it does provide `printk()`, which works pretty much the same as its more familiar cousin. The `printk()` function copies the formatted string into the kernel log buffer, which is normally read by the syslog program. Usage is similar to `printf()`:

```
printk("Hello world! A string '%s' and an integer '%d'\n", str, i);
```

One notable difference between `printf()` and `printk()` is that `printk()` enables you to specify a priority flag. This flag is used by `syslogd` to decide where to display kernel messages. Here is an example of these priorities:

```
printk(KERN_ERR "this is an error!\n");
```

Note there is no comma between `KERN_ERR` and the printed message. This is intentional; the priority flag is a preprocessor-define representing a string literal, which is concatenated onto the printed message during compilation. We use `printk()` throughout this book.

GNU C

Like any self-respecting Unix kernel, the Linux kernel is programmed in C. Perhaps surprisingly, the kernel is not programmed in strict ANSI C. Instead, where applicable, the kernel developers make use of various language extensions available in *gcc* (the GNU Compiler Collection, which contains the C compiler used to compile the kernel and most everything else written in C on a Linux system).

The kernel developers use both ISO C99[1] and GNU C extensions to the C language. These changes wed the Linux kernel to gcc, although recently one other compiler, the Intel C compiler, has sufficiently supported enough gcc features that it, too, can compile the Linux kernel. The earliest supported gcc version is 3.2; gcc version 4.4 or later is recommended. The ISO C99 extensions that the kernel uses are nothing special and, because C99 is an official revision of the C language, are slowly cropping up in a lot of other code. The more unfamiliar deviations from standard ANSI C are those provided by GNU C. Let's look at some of the more interesting extensions that you will see in the kernel; these changes differentiate kernel code from other projects with which you might be familiar.

Inline Functions

Both C99 and GNU C support *inline functions*. An inline function is, as its name suggests, inserted inline into each function call site. This eliminates the overhead of function invocation and return (register saving and restore) and allows for potentially greater optimization as the compiler can optimize both the caller and the called function as one. As a downside (nothing in life is free), code size increases because the contents of the function are copied into all the callers, which increases memory consumption and instruction cache footprint. Kernel developers use inline functions for small time-critical functions.

---

[1] *ISO C99 is the latest major revision to the ISO C standard. C99 adds numerous enhancements to the previous major revision, ISO C90, including designated initializers, variable length arrays, C++-style comments, and the* `long long` *and* `complex` *types. The Linux kernel, however, employs only a subset of C99 features.*

Making large functions inline, especially those used more than once or that are not exceedingly time critical, is frowned upon.

An inline function is declared when the keywords `static` and `inline` are used as part of the function definition. For example

```
static inline void wolf(unsigned long tail_size)
```

The function declaration must precede any usage, or else the compiler cannot make the function inline. Common practice is to place inline functions in header files. Because they are marked `static`, an exported function is not created. If an inline function is used by only one file, it can instead be placed toward the top of just that file.

In the kernel, using inline functions is preferred over complicated macros for reasons of type safety and readability.

Inline Assembly

The gcc C compiler enables the embedding of assembly instructions in otherwise normal C functions. This feature, of course, is used in only those parts of the kernel that are unique to a given system architecture.

The `asm()` compiler directive is used to inline assembly code. For example, this inline assembly directive executes the x86 processor's `rdtsc` instruction, which returns the value of the timestamp (`tsc`) register:

```
unsigned int low, high;
asm volatile("rdtsc" : "=a" (low), "=d" (high));
/* low and high now contain the lower and upper 32-bits of the 64-bit tsc */
```

The Linux kernel is written in a mixture of C and assembly, with assembly relegated to low-level architecture and fast path code. The vast majority of kernel code is programmed in straight C.

Branch Annotation

The gcc C compiler has a built-in directive that optimizes conditional branches as either very likely taken or very unlikely taken. The compiler uses the directive to appropriately optimize the branch. The kernel wraps the directive in easy-to-use macros, `likely()` and `unlikely()`.

For example, consider an `if` statement such as the following:

```
if (error) {
        /* ... */
}
```

To mark this branch as very unlikely taken (that is, likely not taken):

```
/* we predict 'error' is nearly always zero ... */
if (unlikely(error)) {
        /* ... */
}
```

Conversely, to mark a branch as very likely taken:

```
/* we predict 'success' is nearly always nonzero ... */
if (likely(success)) {
        /* ... */
}
```

You should only use these directives when the branch direction is overwhelmingly known *a priori* or when you want to optimize a specific case at the cost of the other case. This is an important point: These directives result in a performance boost when the branch is correctly marked, but a performance *loss* when the branch is mismarked. A common usage, as shown in these examples, for unlikely() and likely() is error conditions. As you might expect, unlikely() finds much more use in the kernel because if statements tend to indicate a special case.

No Memory Protection

When a user-space application attempts an illegal memory access, the kernel can trap the error, send the SIGSEGV signal, and kill the process. If the kernel attempts an illegal memory access, however, the results are less controlled. (After all, who is going to look after the kernel?) Memory violations in the kernel result in an *oops*, which is a major kernel error. It should go without saying that you must not illegally access memory, such as dereferencing a NULL pointer—but within the kernel, the stakes are much higher!

Additionally, kernel memory is not pageable. Therefore, every byte of memory you consume is one less byte of available physical memory. Keep that in mind the next time you need to add *one more feature* to the kernel!

No (Easy) Use of Floating Point

When a user-space process uses floating-point instructions, the kernel manages the transition from integer to floating point mode. What the kernel has to do when using floating-point instructions varies by architecture, but the kernel normally catches a trap and then initiates the transition from integer to floating point mode.

Unlike user-space, the kernel does not have the luxury of seamless support for floating point because it cannot easily trap itself. Using a floating point inside the kernel requires manually saving and restoring the floating point registers, among other possible chores. The short answer is: *Don't do it!* Except in the rare cases, no floating-point operations are in the kernel.

Small, Fixed-Size Stack

User-space can get away with statically allocating many variables on the stack, including huge structures and thousand-element arrays. This behavior is legal because user-space has a large stack that can dynamically grow. (Developers on older, less advanced operating systems—say, DOS—might recall a time when even user-space had a fixed-sized stack.)

The kernel stack is neither large nor dynamic; it is small and fixed in size. The exact size of the kernel's stack varies by architecture. On x86, the stack size is configurable at compile-time and can be either 4KB or 8KB. Historically, the kernel stack is two pages, which generally implies that it is 8KB on 32-bit architectures and 16KB on 64-bit architectures—this size is fixed and absolute. Each process receives its own stack.

The kernel stack is discussed in much greater detail in later chapters.

Synchronization and Concurrency

The kernel is susceptible to race conditions. Unlike a single-threaded user-space application, a number of properties of the kernel allow for concurrent access of shared resources and thus require synchronization to prevent races. Specifically

- Linux is a preemptive multitasking operating system. Processes are scheduled and rescheduled at the whim of the kernel's process scheduler. The kernel must synchronize between these tasks.

- Linux supports symmetrical multiprocessing (SMP). Therefore, without proper protection, kernel code executing simultaneously on two or more processors can concurrently access the same resource.

- Interrupts occur asynchronously with respect to the currently executing code. Therefore, without proper protection, an interrupt can occur in the midst of accessing a resource, and the interrupt handler can then access the same resource.

- The Linux kernel is preemptive. Therefore, without protection, kernel code can be preempted in favor of different code that then accesses the same resource.

Typical solutions to race conditions include spinlocks and semaphores. Later chapters provide a thorough discussion of synchronization and concurrency.

Importance of Portability

Although user-space applications do not *have* to aim for portability, Linux is a portable operating system and should remain one. This means that architecture-independent C code must correctly compile and run on a wide range of systems, and that architecture-dependent code must be properly segregated in system-specific directories in the kernel source tree.

A handful of rules—such as remain endian neutral, be 64-bit clean, do not assume the word or page size, and so on—go a long way. Portability is discussed in depth in a later chapter.

Conclusion

To be sure, the kernel has unique qualities. It enforces its own rules and the stakes, managing the entire system as the kernel does, are certainly higher. That said, the Linux kernel's complexity and barrier-to-entry is not qualitatively different from any other large software project. The most important step on the road to Linux development is the realization that the kernel is not something to fear. Unfamiliar, sure. Insurmountable? Not at all.

This and the previous chapter lay the foundation for the topics we cover through this book's remaining chapters. In each subsequent chapter, we cover a specific kernel concept or subsystem. Along the way, it is imperative that you read and modify the kernel source. Only through actually reading and experimenting with the code can you ever understand it. The source is freely available—use it!

3

Process Management

This chapter introduces the concept of the *process*, one of the fundamental abstractions in Unix operating systems. It defines the process, as well as related concepts such as threads, and then discusses how the Linux kernel manages each process: how they are enumerated within the kernel, how they are created, and how they ultimately die. Because running user applications is the reason we have operating systems, the process management is a crucial part of any operating system kernel, including Linux.

The Process

A *process* is a program (object code stored on some media) in the midst of execution. Processes are, however, more than just the executing program code (often called the *text section* in Unix). They also include a set of resources such as open files and pending signals, internal kernel data, processor state, a memory address space with one or more memory mappings, one or more *threads of execution*, and a *data section* containing global variables. Processes, in effect, are the living result of running program code. The kernel needs to manage all these details efficiently and transparently.

Threads of execution, often shortened to *threads*, are the objects of activity within the process. Each thread includes a unique program counter, process stack, and set of processor registers. The kernel schedules individual threads, not processes. In traditional Unix systems, each process consists of one thread. In modern systems, however, multithreaded programs—those that consist of more than one thread—are common. As you will see later, Linux has a unique implementation of threads: It does not differentiate between threads and processes. To Linux, a thread is just a special kind of process.

On modern operating systems, processes provide two virtualizations: a virtualized processor and virtual memory. The virtual processor gives the process the illusion that it alone monopolizes the system, despite possibly sharing the processor among hundreds of other processes. Chapter 4, "Process Scheduling," discusses this virtualization. Virtual memory lets the process allocate and manage memory as if it alone owned all the memory in the system. Virtual memory is covered in Chapter 12, "Memory Management."

Interestingly, note that threads share the virtual memory abstraction, whereas each receives its own virtualized processor.

A program itself is not a process; a process is an *active* program and related resources. Indeed, two or more processes can exist that are executing the *same* program. In fact, two or more processes can exist that share various resources, such as open files or an address space.

A process begins its life when, not surprisingly, it is created. In Linux, this occurs by means of the `fork()` system call, which creates a new process by duplicating an existing one. The process that calls `fork()` is the *parent,* whereas the new process is the *child.* The parent resumes execution and the child starts execution at the same place: where the call to `fork()` returns. The `fork()` system call returns from the kernel twice: once in the parent process and again in the newborn child.

Often, immediately after a fork it is desirable to execute a new, different program. The `exec()` family of function calls creates a new address space and loads a new program into it. In contemporary Linux kernels, `fork()` is actually implemented via the `clone()` system call, which is discussed in a following section.

Finally, a program exits via the `exit()` system call. This function terminates the process and frees all its resources. A parent process can inquire about the status of a terminated child via the `wait4()`[1] system call, which enables a process to wait for the termination of a specific process. When a process exits, it is placed into a special zombie state that represents terminated processes until the parent calls `wait()` or `waitpid()`.

> **Note**
>
> Another name for a process is a *task*. The Linux kernel internally refers to processes as tasks. In this book, I use the terms interchangeably, although when I say *task* I am generally referring to a process from the kernel's point of view.

Process Descriptor and the Task Structure

The kernel stores the list of processes in a circular doubly linked list called the *task list*.[2] Each element in the task list is a *process descriptor* of the type `struct task_struct`, which is defined in `<linux/sched.h>`. The process descriptor contains all the information about a specific process.

The `task_struct` is a relatively large data structure, at around 1.7 kilobytes on a 32-bit machine. This size, however, is quite small considering that the structure contains all the information that the kernel has and needs about a process. The process descriptor contains

---

[1] The kernel implements the `wait4()` system call. Linux systems, via the C library, typically provide the `wait()`, `waitpid()`, `wait3()`, and `wait4()` functions. All these functions return status about a terminated process, albeit with slightly different semantics.

[2] Some texts on operating system design call this list the task array. Because the Linux implementation is a linked list and not a static array, in Linux it is called the task list.

the data that describes the executing program—open files, the process's address space, pending signals, the process's state, and much more (see Figure 3.1).

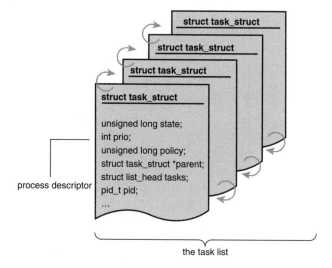

Figure 3.1   The process descriptor and task list.

Allocating the Process Descriptor

The task_struct structure is allocated via the *slab allocator* to provide object reuse and cache coloring (see Chapter 12). Prior to the 2.6 kernel series, struct task_struct was stored at the end of the kernel stack of each process. This allowed architectures with few registers, such as x86, to calculate the location of the process descriptor via the *stack pointer* without using an extra register to store the location. With the process descriptor now dynamically created via the slab allocator, a new structure, struct thread_info, was created that again lives at the bottom of the stack (for stacks that grow down) and at the top of the stack (for stacks that grow up).[3] See Figure 3.2.

The thread_info structure is defined on x86 in <asm/thread_info.h> as

```
struct thread_info {
        struct task_struct    *task;
        struct exec_domain    *exec_domain;
        __u32                 flags;
        __u32                 status;
        __u32                 cpu;
        int                   preempt_count;
```

---

[3] *Register-impaired architectures were not the only reason for creating* struct thread_info. *The new structure also makes it rather easy to calculate offsets of its values for use in assembly code.*

```
mm_segment_t          addr_limit;
struct restart_block  restart_block;
void                  *sysenter_return;
int                   uaccess_err;
};
```

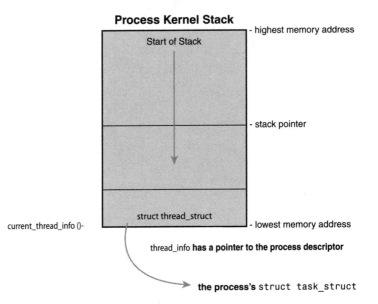

Figure 3.2   The process descriptor and kernel stack.

Each task's `thread_info` structure is allocated at the end of its stack. The `task` element of the structure is a pointer to the task's actual `task_struct`.

Storing the Process Descriptor

The system identifies processes by a unique *process identification* value or *PID*. The PID is a numerical value represented by the opaque type[4] `pid_t`, which is typically an `int`. Because of backward compatibility with earlier Unix and Linux versions, however, the default maximum value is only 32,768 (that of a `short int`), although the value optionally can be increased as high as four million (this is controlled in `<linux/threads.h>`. The kernel stores this value as `pid` inside each process descriptor.

This maximum value is important because it is essentially the maximum number of processes that may exist concurrently on the system. Although 32,768 might be sufficient for a desktop system, large servers may require many more processes. Moreover, the lower the value, the sooner the values will wrap around, destroying the useful notion that higher

---

[4] *An opaque type is a data type whose physical representation is unknown or irrelevant.*

values indicate later-run processes than lower values. If the system is willing to break compatibility with old applications, the administrator may increase the maximum value via /proc/sys/kernel/pid_max.

Inside the kernel, tasks are typically referenced directly by a pointer to their task_struct structure. In fact, most kernel code that deals with processes works directly with struct task_struct. Consequently, it is useful to be able to quickly look up the process descriptor of the currently executing task, which is done via the current macro. This macro must be independently implemented by each architecture. Some architectures save a pointer to the task_struct structure of the currently running process in a register, enabling for efficient access. Other architectures, such as x86 (which has few registers to waste), make use of the fact that struct thread_info is stored on the kernel stack to calculate the location of thread_info and subsequently the task_struct.

On x86, current is calculated by masking out the 13 least-significant bits of the stack pointer to obtain the thread_info structure. This is done by the current_thread_info() function. The assembly is shown here:

```
movl $-8192, %eax
andl %esp, %eax
```

This assumes that the stack size is 8KB. When 4KB stacks are enabled, 4096 is used in lieu of 8192.

Finally, current dereferences the task member of thread_info to return the task_struct:

```
current_thread_info()->task;
```

Contrast this approach with that taken by PowerPC (IBM's modern RISC-based microprocessor), which stores the current task_struct in a register. Thus, current on PPC merely returns the value stored in the register r2. PPC can take this approach because, unlike x86, it has plenty of registers. Because accessing the process descriptor is a common and important job, the PPC kernel developers deem using a register worthy for the task.

Process State

The state field of the process descriptor describes the current condition of the process (see Figure 3.3). Each process on the system is in exactly one of five different states. This value is represented by one of five flags:

- TASK_RUNNING—The process is runnable; it is either currently running or on a runqueue waiting to run (runqueues are discussed in Chapter 4). This is the only possible state for a process executing in user-space; it can also apply to a process in kernel-space that is actively running.

- TASK_INTERRUPTIBLE—The process is sleeping (that is, it is blocked), waiting for some condition to exist. When this condition exists, the kernel sets the process's state to TASK_RUNNING. The process also awakes prematurely and becomes runnable if it receives a signal.

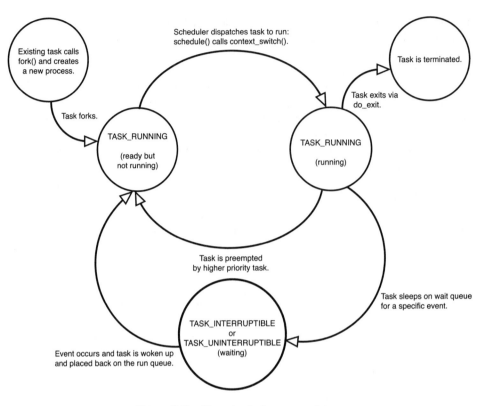

Figure 3.3   Flow chart of process states.

- TASK_UNINTERRUPTIBLE—This state is identical to TASK_INTERRUPTIBLE except that it does *not* wake up and become runnable if it receives a signal. This is used in situations where the process must wait without interruption or when the event is expected to occur quite quickly. Because the task does not respond to signals in this state, TASK_UNINTERRUPTIBLE is less often used than TASK_INTERRUPTIBLE.[5]

- __TASK_TRACED—The process is being *traced* by another process, such as a debugger, via *ptrace*.

- __TASK_STOPPED—Process execution has stopped; the task is not running nor is it eligible to run. This occurs if the task receives the SIGSTOP, SIGTSTP, SIGTTIN, or SIGTTOU signal or if it receives *any* signal while it is being debugged.

---

[5] *This is why you have those dreaded unkillable processes with state D in ps (1). Because the task will not respond to signals, you cannot send it a SIGKILL signal. Further, even if you could terminate the task, it would not be wise because the task is supposedly in the middle of an important operation and may hold a semaphore.*

Manipulating the Current Process State

Kernel code often needs to change a process's state. The preferred mechanism is using

```
set_task_state(task, state);        /* set task 'task' to state 'state' */
```

This function sets the given task to the given state. If applicable, it also provides a memory barrier to force ordering on other processors. (This is only needed on SMP systems.) Otherwise, it is equivalent to

```
task->state = state;
```

The method `set_current_state(state)` is synonymous to `set_task_state(current, state)`. See `<linux/sched.h>` for the implementation of these and related functions.

Process Context

One of the most important parts of a process is the executing program code. This code is read in from an *executable file* and executed within the program's address space. Normal program execution occurs in *user-space*. When a program executes a system call (see Chapter 5, "System Calls") or triggers an exception, it enters *kernel-space*. At this point, the kernel is said to be "executing on behalf of the process" and is in *process context*. When in process context, the `current` macro is valid.[6] Upon exiting the kernel, the process resumes execution in user-space, unless a higher-priority process has become runnable in the interim, in which case the scheduler is invoked to select the higher priority process.

System calls and exception handlers are well-defined interfaces into the kernel. A process can begin executing in kernel-space only through one of these interfaces—*all* access to the kernel is through these interfaces.

The Process Family Tree

A distinct hierarchy exists between processes in Unix systems, and Linux is no exception. All processes are descendants of the `init` process, whose PID is one. The kernel starts `init` in the last step of the boot process. The `init` process, in turn, reads the system *initscripts* and executes more programs, eventually completing the boot process.

Every process on the system has exactly one parent. Likewise, every process has zero or more children. Processes that are all direct children of the same parent are called *siblings*. The relationship between processes is stored in the process descriptor. Each `task_struct` has a pointer to the parent's `task_struct`, named `parent`, and a list of children, named

---

[6] *Other than process context there is interrupt context, which we discuss in Chapter 7, "Interrupts and Interrupt Handlers." In interrupt context, the system is not running on behalf of a process but is executing an interrupt handler. No process is tied to interrupt handlers.*

children. Consequently, given the current process, it is possible to obtain the process descriptor of its parent with the following code:

```
struct task_struct *my_parent = current->parent;
```

Similarly, it is possible to iterate over a process's children with

```
struct task_struct *task;
struct list_head *list;

list_for_each(list, &current->children) {
        task = list_entry(list, struct task_struct, sibling);
        /* task now points to one of current's children */
}
```

The init task's process descriptor is statically allocated as init_task. A good example of the relationship between all processes is the fact that this code will always succeed:

```
struct task_struct *task;

for (task = current; task != &init_task; task = task->parent)
        ;
/* task now points to init */
```

In fact, you can follow the process hierarchy from any one process in the system to *any* other. Oftentimes, however, it is desirable simply to iterate over *all* processes in the system. This is easy because the task list is a circular, doubly linked list. To obtain the next task in the list, given any valid task, use

```
list_entry(task->tasks.next, struct task_struct, tasks)
```

Obtaining the previous task works the same way:

```
list_entry(task->tasks.prev, struct task_struct, tasks)
```

These two routines are provided by the macros next_task(task) and prev_task(task), respectively. Finally, the macro for_each_process(task) is provided, which iterates over the entire task list. On each iteration, task points to the next task in the list:

```
struct task_struct *task;

for_each_process(task) {
        /* this pointlessly prints the name and PID of each task */
        printk("%s[%d]\n", task->comm, task->pid);
}
```

Caution

It is expensive to iterate over every task in a system with many processes; code should have good reason (and no alternative) before doing so.

Process Creation

Process creation in Unix is unique. Most operating systems implement a *spawn* mechanism to create a new process in a new address space, read in an executable, and begin executing it. Unix takes the unusual approach of separating these steps into two distinct functions: fork() and exec().[7] The first, fork(), creates a child process that is a copy of the current task. It differs from the parent only in its PID (which is unique), its PPID (parent's PID, which is set to the original process), and certain resources and statistics, such as pending signals, which are not inherited. The second function, exec(), loads a new executable into the address space and begins executing it. The combination of fork() followed by exec() is similar to the single function most operating systems provide.

Copy-on-Write

Traditionally, upon fork(), all resources owned by the parent are duplicated and the copy is given to the child. This approach is naive and inefficient in that it copies much data that might otherwise be shared. Worse still, if the new process were to immediately execute a new image, all that copying would go to waste. In Linux, fork() is implemented through the use of *copy-on-write* pages. Copy-on-write (or *COW*) is a technique to delay or altogether prevent copying of the data. Rather than duplicate the process address space, the parent and the child can share a single copy.

The data, however, is marked in such a way that if it is written to, a duplicate is made and each process receives a unique copy. Consequently, the duplication of resources occurs only when they are written; until then, they are shared read-only. This technique delays the copying of each page in the address space until it is actually written to. In the case that the pages are never written—for example, if exec() is called immediately after fork()—they never need to be copied.

The only overhead incurred by fork() is the duplication of the parent's page tables and the creation of a unique process descriptor for the child. In the common case that a process executes a new executable image immediately after forking, this optimization prevents the wasted copying of large amounts of data (with the address space, easily tens of megabytes). This is an important optimization because the Unix philosophy encourages quick process execution.

---

[7] By *exec()* I mean any member of the *exec()* family of functions. The kernel implements the *execve()* system call on top of which *execlp()*, *execle()*, *execv()*, and *execvp()* are implemented.

Forking

Linux implements `fork()` via the `clone()` system call. This call takes a series of flags that specify which resources, if any, the parent and child process should share. (See "The Linux Implementation of Threads" section later in this chapter for more about the flags.) The `fork()`, `vfork()`, and `__clone()` library calls all invoke the `clone()` system call with the requisite flags. The `clone()` system call, in turn, calls `do_fork()`.

The bulk of the work in forking is handled by `do_fork()`, which is defined in `kernel/fork.c`. This function calls `copy_process()` and then starts the process running. The interesting work is done by `copy_process()`:

1. It calls `dup_task_struct()`, which creates a new kernel stack, `thread_info` structure, and `task_struct` for the new process. The new values are identical to those of the current task. At this point, the child and parent process descriptors are identical.

2. It then checks that the new child will not exceed the resource limits on the number of processes for the current user.

3. The child needs to differentiate itself from its parent. Various members of the process descriptor are cleared or set to initial values. Members of the process descriptor not inherited are primarily statistically information. The bulk of the values in `task_struct` remain unchanged.

4. The child's state is set to `TASK_UNINTERRUPTIBLE` to ensure that it does not yet run.

5. `copy_process()` calls `copy_flags()` to update the `flags` member of the `task_struct`. The `PF_SUPERPRIV` flag, which denotes whether a task used super-user privileges, is cleared. The `PF_FORKNOEXEC` flag, which denotes a process that has not called `exec()`, is set.

6. It calls `alloc_pid()` to assign an available PID to the new task.

7. Depending on the flags passed to `clone()`, `copy_process()` either duplicates or shares open files, filesystem information, signal handlers, process address space, and namespace. These resources are typically shared between threads in a given process; otherwise they are unique and thus copied here.

8. Finally, `copy_process()` cleans up and returns to the caller a pointer to the new child.

Back in `do_fork()`, if `copy_process()` returns successfully, the new child is woken up and run. Deliberately, the kernel runs the child process first.[8] In the common case of the child simply calling `exec()` immediately, this eliminates any copy-on-write overhead that would occur if the parent ran first and began writing to the address space.

---

[8] *This does not currently function correctly, although the goal is for the child to run first.*

vfork()

The vfork() system call has the same effect as fork(), except that the page table entries of the parent process are not copied. Instead, the child executes as the sole thread in the parent's address space, and the parent is blocked until the child either calls exec() or exits. The child is *not* allowed to write to the address space. This was a welcome optimization in the old days of 3BSD when the call was introduced because at the time copy-on-write pages were not used to implement fork(). Today, with copy-on-write and child-runs-first semantics, the only benefit to vfork() is not copying the parent page tables entries. If Linux one day gains copy-on-write page table entries, there will no longer be any benefit.[9] Because the semantics of vfork() are tricky (what, for example, happens if the exec() fails?), ideally systems would not need vfork() and the kernel would not implement it. It is entirely possible to implement vfork() as a normal fork()—this is what Linux did until version 2.2.

The vfork() system call is implemented via a special flag to the clone() system call:

1. In copy_process(), the task_struct member vfork_done is set to NULL.

2. In do_fork(), if the special flag was given, vfork_done is pointed at a specific address.

3. After the child is first run, the parent—instead of returning—waits for the child to signal it through the vfork_done pointer.

4. In the mm_release() function, which is used when a task exits a memory address space, vfork_done is checked to see whether it is NULL. If it is not, the parent is signaled.

5. Back in do_fork(), the parent wakes up and returns.

If this all goes as planned, the child is now executing in a new address space, and the parent is again executing in its original address space. The overhead is lower, but the implementation is not pretty.

The Linux Implementation of Threads

Threads are a popular modern programming abstraction. They provide multiple threads of execution within the same program in a shared memory address space. They can also share open files and other resources. Threads enable *concurrent programming* and, on multiple processor systems, true *parallelism*.

Linux has a unique implementation of threads. To the Linux kernel, there is no concept of a thread. Linux implements all threads as standard processes. The Linux kernel

---

[9] *Patches are available to add this functionality to Linux. In time, this feature will most likely find its way into the mainline Linux kernel.*

does not provide any special scheduling semantics or data structures to represent threads. Instead, a thread is merely a process that shares certain resources with other processes. Each thread has a unique `task_struct` and appears to the kernel as a normal process— threads just happen to share resources, such as an address space, with other processes.

This approach to threads contrasts greatly with operating systems such as Microsoft Windows or Sun Solaris, which have *explicit* kernel support for threads (and sometimes call threads *lightweight processes*). The name "lightweight process" sums up the difference in philosophies between Linux and other systems. To these other operating systems, threads are an abstraction to provide a lighter, quicker execution unit than the heavy process. To Linux, threads are simply a manner of sharing resources between processes (which are already quite lightweight).[10] For example, assume you have a process that consists of four threads. On systems with explicit thread support, one process descriptor might exist that, in turn, points to the four different threads. The process descriptor describes the shared resources, such as an address space or open files. The threads then describe the resources they alone possess. Conversely, in Linux, there are simply four processes and thus four normal `task_struct` structures. The four processes are set up to share certain resources. The result is quite elegant.

Creating Threads

Threads are created the same as normal tasks, with the exception that the `clone()` system call is passed flags corresponding to the specific resources to be shared:

```
clone(CLONE_VM | CLONE_FS | CLONE_FILES | CLONE_SIGHAND, 0);
```

The previous code results in behavior identical to a normal `fork()`, except that the address space, filesystem resources, file descriptors, and signal handlers are shared. In other words, the new task and its parent are what are popularly called *threads*.

In contrast, a normal `fork()` can be implemented as

```
clone(SIGCHLD, 0);
```

And `vfork()` is implemented as

```
clone(CLONE_VFORK | CLONE_VM | SIGCHLD, 0);
```

The flags provided to `clone()` help specify the behavior of the new process and detail what resources the parent and child will share. Table 3.1 lists the clone flags, which are defined in `<linux/sched.h>`, and their effect.

---

[10] *As an example, benchmark process creation time in Linux versus process (or even thread!) creation time in these other operating systems. The results are favorable for Linux.*

Flag	Meaning
CLONE_FILES	Parent and child share open files.
CLONE_FS	Parent and child share filesystem information.
CLONE_IDLETASK	Set PID to zero (used only by the idle tasks).
CLONE_NEWNS	Create a new namespace for the child.
CLONE_PARENT	Child is to have same parent as its parent.
CLONE_PTRACE	Continue tracing child.
CLONE_SETTID	Write the TID back to user-space.
CLONE_SETTLS	Create a new TLS for the child.
CLONE_SIGHAND	Parent and child share signal handlers and blocked signals.
CLONE_SYSVSEM	Parent and child share System V SEM_UNDO semantics.
CLONE_THREAD	Parent and child are in the same thread group.
CLONE_VFORK	vfork() was used and the parent will sleep until the child wakes it.
CLONE_UNTRACED	Do not let the tracing process force CLONE_PTRACE on the child.
CLONE_STOP	Start process in the TASK_STOPPED state.
CLONE_SETTLS	Create a new TLS (thread-local storage) for the child.
CLONE_CHILD_CLEARTID	Clear the TID in the child.
CLONE_CHILD_SETTID	Set the TID in the child.
CLONE_PARENT_SETTID	Set the TID in the parent.
CLONE_VM	Parent and child share address space.

Kernel Threads

It is often useful for the kernel to perform some operations in the background. The kernel accomplishes this via *kernel threads*—standard processes that exist solely in kernel-space. The significant difference between kernel threads and normal processes is that kernel threads do not have an address space. (Their mm pointer, which points at their address space, is NULL.) They operate only in kernel-space and do not context switch into user-space. Kernel threads, however, are schedulable and preemptable, the same as normal processes.

Linux delegates several tasks to kernel threads, most notably the *flush* tasks and the *ksoftirqd* task. You can see the kernel threads on your Linux system by running the command ps -ef. There are a lot of them! Kernel threads are created on system boot by other kernel threads. Indeed, a kernel thread can be created only by another kernel thread. The kernel handles this automatically by forking all new kernel threads off of the *kthreadd* kernel process. The interface, declared in `<linux/kthread.h>`, for spawning a new kernel thread from an existing one is

```
struct task_struct *kthread_create(int (*threadfn)(void *data),
                                   void *data,
                                   const char namefmt[],
                                   ...)
```

The new task is created via the `clone()` system call by the *kthread* kernel process. The new process will run the `threadfn` function, which is passed the `data` argument. The process will be named `namefmt`, which takes *printf*-style formatting arguments in the variable argument list. The process is created in an unrunnable state; it will not start running until explicitly woken up via `wake_up_process()`. A process can be created and made runnable with a single function, `kthread_run()`:

```
struct task_struct *kthread_run(int (*threadfn)(void *data),
                                void *data,
                                const char namefmt[],
                                ...)
```

This routine, implemented as a macro, simply calls both `kthread_create()` and `wake_up_process()`:

```
#define kthread_run(threadfn, data, namefmt, ...)                    \
({                                                                   \
        struct task_struct *k;                                       \
                                                                     \
        k = kthread_create(threadfn, data, namefmt, ## __VA_ARGS__); \
        if (!IS_ERR(k))                                              \
                wake_up_process(k);                                  \
        k;                                                           \
})
```

When started, a kernel thread continues to exist until it calls `do_exit()` or another part of the kernel calls `kthread_stop()`, passing in the address of the `task_struct` structure returned by `kthread_create()`:

```
int kthread_stop(struct task_struct *k)
```

We discuss specific kernel threads in more detail in later chapters.

Process Termination

It is sad, but eventually processes must die. When a process terminates, the kernel releases the resources owned by the process and notifies the child's parent of its demise.

Generally, process destruction is self-induced. It occurs when the process calls the `exit()` system call, either explicitly when it is ready to terminate or implicitly on return from the main subroutine of any program. (That is, the C compiler places a call to `exit()` after `main()` returns.) A process can also terminate involuntarily. This occurs when the process receives a signal or exception it cannot handle or ignore. Regardless of how a process terminates, the bulk of the work is handled by do_exit(), defined in kernel/exit.c, which completes a number of chores:

1. It sets the PF_EXITING flag in the flags member of the task_struct.

2. It calls del_timer_sync() to remove any kernel timers. Upon return, it is guaranteed that no timer is queued and that no timer handler is running.

3. If BSD process accounting is enabled, do_exit() calls acct_update_integrals() to write out accounting information.

4. It calls exit_mm() to release the mm_struct held by this process. If no other process is using this address space—that it, if the address space is not shared—the kernel then destroys it.

5. It calls exit_sem(). If the process is queued waiting for an IPC semaphore, it is dequeued here.

6. It then calls exit_files() and exit_fs() to decrement the usage count of objects related to file descriptors and filesystem data, respectively. If either usage counts reach zero, the object is no longer in use by any process, and it is destroyed.

7. It sets the task's exit code, stored in the exit_code member of the task_struct, to the code provided by exit() or whatever kernel mechanism forced the termination. The exit code is stored here for optional retrieval by the parent.

8. It calls exit_notify() to send signals to the task's parent, reparents any of the task's children to another thread in their thread group or the init process, and sets the task's exit state, stored in exit_state in the task_struct structure, to EXIT_ZOMBIE.

9. do_exit() calls schedule() to switch to a new process (see Chapter 4). Because the process is now not schedulable, this is the last code the task will ever execute. do_exit() never returns.

At this point, all objects associated with the task (assuming the task was the sole user) are freed. The task is not runnable (and no longer has an address space in which to run) and is in the EXIT_ZOMBIE exit state. The only memory it occupies is its kernel stack, the thread_info structure, and the task_struct structure. The task exists solely to provide information to its parent. After the parent retrieves the information, or notifies the kernel that it is uninterested, the remaining memory held by the process is freed and returned to the system for use.

Removing the Process Descriptor

After do_exit() completes, the process descriptor for the terminated process still exists, but the process is a zombie and is unable to run. As discussed, this enables the system to obtain information about a child process after it has terminated. Consequently, the acts of cleaning up after a process and removing its process descriptor are separate. After the parent has obtained information on its terminated child, or signified to the kernel that it does not care, the child's task_struct is deallocated.

The wait() family of functions are implemented via a single (and complicated) system call, wait4(). The standard behavior is to suspend execution of the calling task until one of its children exits, at which time the function returns with the PID of the exited child. Additionally, a pointer is provided to the function that on return holds the exit code of the terminated child.

When it is time to finally deallocate the process descriptor, release_task() is invoked. It does the following:

1. It calls __exit_signal(), which calls __unhash_process(), which in turns calls detach_pid() to remove the process from the pidhash and remove the process from the task list.

2. __exit_signal() releases any remaining resources used by the now dead process and finalizes statistics and bookkeeping.

3. If the task was the last member of a thread group, and the leader is a zombie, then release_task() notifies the zombie leader's parent.

4. release_task() calls put_task_struct() to free the pages containing the process's kernel stack and thread_info structure and deallocate the slab cache containing the task_struct.

At this point, the process descriptor and all resources belonging solely to the process have been freed.

The Dilemma of the Parentless Task

If a parent exits before its children, some mechanism must exist to *reparent* any child tasks to a new process, or else parentless terminated processes would forever remain zombies, wasting system memory. The solution is to reparent a task's children on exit to either another process in the current thread group or, if that fails, the init process. do_exit() calls exit_notify(), which calls forget_original_parent(), which, in turn, calls find_new_reaper() to perform the reparenting:

```
static struct task_struct *find_new_reaper(struct task_struct *father)
{
        struct pid_namespace *pid_ns = task_active_pid_ns(father);
        struct task_struct *thread;

        thread = father;
        while_each_thread(father, thread) {
                if (thread->flags & PF_EXITING)
                        continue;
                if (unlikely(pid_ns->child_reaper == father))
```

```
                    pid_ns->child_reaper = thread;
              return thread;
      }

      if (unlikely(pid_ns->child_reaper == father)) {
              write_unlock_irq(&tasklist_lock);
              if (unlikely(pid_ns == &init_pid_ns))
                      panic("Attempted to kill init!");

              zap_pid_ns_processes(pid_ns);
              write_lock_irq(&tasklist_lock);
              /*
               * We can not clear ->child_reaper or leave it alone.
               * There may by stealth EXIT_DEAD tasks on ->children,
               * forget_original_parent() must move them somewhere.
               */
              pid_ns->child_reaper = init_pid_ns.child_reaper;
      }
      return pid_ns->child_reaper;
}
```

This code attempts to find and return another task in the process's thread group. If another task is not in the thread group, it finds and returns the init process. Now that a suitable new parent for the children is found, each child needs to be located and reparented to reaper:

```
reaper = find_new_reaper(father);
list_for_each_entry_safe(p, n, &father->children, sibling) {
              p->real_parent = reaper;
              if (p->parent == father) {
                      BUG_ON(p->ptrace);
                      p->parent = p->real_parent;
              }
              reparent_thread(p, father);
      }
```

ptrace_exit_finish() is then called to do the same reparenting but to a list of *ptraced* children:

```
void exit_ptrace(struct task_struct *tracer)
{
      struct task_struct *p, *n;
      LIST_HEAD(ptrace_dead);

      write_lock_irq(&tasklist_lock);
      list_for_each_entry_safe(p, n, &tracer->ptraced, ptrace_entry) {
              if (__ptrace_detach(tracer, p))
                      list_add(&p->ptrace_entry, &ptrace_dead);
```

```
        }
        write_unlock_irq(&tasklist_lock);

        BUG_ON(!list_empty(&tracer->ptraced));

        list_for_each_entry_safe(p, n, &ptrace_dead, ptrace_entry) {
                list_del_init(&p->ptrace_entry);
                release_task(p);
        }
}
```

The rationale behind having both a child list and a ptraced list is interesting; it is a new feature in the 2.6 kernel. When a task is *ptraced,* it is temporarily reparented to the debugging process. When the task's parent exits, however, it must be reparented along with its other siblings. In previous kernels, this resulted in a loop over *every process in the system* looking for children. The solution is simply to keep a separate list of a process's children being ptraced—reducing the search for one's children from every process to just two relatively small lists.

With the process successfully reparented, there is no risk of stray zombie processes. The init process routinely calls wait() on its children, cleaning up any zombies assigned to it.

Conclusion

In this chapter, we looked at the core operating system abstraction of the *process.* We discussed the generalities of the process, why it is important, and the relationship between processes and threads. We then discussed how Linux stores and represents processes (with task_struct and thread_info), how processes are created (via fork() and ultimately clone()), how new executable images are loaded into address spaces (via the exec() family of system calls), the hierarchy of processes, how parents glean information about their deceased children (via the wait() family of system calls), and how processes ultimately die (forcefully or intentionally via exit()). The process is a fundamental and crucial abstraction, at the heart of every modern operating system, and ultimately the reason we have operating systems altogether (to run programs).

The next chapter discusses process scheduling, which is the delicate and interesting manner in which the kernel decides which processes to run, at what time, and in what order.

4

Process Scheduling

The prior chapter discussed *processes*, the operating system abstraction of active program code. This chapter discusses the *process scheduler*, the kernel subsystem that puts those processes to work.

The process scheduler decides which process runs, when, and for how long. The process scheduler (or simply the *scheduler*, to which it is often shortened) divides the finite resource of processor time between the runnable processes on a system. The scheduler is the basis of a multitasking operating system such as Linux. By deciding which process runs next, the scheduler is responsible for best utilizing the system and giving users the impression that multiple processes are executing simultaneously.

The idea behind the scheduler is simple. To best utilize processor time, assuming there are *runnable* processes, a process should always be running. If there are more runnable processes than processors in a system, some processes will not be running at a given moment. These processes are *waiting to run*. Deciding which process runs next, given a set of runnable processes, is the fundamental decision that the scheduler must make.

Multitasking

A *multitasking* operating system is one that can simultaneously interleave execution of more than one process. On single processor machines, this gives the illusion of multiple processes running concurrently. On multiprocessor machines, such functionality enables processes to actually run concurrently, in parallel, on different processors. On either type of machine, it also enables many processes to *block* or *sleep*, not actually executing until work is available. These processes, although in memory, are not *runnable*. Instead, such processes utilize the kernel to wait until some event (keyboard input, network data, passage of time, and so on) occurs. Consequently, a modern Linux system can have many processes in memory but, say, only one in a runnable state.

Multitasking operating systems come in two flavors: *cooperative multitasking* and *preemptive multitasking*. Linux, like all Unix variants and most modern operating systems, implements preemptive multitasking. In preemptive multitasking, the scheduler decides when a process is to cease running and a new process is to begin running. The act of involuntarily suspending a running process is called *preemption*. The time a process runs before it is preempted is usually predetermined, and it is called the *timeslice* of the process. The timeslice, in effect, gives each runnable process a *slice* of the processor's time. Managing the timeslice enables the scheduler to make global scheduling decisions for the system. It also prevents any one process from monopolizing the processor. On many modern operating systems, the timeslice is dynamically calculated as a function of process behavior and configurable system policy. As we shall see, Linux's unique "fair" scheduler does not employ timeslices *per se*, to interesting effect.

Conversely, in *cooperative multitasking,* a process does not stop running until it voluntary decides to do so. The act of a process voluntarily suspending itself is called *yielding*. Ideally, processes yield often, giving each runnable process a decent chunk of the processor, but the operating system cannot enforce this. The shortcomings of this approach are manifest: The scheduler cannot make global decisions regarding how long processes run; processes can monopolize the processor for longer than the user desires; and a hung process that never yields can potentially bring down the entire system. Thankfully, most operating systems designed in the last two decades employ preemptive multitasking, with Mac OS 9 (and earlier) and Windows 3.1 (and earlier) being the most notable (and embarrassing) exceptions. Of course, Unix has sported preemptive multitasking since its inception.

Linux's Process Scheduler

From Linux's first version in 1991 through the 2.4 kernel series, the Linux scheduler was simple, almost pedestrian, in design. It was easy to understand, but scaled poorly in light of many runnable processes or many processors.

In response, during the 2.5 kernel development series, the Linux kernel received a scheduler overhaul. A new scheduler, commonly called the *O(1) scheduler* because of its algorithmic behavior,[1] solved the shortcomings of the previous Linux scheduler and introduced powerful new features and performance characteristics. By introducing a constant-time algorithm for timeslice calculation and per-processor runqueues, it rectified the design limitations of the earlier scheduler.

The O(1) scheduler performed admirably and scaled effortlessly as Linux supported large "iron" with tens if not hundreds of processors. Over time, however, it became evident that the O(1) scheduler had several pathological failures related to scheduling latency-sensitive applications. These applications, called *interactive processes*, include any application with which the user interacts. Thus, although the O(1) scheduler was ideal for large server workloads—which lack interactive processes—it performed below par on desktop systems, where interactive applications are the *raison d'être*. Beginning early in the

---

[1] *O(1) is an example of big-o notation. In short, it means the scheduler can perform its work in constant time, regardless of the size of any inputs. A full explanation of big-o notation is in Chapter 6, "Kernel Data Structures."*

2.6 kernel series, developers introduced new process schedulers aimed at improving the interactive performance of the o(1) scheduler. The most notable of these was the *Rotating Staircase Deadline* scheduler, which introduced the concept of *fair scheduling*, borrowed from queuing theory, to Linux's process scheduler. This concept was the inspiration for the o(1) scheduler's eventual replacement in kernel version 2.6.23, the *Completely Fair Scheduler*, or *CFS*.

This chapter discusses the fundamentals of scheduler design and how they apply to the Completely Fair Scheduler and its goals, design, implementation, algorithms, and related system calls. We also discuss the o(1) scheduler because its implementation is a more "classic" Unix process scheduler model.

Policy

Policy is the behavior of the scheduler that determines what runs when. A scheduler's policy often determines the overall feel of a system and is responsible for optimally utilizing processor time. Therefore, it is very important.

I/O-Bound Versus Processor-Bound Processes

Processes can be classified as either *I/O-bound* or *processor-bound*. The former is characterized as a process that spends much of its time submitting and waiting on I/O requests. Consequently, such a process is runnable for only short durations, because it eventually blocks waiting on more I/O. (Here, by *I/O*, we mean any type of blockable resource, such as keyboard input or network I/O, and not just disk I/O.) Most graphical user interface (GUI) applications, for example, are I/O-bound, even if they never read from or write to the disk, because they spend most of their time waiting on user interaction via the keyboard and mouse.

Conversely, processor-bound processes spend much of their time executing code. They tend to run until they are preempted because they do not block on I/O requests very often. Because they are not I/O-driven, however, system response does not dictate that the scheduler run them often. A scheduler policy for processor-bound processes, therefore, tends to run such processes less frequently but for longer durations. The ultimate example of a processor-bound process is one executing an infinite loop. More palatable examples include programs that perform a lot of mathematical calculations, such as *ssh-keygen* or *MATLAB*.

Of course, these classifications are not mutually exclusive. Processes can exhibit both behaviors simultaneously: The X Window server, for example, is both processor and I/O-intense. Other processes can be I/O-bound but dive into periods of intense processor action. A good example of this is a word processor, which normally sits waiting for key presses but at any moment might peg the processor in a rabid fit of spell checking or macro calculation.

The scheduling policy in a system must attempt to satisfy two conflicting goals: fast process response time (low latency) and maximal system utilization (high throughput). To satisfy these at-odds requirements, schedulers often employ complex algorithms to determine the most worthwhile process to run while not compromising fairness to other, lower priority, processes. The scheduler policy in Unix systems tends to explicitly favor I/O-bound processes, thus providing good process response time. Linux, aiming to provide good interactive response and desktop performance, optimizes for process response (low latency), thus favoring I/O-bound processes over processor-bound processors. As we will see, this is done in a creative manner that does not neglect processor-bound processes.

Process Priority

A common type of scheduling algorithm is *priority-based* scheduling. The goal is to rank processes based on their worth and need for processor time. The general idea, which isn't exactly implemented on Linux, is that processes with a higher priority run before those with a lower priority, whereas processes with the same priority are scheduled *round-robin* (one after the next, repeating). On some systems, processes with a higher priority also receive a longer timeslice. The runnable process with timeslice remaining and the highest priority always runs. Both the user and the system can set a process's priority to influence the scheduling behavior of the system.

The Linux kernel implements two separate priority ranges. The first is the *nice* value, a number from −20 to +19 with a default of 0. Larger nice values correspond to a lower priority—you are being "nice" to the other processes on the system. Processes with a lower nice value (higher priority) receive a larger proportion of the system's processor compared to processes with a higher nice value (lower priority). Nice values are the standard priority range used in all Unix systems, although different Unix systems apply them in different ways, reflective of their individual scheduling algorithms. In other Unix-based systems, such as Mac OS X, the nice value is a control over the *absolute* timeslice allotted to a process; in Linux, it is a control over the *proportion* of timeslice. You can see a list of the processes on your system and their respective nice values (under the column marked *NI*) with the command ps -el.

The second range is the *real-time priority*. The values are configurable, but by default range from 0 to 99, inclusive. Opposite from nice values, higher real-time priority values correspond to a greater priority. All real-time processes are at a higher priority than normal processes; that is, the real-time priority and nice value are in disjoint value spaces. Linux implements real-time priorities in accordance with the relevant Unix standards, specifically POSIX.1b. All modern Unix systems implement a similar scheme. You can see a list of the processes on your system and their respective real-time priority (under the column marked *RTPRIO*) with the command

```
ps -eo state,uid,pid,ppid,rtprio,time,comm.
```

A value of "-" means the process is not real-time.

Timeslice

The timeslice[2] is the numeric value that represents how long a task can run until it is preempted. The scheduler policy must dictate a default timeslice, which is not a trivial exercise. Too long a timeslice causes the system to have poor interactive performance; the system will no longer feel as if applications are concurrently executed. Too short a timeslice causes significant amounts of processor time to be wasted on the overhead of switching processes because a significant percentage of the system's time is spent switching from one process with a short timeslice to the next. Furthermore, the conflicting goals of I/O-bound versus processor-bound processes again arise: I/O-bound processes do not need longer timeslices (although they do like to run often), whereas processor-bound processes crave long timeslices (to keep their caches hot).

With this argument, it would seem that *any* long timeslice would result in poor interactive performance. In many operating systems, this observation is taken to heart, and the default timeslice is rather low—for example, 10 milliseconds. Linux's CFS scheduler, however, does not directly assign timeslices to processes. Instead, in a novel approach, CFS assigns processes a *proportion* of the processor. On Linux, therefore, the amount of processor time that a process receives is a function of the load of the system. This assigned proportion is further affected by each process's nice value. The nice value acts as a weight, changing the proportion of the processor time each process receives. Processes with higher nice values (a lower priority) receive a deflationary weight, yielding them a smaller proportion of the processor; processes with smaller nice values (a higher priority) receive an inflationary weight, netting them a larger proportion of the processor.

As mentioned, the Linux operating system is *preemptive*. When a process enters the runnable state, it becomes eligible to run. In most operating systems, whether the process runs immediately, preempting the currently running process, is a function of the process's priority and available timeslice. In Linux, under the new CFS scheduler, the decision is a function of how much of a proportion of the processor the newly runnable processor has consumed. If it has consumed a smaller proportion of the processor than the currently executing process, it runs immediately, preempting the current process. If not, it is scheduled to run at a later time.

The Scheduling Policy in Action

Consider a system with two runnable tasks: a text editor and a video encoder. The text editor is I/O-bound because it spends nearly all its time waiting for user key presses. (No matter how fast the user types, it is not *that* fast.) Despite this, when the text editor does receive a key press, the user expects the editor to respond immediately. Conversely, the video encoder is processor-bound. Aside from reading the raw data stream from the disk

---

[2] *Timeslice is sometimes called* quantum *or* processor slice *in other systems. Linux calls it timeslice, thus so should you.*

and later writing the resulting video, the encoder spends all its time applying the video codec to the raw data, easily consuming 100% of the processor. The video encoder does not have any strong time constraints on when it runs—if it started running now or in half a second, the user could not tell and would not care. Of course, the sooner it finishes the better, but latency is not a primary concern.

In this scenario, ideally the scheduler gives the text editor a larger proportion of the available processor than the video encoder, because the text editor is interactive. We have two goals for the text editor. First, we want it to have a large amount of processor time available to it; not because it needs a lot of processor (it does not) but because we want it to always have processor time available the moment it needs it. Second, we want the text editor to preempt the video encoder the moment it wakes up (say, when the user presses a key). This can ensure the text editor has good *interactive performance* and is responsive to user input. On most operating systems, these goals are accomplished (if at all) by giving the text editor a higher priority and larger timeslice than the video encoder. Advanced operating systems do this automatically, by detecting that the text editor is interactive. Linux achieves these goals too, but by different means. Instead of assigning the text editor a specific priority and timeslice, it guarantees the text editor a specific proportion of the processor. If the video encoder and text editor are the only running processes and both are at the same nice level, this proportion would be 50%—each would be guaranteed half of the processor's time. Because the text editor spends most of its time blocked, waiting for user key presses, it does not use anywhere near 50% of the processor. Conversely, the video encoder is free to use *more* than its allotted 50%, enabling it to finish the encoding quickly.

The crucial concept is what happens when the text editor wakes up. Our primary goal is to ensure it runs immediately upon user input. In this case, when the editor wakes up, CFS notes that it is allotted 50% of the processor but has used considerably less. Specifically, CFS determines that the text editor has run for *less time* than the video encoder. Attempting to give all processes a *fair share* of the processor, it then preempts the video encoder and enables the text editor to run. The text editor runs, quickly processes the user's key press, and again sleeps, waiting for more input. As the text editor has not consumed its allotted 50%, we continue in this manner, with CFS always enabling the text editor to run when it wants and the video encoder to run the rest of the time.

The Linux Scheduling Algorithm

In the previous sections, we discussed process scheduling in the abstract, with only occasional mention of how Linux applies a given concept to reality. With the foundation of scheduling now built, we can dive into Linux's process scheduler.

Scheduler Classes

The Linux scheduler is modular, enabling different algorithms to schedule different types of processes. This modularity is called *scheduler classes*. Scheduler classes enable different, pluggable algorithms to coexist, scheduling their own types of processes. Each scheduler class has a priority. The base scheduler code, which is defined in `kernel/sched.c`, iterates over each scheduler class in order of priority. The highest priority scheduler class that has a runnable process wins, selecting who runs next.

The Completely Fair Scheduler (CFS) is the registered scheduler class for normal processes, called `SCHED_NORMAL` in Linux (and `SCHED_OTHER` in POSIX). CFS is defined in `kernel/sched_fair.c`. The rest of this section discusses the CFS algorithm and is germane to any Linux kernel since 2.6.23. We discuss the scheduler class for real-time processes in a later section.

Process Scheduling in Unix Systems

To discuss fair scheduling, we must first describe how traditional Unix systems schedule processes. As mentioned in the previous section, modern process schedulers have two common concepts: process priority and timeslice. Timeslice is how long a process runs; processes start with some default timeslice. Processes with a higher priority run more frequently and (on many systems) receive a higher timeslice. On Unix, the priority is exported to user-space in the form of nice values. This sounds simple, but in practice it leads to several pathological problems, which we now discuss.

First, mapping nice values onto timeslices requires a decision about what absolute timeslice to allot each nice value. This leads to suboptimal switching behavior. For example, let's assume we assign processes of the default nice value (zero) a timeslice of 100 milliseconds and processes at the highest nice value (+20, the lowest priority) a timeslice of 5 milliseconds. Further, let's assume one of each of these processes is runnable. Our default-priority process thus receives 20/21 (100 out of 105 milliseconds) of the processor, whereas our low priority process receives 1/21 (5 out of 105 milliseconds) of the processor. We could have used any numbers for this example, but we assume this allotment is optimal since we chose it. Now, what happens if we run exactly two low priority processes? We'd expect they each receive 50% of the processor, which they do. But they each enjoy the processor for only 5 milliseconds at a time (5 out of 10 milliseconds each)! That is, instead of context switching twice every 105 milliseconds, we now context switch twice every 10 milliseconds. Conversely, if we have two normal priority processes, each again receives the correct 50% of the processor, but in 100 millisecond increments. Neither of these timeslice allotments are necessarily ideal; each is simply a byproduct of a given nice value to timeslice mapping coupled with a specific runnable process priority mix. Indeed, given that high nice value (low priority) processes tend to be background, processor-intensive tasks, while normal priority processes tend to be foreground user tasks, this timeslice allotment is exactly *backward* from ideal!

A second problem concerns relative nice values and again the nice value to timeslice mapping. Say we have two processes, each a single nice value apart. First, let's assume they are at nice values 0 and 1. This might map (and indeed did in the `O(1)` scheduler) to timeslices of 100 and 95 milliseconds, respectively. These two values are nearly identical, and thus the difference here between a single nice value is small. Now, instead, let's assume our two processes are at nice values of 18 and 19. This now maps to timeslices of

10 and 5 milliseconds, respectively—the former receiving twice the processor time as the latter! Because nice values are most commonly used in relative terms (as the system call accepts an increment, not an absolute value), this behavior means that "nicing down a process by one" has wildly different effects depending on the starting nice value.

Third, if performing a nice value to timeslice mapping, we need the ability to assign an absolute timeslice. This absolute value must be measured in terms the kernel can measure. In most operating systems, this means the timeslice must be some integer multiple of the timer tick. (See Chapter 11, "Timers and Time Management," for a discussion on time.) This introduces several problems. First, the minimum timeslice has a floor of the period of the timer tick, which might be as high as 10 milliseconds or as low as 1 millisecond. Second, the system timer limits the difference between two timeslices; successive nice values might map to timeslices as much as 10 milliseconds or as little as 1 millisecond apart. Finally, timeslices change with different timer ticks. (If this paragraph's discussion of timer ticks is foreign, reread it after reading Chapter 11. This is only one motivation behind CFS.)

The fourth and final problem concerns handling process wake up in a priority-based scheduler that wants to optimize for interactive tasks. In such a system, you might want to give freshly woken-up tasks a priority boost by allowing them to run immediately, even if their timeslice was expired. Although this improves interactive performance in many, if not most, situations, it also opens the door to pathological cases where certain sleep/wake up use cases can game the scheduler into providing one process an unfair amount of processor time, at the expense of the rest of the system.

Most of these problems are solvable by making substantial but not paradigm-shifting changes to the old-school Unix scheduler. For example, making nice values geometric instead of additive solves the second problem. And mapping nice values to timeslices using a measurement decoupled from the timer tick solves the third problem. But such solutions belie the true problem, which is that assigning absolute timeslices yields a constant switching rate but variable fairness. The approach taken by CFS is a radical (for process schedulers) rethinking of timeslice allotment: Do away with timeslices completely and assign each process a proportion of the processor. CFS thus yields constant fairness but a variable switching rate.

Fair Scheduling

CFS is based on a simple concept: Model process scheduling as if the system had an ideal, perfectly multitasking processor. In such a system, each process would receive $1/n$ of the processor's time, where n is the number of runnable processes, and we'd schedule them for infinitely small durations, so that in any measurable period we'd have run all n processes for the same amount of time. As an example, assume we have two processes. In the standard Unix model, we might run one process for 5 milliseconds and then another process for 5 milliseconds. While running, each process would receive 100% of the processor. In an ideal, perfectly multitasking processor, we would run both processes *simultaneously* for 10 milliseconds, each at 50% power. This latter model is called *perfect multitasking*.

Of course, such a model is also impractical, because it is not possible on a single processor to *literally* run multiple processes simultaneously. Moreover, it is not efficient to run processes for infinitely small durations. That is, there is a *switching cost* to preempting one process for another: the overhead of swapping one process for another and the effects on caches, for example. Thus, although we'd like to run processes for very small durations, CFS is mindful of the overhead and performance hit in doing so. Instead, CFS will run each process for some amount of time, round-robin, selecting next the process that has run the least. Rather than assign each process a timeslice, CFS calculates how long a process should run as a function of the total number of runnable processes. Instead of using the nice value to calculate a timeslice, CFS uses the nice value to *weight* the proportion of processor a process is to receive: Higher valued (lower priority) processes receive a fractional weight relative to the default nice value, whereas lower valued (higher priority) processes receive a larger weight.

Each process then runs for a "timeslice" proportional to its weight divided by the total weight of all runnable threads. To calculate the actual timeslice, CFS sets a target for its approximation of the "infinitely small" scheduling duration in perfect multitasking. This target is called the *targeted latency*. Smaller targets yield better interactivity and a closer approximation to perfect multitasking, at the expense of higher switching costs and thus worse overall throughput. Let's assume the targeted latency is 20 milliseconds and we have two runnable tasks at the same priority. *Regardless of those task's priority*, each will run for 10 milliseconds before preempting in favor of the other. If we have four tasks at the same priority, each will run for 5 milliseconds. If there are 20 tasks, each will run for 1 millisecond.

Note as the number of runnable tasks approaches infinity, the proportion of allotted processor and the assigned timeslice approaches zero. As this will eventually result in unacceptable switching costs, CFS imposes a floor on the timeslice assigned to each process. This floor is called the *minimum granularity*. By default it is 1 millisecond. Thus, even as the number of runnable processes approaches infinity, each will run for at least 1 millisecond, to ensure there is a ceiling on the incurred switching costs. (Astute readers will note that CFS is thus not perfectly fair when the number of processes grows so large that the calculated proportion is floored by the minimum granularity. This is true. Although modifications to fair queuing exist to improve upon this fairness, CFS was explicitly designed to make this trade-off. In the common case of only a handful of runnable processes, CFS is perfectly fair.)

Now, let's again consider the case of two runnable processes, except with dissimilar nice values—say, one with the default nice value (zero) and one with a nice value of 5. These nice values have dissimilar weights and thus our two processes receive different proportions of the processor's time. In this case, the weights work out to about a 1/3 penalty for the nice-5 process. If our target latency is again 20 milliseconds, our two processes will receive 15 milliseconds and 5 milliseconds each of processor time, respectively. Say our two runnable processes instead had nice values of 10 and 15. What would be the allotted timeslices? Again 15 and 5 milliseconds each! Absolute nice values no longer affect scheduling decisions; only relative values affect the proportion of processor time allotted.

Put generally, the proportion of processor time that any process receives is determined only by the relative difference in niceness between it and the other runnable processes. The nice values, instead of yielding additive increases to timeslices, yield geometric differences. The absolute timeslice allotted any nice value is not an absolute number, but a given proportion of the processor. CFS is called a *fair scheduler* because it gives each process a fair share—a proportion—of the processor's time. As mentioned, note that CFS isn't perfectly fair, because it only approximates perfect multitasking, but it *can* place a lower bound on latency of *n* for *n* runnable processes on the unfairness.

The Linux Scheduling Implementation

With the discussion of the motivation for and logic of CFS behind us, we can now explore CFS's actual implementation, which lives in `kernel/sched_fair.c`. Specifically, we discuss four components of CFS:

- Time Accounting
- Process Selection
- The Scheduler Entry Point
- Sleeping and Waking Up

Time Accounting

All process schedulers must account for the time that a process runs. Most Unix systems do so, as discussed earlier, by assigning each process a timeslice. On each tick of the system clock, the timeslice is decremented by the tick period. When the timeslice reaches zero, the process is preempted in favor of another runnable process with a nonzero timeslice.

The Scheduler Entity Structure

CFS does not have the notion of a timeslice, but it must still keep account for the time that each process runs, because it needs to ensure that each process runs only for its fair share of the processor. CFS uses the *scheduler entity structure*, `struct sched_entity`, defined in `<linux/sched.h>`, to keep track of process accounting:

```
struct sched_entity {
        struct load_weight      load;
        struct rb_node          run_node;
        struct list_head        group_node;
        unsigned int            on_rq;
        u64                     exec_start;
        u64                     sum_exec_runtime;
        u64                     vruntime;
        u64                     prev_sum_exec_runtime;
```

```
u64                    last_wakeup;
u64                    avg_overlap;
u64                    nr_migrations;
u64                    start_runtime;
u64                    avg_wakeup;

/* many stat variables elided, enabled only if CONFIG_SCHEDSTATS is set */
};
```

The scheduler entity structure is embedded in the *process descriptor*, struct task_stuct, as a member variable named se. We discussed the process descriptor in Chapter 3, "Process Management."

The Virtual Runtime

The vruntime variable stores the *virtual runtime* of a process, which is the actual runtime (the amount of time spent running) normalized (or weighted) by the number of runnable processes. The virtual runtime's units are nanoseconds and therefore vruntime is decoupled from the timer tick. The virtual runtime is used to help us approximate the "ideal multitasking processor" that CFS is modeling. With such an ideal processor, we wouldn't need vruntime, because all runnable processes would perfectly multitask. That is, on an ideal processor, the virtual runtime of all processes of the same priority would be identical—all tasks would have received an equal, fair share of the processor. Because processors are not capable of perfect multitasking and we must run each process in succession, CFS uses vruntime to account for how long a process has run and thus how much longer it ought to run.

The function update_curr(), defined in kernel/sched_fair.c, manages this accounting:

```
static void update_curr(struct cfs_rq *cfs_rq)
{
        struct sched_entity *curr = cfs_rq->curr;
        u64 now = rq_of(cfs_rq)->clock;
        unsigned long delta_exec;

        if (unlikely(!curr))
                return;

        /*
         * Get the amount of time the current task was running
         * since the last time we changed load (this cannot
         * overflow on 32 bits):
         */
        delta_exec = (unsigned long)(now - curr->exec_start);
        if (!delta_exec)
                return;
```

```
              __update_curr(cfs_rq, curr, delta_exec);
              curr->exec_start = now;

              if (entity_is_task(curr)) {
                      struct task_struct *curtask = task_of(curr);

                      trace_sched_stat_runtime(curtask, delta_exec, curr->vruntime);
                      cpuacct_charge(curtask, delta_exec);
                      account_group_exec_runtime(curtask, delta_exec);
              }
      }
```

update_curr() calculates the execution time of the current process and stores that value in delta_exec. It then passes that runtime to __update_curr(), which weights the time by the number of runnable processes. The current process's vruntime is then incremented by the weighted value:

```
/*
 * Update the current task's runtime statistics. Skip current tasks that
 * are not in our scheduling class.
 */
static inline void
__update_curr(struct cfs_rq *cfs_rq, struct sched_entity *curr,
              unsigned long delta_exec)
{
      unsigned long delta_exec_weighted;

      schedstat_set(curr->exec_max, max((u64)delta_exec, curr->exec_max));

      curr->sum_exec_runtime += delta_exec;
      schedstat_add(cfs_rq, exec_clock, delta_exec);
      delta_exec_weighted = calc_delta_fair(delta_exec, curr);

      curr->vruntime += delta_exec_weighted;
      update_min_vruntime(cfs_rq);
}
```

update_curr() is invoked periodically by the system timer and also whenever a process becomes runnable or blocks, becoming unrunnable. In this manner, vruntime is an accurate measure of the runtime of a given process and an indicator of what process should run next.

Process Selection

In the last section, we discussed how vruntime on an ideal, perfectly multitasking processor would be identical among all runnable processes. In reality, we cannot perfectly multitask, so CFS attempts to balance a process's virtual runtime with a simple rule: When CFS is deciding what process to run next, it picks the process with the smallest vruntime. This is, in fact, the core of CFS's scheduling algorithm: Pick the task with the smallest vruntime. That's it! The rest of this subsection describes how the selection of the process with the smallest vruntime is implemented.

CFS uses a *red-black tree* to manage the list of runnable processes and efficiently find the process with the smallest vruntime. A red-black tree, called an *rbtree* in Linux, is a type of *self-balancing binary search tree*. We discuss self-balancing binary search trees in general and red-black trees in particular in Chapter 6. For now, if you are unfamiliar, you need to know only that red-black trees are a data structure that store *nodes* of arbitrary data, identified by a specific *key*, and that they enable efficient search for a given *key*. (Specifically, obtaining a node identified by a given key is logarithmic in time as a function of total nodes in the tree.)

Picking the Next Task

Let's start with the assumption that we have a red-black tree populated with every runnable process in the system where the key for each node is the runnable process's virtual runtime. We'll look at how we build that tree in a moment, but for now let's assume we have it. Given this tree, the process that CFS wants to run next, which is the process with the smallest vruntime, is the leftmost node in the tree. That is, if you follow the tree from the root down through the left child, and continue moving to the left until you reach a leaf node, you find the process with the smallest vruntime. (Again, if you are unfamiliar with binary search trees, don't worry. Just know that this process is efficient.) CFS's process selection algorithm is thus summed up as "run the process represented by the leftmost node in the rbtree." The function that performs this selection is __pick_next_entity(), defined in kernel/sched_fair.c:

```
static struct sched_entity *__pick_next_entity(struct cfs_rq *cfs_rq)
{
        struct rb_node *left = cfs_rq->rb_leftmost;

        if (!left)
                return NULL;

        return rb_entry(left, struct sched_entity, run_node);
}
```

Note that __pick_next_entity() does not actually traverse the tree to find the leftmost node, because the value is cached by rb_leftmost. Although it is efficient to walk the tree to find the leftmost node—O(height of tree), which is O(log N) for N nodes if the tree is balanced—it is even easier to cache the leftmost node. The return value from this function is the process that CFS next runs. If the function returns NULL, there is no leftmost node, and thus no nodes in the tree. In that case, there are no runnable processes, and CFS schedules the idle task.

Adding Processes to the Tree

Now let's look at how CFS adds processes to the rbtree and caches the leftmost node. This would occur when a process becomes runnable (wakes up) or is first created via fork(), as discussed in Chapter 3. Adding processes to the tree is performed by enqueue_entity():

```
static void
enqueue_entity(struct cfs_rq *cfs_rq, struct sched_entity *se, int flags)
{
        /*
         * Update the normalized vruntime before updating min_vruntime
         * through callig update_curr().
         */
        if (!(flags & ENQUEUE_WAKEUP) || (flags & ENQUEUE_MIGRATE))
                se->vruntime += cfs_rq->min_vruntime;

        /*
         * Update run-time statistics of the 'current'.
         */
        update_curr(cfs_rq);
        account_entity_enqueue(cfs_rq, se);

        if (flags & ENQUEUE_WAKEUP) {
                place_entity(cfs_rq, se, 0);
                enqueue_sleeper(cfs_rq, se);
        }

        update_stats_enqueue(cfs_rq, se);
        check_spread(cfs_rq, se);
        if (se != cfs_rq->curr)
                __enqueue_entity(cfs_rq, se);
}
```

This function updates the runtime and other statistics and then invokes __enqueue_entity() to perform the actual heavy lifting of inserting the entry into the red-black tree:

```
/*
 * Enqueue an entity into the rb-tree:
 */
static void __enqueue_entity(struct cfs_rq *cfs_rq, struct sched_entity *se)
{
        struct rb_node **link = &cfs_rq->tasks_timeline.rb_node;
        struct rb_node *parent = NULL;
        struct sched_entity *entry;
        s64 key = entity_key(cfs_rq, se);
        int leftmost = 1;
```

```
/*
 * Find the right place in the rbtree:
 */
while (*link) {
        parent = *link;
        entry = rb_entry(parent, struct sched_entity, run_node);
        /*
         * We dont care about collisions. Nodes with
         * the same key stay together.
         */
        if (key < entity_key(cfs_rq, entry)) {
                link = &parent->rb_left;
        } else {
                link = &parent->rb_right;
                leftmost = 0;
        }
}

/*
 * Maintain a cache of leftmost tree entries (it is frequently
 * used):
 */
if (leftmost)
        cfs_rq->rb_leftmost = &se->run_node;

rb_link_node(&se->run_node, parent, link);
rb_insert_color(&se->run_node, &cfs_rq->tasks_timeline);
}
```

Let's look at this function. The body of the while() loop traverses the tree in search of a matching key, which is the inserted process's vruntime. Per the rules of the balanced tree, it moves to the left child if the key is smaller than the current node's key and to the right child if the key is larger. If it ever moves to the right, even once, it knows the inserted process cannot be the new leftmost node, and it sets leftmost to zero. If it moves only to the left, leftmost remains one, and we have a new leftmost node and can update the cache by setting rb_leftmost to the inserted process. The loop terminates when we compare ourselves to a node that has no child in the direction we move; link is then NULL and the loop terminates. When out of the loop, the function calls rb_link_node() on the parent node, making the inserted process the new child. The function rb_insert_color() updates the self-balancing properties of the tree; we discuss the coloring in Chapter 6.

Removing Processes from the Tree

Finally, let's look at how CFS removes processes from the red-black tree. This happens when a process blocks (becomes unrunnable) or terminates (ceases to exist):

```
static void
dequeue_entity(struct cfs_rq *cfs_rq, struct sched_entity *se, int sleep)
{
        /*
         * Update run-time statistics of the 'current'.
         */
        update_curr(cfs_rq);

        update_stats_dequeue(cfs_rq, se);
        clear_buddies(cfs_rq, se);

        if (se != cfs_rq->curr)
                __dequeue_entity(cfs_rq, se);
        account_entity_dequeue(cfs_rq, se);
        update_min_vruntime(cfs_rq);

        /*
         * Normalize the entity after updating the min_vruntime because the
         * update can refer to the ->curr item and we need to reflect this
         * movement in our normalized position.
         */
        if (!sleep)
                se->vruntime -= cfs_rq->min_vruntime;
}
```

As with adding a process to the red-black tree, the real work is performed by a helper function, `__dequeue_entity()`:

```
static void __dequeue_entity(struct cfs_rq *cfs_rq, struct sched_entity *se)
{
        if (cfs_rq->rb_leftmost == &se->run_node) {
                struct rb_node *next_node;

                next_node = rb_next(&se->run_node);
                cfs_rq->rb_leftmost = next_node;
        }

        rb_erase(&se->run_node, &cfs_rq->tasks_timeline);
}
```

Removing a process from the tree is much simpler because the rbtree implementation provides the `rb_erase()` function that performs all the work. The rest of this function updates the `rb_leftmost` cache. If the process-to-remove is the leftmost node, the function invokes `rb_next()` to find what would be the next node in an in-order traversal. This is what will be the leftmost node when the current leftmost node is removed.

The Scheduler Entry Point

The main entry point into the process schedule is the function `schedule()`, defined in `kernel/sched.c`. This is the function that the rest of the kernel uses to invoke the process scheduler, deciding which process to run and then running it. `schedule()` is generic with respect to scheduler classes. That is, it finds the highest priority scheduler class with a runnable process and asks it what to run next. Given that, it should be no surprise that `schedule()` is simple. The only important part of the function—which is otherwise too uninteresting to reproduce here—is its invocation of `pick_next_task()`, also defined in `kernel/sched.c`. The `pick_next_task()` function goes through each scheduler class, starting with the highest priority, and selects the highest priority process in the highest priority class:

```
/*
 * Pick up the highest-prio task:
 */
static inline struct task_struct *
pick_next_task(struct rq *rq)
{
        const struct sched_class *class;
        struct task_struct *p;

        /*
         * Optimization: we know that if all tasks are in
         * the fair class we can call that function directly:
         */
        if (likely(rq->nr_running == rq->cfs.nr_running)) {
                p = fair_sched_class.pick_next_task(rq);
                if (likely(p))
                        return p;
        }

        class = sched_class_highest;
        for ( ; ; ) {
                p = class->pick_next_task(rq);
                if (p)
                        return p;
                /*
                 * Will never be NULL as the idle class always
                 * returns a non-NULL p:
                 */
                class = class->next;
        }
}
```

Note the optimization at the beginning of the function. Because CFS is the scheduler class for normal processes, and most systems run mostly normal processes, there is a small hack to quickly select the next CFS-provided process if the number of runnable processes is equal to the number of CFS runnable processes (which suggests that all runnable processes are provided by CFS).

The core of the function is the `for()` loop, which iterates over each class in priority order, starting with the highest priority class. Each class implements the `pick_next_task()` function, which returns a pointer to its next runnable process or, if there is not one, `NULL`. The first class to return a non-`NULL` value has selected the next runnable process. CFS's implementation of `pick_next_task()` calls `pick_next_entity()`, which in turn calls the `__pick_next_entity()` function that we discussed in the previous section.

Sleeping and Waking Up

Tasks that are sleeping (blocked) are in a special nonrunnable state. This is important because without this special state, the scheduler would select tasks that did not want to run or, worse, sleeping would have to be implemented as busy looping. A task sleeps for a number of reasons, but always while it is waiting for some event. The event can be a specified amount of time, more data from a file I/O, or another hardware event. A task can also involuntarily go to sleep when it tries to obtain a contended semaphore in the kernel (this is covered in Chapter 9, "An Introduction to Kernel Synchronization"). A common reason to sleep is file I/O—for example, the task issued a `read()` request on a file, which needs to be read in from disk. As another example, the task could be waiting for keyboard input. Whatever the case, the kernel behavior is the same: The task marks itself as sleeping, puts itself on a wait queue, removes itself from the red-black tree of runnable, and calls `schedule()` to select a new process to execute. Waking back up is the inverse: The task is set as runnable, removed from the wait queue, and added back to the red-black tree.

As discussed in the previous chapter, two states are associated with sleeping, `TASK_INTERRUPTIBLE` and `TASK_UNINTERRUPTIBLE`. They differ only in that tasks in the `TASK_UNINTERRUPTIBLE` state ignore signals, whereas tasks in the `TASK_INTERRUPTIBLE` state wake up prematurely and respond to a signal if one is issued. Both types of sleeping tasks sit on a wait queue, waiting for an event to occur, and are not runnable.

Wait Queues

Sleeping is handled via wait queues. A wait queue is a simple list of processes waiting for an event to occur. Wait queues are represented in the kernel by `wake_queue_head_t`. Wait queues are created statically via `DECLARE_WAITQUEUE()` or dynamically via `init_waitqueue_head()`. Processes put themselves on a wait queue and mark themselves not runnable. When the event associated with the wait queue occurs, the processes on the queue are awakened. It is important to implement sleeping and waking correctly, to avoid race conditions.

Some simple interfaces for sleeping used to be in wide use. These interfaces, however, have races: It is possible to go to sleep *after* the condition becomes true. In that case, the task might sleep indefinitely. Therefore, the recommended method for sleeping in the kernel is a bit more complicated:

```
/* 'q' is the wait queue we wish to sleep on */
DEFINE_WAIT(wait);

add_wait_queue(q, &wait);
while (!condition) {    /* condition is the event that we are waiting for */
        prepare_to_wait(&q, &wait, TASK_INTERRUPTIBLE);
        if (signal_pending(current))
                /* handle signal */
        schedule();
}
finish_wait(&q, &wait);
```

The task performs the following steps to add itself to a wait queue:

1. Creates a wait queue entry via the macro DEFINE_WAIT().

2. Adds itself to a wait queue via add_wait_queue(). This wait queue awakens the process when the condition for which it is waiting occurs. Of course, there needs to be code elsewhere that calls wake_up() on the queue when the event actually does occur.

3. Calls prepare_to_wait() to change the process state to either TASK_INTERRUPTIBLE or TASK_UNINTERRUPTIBLE. This function also adds the task back to the wait queue if necessary, which is needed on subsequent iterations of the loop.

4. If the state is set to TASK_INTERRUPTIBLE, a signal wakes the process up. This is called a *spurious wake up* (a wake-up not caused by the occurrence of the event). So check and handle signals.

5. When the task awakens, it again checks whether the condition is true. If it is, it exits the loop. Otherwise, it again calls schedule() and repeats.

6. Now that the condition is true, the task sets itself to TASK_RUNNING and removes itself from the wait queue via finish_wait().

If the condition occurs before the task goes to sleep, the loop terminates, and the task does not erroneously go to sleep. Note that kernel code often has to perform various other tasks in the body of the loop. For example, it might need to release locks before calling schedule() and reacquire them after or react to other events.

The function `inotify_read()` in `fs/notify/inotify/inotify_user.c`, which handles reading from the inotify file descriptor, is a straightforward example of using wait queues:

```c
static ssize_t inotify_read(struct file *file, char __user *buf,
                            size_t count, loff_t *pos)
{
        struct fsnotify_group *group;
        struct fsnotify_event *kevent;
        char __user *start;
        int ret;
        DEFINE_WAIT(wait);

        start = buf;
        group = file->private_data;

        while (1) {
                prepare_to_wait(&group->notification_waitq,
                                &wait,
                                TASK_INTERRUPTIBLE);

                mutex_lock(&group->notification_mutex);
                kevent = get_one_event(group, count);
                mutex_unlock(&group->notification_mutex);

                if (kevent) {
                        ret = PTR_ERR(kevent);
                        if (IS_ERR(kevent))
                                break;
                        ret = copy_event_to_user(group, kevent, buf);
                        fsnotify_put_event(kevent);
                        if (ret < 0)
                                break;
                        buf += ret;
                        count -= ret;
                        continue;
                }

                ret = -EAGAIN;
                if (file->f_flags & O_NONBLOCK)
                        break;
                ret = -EINTR;
                if (signal_pending(current))
                        break;

                if (start != buf)
                        break;

                schedule();
```

```
    }
    finish_wait(&group->notification_waitq, &wait);

    if (start != buf && ret != -EFAULT)
            ret = buf - start;
    return ret;
}
```

This function follows the pattern laid out in our example. The main difference is that it checks for the condition in the body of the `while()` loop, instead of in the `while()` statement itself. This is because checking the condition is complicated and requires grabbing locks. The loop is terminated via `break`.

Waking Up

Waking is handled via `wake_up()`, which wakes up all the tasks waiting on the given wait queue. It calls `try_to_wake_up()`, which sets the task's state to `TASK_RUNNING`, calls `enqueue_task()` to add the task to the red-black tree, and sets `need_resched` if the awakened task's priority is higher than the priority of the current task. The code that causes the event to occur typically calls `wake_up()` itself. For example, when data arrives from the hard disk, the VFS calls `wake_up()` on the wait queue that holds the processes waiting for the data.

An important note about sleeping is that there are spurious wake-ups. Just because a task is awakened does not mean that the event for which the task is waiting has occurred; sleeping should always be handled in a loop that ensures that the condition for which the task is waiting has indeed occurred. Figure 4.1 depicts the relationship between each scheduler state.

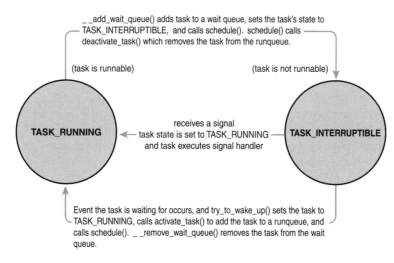

Figure 4.1   Sleeping and waking up.

Preemption and Context Switching

Context switching, the switching from one runnable task to another, is handled by the `context_switch()` function defined in `kernel/sched.c`. It is called by `schedule()` when a new process has been selected to run. It does two basic jobs:

- Calls `switch_mm()`, which is declared in `<asm/mmu_context.h>`, to switch the virtual memory mapping from the previous process's to that of the new process.
- Calls `switch_to()`, declared in `<asm/system.h>`, to switch the processor state from the previous process's to the current's. This involves saving and restoring stack information and the processor registers and any other architecture-specific state that must be managed and restored on a per-process basis.

The kernel, however, must know when to call `schedule()`. If it called `schedule()` only when code explicitly did so, user-space programs could run indefinitely. Instead, the kernel provides the `need_resched` flag to signify whether a reschedule should be performed (see Table 4.1). This flag is set by `scheduler_tick()` when a process should be preempted, and by `try_to_wake_up()` when a process that has a higher priority than the currently running process is awakened. The kernel checks the flag, sees that it is set, and calls `schedule()` to switch to a new process. The flag is a message to the kernel that the scheduler should be invoked as soon as possible because another process deserves to run.

Table 4.1   **Functions for Accessing and Manipulating need_resched**

Function	Purpose
`set_tsk_need_resched()`	Set the `need_resched` flag in the given process.
`clear_tsk_need_resched()`	Clear the `need_resched` flag in the given process.
`need_resched()`	Test the value of the `need_resched` flag; return true if set and false otherwise.

Upon returning to user-space or returning from an interrupt, the `need_resched` flag is checked. If it is set, the kernel invokes the scheduler before continuing.

The flag is per-process, and not simply global, because it is faster to access a value in the process descriptor (because of the speed of `current` and high probability of it being cache hot) than a global variable. Historically, the flag was global before the 2.2 kernel. In 2.2 and 2.4, the flag was an `int` inside the `task_struct`. In 2.6, it was moved into a single bit of a special flag variable inside the `thread_info` structure.

User Preemption

User preemption occurs when the kernel is about to return to user-space, `need_resched` is set, and therefore, the scheduler is invoked. If the kernel is returning to user-space, it knows it is in a safe quiescent state. In other words, if it is safe to continue executing the current task, it is also safe to pick a new task to execute. Consequently, whenever the kernel is preparing to return to user-space either on return from an interrupt or after a system call, the value of `need_resched` is checked. If it is set, the scheduler is invoked to select a new (more fit) process to execute. Both the return paths for return from interrupt and return from system call are architecture-dependent and typically implemented in assembly in `entry.s` (which, aside from kernel entry code, also contains kernel exit code).

In short, user preemption can occur

- When returning to user-space from a system call
- When returning to user-space from an interrupt handler

Kernel Preemption

The Linux kernel, unlike most other Unix variants and many other operating systems, is a fully preemptive kernel. In nonpreemptive kernels, kernel code runs until completion. That is, the scheduler cannot reschedule a task while it is in the kernel—kernel code is scheduled cooperatively, not preemptively. Kernel code runs until it finishes (returns to user-space) or explicitly blocks. In the 2.6 kernel, however, the Linux kernel became preemptive: It is now possible to preempt a task at any point, so long as the kernel is in a state in which it is safe to reschedule.

So when is it safe to reschedule? The kernel can preempt a task running in the kernel so long as it does not hold a lock. That is, locks are used as markers of regions of nonpreemptibility. Because the kernel is SMP-safe, if a lock is not held, the current code is reentrant and capable of being preempted.

The first change in supporting kernel preemption was the addition of a preemption counter, `preempt_count`, to each process's `thread_info`. This counter begins at zero and increments once for each lock that is acquired and decrements once for each lock that is released. When the counter is zero, the kernel is preemptible. Upon return from interrupt, if returning to kernel-space, the kernel checks the values of `need_resched` and `preempt_count`. If `need_resched` is set and `preempt_count` is zero, then a more important task is runnable, and it is safe to preempt. Thus, the scheduler is invoked. If `preempt_count` is nonzero, a lock is held, and it is unsafe to reschedule. In that case, the interrupt returns as usual to the currently executing task. When all the locks that the current task is holding are released, `preempt_count` returns to zero. At that time, the unlock code checks whether `need_resched` is set. If so, the scheduler is invoked. Enabling and disabling kernel preemption is sometimes required in kernel code and is discussed in Chapter 9.

Kernel preemption can also occur explicitly, when a task in the kernel blocks or explicitly calls `schedule()`. This form of kernel preemption has always been supported because no additional logic is required to ensure that the kernel is in a state that is safe to preempt. It is assumed that the code that explicitly calls `schedule()` knows it is safe to reschedule.

Kernel preemption can occur

- When an interrupt handler exits, before returning to kernel-space
- When kernel code becomes preemptible again
- If a task in the kernel explicitly calls `schedule()`
- If a task in the kernel blocks (which results in a call to `schedule()`)

Real-Time Scheduling Policies

Linux provides two real-time scheduling policies, `SCHED_FIFO` and `SCHED_RR`. The normal, not real-time scheduling policy is `SCHED_NORMAL`. Via the *scheduling classes* framework, these real-time policies are managed not by the Completely Fair Scheduler, but by a special real-time scheduler, defined in `kernel/sched_rt.c`. The rest of this section discusses the real-time scheduling policies and algorithm.

`SCHED_FIFO` implements a simple first-in, first-out scheduling algorithm without timeslices. A runnable `SCHED_FIFO` task is always scheduled over any `SCHED_NORMAL` tasks. When a `SCHED_FIFO` task becomes runnable, it continues to run until it blocks or explicitly yields the processor; it has no timeslice and can run indefinitely. Only a higher priority `SCHED_FIFO` or `SCHED_RR` task can preempt a `SCHED_FIFO` task. Two or more `SCHED_FIFO` tasks at the same priority run round-robin, but again only yielding the processor when they explicitly choose to do so. If a `SCHED_FIFO` task is runnable, all tasks at a lower priority cannot run until it becomes unrunnable.

`SCHED_RR` is identical to `SCHED_FIFO` except that each process can run only until it exhausts a predetermined timeslice. That is, `SCHED_RR` is `SCHED_FIFO` with timeslices—it is a real-time, round-robin scheduling algorithm. When a `SCHED_RR` task exhausts its timeslice, any other real-time processes at its priority are scheduled round-robin. The timeslice is used to allow only rescheduling of same-priority processes. As with `SCHED_FIFO`, a higher-priority process always immediately preempts a lower-priority one, and a lower-priority process can never preempt a `SCHED_RR` task, even if its timeslice is exhausted.

Both real-time scheduling policies implement static priorities. The kernel does not calculate dynamic priority values for real-time tasks. This ensures that a real-time process at a given priority *always* preempts a process at a lower priority.

The real-time scheduling policies in Linux provide soft real-time behavior. *Soft real-time* refers to the notion that the kernel tries to schedule applications within timing deadlines, but the kernel does not promise to always achieve these goals. Conversely, *hard real-time* systems are guaranteed to meet any scheduling requirements within certain limits. Linux makes no guarantees on the capability to schedule real-time tasks. Despite not having a design that guarantees hard real-time behavior, the real-time scheduling performance in Linux is quite good. The 2.6 Linux kernel is capable of meeting stringent timing requirements.

Real-time priorities range inclusively from zero to MAX_RT_PRIO minus 1. By default, MAX_RT_PRIO is 100—therefore, the default real-time priority range is zero to 99. This priority space is shared with the nice values of SCHED_NORMAL tasks: They use the space from MAX_RT_PRIO to (MAX_RT_PRIO + 40). By default, this means the −20 to +19 nice range maps directly onto the priority space from 100 to 139.

Scheduler-Related System Calls

Linux provides a family of system calls for the management of scheduler parameters. These system calls allow manipulation of process priority, scheduling policy, and processor affinity, as well as provide an explicit mechanism to *yield* the processor to other tasks.

Various books—and your friendly system man pages—provide reference to these system calls (which are all implemented in the C library without much wrapper—they just invoke the system call). Table 4.2 lists the system calls and provides a brief description. How system calls are implemented in the kernel is discussed in Chapter 5, "System Calls."

Table 4.2   **Scheduler-Related System Calls**

System Call	Description
nice()	Sets a process's nice value
sched_setscheduler()	Sets a process's scheduling policy
sched_getscheduler()	Gets a process's scheduling policy
sched_setparam()	Sets a process's real-time priority
sched_getparam()	Gets a process's real-time priority
sched_get_priority_max()	Gets the maximum real-time priority
sched_get_priority_min()	Gets the minimum real-time priority
sched_rr_get_interval()	Gets a process's timeslice value
sched_setaffinity()	Sets a process's processor affinity
sched_getaffinity()	Gets a process's processor affinity
sched_yield()	Temporarily yields the processor

Scheduling Policy and Priority-Related System Calls

The sched_setscheduler() and sched_getscheduler() system calls set and get a given process's scheduling policy and real-time priority, respectively. Their implementation, like most system calls, involves a lot of argument checking, setup, and cleanup. The important work, however, is merely to read or write the policy and rt_priority values in the process's task_struct.

The sched_setparam() and sched_getparam() system calls set and get a process's real-time priority. These calls merely encode rt_priority in a special sched_param structure. The calls sched_get_priority_max() and sched_get_priority_min() return the maximum and minimum priorities, respectively, for a given scheduling policy. The maximum priority for the real-time policies is MAX_USER_RT_PRIO minus one; the minimum is one.

For normal tasks, the nice() function increments the given process's static priority by the given amount. Only root can provide a negative value, thereby lowering the nice value and increasing the priority. The nice() function calls the kernel's set_user_nice() function, which sets the static_prio and prio values in the task's task_struct as appropriate.

Processor Affinity System Calls

The Linux scheduler enforces hard processor affinity. That is, although it tries to provide soft or natural affinity by attempting to keep processes on the same processor, the scheduler also enables a user to say, "This task must remain on this subset of the available processors no matter what." This hard affinity is stored as a bitmask in the task's task_struct as cpus_allowed. The bitmask contains one bit per possible processor on the system. By default, all bits are set and, therefore, a process is potentially runnable on any processor. The user, however, via sched_setaffinity(), can provide a different bitmask of any combination of one or more bits. Likewise, the call sched_getaffinity() returns the current cpus_allowed bitmask.

The kernel enforces hard affinity in a simple manner. First, when a process is initially created, it inherits its parent's affinity mask. Because the parent is running on an allowed processor, the child thus runs on an allowed processor. Second, when a processor's affinity is changed, the kernel uses the *migration threads* to push the task onto a legal processor. Finally, the load balancer pulls tasks to only an allowed processor. Therefore, a process only ever runs on a processor whose bit is set in the cpus_allowed field of its process descriptor.

Yielding Processor Time

Linux provides the sched_yield() system call as a mechanism for a process to explicitly yield the processor to other waiting processes. It works by removing the process from the active array (where it currently is, because it is running) and inserting it into the expired array. This has the effect of not only preempting the process and putting it at the end of its priority list, but also putting it on the expired list—guaranteeing it will not run for a while. Because real-time tasks never expire, they are a special case. Therefore, they are merely moved to the end of their priority list (and not inserted into the expired array). In earlier versions of Linux, the semantics of the `sched_yield()` call were quite different; at best, the task was moved only to the end of its priority list. The yielding was often not for a long time. Nowadays, applications and even kernel code should be certain they truly want to give up the processor before calling `sched_yield()`.

Kernel code, as a convenience, can call `yield()`, which ensures that the task's state is `TASK_RUNNING` and then call `sched_yield()`. User-space applications use the `sched_yield()` system call.

Conclusion

The process scheduler is an important part of any kernel because running processes is (for most of us, at least) the point of using the computer in the first place. Juggling the demands of process scheduling is nontrivial, however: A large number of runnable processes, scalability concerns, trade-offs between latency and throughput, and the demands of various workloads make a one-size-fits-all algorithm hard to achieve. The Linux kernel's new CFS process scheduler, however, comes close to appeasing all parties and providing an optimal solution for most use cases with good scalability through a novel, interesting approach.

The previous chapter covered process management. This chapter ruminated on the theory behind process scheduling and the specific implementation, algorithms, and interfaces used by the current Linux kernel. The next chapter covers the primary interface that the kernel provides to running processes: system calls.

5

System Calls

In any modern operating system, the kernel provides a set of interfaces by which processes running in user-space can interact with the system. These interfaces give applications controlled access to hardware, a mechanism with which to create new processes and communicate with existing ones, and the capability to request other operating system resources. The interfaces act as the messengers between applications and the kernel, with the applications issuing various requests and the kernel fulfilling them (or returning an error). The existence of these interfaces, and the fact that applications are not free to directly do whatever they want, is key to providing a stable system.

Communicating with the Kernel

System calls provide a layer between the hardware and user-space processes. This layer serves three primary purposes. First, it provides an abstracted hardware interface for user-space. When reading or writing from a file, for example, applications are not concerned with the type of disk, media, or even the type of filesystem on which the file resides. Second, system calls ensure system security and stability. With the kernel acting as a middleman between system resources and user-space, the kernel can arbitrate access based on permissions, users, and other criteria. For example, this arbitration prevents applications from incorrectly using hardware, stealing other processes' resources, or otherwise doing harm to the system. Finally, a single common layer between user-space and the rest of the system allows for the virtualized system provided to processes, discussed in Chapter 3, "Process Management." If applications were free to access system resources without the kernel's knowledge, it would be nearly impossible to implement multitasking and virtual memory, and certainly impossible to do so with stability and security. In Linux, system calls are the only means user-space has of interfacing with the kernel; they are the only legal entry point into the kernel other than exceptions and traps. Indeed, other interfaces, such as device files or /proc, are ultimately accessed via system calls. Interestingly, Linux implements far fewer system calls than most systems.[1] This chapter addresses the role and implementation of system calls in Linux.

APIs, POSIX, and the C Library

Typically, applications are programmed against an Application Programming Interface (API) implemented in user-space, not directly to system calls. This is important because no direct correlation is needed between the interfaces that applications make use of and the actual interface provided by the kernel. An API defines a set of programming interfaces used by applications. Those interfaces can be implemented as a system call, implemented through multiple system calls, or implemented without the use of system calls at all. The same API can exist on multiple systems and provide the same interface to applications while the implementation of the API itself can differ greatly from system to system. See Figure 5.1 for an example of the relationship between a POSIX API, the C library, and system calls.

| call to printf() | printf() in the C library | write() in the C library | write() system call |

Application ──────────────────────► C library ──────────────────► Kernel

Figure 5.1   The relationship between applications, the C library, and the kernel with a call to `printf()`.

One of the more common application programming interfaces in the Unix world is based on the POSIX standard. Technically, POSIX is composed of a series of standards from the IEEE[2] that aim to provide a portable operating system standard roughly based on Unix. Linux strives to be POSIX- and SUSv3-compliant where applicable.

POSIX is an excellent example of the relationship between APIs and system calls. On most Unix systems, the POSIX-defined API calls have a strong correlation to the system calls. Indeed, the POSIX standard was created to resemble the interfaces provided by earlier Unix systems. On the other hand, some systems that are rather un-Unix, such as Microsoft Windows, offer POSIX-compatible libraries.

---

[1] *There are about 335 system calls are on x86. (Each architecture is allowed to define unique system calls.) Although not all operating systems publish their exact system calls, some operating systems are estimated to have more than one thousand. In the previous edition of this book, x86 had only 250 system calls.*

[2] *IEEE (eye-triple-E) is the Institute of Electrical and Electronics Engineers. It is a nonprofit professional association involved in numerous technical areas and responsible for many important standards, such as POSIX. For more information, visit http://www.ieee.org.*

The system call interface in Linux, as with most Unix systems, is provided in part by the C library. The C library implements the main API on Unix systems, including the standard C library and the system call interface. The C library is used by all C programs and, because of C's nature, is easily wrapped by other programming languages for use in their programs. The C library additionally provides the majority of the POSIX API.

From the application programmer's point of view, system calls are irrelevant; all the programmer is concerned with is the API. Conversely, the kernel is concerned only with the system calls; what library calls and applications make use of the system calls is not of the kernel's concern. Nonetheless, it is important for the kernel to keep track of the potential uses of a system call and keep the system call as general and flexible as possible.

A meme related to interfaces in Unix is "Provide mechanism, not policy." In other words, Unix system calls exist to provide a specific function in an abstract sense. The manner in which the function is used is not any of the kernel's business.

Syscalls

System calls (often called *syscalls* in Linux) are typically accessed via function calls defined in the C library. They can define zero, one, or more arguments (inputs) and might result in one or more side effects,[3] for example writing to a file or copying some data into a provided pointer. System calls also provide a return value of type long[4] that signifies success or error—usually, although not always, a negative return value denotes an error. A return value of zero is usually (but again not always) a sign of success. The C library, when a system call returns an error, writes a special error code into the global errno variable. This variable can be translated into human-readable errors via library functions such as perror().

Finally, system calls have a defined behavior. For example, the system call getpid() is defined to return an integer that is the current process's PID. The implementation of this syscall in the kernel is simple:

```
SYSCALL_DEFINE0(getpid)
{
        return task_tgid_vnr(current); // returns current->tgid
}
```

Note that the definition says nothing of the implementation. The kernel must provide the intended behavior of the system call but is free to do so with whatever implementation

---

[3] Note the "might" here. Although nearly all system calls have a side effect (that is, they result in some change of the system's state), a few syscalls, such as getpid(), merely return some data from the kernel.

[4] The use of type long is for compatibility with 64-bit architectures.

it wants as long as the result is correct. Of course, this system call is as simple as they come, and there are not too many other ways to implement it.[5]

SYSCALL_DEFINE0 is simply a macro that defines a system call with no parameters (hence the *0*). The expanded code looks like this:

```
asmlinkage long sys_getpid(void)
```

Let's look at how system calls are defined. First, note the asmlinkage modifier on the function definition. This is a directive to tell the compiler to look only on the stack for this function's arguments. This is a required modifier for all system calls. Second, the function returns a long. For compatibility between 32- and 64-bit systems, system calls defined to return an int in user-space return a long in the kernel. Third, note that the getpid() system call is defined as sys_getpid() in the kernel. This is the naming convention taken with all system calls in Linux: System call bar() is implemented in the kernel as function sys_bar().

System Call Numbers

In Linux, each system call is assigned a *syscall number*. This is a unique number that is used to reference a specific system call. When a user-space process executes a system call, the syscall number identifies which syscall was executed; the process does not refer to the syscall by name.

The syscall number is important; when assigned, it cannot change, or compiled applications will break. Likewise, if a system call is removed, its system call number cannot be recycled, or previously compiled code would aim to invoke one system call but would in reality invoke another. Linux provides a "not implemented" system call, sys_ni_syscall(), which does nothing except return -ENOSYS, the error corresponding to an invalid system call. This function is used to "plug the hole" in the rare event that a syscall is removed or otherwise made unavailable.

The kernel keeps a list of all registered system calls in the system call table, stored in sys_call_table. This table is explicitly defined for each architecture; on x86-64 it is defined in arch/x86/kernel/syscall_64.c. This table assigns each valid syscall to a unique syscall number.

System Call Performance

System calls in Linux are faster than in many other operating systems. This is partly because of Linux's fast context switch times; entering and exiting the kernel is a stream-lined and simple affair. The other factor is the simplicity of the system call handler and the individual system calls themselves.

---

[5] *You might be wondering* why does getpid() return tgid, the thread group ID? *In normal processes, the TGID is equal to the PID. With threads, the TGID is the same for all threads in a thread group. This enables the threads to call* getpid() *and get the same PID.*

System Call Handler

It is not possible for user-space applications to execute kernel code directly. They cannot simply make a function call to a method existing in kernel-space because the kernel exists in a protected memory space. If applications could directly read and write to the kernel's address space, system security and stability would be nonexistent.

Instead, user-space applications must somehow signal to the kernel that they want to execute a system call and have the system switch to kernel mode, where the system call can be executed in kernel-space by the kernel on behalf of the application.

The mechanism to signal the kernel is a software interrupt: Incur an exception, and the system will switch to kernel mode and execute the exception handler. The exception handler, in this case, is actually the system call handler. The defined software interrupt on x86 is interrupt number 128, which is incurred via the `int $0x80` instruction. It triggers a switch to kernel mode and the execution of exception vector 128, which is the system call handler. The system call handler is the aptly named function `system_call()`. It is architecture-dependent; on x86-64 it is implemented in assembly in `entry_64.S`.[6] Recently, x86 processors added a feature known as *sysenter*. This feature provides a faster, more specialized way of trapping into a kernel to execute a system call than using the `int` interrupt instruction. Support for this feature was quickly added to the kernel. Regardless of how the system call handler is invoked, however, the important notion is that somehow user-space causes an exception or trap to enter the kernel.

Denoting the Correct System Call

Simply entering kernel-space alone is not sufficient because multiple system calls exist, all of which enter the kernel in the same manner. Thus, the system call number must be passed into the kernel. On x86, the syscall number is fed to the kernel via the `eax` register. Before causing the trap into the kernel, user-space sticks in `eax` the number corresponding to the desired system call. The system call handler then reads the value from `eax`. Other architectures do something similar.

The `system_call()` function checks the validity of the given system call number by comparing it to `NR_syscalls`. If it is larger than or equal to `NR_syscalls`, the function returns `-ENOSYS`. Otherwise, the specified system call is invoked:

```
call *sys_call_table(,%rax,8)
```

Because each element in the system call table is 64 bits (8 bytes), the kernel multiplies the given system call number by four to arrive at its location in the system call table. On x86-32, the code is similar, with the 8 replaced by 4. See Figure 5.2.

---

[6] *Much of the following description of the system call handler is based on the x86 version. They are all similar.*

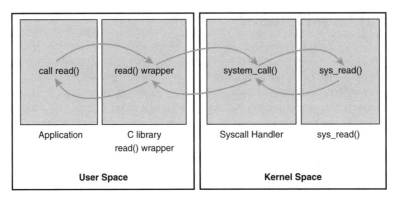

Figure 5.2   Invoking the system call handler and executing a system call.

Parameter Passing

In addition to the system call number, most syscalls require that one or more parameters be passed to them. Somehow, user-space must relay the parameters to the kernel during the trap. The easiest way to do this is via the same means that the syscall number is passed: The parameters are stored in registers. On x86-32, the registers ebx, ecx, edx, esi, and edi contain, in order, the first five arguments. In the unlikely case of six or more arguments, a single register is used to hold a pointer to user-space where all the parameters are stored.

The return value is sent to user-space also via register. On x86, it is written into the eax register.

System Call Implementation

The actual implementation of a system call in Linux does not need to be concerned with the behavior of the system call handler. Thus, adding a new system call to Linux is relatively easy. The hard work lies in designing and implementing the system call; registering it with the kernel is simple. Let's look at the steps involved in writing a new system call for Linux.

Implementing System Calls

The first step in implementing a system call is defining its purpose. What will it do? The syscall should have exactly one purpose. Multiplexing syscalls (a single system call that does wildly different things depending on a flag argument) is discouraged in Linux. Look at ioctl() as an example of what *not* to do.

What are the new system call's arguments, return value, and error codes? The system call should have a clean and simple interface with the smallest number of arguments possible. The semantics and behavior of a system call are important; they must not change, because existing applications will come to rely on them. Be forward thinking; consider how the function might change over time. Can new functionality be added to your system call or will any change require an entirely new function? Can you easily fix bugs without breaking backward compatibility? Many system calls provide a flag argument to address forward compatibility. The flag is not used to multiplex different behavior across a single system call—as mentioned, that is not acceptable—but to enable new functionality and options without breaking backward compatibility or needing to add a new system call.

Designing the interface with an eye toward the future is important. Are you needlessly limiting the function? Design the system call to be as general as possible. Do not assume its use today will be the same as its use tomorrow. The *purpose* of the system call will remain constant but its *uses* may change. Is the system call portable? Do not make assumptions about an architecture's word size or endianness. Chapter 19, "Portability," discusses these issues. Make sure you are not making poor assumptions that will break the system call in the future. Remember the Unix motto: "Provide mechanism, not policy."

When you write a system call, you need to realize the need for portability and robustness, not just today but in the future. The basic Unix system calls have survived this test of time; most of them are just as useful and applicable today as they were 30 years ago!

Verifying the Parameters

System calls must carefully verify all their parameters to ensure that they are valid and legal. The system call runs in kernel-space, and if the user can pass invalid input into the kernel without restraint, the system's security and stability can suffer.

For example, file I/O syscalls must check whether the file descriptor is valid. Process-related functions must check whether the provided PID is valid. Every parameter must be checked to ensure it is not just valid and legal, but correct. Processes must not ask the kernel to access resources to which the process does not have access.

One of the most important checks is the validity of any pointers that the user provides. Imagine if a process could pass any pointer into the kernel, unchecked, with warts and all, even passing a pointer to which it did not have read access! Processes could then trick the kernel into copying data for which they did not have access permission, such as data belonging to another process or data mapped unreadable. Before following a pointer into user-space, the system must ensure that

- The pointer points to a region of memory in user-space. Processes must not be able to trick the kernel into reading data in kernel-space on their behalf.

- The pointer points to a region of memory in the process's address space. The process must not be able to trick the kernel into reading someone else's data.

- If reading, the memory is marked readable. If writing, the memory is marked writable. If executing, the memory is marked executable. The process must not be able to bypass memory access restrictions.

The kernel provides two methods for performing the requisite checks and the desired copy to and from user-space. Note kernel code must never blindly follow a pointer into user-space! One of these two methods must always be used.

For writing into user-space, the method `copy_to_user()` is provided. It takes three parameters. The first is the destination memory address in the process's address space. The second is the source pointer in kernel-space. Finally, the third argument is the size in bytes of the data to copy.

For reading from user-space, the method `copy_from_user()` is analogous to `copy_to_user()`. The function reads from the second parameter into the first parameter the number of bytes specified in the third parameter.

Both of these functions return the number of bytes they failed to copy on error. On success, they return zero. It is standard for the syscall to return `-EFAULT` in the case of such an error.

Let's consider an example system call that uses both `copy_from_user()` and `copy_to_user()`. This syscall, `silly_copy()`, is utterly worthless; it copies data from its first parameter into its second. This is suboptimal in that it involves an intermediate and extraneous copy into kernel-space for no gain. But it helps illustrate the point.

```
/*
 * silly_copy - pointless syscall that copies the len bytes from
 * 'src' to 'dst' using the kernel as an intermediary in the copy.
 * Intended as an example of copying to and from the kernel.
 */
SYSCALL_DEFINE3(silly_copy,
                unsigned long *, src,
                unsigned long *, dst,
                unsigned long, len)
{
        unsigned long buf;

        /* copy src, which is in the user's address space, into buf */
        if (copy_from_user(&buf, src, len))
                return -EFAULT;

        /* copy buf into dst, which is in the user's address space */
        if (copy_to_user(dst, &buf, len))
                return -EFAULT;

        /* return amount of data copied */
        return len;
}
```

Both `copy_to_user()` and `copy_from_user()` may block. This occurs, for example, if the page containing the user data is not in physical memory but is swapped to disk. In that case, the process sleeps until the page fault handler can bring the page from the swap file on disk into physical memory.

A final possible check is for valid permission. In older versions of Linux, it was standard for syscalls that require *root* privilege to use `suser()`. This function merely checked whether a user was root; this is now removed and a finer-grained "capabilities" system is in place. The new system enables specific access checks on specific resources. A call to capable() with a valid capabilities flag returns nonzero if the caller holds the specified capability and zero otherwise. For example, capable(CAP_SYS_NICE) checks whether the caller has the ability to modify nice values of other processes. By default, the superuser possesses all capabilities and nonroot possesses none. For example, here is the reboot() system call. Note how its first step is ensuring that the calling process has the CAP_SYS_REBOOT. If that one conditional statement were removed, any process could reboot the system.

```
SYSCALL_DEFINE4(reboot,
                int, magic1,
                int, magic2,
                unsigned int, cmd,
                void __user *, arg)
{
        char buffer[256];

        /* We only trust the superuser with rebooting the system. */
        if (!capable(CAP_SYS_BOOT))
                return -EPERM;

        /* For safety, we require "magic" arguments. */
        if (magic1 != LINUX_REBOOT_MAGIC1 ||
            (magic2 != LINUX_REBOOT_MAGIC2 &&
                        magic2 != LINUX_REBOOT_MAGIC2A &&
                        magic2 != LINUX_REBOOT_MAGIC2B &&
                        magic2 != LINUX_REBOOT_MAGIC2C))
                return -EINVAL;

        /* Instead of trying to make the power_off code look like
         * halt when pm_power_off is not set do it the easy way.
         */
        if ((cmd == LINUX_REBOOT_CMD_POWER_OFF) && !pm_power_off)
                cmd = LINUX_REBOOT_CMD_HALT;

        lock_kernel();
        switch (cmd) {
        case LINUX_REBOOT_CMD_RESTART:
                kernel_restart(NULL);
                break;

        case LINUX_REBOOT_CMD_CAD_ON:
                C_A_D = 1;
                break;
```

```
        case LINUX_REBOOT_CMD_CAD_OFF:
                C_A_D = 0;
                break;

        case LINUX_REBOOT_CMD_HALT:
                kernel_halt();
                unlock_kernel();
                do_exit(0);
                break;

        case LINUX_REBOOT_CMD_POWER_OFF:
                kernel_power_off();
                unlock_kernel();
                do_exit(0);
                break;

        case LINUX_REBOOT_CMD_RESTART2:
                if (strncpy_from_user(&buffer[0], arg, sizeof(buffer) - 1) < 0) {
                        unlock_kernel();
                        return -EFAULT;
                }
                buffer[sizeof(buffer) - 1] = '\0';

                kernel_restart(buffer);
                break;

        default:
                unlock_kernel();
                return -EINVAL;
        }
        unlock_kernel();
        return 0;
}
```

See <linux/capability.h> for a list of all capabilities and what rights they entail.

System Call Context

As discussed in Chapter 3, the kernel is in process context during the execution of a system call. The current pointer points to the current task, which is the process that issued the syscall.

In process context, the kernel is capable of sleeping (for example, if the system call blocks on a call or explicitly calls schedule()) and is fully preemptible. These two points are important. First, the capability to sleep means that system calls can make use of the majority of the kernel's functionality. As we will see in Chapter 7, "Interrupts and

Interrupt Handlers," the capability to sleep greatly simplifies kernel programming.[7] The fact that process context is preemptible implies that, like user-space, the current task may be preempted by another task. Because the new task may then execute the same system call, care must be exercised to ensure that system calls are reentrant. Of course, this is the same concern that symmetrical multiprocessing introduces. Synchronizing reentrancy is covered in Chapter 9, "An Introduction to Kernel Synchronization," and Chapter 10, "Kernel Synchronization Methods."

When the system call returns, control continues in `system_call()`, which ultimately switches to user-space and continues the execution of the user process.

Final Steps in Binding a System Call

After the system call is written, it is trivial to register it as an official system call:

1. Add an entry to the end of the system call table. This needs to be done for each architecture that supports the system call (which, for most calls, is all the architectures). The position of the syscall in the table, starting at zero, is its system call number. For example, the tenth entry in the list is assigned syscall number nine.

2. For each supported architecture, define the syscall number in `<asm/unistd.h>`.

3. Compile the syscall into the kernel image (as opposed to compiling as a module). This can be as simple as putting the system call in a relevant file in `kernel/`, such as `sys.c`, which is home to miscellaneous system calls.

Look at these steps in more detail with a fictional system call, `foo()`. First, we want to add `sys_foo()` to the system call table. For most architectures, the table is located in `entry.S` and looks like this:

```
ENTRY(sys_call_table)
        .long sys_restart_syscall    /* 0 */
        .long sys_exit
        .long sys_fork
        .long sys_read
        .long sys_write
        .long sys_open               /* 5 */

    ...

        .long sys_eventfd2
        .long sys_epoll_create1
        .long sys_dup3               /* 330 */
```

---

[7] Interrupt handlers cannot sleep and thus are much more limited in what they can do than system calls running in process context.

```
.long sys_pipe2
.long sys_inotify_init1
.long sys_preadv
.long sys_pwritev
.long sys_rt_tgsigqueueinfo        /* 335 */
.long sys_perf_event_open
.long sys_recvmmsg
```

The new system call is then appended to the tail of this list:

```
.long sys_foo
```

Although it is not explicitly specified, the system call is then given the next subsequent syscall number—in this case, 338. For each architecture you want to support, the system call must be added to the architecture's system call table. The system call does not need to receive the same syscall number under each architecture, as the system call number is part of the architecture's unique ABI. Usually, you would want to make the system call available to each architecture. Note the convention of placing the number in a comment every five entries; this makes it easy to find out which syscall is assigned which number.

Next, the system call number is added to <asm/unistd.h>, which currently looks somewhat like this:

```
/*
 * This file contains the system call numbers.
 */

#define __NR_restart_syscall       0
#define __NR_exit                  1
#define __NR_fork                  2
#define __NR_read                  3
#define __NR_write                 4
#define __NR_open                  5


...
#define __NR_signalfd4           327
#define __NR_eventfd2            328
#define __NR_epoll_create1       329
#define __NR_dup3                330
#define __NR_pipe2               331
#define __NR_inotify_init1       332
#define __NR_preadv              333
#define __NR_pwritev             334
#define __NR_rt_tgsigqueueinfo   335
#define __NR_perf_event_open     336
#define __NR_recvmmsg            337
```

The following is then added to the end of the list:

```
#define __NR_foo                 338
```

Finally, the actual `foo()` system call is implemented. Because the system call must be compiled into the core kernel image in all configurations, in this example we define it in `kernel/sys.c`. You should put it wherever the function is most relevant; for example, if the function is related to scheduling, you could define it in `kernel/sched.c`.

```
#include <asm/page.h>


/*
 * sys_foo - everyone's favorite system call.
 *
 * Returns the size of the per-process kernel stack.
 */
asmlinkage long sys_foo(void)
{
        return THREAD_SIZE;
}
```

That is it! Boot this kernel and user-space can invoke the `foo()` system call.

Accessing the System Call from User-Space

Generally, the C library provides support for system calls. User applications can pull in function prototypes from the standard headers and link with the C library to use your system call (or the library routine that, in turn, uses your syscall call). If you just wrote the system call, however, it is doubtful that glibc already supports it!

Thankfully, Linux provides a set of macros for wrapping access to system calls. It sets up the register contents and issues the trap instructions. These macros are named `_syscalln()`, where *n* is between 0 and 6. The number corresponds to the number of parameters passed into the syscall because the macro needs to know how many parameters to expect and, consequently, push into registers. For example, consider the system call `open()`, defined as

```
long open(const char *filename, int flags, int mode)
```

The syscall macro to use this system call without explicit library support would be

```
#define __NR_open 5
_syscall3(long, open, const char *, filename, int, flags, int, mode)
```

Then, the application can simply call `open()`.

For each macro, there are 2 + 2 × n parameters. The first parameter corresponds to the return type of the syscall. The second is the name of the system call. Next follows the type and name for each parameter in order of the system call. The `__NR_open` define is in `<asm/unistd.h>`; it is the system call number. The `_syscall3` macro expands into a C function with inline assembly; the assembly performs the steps discussed in the previous section to push the system call number and parameters into the correct registers and issue the software interrupt to trap into the kernel. Placing this macro in an application is all that is required to use the open() system call.

Let's write the macro to use our splendid new foo() system call and then write some test code to show off our efforts.

```
#define __NR_foo 283
__syscall0(long, foo)

int main ()
{
        long stack_size;

        stack_size = foo ();
        printf ("The kernel stack size is %ld\n", stack_size);

        return 0;
}
```

Why Not to Implement a System Call

The previous sections have shown that it is easy to implement a new system call, but that in no way should encourage you to do so. Indeed, you should exercise caution and restraint in adding new syscalls. Often, much more viable alternatives to providing a new system call are available. Let's look at the pros, cons, and alternatives.

The pros of implementing a new interface as a syscall are as follows:

- System calls are simple to implement and easy to use.
- System call performance on Linux is fast.

The cons:

- You need a syscall number, which needs to be officially assigned to you.
- After the system call is in a stable series kernel, it is written in stone. The interface cannot change without breaking user-space applications.
- Each architecture needs to separately register the system call and support it.
- System calls are not easily used from scripts and cannot be accessed directly from the filesystem.
- Because you need an assigned syscall number, it is hard to maintain and use a system call outside of the master kernel tree.
- For simple exchanges of information, a system call is overkill.

The alternatives:

- Implement a device node and read() and write() to it. Use ioctl() to manipulate specific settings or retrieve specific information.

- Certain interfaces, such as semaphores, can be represented as file descriptors and manipulated as such.
- Add the information as a file to the appropriate location in sysfs.

For many interfaces, system calls *are* the correct answer. Linux, however, has tried to avoid simply adding a system call to support each new abstraction that comes along. The result has been an incredibly clean system call layer with few regrets or deprecations (interfaces no longer used or supported). The slow rate of addition of new system calls is a sign that Linux is a relatively stable and feature-complete operating system.

Conclusion

In this chapter, we discussed what system calls are and how they relate to library calls and the application programming interface (API). We then looked at how the Linux kernel implements system calls and the chain of events required to execute a system call: trapping into the kernel, transmitting the syscall number and any arguments, executing the correct system call function, and returning to user-space with the syscall's return value.

We then went over how to add system calls and provided a simple example of using a new system call from user-space. The whole process was quite easy! As the simplicity of adding a new system call demonstrates, the work is all in the syscall's implementation. The rest of this book discusses concepts and kernel interfaces needed to write well-behaved, optimal, and safe system calls.

Finally, we wrapped up the chapter with a discussion on the pros and cons of implementing system calls and a brief list of the alternatives to adding new ones.

6

Kernel Data Structures

This chapter introduces several built-in data structures for use in Linux kernel code. As with any large software project, the Linux kernel provides these generic data structures and primitives to encourage code reuse. Kernel developers should use these data structures whenever possible and not "roll your own" solutions. In the following sections, we cover the most useful of these generic data structures, which are the following:

- Linked lists
- Queues
- Maps
- Binary trees

We conclude the chapter with a discussion on algorithmic complexity, the ease with which algorithms and data structures scale to support ever larger inputs.

Linked Lists

The linked list is the simplest and most common data structure in the Linux kernel. A *linked list* is a data structure that allows the storage and manipulation of a variable number of *elements*, called the *nodes* of the list. Unlike in a static array, the elements in a linked list are dynamically created and inserted into the list. This enables the management of a varying number of elements unknown at compile time. Because the elements are created at different times, they do not necessarily occupy contiguous regions in memory. Therefore, the elements need to be *linked* together; thus each element in the list contains a pointer to the *next* element. As elements are added to or removed from the list, the pointer to the next node is simply adjusted.

Singly and Doubly Linked Lists

The simplest data structure representing such a linked list might look similar to the following:

```
/* an element in a linked list */
struct list_element {
        void *data;                    /* the payload */
        struct list_element *next;     /* pointer to the next element */
};
```

Figure 6.1 is a linked list.

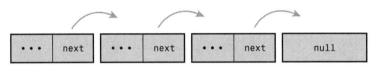

Figure 6.1   A singly linked list.

In some linked lists, each element also contains a pointer to the *previous* element. These lists are called *doubly linked lists* because they are linked both forward and backward. Linked lists, such as the list in Figure 6.1, that do not have a pointer to the previous element are called *singly linked lists*.

A data structure representing a doubly linked list would look similar to this:

```
/* an element in a linked list */
struct list_element {
        void *data;                    /* the payload */
        struct list_element *next;     /* pointer to the next element */
        struct list_element *prev;     /* pointer to the previous element */
};
```

Figure 6.2 is a doubly linked list.

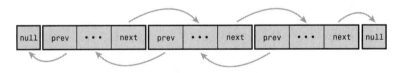

Figure 6.2   A doubly linked list.

Circular Linked Lists

Normally, because the last element in a linked list has no next element, it is set to point to a special value, such as NULL, to indicate it is the last element in the list. In some linked lists, the last element does *not* point to a special value. Instead, it points back to the first value. This linked list is called a *circular linked list* because the list is cyclic. Circular linked lists can come in both doubly and singly linked versions. In a circular doubly linked list, the first node's "previous" pointer points at the last node. Figures 6.3 and 6.4 are singly and doubly circular linked lists, respectively.

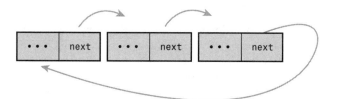

Figure 6.3   A circular singly linked list.

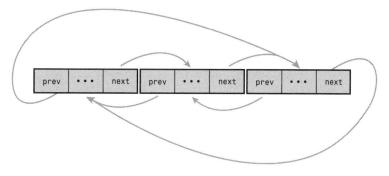

Figure 6.4   A circular doubly linked list.

Although the Linux kernel's linked list implementation is unique, it is fundamentally a *circular doubly linked list*. Using this type of linked list provides the greatest flexibility.

Moving Through a Linked List

Movement through a linked list occurs linearly. You visit one element, follow the next pointer, and visit the next element. Rinse and repeat. This is the easiest method of moving through a linked list, and the one for which linked lists are best suited. Linked lists are ill-suited for use cases where random access is an important operation. Instead, you use linked lists when iterating over the whole list is important and the dynamic addition and removal of elements is required.

In linked list implementations, the first element is often represented by a special pointer—called the *head*—that enables easy access to the "start" of the list. In a noncircular-linked list, the last element is delineated by its next pointer being NULL. In a circular-linked list, the last element is delineated because it points to the head element. Traversing the list, therefore, occurs linearly through each element from the first to the last. In a doubly linked list, movement can also occur backward, linearly from the last element to the first. Of course, given a specific element in the list, you can iterate backward and forward any number of elements, too. You need not traverse the whole list.

The Linux Kernel's Implementation

In comparison to most linked list implementations—including the generic approach described in the previous sections—the Linux kernel's implementation is unique. Recall from the earlier discussion that data (or a grouping of data, such as a `struct`) is maintained in a linked list by adding a *next* (and perhaps a *previous*) node pointer to the data. For example, assume we had a `fox` structure to describe that member of the *Canidae* family:

```
struct fox {
        unsigned long  tail_length;  /* length in centimeters of tail */
        unsigned long  weight;       /* weight in kilograms */
        bool           is_fantastic; /* is this fox fantastic? */
};
```

The common pattern for storing this structure in a linked list is to embed the list pointer in the structure. For example:

```
struct fox {
        unsigned long  tail_length;  /* length in centimeters of tail */
        unsigned long  weight;       /* weight in kilograms */
        bool           is_fantastic; /* is this fox fantastic? */
        struct fox     *next;        /* next fox in linked list */
        struct fox     *prev;        /* previous fox in linked list */
};
```

The Linux kernel approach is different. Instead of turning the structure into a linked list, the Linux approach is to *embed a linked list node in the structure*!

The Linked List Structure

In the old days, there were multiple implementations of linked lists in the kernel. A single, powerful linked list implementation was needed to remove duplicate code. During the 2.1 kernel development series, the official kernel linked-list implementation was introduced. All existing uses of linked lists now use the official implementation; do not reinvent the wheel!

The linked-list code is declared in the header file `<linux/list.h>` and the data structure is simple:

```
struct list_head {
        struct list_head *next
        struct list_head *prev;
};
```

The `next` pointer points to the next list node, and the `prev` pointer points to the previous list node. Yet, seemingly, this is not particularly useful. What value is a giant linked list...of linked list nodes? The utility is in *how* the `list_head` structure is used:

```
struct fox {
        unsigned long    tail_length; /* length in centimeters of tail */
        unsigned long    weight;      /* weight in kilograms */
        bool             is_fantastic; /* is this fox fantastic? */
        struct list_head list;        /* list of all fox structures */
};
```

With this, `list.next` in `fox` points to the next element, and `list.prev` in `fox` points to the previous. Now this is becoming useful, but it gets better. The kernel provides a family of routines to manipulate linked lists. For example, the `list_add()` method adds a new node to an existing linked list. These methods, however, are generic: They accept only `list_head` structures. Using the macro `container_of()`, we can easily find the parent structure containing any given member variable. This is because in C, the offset of a given variable into a structure is fixed by the ABI at compile time.

```
#define container_of(ptr, type, member) ({                       \
        const typeof( ((type *)0)->member ) *__mptr = (ptr);     \
        (type *)( (char *)__mptr - offsetof(type,member) );})
```

Using `container_of()`, we can define a simple function to return the parent structure containing any `list_head`:

```
#define list_entry(ptr, type, member) \
        container_of(ptr, type, member)
```

Armed with `list_entry()`, the kernel provides routines to create, manipulate, and otherwise manage linked lists—all without knowing anything about the structures that the `list_head` resides within.

Defining a Linked List

As shown, a `list_head` by itself is worthless; it is normally embedded inside your own structure:

```
struct fox {
        unsigned long    tail_length; /* length in centimeters of tail */
        unsigned long    weight;      /* weight in kilograms */
        bool             is_fantastic; /* is this fox fantastic? */
        struct list_head list;        /* list of all fox structures */
};
```

The list needs to be initialized before it can be used. Because most of the elements are created dynamically (probably why you need a linked list), the most common way of initializing the linked list is at runtime:

```
struct fox *red_fox;
red_fox = kmalloc(sizeof(*red_fox), GFP_KERNEL);
red_fox->tail_length = 40;
red_fox->weight = 6;
red_fox->is_fantastic = false;
INIT_LIST_HEAD(&red_fox->list);
```

If the structure is statically created at compile time, and you have a direct reference to it, you can simply do this:

```
struct fox red_fox = {
  .tail_length = 40,
  .weight = 6,
  .list  = LIST_HEAD_INIT(red_fox.list),
};
```

List Heads

The previous section shows how easy it is to take an existing structure—such as our struct fox example—and turn it into a linked list. With simple code changes, our structure is now manageable by the kernel's linked list routines. But before we can use those routines, we need a canonical pointer to refer to the list as a whole—a *head* pointer.

One nice aspect of the kernel's linked list implementation is that our fox nodes are indistinguishable. Each contains a list_head, and we can iterate from any one node to the next, until we have seen every node. This approach is elegant, but you will generally want a special pointer that refers to your linked list, without being a list node itself. Interestingly, this special node is in fact a normal list_head:

```
static LIST_HEAD(fox_list);
```

This defines and initializes a list_head named fox_list. The majority of the linked list routines accept one or two parameters: the head node or the head node plus an actual list node. Let's look at those routines.

Manipulating Linked Lists

The kernel provides a family of functions to manipulate linked lists. They all take pointers to one or more list_head structures. The functions are implemented as inline functions in generic C and can be found in <linux/list.h>.

Interestingly, all these functions are O(1).[1] This means they execute in *constant time*, regardless of the size of the list or any other inputs. For example, it takes the same amount of time to add or remove an entry to or from a list whether that list has 3 or 3,000 entries. This is perhaps not surprising, but still good to know.

Adding a Node to a Linked List

To add a node to a linked list:

```
list_add(struct list_head *new, struct list_head *head)
```

---

[1] *See the section "Algorithmic Complexity," later in this chapter, for a discussion on O(1).*

This function adds the `new` node to the given list immediately *after* the `head` node. Because the list is circular and generally has no concept of *first* or *last* nodes, you can pass any element for `head`. If you do pass the "last" element, however, this function can be used to implement a stack.

Returning to our fox example, assume we had a new `struct fox` that we wanted to add to the `fox_list` list. We'd do this:

```
list_add(&f->list, &fox_list);
```

To add a node to the end of a linked list:

```
list_add_tail(struct list_head *new, struct list_head *head)
```

This function adds the `new` node to the given list immediately *before* the `head` node. As with `list_add()`, because the lists are circular, you can generally pass any element for `head`. This function can be used to implement a queue, however, if you pass the "first" element.

Deleting a Node from a Linked List

After adding a node to a linked list, deleting a node from a list is the next most important operation. To delete a node from a linked list, use `list_del()`:

```
list_del(struct list_head *entry)
```

This function removes the element `entry` from the list. Note that it does not free any memory belonging to `entry` or the data structure in which it is embedded; this function merely removes the element from the list. After calling this, you would typically destroy your data structure and the `list_head` inside it.

For example, to delete the fox node we previous added to `fox_list`:

```
list_del(&f->list);
```

Note the function does not receive as input `fox_list`. It simply receives a specific node and modifies the pointers of the previous and subsequent nodes such that the given node is no longer part of the list. The implementation is instructive:

```
static inline void __list_del(struct list_head *prev, struct list_head *next)
{
        next->prev = prev;
        prev->next = next;
}

static inline void list_del(struct list_head *entry)
{
        __list_del(entry->prev, entry->next);
}
```

To delete a node from a linked list and reinitialize it, the kernel provides `list_del_init()`:

```
list_del_init(struct list_head *entry)
```

This function behaves the same as `list_del()`, except it also reinitializes the given `list_head` with the rationale that you no longer want the entry in the list, but you can reuse the data structure itself.

Moving and Splicing Linked List Nodes

To move a node from one list to another

```
list_move(struct list_head *list, struct list_head *head)
```

This function removes the `list` entry from its linked list and adds it to the given list *after* the `head` element.

To move a node from one list to the end of another

```
list_move_tail(struct list_head *list, struct list_head *head)
```

This function does the same as `list_move()`, but inserts the `list` element *before* the head entry.

To check whether a list is empty

```
list_empty(struct list_head *head)
```

This returns nonzero if the given list is empty; otherwise, it returns zero.

To splice two unconnected lists together

```
list_splice(struct list_head *list, struct list_head *head)
```

This function splices together two lists by inserting the list pointed to by `list` to the given list after the element `head`.

To splice two unconnected lists together and reinitialize the old list

```
list_splice_init(struct list_head *list, struct list_head *head)
```

This function works the same as `list_splice()`, except that the emptied list pointed to by `list` is reinitialized.

Saving a Couple Dereferences

If you happen to already have the `next` and `prev` pointers available, you can save a couple cycles (specifically, the dereferences to get the pointers) by calling the internal list functions directly. Every previously discussed function actually does nothing except find the `next` and `prev` pointers and then call the internal functions. The internal functions generally have the same name as their wrappers, except they are prefixed by double underscores. For example, rather than call `list_del(list)`, you can call `__list_del(prev, next)`. This is useful only if the next and previous pointers are *already* dereferenced. Otherwise, you are just writing ugly code. See the header `<linux/list.h>` for the exact interfaces.

Traversing Linked Lists

Now you know how to declare, initialize, and manipulate a linked list in the kernel. This is all very well and good, but it is meaningless if you have no way to access your data! The linked lists are just containers that hold your important data; you need a way to use lists to move around and access the actual structures that contain the data. The kernel (thank goodness) provides a nice set of interfaces for traversing linked lists and referencing the data structures that include them.

Note that, unlike the list manipulation routines, iterating over a linked list in its entirety is clearly an $O(n)$ operation, for n entries in the list.

The Basic Approach

The most basic way to iterate over a list is with the `list_for_each()` macro. The macro takes two parameters, both `list_head` structures. The first is a pointer used to point to the current entry; it is a temporary variable that you must provide. The second is the `list_head` acting as the head node of the list you want to traverse (see the earlier section, "List Heads"). On each iteration of the loop, the first parameter points to the next entry in the list, until each entry has been visited. Usage is as follows:

```
struct list_head *p;

list_for_each(p, fox_list) {
        /* p points to an entry in the list */
}
```

Well, that is still worthless! A pointer to the list structure is usually no good; what we need is a pointer to the structure that contains the `list_head`. For example, with the previous fox structure example, we want a pointer to each `fox`, not a pointer to the `list` member in the structure. We can use the macro `list_entry()`, which we discussed earlier, to retrieve the structure that contains a given `list_head`. For example:

```
struct list_head *p;
struct fox *f;

list_for_each(p, &fox_list) {
        /* f points to the structure in which the list is embedded */
        f = list_entry(p, struct fox, list);
}
```

The Usable Approach

The previous approach does not make for particularly intuitive or elegant code, although it does illustrate how `list_head` nodes function. Consequently, most kernel code uses the `list_for_each_entry()` macro to iterate over a linked list. This macro handles the work performed by `list_entry()`, making list iteration simple:

```
list_for_each_entry(pos, head, member)
```

Here, `pos` is a pointer to the object containing the `list_head` nodes. Think of it as the return value from `list_entry()`. `head` is a pointer to the `list_head` head node from which you want to start iterating—in our previous example, `fox_list`. `member` is the variable name of the `list_head` structure in `pos`—`list` in our example. This sounds confusing, but it is easy to use. Here is how we would rewrite the previous `list_for_each()` to iterate over every fox node:

```
struct fox *f;

list_for_each_entry(f, &fox_list, list) {
        /* on each iteration, 'f' points to the next fox structure ... */
}
```

Now let's look at a real example, from *inotify*, the kernel's filesystem notification system:

```
static struct inotify_watch *inode_find_handle(struct inode *inode,
                                               struct inotify_handle *ih)
{
        struct inotify_watch *watch;

        list_for_each_entry(watch, &inode->inotify_watches, i_list) {
                if (watch->ih == ih)
                        return watch;
        }

        return NULL;
}
```

This function iterates over all the entries in the `inode->inotify_watches` list. Each entry is of type `struct inotify_watch` and the `list_head` in that structure is named `i_list`. With each iteration of the loop, `watch` points at a new node in the list. The purpose of this simple function is to search the `inotify_watches` list in the provided `inode` structure to find an `inotify_watch` entry whose `inotify_handle` matches the provided handle.

Iterating Through a List Backward

The macro `list_for_each_entry_reverse()` works just like `list_for_each_entry()`, except that it moves through the list in reverse. That is, instead of following the next pointers *forward* through the list, it follows the `prev` pointers *backward*. Usage is the same as with `list_for_each_entry()`:

```
list_for_each_entry_reverse(pos, head, member)
```

There are only a handful of reasons to favor moving through a list in reverse. One is performance: If you know the item you are searching for is likely *behind* the node you are starting your search from, you can move backward in hopes of finding it sooner. A second reason is if ordering is important. For example, if you use a linked list as a stack, you can walk the list from the tail backward to achieve *last-in/first-out (LIFO)* ordering. If you do not have an explicit reason to move through the list in reverse, don't—just use `list_for_each_entry()`.

Iterating While Removing

The standard list iteration methods are not appropriate if you are removing entries from the list as you iterate. The standard methods rely on the fact that the list entries are not changing out from under them, and thus if the current entry is removed in the body of the loop, the subsequent iteration cannot advance to the next (or previous) pointer. This is a common pattern in loops, and programmers solve it by storing the next (or previous) pointer in a temporary variable *prior* to a potential removal operation. The Linux kernel provides a routine to handle this situation for you:

```
list_for_each_entry_safe(pos, next, head, member)
```

You use this version in the same manner as `list_for_each_entry()`, except that you provide the `next` pointer, which is of the same type as `pos`. The next pointer is used by the `list_for_each_entry_safe()` macro to store the next entry in the list, making it safe to remove the current entry. Let's consider an example, again in inotify:

```
void inotify_inode_is_dead(struct inode *inode)
{
        struct inotify_watch *watch, *next;

        mutex_lock(&inode->inotify_mutex);
        list_for_each_entry_safe(watch, next, &inode->inotify_watches, i_list) {
                struct inotify_handle *ih = watch->ih;
                mutex_lock(&ih->mutex);
                inotify_remove_watch_locked(ih, watch); /* deletes watch */
                mutex_unlock(&ih->mutex);
        }
        mutex_unlock(&inode->inotify_mutex);
}
```

This function iterates over and removes all the entries in the `inotify_watches` list. If the standard `list_for_each_entry()` were used, this code would introduce a use-after-free bug, as moving to the next item in the list would require accessing `watch`, which was destroyed.

If you need to iterate over a linked list in reverse and potentially remove elements, the kernel provides `list_for_each_entry_safe_reverse()`:

```
list_for_each_entry_safe_reverse(pos, n, head, member)
```

Usage is the same as with `list_for_each_entry_safe()`.

> ### You May Still Need Locking!
>
> The "safe" variants of `list_for_each_entry()` protect you *only* from removals from the list *within* the body of the loop. If there is a chance of concurrent removals from other code—or any other form of concurrent list manipulation—you need to properly lock access to the list.
>
> See Chapters 9, "An Introduction to Kernel Synchronization," and Chapter 10, "Kernel Synchronization Methods," for a discussion on synchronization and locking.

Other Linked List Methods

Linux provides myriad other list methods, enabling seemingly every conceivable way to access and manipulate a linked list. All these methods are defined in the header file `<linux/list.h>`.

Queues

A common programming pattern in any operating system kernel is *producer and consumer*. In this pattern, a producer creates data—say, error messages to be read or networking packets to be processed—while a consumer, in turn, reads, processes, or otherwise *consumes* the data. Often the easiest way to implement this pattern is with a *queue*. The producer pushes data onto the queue and the consumer pulls data off the queue. The consumer retrieves the data in the order it was enqueued. That is, the first data on the queue is the first data off the queue. For this reason, queues are also called *FIFOs*, short for *first-in, first-out*. See Figure 6.5 for an example of a standard queue.

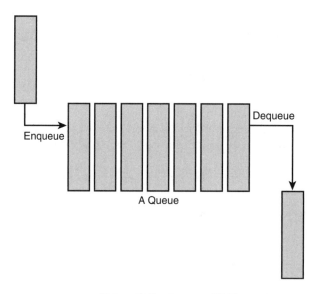

Figure 6.5   A queue (FIFO).

The Linux kernel's generic queue implementation is called *kfifo* and is implemented in
`kernel/kfifo.c` and declared in `<linux/kfifo.h>`. This section discusses the API after
an update in 2.6.33. Usage is slightly different in kernel versions prior to 2.6.33—double-
check `<linux/kfifo.h>` before writing code.

kfifo

Linux's kfifo works like most other queue abstractions, providing two primary operations:
enqueue (unfortunately named *in*) and dequeue (*out*). The kfifo object maintains two offsets into the queue: an *in offset* and an *out offset*. The in offset is the location in the queue
to which the next enqueue will occur. The out offset is the location in the queue from
which the next dequeue will occur. The out offset is always less than or equal to the in
offset. It wouldn't make sense for it to be greater; otherwise, you could dequeue data that
had not yet been enqueued.

The enqueue (in) operation copies data into the queue, starting at the in offset. When
complete, the in offset is incremented by the amount of data enqueued. The dequeue
(out) operation copies data out of the queue, starting from the out offset. When complete,
the out offset is incremented by the amount of data enqueued. When the out offset is
equal to the in offset, the queue is empty: No more data can be dequeued until more data
is enqueued. When the in offset is equal to the length of the queue, no more data can be
enqueued until the queue is reset.

Creating a Queue

To use a kfifo, you must first define and initialize it. As with most kernel objects, you can
do this dynamically or statically. The most common method is dynamic:

```
int kfifo_alloc(struct kfifo *fifo, unsigned int size, gfp_t gfp_mask);
```

This function creates and initializes a kfifo with a queue of `size` bytes. The kernel uses
the *gfp mask* `gfp_mask` to allocate the queue. (We discuss memory allocations in Chapter
12, "Memory Management"). Upon success, `kfifo_alloc()` returns zero; on error it
returns a negative error code. Following is a simple example:

```
struct kfifo fifo;
int ret;

ret = kfifo_alloc(&kifo, PAGE_SIZE, GFP_KERNEL);
if (ret)
        return ret;

/* 'fifo' now represents a PAGE_SIZE-sized queue ... */
```

If you want to allocate the buffer yourself, you can:

```
void kfifo_init(struct kfifo *fifo, void *buffer, unsigned int size);
```

This function creates and initializes a kfifo that will use the `size` bytes of memory pointed at by `buffer` for its queue. With both `kfifo_alloc()` and `kfifo_init()`, `size` must be a power of two.

Statically declaring a kfifo is simpler, but less common:

```
DECLARE_KFIFO(name, size);
INIT_KFIFO(name);
```

This creates a static kfifo named `name` with a queue of `size` bytes. As before, `size` must be a power of 2.

Enqueuing Data

When your kfifo is created and initialized, enqueuing data into the queue is performed via the `kfifo_in()` function:

```
unsigned int kfifo_in(struct kfifo *fifo, const void *from, unsigned int len);
```

This function copies the `len` bytes starting at `from` into the queue represented by `fifo`. On success it returns the number of bytes enqueued. If less than `len` bytes are free in the queue, the function copies only up to the amount of available bytes. Thus the return value can be less than `len` or even zero, if nothing was copied.

Dequeuing Data

When you add data to a queue with `kfifo_in()`, you can remove it with `kfifo_out()`:

```
unsigned int kfifo_out(struct kfifo *fifo, void *to, unsigned int len);
```

This function copies at most `len` bytes from the queue pointed at by `fifo` to the buffer pointed at by `to`. On success the function returns the number of bytes copied. If less than `len` bytes are in the queue, the function copies less than requested.

When dequeued, data is no longer accessible from the queue. This is the normal usage of a queue, but if you want to "peek" at data within the queue without removing it, you can use `kfifo_out_peek()`:

```
unsigned int kfifo_out_peek(struct kfifo *fifo, void *to, unsigned int len,
                            unsigned offset);
```

This works the same as `kfifo_out()`, except that the out offset is not incremented, and thus the dequeued data is available to read on a subsequent call to `kfifo_out()`. The parameter `offset` specifies an index into the queue; specify zero to read from the head of the queue, as `kfifo_out()` does.

Obtaining the Size of a Queue

To obtain the total size in bytes of the buffer used to store a kfifo's queue, call `kfifo_size()`:

```
static inline unsigned int kfifo_size(struct kfifo *fifo);
```

In another example of horrible kernel naming, use `kfifo_len()` to obtain the number of bytes enqueued in a kfifo:

```
static inline unsigned int kfifo_len(struct kfifo *fifo);
```

To find out the number of bytes available to write into a kfifo, call `kfifo_avail()`:

```
static inline unsigned int kfifo_avail(struct kfifo *fifo);
```

Finally, `kfifo_is_empty()` and `kfifo_is_full()` return nonzero if the given kfifo is empty or full, respectively, and zero if not:

```
static inline int kfifo_is_empty(struct kfifo *fifo);
static inline int kfifo_is_full(struct kfifo *fifo);
```

Resetting and Destroying the Queue

To reset a kfifo, jettisoning all the contents of the queue, call `kfifo_reset()`:

```
static inline void kfifo_reset(struct kfifo *fifo);
```

To destroy a kfifo allocated with `kfifo_alloc()`, call `kfifo_free()`:

```
void kfifo_free(struct kfifo *fifo);
```

If you created your kfifo with `kfifo_init()`, it is your responsibility to free the associated buffer. How you do so depends on how you created it. See Chapter 12 for a discussion on allocating and freeing dynamic memory.

Example Queue Usage

With these interfaces under our belt, let's take a look at a simple example of using a kfifo. Assume we created a kfifo pointed at by `fifo` with a queue size of 8KB. We can now enqueue data onto the queue. In this example, we enqueue simple integers. In your own code, you will likely enqueue more complicated, task-specific structures. Using integers in this example, let's see exactly how the kfifo works:

```
unsigned int i;

/* enqueue [0, 32) to the kfifo named 'fifo' */
for (i = 0; i < 32; i++)
        kfifo_in(fifo, &i; sizeof(i));
```

The kfifo named `fifo` now contains 0 through 31, inclusive. We can take a peek at the first item in the queue and verify it is 0:

```
unsigned int val;
int ret;

ret = kfifo_out_peek(fifo, &val, sizeof(val), 0);
if (ret != sizeof(val))
        return -EINVAL;
```

```
printk(KERN_INFO "%u\n", val); /* should print 0 */
```

To dequeue and print all the items in the kfifo, we can use `kfifo_out()`:

```
/* while there is data in the queue ... */
while (kfifo_avail(fifo)) {
        unsigned int val;
        int ret;

        /* ... read it, one integer at a time */
        ret = kfifo_out(fifo, &val, sizeof(val));
        if (ret != sizeof(val))
                return -EINVAL;

        printk(KERN_INFO "%u\n", val);
}
```

This prints 0 through 31, inclusive, and in that order. (If this code snippet printed the numbers backward, from 31 to 0, we would have a stack, not a queue.)

Maps

A *map*, also known as an *associative array*, is a collection of unique keys, where each key is associated with a specific value. The relationship between a key and its value is called a *mapping*. Maps support at least three operations:

- Add (key, value)
- Remove (key)
- value = Lookup (key)

Although a hash table is a type of map, not all maps are implemented via hashes. Instead of a hash table, maps can also use a self-balancing binary search tree to store their data. Although a hash offers better average-case asymptotic complexity (see the section "Algorithmic Complexity" later in this chapter), a binary search tree has better worst-case behavior (logarithmic versus linear). A binary search tree also enables *order preservation*, enabling users to efficiently iterate over the entire collection in a sorted order. Finally, a binary search tree does not require a hash function; instead, any key type is suitable so long as it can define the `<=` operator.

Although the general term for all collections mapping a key to a value, the name *maps* often refers specifically to an associated array implemented using a binary search tree as opposed to a hash table. For example, the C++ STL container `std::map` is implemented using a self-balancing binary search tree (or similar data structure), because it provides the ability to in-order traverse the collection.

The Linux kernel provides a simple and efficient map data structure, but it is not a general-purpose map. Instead, it is designed for one specific use case: mapping a unique identification number (UID) to a pointer. In addition to providing the three main map operations, Linux's implementation also piggybacks an *allocate* operation on top of the *add* operation. This allocate operation not only adds a UID/value pair to the map but also generates the UID.

The idr data structure is used for mapping user-space UIDs, such as inotify watch descriptors or POSIX timer IDs, to their associated kernel data structure, such as the `inotify_watch` or `k_itimer` structures, respectively. Following the Linux kernel's scheme of obfuscated, confusing names, this map is called *idr*.

Initializing an idr

Setting up an idr is easy. First you statically define or dynamically allocate an `idr` structure. Then you call `idr_init()`:

```
void idr_init(struct idr *idp);
```

For example:

```
struct idr id_huh;   /* statically define idr structure */
idr_init(&id_huh);   /* initialize provided idr structure */
```

Allocating a New UID

Once you have an idr set up, you can allocate a new UID, which is a two-step process. First you tell the idr that you want to allocate a new UID, allowing it to resize the backing tree as necessary. Then, with a second call, you actually request the new UID. This complication exists to allow you to perform the initial resizing, which may require a memory allocation, without a lock. We discuss memory allocations in Chapter 12 and locking in Chapters 9 and 10. For now, let's concentrate on using idr without concern to how we handle locking.

The first function, to resize the backing tree, is `idr_pre_get()`:

```
int idr_pre_get(struct idr *idp, gfp_t gfp_mask);
```

This function will, if needed to fulfill a new UID allocation, resize the idr pointed at by `idp`. If a resize is needed, the memory allocation will use the *gfp flags* `gfp_mask` (gfp flags are discussed in Chapter 12). You do not need to synchronize concurrent access to this call. Inverted from nearly every other function in the kernel, `idr_pre_get()` returns one on success and zero on error—be careful!

The second function, to actually obtain a new UID and add it to the idr, is `idr_get_new()`:

```
int idr_get_new(struct idr *idp, void *ptr, int *id);
```

This function uses the idr pointed at by idp to allocate a new UID and associate it with the pointer `ptr`. On success, the function returns zero and stores the new UID in id. On error, it returns a nonzero error code: `-EAGAIN` if you need to (again) call `idr_pre_get()` and `-ENOSPC` if the idr is full.

Let's look at a full example:

```
int id;

do {
        if (!idr_pre_get(&idr_huh, GFP_KERNEL))
                return -ENOSPC;
        ret = idr_get_new(&idr_huh, ptr, &id);
} while (ret == -EAGAIN);
```

If successful, this snippet obtains a new UID, which is stored in the integer `id` and maps that UID to `ptr` (which we don't define in the snippet).

The function `idr_get_new_above()` enables the caller to specify a minimum UID value to return:

```
int idr_get_new_above(struct idr *idp, void *ptr, int starting_id, int *id);
```

This works the same as `idr_get_new()`, except that the new UID is guaranteed to be equal to or greater than `starting_id`. Using this variant of the function allows idr users to ensure that a UID is never reused, allowing the value to be unique not only among currently allocated IDs but across the entirety of a system's uptime. This code snippet is the same as our previous example, except that we request strictly increasing UID values:

```
int id;

do {
        if (!idr_pre_get(&idr_huh, GFP_KERNEL))
                return -ENOSPC;
        ret = idr_get_new_above(&idr_huh, ptr, next_id, &id);
} while (ret == -EAGAIN);

if (!ret)
        next_id = id + 1;
```

Looking Up a UID

When we have allocated some number of UIDs in an idr, we can look them up: The caller provides the UID, and the idr returns the associated pointer. This is accomplished, in a much simpler manner than allocating a new UID, with the `idr_find()` function:

```
void *idr_find(struct idr *idp, int id);
```

A successful call to this function returns the pointer associated with the UID `id` in the idr pointed at by `idp`. On error, the function returns NULL. Note if you mapped NULL to a UID with `idr_get_new()` or `idr_get_new_above()`, this function successfully returns NULL, giving you no way to distinguish success from failure. Consequently, you should not map UIDs to NULL.

Usage is simple:

```
struct my_struct *ptr = idr_find(&idr_huh, id);
if (!ptr)
        return -EINVAL;  /* error */
```

Removing a UID

To remove a UID from an idr, use `idr_remove()`:

```
void idr_remove(struct idr *idp, int id);
```

A successful call to `idr_remove()` removes the UID `id` from the idr pointed at by `idp`. Unfortunately, `idr_remove()` has no way to signify error (for example if `id` is not in `idp`).

Destroying an idr

Destroying an idr is a simple affair, accomplished with the `idr_destroy()` function:

```
void idr_destroy(struct idr *idp);
```

A successful call to `idr_destroy()` deallocates only unused memory associated with the idr pointed at by `idp`. It does not free any memory currently in use by allocated UIDs. Generally, kernel code wouldn't destroy its idr facility until it was shutting down or unloading, and it wouldn't unload until it had no more users (and thus no more UIDs), but to force the removal of all UIDs, you can call `idr_remove_all()`:

```
void idr_remove_all(struct idr *idp);
```

You would call `idr_remove_all()` on the idr pointed at by `idp` *before* calling `idr_destroy()`, ensuring that all idr memory was freed.

Binary Trees

A *tree* is a data structure that provides a hierarchical tree-like structure of data. Mathematically, it is an *acyclic, connected, directed graph* in which each vertex (called a *node*) has zero or more outgoing edges and zero or one incoming edges. A *binary tree* is a tree in which nodes have at most two outgoing edges—that is, a tree in which nodes have zero, one, or two children. See Figure 6.6 for a sample binary tree.

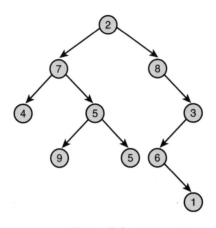

Figure 6.6   A binary tree.

Binary Search Trees

A *binary search tree* (often abbreviated *BST*) is a binary tree with a specific ordering imposed on its nodes. The ordering is often defined via the following induction:

- The left subtree of the root contains only nodes with values less than the root.
- The right subtree of the root contains only nodes with values greater than the root.
- All subtrees are also binary search trees.

A binary search tree is thus a binary tree in which all nodes are *ordered* such that left children are less than their parent in value and right children are greater than their parent. Consequently, both searching for a given node and in-order traversal are efficient (logarithmic and linear, respectively). See Figure 6.7 for a sample binary search tree.

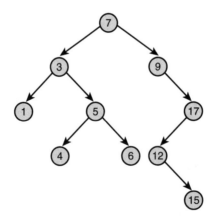

Figure 6.7   A binary search tree (BST).

Self-Balancing Binary Search Trees

The *depth* of a node is measured by how many parent nodes it is from the root. Nodes at the "bottom" of the tree—those with no children—are called *leaves*. The *height* of a tree is the depth of the deepest node in the tree. A *balanced binary search tree* is a binary search tree in which the depth of all leaves differs by at most one (see Figure 6.8). A *self-balancing binary search tree* is a binary search tree that attempts, as part of its normal operations, to remain (semi) balanced.

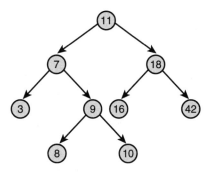

Figure 6.8   A balanced binary search tree.

Red-Black Trees

A *red-black tree* is a type of self-balancing binary search tree. Linux's primary binary tree data structure is the red-black tree. Red-black trees have a special color attribute, which is either *red* or *black*. Red-black trees remain semi-balanced by enforcing that the following six properties remain true:

1. All nodes are either red or black.

2. Leaf nodes are black.

3. Leaf nodes do not contain data.

4. All non-leaf nodes have two children.

5. If a node is red, both of its children are black.

6. The path from a node to one of its leaves contains the same number of black nodes as the shortest path to any of its other leaves.

Taken together, these properties ensure that the deepest leaf has a depth of no more than double that of the shallowest leaf. Consequently, the tree is always semi-balanced. Why this is true is surprisingly simple. First, by property five, a red node cannot be the child or parent of another red node. By property six, all paths through the tree to its leaves have the same number of black nodes. The longest path through the tree alternates red and black nodes. Thus the shortest path, which must have the same number of black nodes, contains only black nodes. Therefore, the longest path from the root to a leaf is no more than double the shortest path from the root to any other leaf.

If the insertion and removal operations enforce these six properties, the tree remains semi-balanced. Now, it might seem odd to require insert and remove to maintain *these* particular properties. Why not implement the operations such that they enforce other, simpler rules that result in a balanced tree? It turns out that these properties are relatively easy to enforce (although complex to implement), allowing insert and remove to guarantee a semi-balanced tree without burdensome extra overhead.

Describing *how* insert and remove enforce these rules is beyond the scope of this book. Although simple rules, the implementation is complex. Any good undergraduate-level data structures textbook ought to give a full treatment.

rbtrees

The Linux implementation of red-black trees is called *rbtrees*. They are defined in `lib/rbtree.c` and declared in `<linux/rbtree.h>`. Aside from optimizations, Linux's rbtrees resemble the "classic" red-black tree as described in the previous section. They remain balanced such that inserts are always logarithmic with respect to the number of nodes in the tree.

The root of an rbtree is represented by the `rb_root` structure. To create a new tree, we allocate a new `rb_root` and initialize it to the special value `RB_ROOT`:

```
struct rb_root root = RB_ROOT;
```

Individual nodes in an rbtree are represented by the `rb_node` structure. Given an `rb_node`, we can move to its left or right child by following pointers off the node of the same name.

The rbtree implementation does not provide search and insert routines. Users of rbtrees are expected to define their own. This is because C does not make generic programming easy, and the Linux kernel developers believed the most efficient way to implement search and insert was to require each user to do so manually, using provided rbtree helper functions but their own comparison operators.

The best way to demonstrate search and insert is to show a real-world example. First, let's look at search. The following function implements a search of Linux's page cache for a chunk of a file (represented by an inode and offset pair). Each inode has its own rbtree, keyed off of page offsets into file. This function thus searches the given inode's rbtree for a matching offset value:

```
struct page * rb_search_page_cache(struct inode *inode,
                                   unsigned long offset)
{
        struct rb_node *n = inode->i_rb_page_cache.rb_node;

        while (n) {
                struct page *page = rb_entry(n, struct page, rb_page_cache);
```

```
                if (offset < page->offset)
                        n = n->rb_left;
                else if (offset > page->offset)
                        n = n->rb_right;
                else
                        return page;
        }
        return NULL;
}
```

In this example, the while loop iterates over the rbtree, traversing as needed to the left or right child in the direction of the given offset. The `if` and `else` statements implement the rbtree's comparison function, thus enforcing the tree's ordering. If the loop finds a node with a matching offset, the search is complete, and the function returns the associated `page` structure. If the loop reaches the end of the rbtree without finding a match, one does not exist in the tree, and the function returns `NULL`.

Insert is even more complicated because it implements both search and insertion logic. The following isn't a trivial function, but if you need to implement your own insert routine, this is a good guide:

```
struct page * rb_insert_page_cache(struct inode *inode,
                                    unsigned long offset,
                                    struct rb_node *node)
{
        struct rb_node **p = &inode->i_rb_page_cache.rb_node;
        struct rb_node *parent = NULL;
        struct page *page;

        while (*p) {
                parent = *p;
                page = rb_entry(parent, struct page, rb_page_cache);

                if (offset < page->offset)
                        p = &(*p)->rb_left;
                else if (offset > page->offset)
                        p = &(*p)->rb_right;
                else
                        return page;
        }

        rb_link_node(node, parent, p);
        rb_insert_color(node, &inode->i_rb_page_cache);

        return NULL;
}
```

As with our search function, the while loop is iterating over the tree, moving in the direction of the provided offset. Unlike with search, however, the function is hoping *not* to find a matching offset but, instead, reach the leaf node that is the correct insertion point for the new offset. When the insertion point is found, rb_link_node() is called to insert the new node at the given spot. rb_insert_color() is then called to perform the complicated rebalancing dance. The function returns NULL if the page was added to the page cache and the address of an existing page structure if the page is already in the cache.

What Data Structure to Use, When

Thus far we've discussed four of Linux's most important data structures: linked lists, queues, maps, and red-black trees. In this section, we cover some tips to help you decide which data structure to use in your own code.

If your primary access method is iterating over all your data, use a linked list. Intuitively, no data structure can provide better than linear complexity when visiting every element, so you should favor the simplest data structure for that simple job. Also consider linked lists when performance is not important, when you need to store a relatively small number of items, or when you need to interface with other kernel code that uses linked lists.

If your code follows the producer/consumer pattern, use a queue, particularly if you want (or can cope with) a fixed-size buffer. Queues make adding and removing items simple and efficient, and they provide first-in, first-out (FIFO) semantics, which is what most producer/consumer use cases demand. On the other hand, if you need to store an unknown, potentially large number of items, a linked list may make more sense, because you can dynamically add any number of items to the list.

If you need to map a UID to an object, use a map. Maps make such mappings easy and efficient, and they also maintain and allocate the UID for you. Linux's map interface, being specific to UID-to-pointer mappings, isn't good for much else, however. If you are dealing with descriptors handed out to user-space, consider this option.

If you need to store a large amount of data and look it up efficiently, consider a red-black tree. Red-black trees enable the searching in logarithmic time, while still providing an efficient linear time in-order traversal. Although more complicated to implement than the other data structures, their in-memory footprint isn't significantly worse. If you are not performing many time-critical look-up operations, a red-black tree probably isn't your best bet. In that case, favor a linked list.

None of these data structures fit your needs? The kernel implements other seldom-used data structures that might meet your needs, such as radix trees (a type of *trie*) and bitmaps. Only after exhausting all kernel-provided solutions should you consider "rolling your own" data structure. One common data structure often implemented in individual source files is the hash table. Because a hash table is little more than some buckets and a hash function, and the hash function is so specific to each use case, there is little value in providing a kernelwide solution in a nongeneric programming language such as C.

Algorithmic Complexity

Often, in computer science and related disciplines, it is useful to express the algorithmic complexity—or *scalability*—of algorithms quantitatively. Various methods exist for representing scalability. One common technique is to study the *asymptotic behavior* of the algorithm. This is the behavior of the algorithm because its inputs grow exceedingly large and approach infinity. Asymptotic behavior shows how well an algorithm scales as its input grows larger and larger. Studying an algorithm's scalability—how it performs as the size of its input increases—enables us to model the algorithm against a benchmark and better understand its behavior.

Algorithms

An algorithm is a series of instructions, possibly one or more inputs, and ultimately a result or output. For example, the steps carried out to count the number of people in a room are an algorithm, with the people being the input and the count being the output. In the Linux kernel, both page eviction and the process scheduler are examples of algorithms. Mathematically, an algorithm is like a function. (Or at least, you can model it as one.) For example, if you call the people counting algorithm f and the number of people to count x, you can write

```
y = f(x)          people counting function
```

where y is the time required to count the x people.

Big-O Notation

One useful asymptotic notation is the upper bound, which is a function whose value, after an initial point, is always greater than the value of the function that you are studying. It is said that the upper bound grows as fast or faster than the function in question. A special notation, big-o (pronounced *big oh*) notation, is used to describe this growth. It is written f(x) is O(g(x)) and is read as *f is big-oh of g*. The formal mathematical definition is

If f(x) is O(g(x)), then
$\exists c, x'$ such that $f(x) \leq c \cdot g(x), \forall x > x'$

In English, the time to complete f(x) is always less than or equal to the time to complete g(x) multiplied by some arbitrary constant, so long as the input x is larger than some initial value x'.

Essentially, you are looking for a function whose behavior is as bad as or worse than the algorithm. You can then look at the result of large inputs to this function and obtain an understanding of the bound of your algorithm.

Big Theta Notation

When most people talk about big-o notation, they are more accurately referring to what Donald Knuth describes as *big-theta notation*. Technically, big-o notation refers to an upper bound. For example, 7 is an upper bound of 6; so are 9, 12, and 65. Subsequently, when most people discuss function growth, they talk about the *least upper bound,* or a function that models both the upper and lower bounds.[2] Professor Knuth, the father of the field of algorithmic analysis, describes this as big-theta notation and gives the following definition:

```
If f(x) is big-theta of g(x), then
g(x) is both an upper bound and a
lower bound for f(x).
```

Then, you can say that `f(x)` is of *order* `g(x)`. The order, or big-theta, of an algorithm is one of the most important mathematical tools for understanding algorithms in the kernel.

Consequently, when people refer to big-o notation, they are more often talking about the least such big-o, the big-theta. You really do not have to worry about this, unless you want to make Professor Knuth really happy.

Time Complexity

Consider the original example of having to count the number of people in a room. Pretend you can count one person per second. Then, if there are 7 people in the room, it will take 7 seconds to count them. More generally, given n people it will take n seconds to count everyone. Thus, you can say this algorithm is `O(n)`. What if the task was to dance in front of everyone in the room? Because it would take the same amount of time to dance whether there were 5 or 5,000 people in the room, this task is `O(1)`. See Table 6.1 for other common complexities.

Table 6.1   **Table of Common Time Complexity Values**

O(g(x))	Name
1	Constant (perfect scalability)
log n	Logarithmic
n	Linear
n^2	Quadratic
n^3	Cubic
2^n	Exponential
n!	Factorial

[2] *If you're curious, the lower bound is modeled by big-omega notation. The definition is the same as big-o, except g (x) is always less than or equal to f (x), not greater than or equal to. Big-omega notation is less useful than big-o because finding functions smaller than your function is rarely indicative of behavior.*

What is the complexity of introducing everyone in the room to everyone else? What is a possible function that models this algorithm? If it took 30 seconds to introduce each person, how long would it take to introduce 10 people to each other? What about 100 people to each other? Understanding how an algorithm performs as it has ever more work to do is a crucial component in determining the best algorithm for a given job.

Of course, it is wise to avoid complexities such as `O(n!)` or `O(2ⁿ)`. Likewise, it is usually an improvement to replace an `O(n)` algorithm with a functionally equivalent `O(log n)` algorithm. This is not always the case, however, and a blind assumption should not be made based solely on big-o notation. Recall that, given `O(g(x))`, there is a constant, c, multiplied by `g(x)`. Therefore, it is possible that an `O(1)` algorithm takes 3 hours to complete. Sure, it is *always* 3 hours, regardless of how large the input, but that can still be a long time compared to an `O(n)` algorithm with few inputs. The typical input size should always be taken into account when comparing algorithms.

Favor less complex algorithms, but keep in mind the overhead of the algorithm in relation to the typical input size. Do not blindly optimize to a level of scalability you will never need to support!

Conclusion

In this chapter, we discussed many of the generic data structures that Linux kernel developers use to implement everything from the process scheduler to device drivers. You will find these data structures useful as we continue our study of the Linux kernel. When writing your own kernel code, always reuse existing kernel infrastructure and don't reinvent the wheel.

We also covered algorithmic complexity and tools for measuring and expressing it, the most notable being *big-o* notation. Throughout this book and the Linux kernel, big-o notation is an important notion of how well algorithms and kernel components scale in light of many users, processes, processors, network connections, and other ever-expanding inputs.

7

Interrupts and
Interrupt Handlers

A core responsibility of any operating system kernel is managing the hardware connected to the machine—hard drives and Blu-ray discs, keyboards and mice, 3D processors and wireless radios. To meet this responsibility, the kernel needs to communicate with the machine's individual devices. Given that processors can be orders of magnitudes faster than the hardware they talk to, it is not ideal for the kernel to issue a request and wait for a response from the significantly slower hardware. Instead, because the hardware is comparatively slow to respond, the kernel must be free to go and handle other work, dealing with the hardware only after that hardware has actually completed its work.

How can the processor work with hardware without impacting the machine's overall performance? One answer to this question is *polling*. Periodically, the kernel can check the status of the hardware in the system and respond accordingly. Polling incurs overhead, however, because it must occur repeatedly regardless of whether the hardware is active or ready. A better solution is to provide a mechanism for the hardware to signal to the kernel when attention is needed. This mechanism is called an *interrupt*. In this chapter, we discuss interrupts and how the kernel responds to them, with special functions called *interrupt handlers*.

Interrupts

Interrupts enable hardware to signal to the processor. For example, as you type, the keyboard controller (the hardware device that manages the keyboard) issues an electrical signal to the processor to alert the operating system to newly available key presses. These electrical signals are interrupts. The processor receives the interrupt and signals the operating system to enable the operating system to respond to the new data. Hardware devices generate interrupts asynchronously with respect to the processor clock—they can occur at any time. Consequently, the kernel can be interrupted at any time to process interrupts.

An interrupt is physically produced by electronic signals originating from hardware devices and directed into input pins on an interrupt controller, a simple chip that multiplexes multiple interrupt lines into a single line to the processor. Upon receiving an interrupt, the interrupt controller sends a signal to the processor. The processor detects this signal and interrupts its current execution to handle the interrupt. The processor can then notify the operating system that an interrupt has occurred, and the operating system can handle the interrupt appropriately.

Different devices can be associated with different interrupts by means of a unique value associated with each interrupt. This way, interrupts from the keyboard are distinct from interrupts from the hard drive. This enables the operating system to differentiate between interrupts and to know which hardware device caused which interrupt. In turn, the operating system can service each interrupt with its corresponding handler.

These interrupt values are often called *interrupt request (IRQ)* lines. Each IRQ line is assigned a numeric value—for example, on the classic PC, IRQ zero is the timer interrupt and IRQ one is the keyboard interrupt. Not all interrupt numbers, however, are so rigidly defined. Interrupts associated with devices on the PCI bus, for example, generally are dynamically assigned. Other non–PC architectures have similar dynamic assignments for interrupt values. The important notion is that a specific interrupt is associated with a specific device, and the kernel knows this. The hardware then issues interrupts to get the kernel's attention: *Hey, I have new key presses waiting! Read and process these bad boys!*

Exceptions

In OS texts, *exceptions* are often discussed at the same time as interrupts. Unlike interrupts, exceptions occur synchronously with respect to the processor clock. Indeed, they are often called *synchronous interrupts*. Exceptions are produced by the processor while executing instructions either in response to a programming error (for example, divide by zero) or abnormal conditions that must be handled by the kernel (for example, a page fault). Because many processor architectures handle exceptions in a similar manner to interrupts, the kernel infrastructure for handling the two is similar. Much of the discussion of interrupts (asynchronous interrupts generated by hardware) in this chapter also pertains to exceptions (synchronous interrupts generated by the processor).

You are already familiar with one exception: In the previous chapter, you saw how system calls on the x86 architecture are implemented by the issuance of a software interrupt, which traps into the kernel and causes execution of a special system call handler. Interrupts work in a similar way, you will see, except hardware—not software—issues interrupts.

Interrupt Handlers

The function the kernel runs in response to a specific interrupt is called an *interrupt handler* or *interrupt service routine (ISR)*. Each device that generates interrupts has an associated interrupt handler. For example, one function handles interrupts from the system timer, whereas another function handles interrupts generated by the keyboard. The interrupt handler for a device is part of the device's *driver*—the kernel code that manages the device.

In Linux, interrupt handlers are normal C functions. They match a specific prototype, which enables the kernel to pass the handler information in a standard way, but otherwise they are ordinary functions. What differentiates interrupt handlers from other kernel functions is that the kernel invokes them in response to interrupts and that they run in a special context (discussed later in this chapter) called *interrupt context*. This special context is occasionally called *atomic context* because, as we shall see, code executing in this context is unable to block. In this book, we will use the term interrupt context.

Because an interrupt can occur at any time, an interrupt handler can, in turn, be executed at any time. It is imperative that the handler runs quickly, to resume execution of the interrupted code as soon as possible. Therefore, while it is important to the hardware that the operating system services the interrupt without delay, it is also important to the rest of the system that the interrupt handler executes in as short a period as possible.

At the very least, an interrupt handler's job is to acknowledge the interrupt's receipt to the hardware: *Hey, hardware, I hear ya; now get back to work!* Often, however, interrupt handlers have a large amount of work to perform. For example, consider the interrupt handler for a network device. On top of responding to the hardware, the interrupt handler needs to copy networking packets from the hardware into memory, process them, and push the packets down to the appropriate protocol stack or application. Obviously, this can be a lot of work, especially with today's gigabit and 10-gigabit Ethernet cards.

Top Halves Versus Bottom Halves

These two goals—that an interrupt handler execute quickly *and* perform a large amount of work—clearly conflict with one another. Because of these competing goals, the processing of interrupts is split into two parts, or halves. The interrupt handler is the *top half*. The top half is run immediately upon receipt of the interrupt and performs only the work that is time-critical, such as acknowledging receipt of the interrupt or resetting the hardware. Work that can be performed later is deferred until the *bottom half*. The bottom half runs in the future, at a more convenient time, with all interrupts enabled. Linux provides various mechanisms for implementing bottom halves, and they are all discussed in Chapter 8, "Bottom Halves and Deferring Work."

Let's look at an example of the top-half/bottom-half dichotomy, using our old friend, the network card. When network cards receive packets from the network, they need to alert the kernel of their availability. They want and need to do this immediately, to optimize network throughput and latency and avoid timeouts. Thus, they immediately issue an interrupt: *Hey, kernel, I have some fresh packets here!* The kernel responds by executing the network card's registered interrupt.

The interrupt runs, acknowledges the hardware, copies the new networking packets into main memory, and readies the network card for more packets. These jobs are the important, time-critical, and hardware-specific work. The kernel generally needs to quickly copy the networking packet into main memory because the network data buffer on the networking card is fixed and miniscule in size, particularly compared to main memory. Delays in copying the packets can result in a buffer overrun, with incoming packets overwhelming the networking card's buffer and thus packets being dropped. After the networking data is safely in the main memory, the interrupt's job is done, and it can return control of the system to whatever code was interrupted when the interrupt was generated. The rest of the processing and handling of the packets occurs later, in the bottom half. In this chapter, we look at the top half; in the next chapter, we study the bottom.

Registering an Interrupt Handler

Interrupt handlers are the responsibility of the driver managing the hardware. Each device has one associated driver and, if that device uses interrupts (and most do), then that driver must register one interrupt handler.

Drivers can register an interrupt handler and enable a given interrupt line for handling with the function request_irq(), which is declared in <linux/interrupt.h>:

```
/* request_irq: allocate a given interrupt line */
int request_irq(unsigned int irq,
                irq_handler_t handler,
                unsigned long flags,
                const char *name,
                void *dev)
```

The first parameter, irq, specifies the interrupt number to allocate. For some devices, for example legacy PC devices such as the system timer or keyboard, this value is typically hard-coded. For most other devices, it is probed or otherwise determined programmatically and dynamically.

The second parameter, handler, is a function pointer to the actual interrupt handler that services this interrupt. This function is invoked whenever the operating system receives the interrupt.

```
typedef irqreturn_t (*irq_handler_t)(int, void *);
```

Note the specific prototype of the handler function: It takes two parameters and has a return value of irqreturn_t. This function is discussed later in this chapter.

Interrupt Handler Flags

The third parameter, flags, can be either zero or a bit mask of one or more of the flags defined in <linux/interrupt.h>. Among these flags, the most important are

- IRQF_DISABLED—When set, this flag instructs the kernel to disable all interrupts when executing this interrupt handler. When unset, interrupt handlers run with all interrupts except their own enabled. Most interrupt handlers do not set this flag, as disabling all interrupts is bad form. Its use is reserved for performance-sensitive interrupts that execute quickly. This flag is the current manifestation of the SA_INTERRUPT flag, which in the past distinguished between "fast" and "slow" interrupts.

- IRQF_SAMPLE_RANDOM—This flag specifies that interrupts generated by this device should contribute to the kernel entropy pool. The kernel entropy pool provides truly random numbers derived from various random events. If this flag is specified, the timing of interrupts from this device are fed to the pool as entropy. Do *not* set this if your device issues interrupts at a predictable rate (for example, the system timer) or can be influenced by external attackers (for example, a networking device). On the other hand, most other hardware generates interrupts at nondeterministic times and is, therefore, a good source of entropy.

- IRQF_TIMER—This flag specifies that this handler processes interrupts for the system timer.

- IRQF_SHARED—This flag specifies that the interrupt line can be shared among multiple interrupt handlers. Each handler registered on a given line must specify this flag; otherwise, only one handler can exist per line. More information on shared handlers is provided in a following section.

The fourth parameter, name, is an ASCII text representation of the device associated with the interrupt. For example, this value for the keyboard interrupt on a PC is keyboard. These text names are used by /proc/irq and /proc/interrupts for communication with the user, which is discussed shortly.

The fifth parameter, dev, is used for shared interrupt lines. When an interrupt handler is freed (discussed later), dev provides a unique cookie to enable the removal of only the desired interrupt handler from the interrupt line. Without this parameter, it would be impossible for the kernel to know *which* handler to remove on a given interrupt line. You can pass NULL here if the line is not shared, but you must pass a unique cookie if your interrupt line is shared. (And unless your device is old and crusty and lives on the ISA bus, there is a good chance it must support sharing.) This pointer is also passed into the interrupt handler on each invocation. A common practice is to pass the driver's device structure: This pointer is unique and might be useful to have within the handlers.

On success, request_irq() returns zero. A nonzero value indicates an error, in which case the specified interrupt handler was not registered. A common error is -EBUSY, which denotes that the given interrupt line is already in use (and either the current user or you did not specify IRQF_SHARED).

Note that request_irq() can sleep and therefore cannot be called from interrupt context or other situations where code cannot block. It is a common mistake to call request_irq() when it is unsafe to sleep. This is partly because of *why* request_irq() can block: It is indeed unclear. On registration, an entry corresponding to the interrupt is created in /proc/irq. The function proc_mkdir() creates new procfs entries. This function calls proc_create() to set up the new procfs entries, which in turn calls kmalloc() to allocate memory. As you will see in Chapter 12, "Memory Management," kmalloc() can sleep. So there you go!

An Interrupt Example

In a driver, requesting an interrupt line and installing a handler is done via request_irq():

```
if (request_irq(irqn, my_interrupt, IRQF_SHARED, "my_device", my_dev)) {
        printk(KERN_ERR "my_device: cannot register IRQ %d\n", irqn);
        return -EIO;
}
```

In this example, `irqn` is the requested interrupt line; `my_interrupt` is the handler; we specify via flags that the line can be shared; the device is named `my_device`; and we passed `my_dev` for `dev`. On failure, the code prints an error and returns. If the call returns zero, the handler has been successfully installed. From that point forward, the handler is invoked in response to an interrupt. It is important to initialize hardware and register an interrupt handler in the proper order to prevent the interrupt handler from running before the device is fully initialized.

Freeing an Interrupt Handler

When your driver unloads, you need to unregister your interrupt handler and potentially disable the interrupt line. To do this, call

```
void free_irq(unsigned int irq, void *dev)
```

If the specified interrupt line is not shared, this function removes the handler and disables the line. If the interrupt line is shared, the handler identified via `dev` is removed, but the interrupt line is disabled only when the last handler is removed. Now you can see why a unique `dev` is important. With shared interrupt lines, a unique cookie is required to differentiate between the multiple handlers that can exist on a single line and enable `free_irq()` to remove only the correct handler. In either case (shared or unshared), if `dev` is non-NULL, it must match the desired handler. A call to `free_irq()` must be made from process context.

Table 7.1 reviews the functions for registering and deregistering an interrupt handler.

Table 7.1   **Interrupt Registration Methods**

Function	Description
`request_irq()`	Register a given interrupt handler on a given interrupt line.
`free_irq()`	Unregister a given interrupt handler; if no handlers remain on the line, the given interrupt line is disabled.

Writing an Interrupt Handler

The following is a declaration of an interrupt handler:

```
static irqreturn_t intr_handler(int irq, void *dev)
```

Note that this declaration matches the prototype of the `handler` argument given to `request_irq()`. The first parameter, `irq`, is the numeric value of the interrupt line the handler is servicing. This value is passed into the handler, but it is not used very often, except in printing log messages. Before version 2.0 of the Linux kernel, there was not a `dev` parameter and thus `irq` was used to differentiate between multiple devices using the same driver and therefore the same interrupt handler. As an example of this, consider a computer with multiple hard drive controllers of the same type.

The second parameter, `dev`, is a generic pointer to the same `dev` that was given to `request_irq()` when the interrupt handler was registered. If this value is unique (which is required to support sharing), it can act as a cookie to differentiate between multiple devices potentially using the same interrupt handler. `dev` might also point to a structure of use to the interrupt handler. Because the `device` structure is both unique to each device and potentially useful to have within the handler, it is typically passed for `dev`.

The return value of an interrupt handler is the special type `irqreturn_t`. An interrupt handler can return two special values, `IRQ_NONE` or `IRQ_HANDLED`. The former is returned when the interrupt handler detects an interrupt for which its device was not the originator. The latter is returned if the interrupt handler was correctly invoked, and its device did indeed cause the interrupt. Alternatively, `IRQ_RETVAL(val)` may be used. If `val` is nonzero, this macro returns `IRQ_HANDLED`. Otherwise, the macro returns `IRQ_NONE`. These special values are used to let the kernel know whether devices are issuing spurious (that is, unrequested) interrupts. If all the interrupt handlers on a given interrupt line return `IRQ_NONE`, then the kernel can detect the problem. Note the curious return type, `irqreturn_t`, which is simply an `int`. This value provides backward compatibility with earlier kernels, which did not have this feature; before 2.6, interrupt handlers returned `void`. Drivers may simply typedef `irqreturn_t` to `void` and define the different return values to no-ops and then work in 2.4 without further modification. The interrupt handler is normally marked `static` because it is never called directly from another file.

The role of the interrupt handler depends entirely on the device and its reasons for issuing the interrupt. At a minimum, most interrupt handlers need to provide acknowledgment to the device that they received the interrupt. Devices that are more complex need to additionally send and receive data and perform extended work in the interrupt handler. As mentioned, the extended work is pushed as much as possible into the bottom half handler, which is discussed in the next chapter.

Reentrancy and Interrupt Handlers

Interrupt handlers in Linux need not be reentrant. When a given interrupt handler is executing, the corresponding interrupt line is masked out on all processors, preventing another interrupt on the same line from being received. Normally all other interrupts are enabled, so other interrupts are serviced, but the current line is always disabled. Consequently, the same interrupt handler is never invoked concurrently to service a nested interrupt. This greatly simplifies writing your interrupt handler.

Shared Handlers

A shared handler is registered and executed much like a nonshared handler. Following are three main differences:

- The `IRQF_SHARED` flag must be set in the `flags` argument to `request_irq()`.
- The `dev` argument must be unique to each registered handler. A pointer to any per-device structure is sufficient; a common choice is the `device` structure as it is

both unique and potentially useful to the handler. You *cannot* pass NULL for a shared handler!

- The interrupt handler must be capable of distinguishing whether its device actually generated an interrupt. This requires both hardware support and associated logic in the interrupt handler. If the hardware did not offer this capability, there would be no way for the interrupt handler to know whether its associated device or some other device sharing the line caused the interrupt.

All drivers sharing the interrupt line must meet the previous requirements. If any one device does not share fairly, none can share the line. When request_irq() is called with IRQF_SHARED specified, the call succeeds only if the interrupt line is currently not registered, or if all registered handlers on the line also specified IRQF_SHARED. Shared handlers, however, can mix usage of IRQF_DISABLED.

When the kernel receives an interrupt, it invokes sequentially each registered handler on the line. Therefore, it is important that the handler be capable of distinguishing whether it generated a given interrupt. The handler must quickly exit if its associated device did not generate the interrupt. This requires the hardware device to have a status register (or similar mechanism) that the handler can check. Most hardware does indeed have such a feature.

A Real-Life Interrupt Handler

Let's look at a real interrupt handler, from the real-time clock (RTC) driver, found in drivers/char/rtc.c. An RTC is found in many machines, including PCs. It is a device, separate from the system timer, which sets the system clock, provides an alarm, or supplies a periodic timer. On most architectures, the system clock is set by writing the desired time into a specific register or I/O range. Any alarm or periodic timer functionality is normally implemented via interrupt. The interrupt is equivalent to a real-world clock alarm: The receipt of the interrupt is analogous to a buzzing alarm.

When the RTC driver loads, the function rtc_init() is invoked to initialize the driver. One of its duties is to register the interrupt handler:

```
/* register rtc_interrupt on rtc_irq */
if (request_irq(rtc_irq, rtc_interrupt, IRQF_SHARED, "rtc", (void *)&rtc_port)) {
        printk(KERN_ERR "rtc: cannot register IRQ %d\n", rtc_irq);
        return -EIO;
}
```

In this example, the interrupt line is stored in rtc_irq. This variable is set to the RTC interrupt for a given architecture. On a PC, the RTC is located at IRQ 8. The second parameter is the interrupt handler, rtc_interrupt, which is willing to share the interrupt line with other handlers, thanks to the IRQF_SHARED flag. From the fourth parameter, you can see that the driver name is rtc. Because this device shares the interrupt line, it passes a unique per-device value for dev.

Finally, the handler itself:

```
static irqreturn_t rtc_interrupt(int irq, void *dev)
{
        /*
         * Can be an alarm interrupt, update complete interrupt,
         * or a periodic interrupt. We store the status in the
         * low byte and the number of interrupts received since
         * the last read in the remainder of rtc_irq_data.
         */

        spin_lock(&rtc_lock);

        rtc_irq_data += 0x100;
        rtc_irq_data &= ~0xff;
        rtc_irq_data |= (CMOS_READ(RTC_INTR_FLAGS) & 0xF0);

        if (rtc_status & RTC_TIMER_ON)
            mod_timer(&rtc_irq_timer, jiffies + HZ/rtc_freq + 2*HZ/100);

        spin_unlock(&rtc_lock);

        /*
         * Now do the rest of the actions
         */
        spin_lock(&rtc_task_lock);
        if (rtc_callback)
                rtc_callback->func(rtc_callback->private_data);
        spin_unlock(&rtc_task_lock);
        wake_up_interruptible(&rtc_wait);

        kill_fasync(&rtc_async_queue, SIGIO, POLL_IN);

        return IRQ_HANDLED;
}
```

This function is invoked whenever the machine receives the RTC interrupt. First, note the spin lock calls: The first set ensures that rtc_irq_data is not accessed concurrently by another processor on an SMP machine, and the second set protects rtc_callback from the same. Locks are discussed in Chapter 10, "Kernel Synchronization Methods."

The rtc_irq_data variable is an unsigned long that stores information about the RTC and is updated on each interrupt to reflect the status of the interrupt.

Next, if an RTC periodic timer is set, it is updated via mod_timer(). Timers are discussed in Chapter 11, "Timers and Time Management."

The final bunch of code, under the comment "now do the rest of the actions," executes a possible preset callback function. The RTC driver enables a callback function to be registered and executed on each RTC interrupt.

Finally, this function returns IRQ_HANDLED to signify that it properly handled this device. Because the interrupt handler does not support sharing, and there is no mechanism for the RTC to detect a spurious interrupt, this handler always returns IRQ_HANDLED.

Interrupt Context

When executing an interrupt handler, the kernel is in *interrupt context*. Recall that process context is the mode of operation the kernel is in while it is executing on behalf of a process—for example, executing a system call or running a kernel thread. In process context, the current macro points to the associated task. Furthermore, because a process is coupled to the kernel in process context, process context can sleep or otherwise invoke the scheduler.

Interrupt context, on the other hand, is not associated with a process. The current macro is not relevant (although it points to the interrupted process). Without a backing process, interrupt context cannot sleep—how would it ever reschedule? Therefore, you cannot call certain functions from interrupt context. If a function sleeps, you cannot use it from your interrupt handler—this limits the functions that one can call from an interrupt handler.

Interrupt context is time-critical because the interrupt handler interrupts other code. Code should be quick and simple. Busy looping is possible, but discouraged. This is an important point; always keep in mind that your interrupt handler has interrupted other code (possibly even another interrupt handler on a different line!). Because of this asynchronous nature, it is imperative that all interrupt handlers be as quick and as simple as possible. As much as possible, work should be pushed out from the interrupt handler and performed in a bottom half, which runs at a more convenient time.

The setup of an interrupt handler's stacks is a configuration option. Historically, interrupt handlers did not receive their own stacks. Instead, they would share the stack of the process that they interrupted.[1] The kernel stack is two pages in size; typically, that is 8KB on 32-bit architectures and 16KB on 64-bit architectures. Because in this setup interrupt handlers share the stack, they must be exceptionally frugal with what data they allocate there. Of course, the kernel stack is limited to begin with, so all kernel code should be cautious.

Early in the 2.6 kernel process, an option was added to reduce the stack size from two pages down to one, providing only a 4KB stack on 32-bit systems. This reduced memory pressure because every process on the system previously needed two pages of contiguous, nonswappable kernel memory. To cope with the reduced stack size, interrupt handlers were given their own stack, one stack per processor, one page in size. This stack is referred to as the *interrupt stack*. Although the total size of the interrupt stack is half that of the original shared stack, the average stack space available is greater because interrupt handlers get the full page of memory to themselves.

---

[1] A process is always running. When nothing else is schedulable, the idle task runs.

Your interrupt handler should not care what stack setup is in use or what the size of the kernel stack is. Always use an absolute minimum amount of stack space.

Implementing Interrupt Handlers

Perhaps not surprising, the implementation of the interrupt handling system in Linux is architecture-dependent. The implementation depends on the processor, the type of interrupt controller used, and the design of the architecture and machine.

Figure 7.1 is a diagram of the path an interrupt takes through hardware and the kernel.

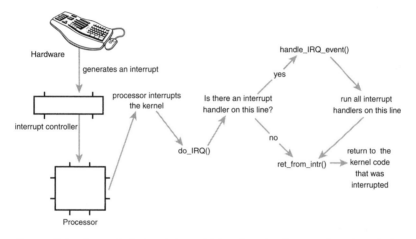

Figure 7.1   The path that an interrupt takes from hardware and on through the kernel.

A device issues an interrupt by sending an electric signal over its bus to the interrupt controller. If the interrupt line is enabled (they can be masked out), the interrupt controller sends the interrupt to the processor. In most architectures, this is accomplished by an electrical signal sent over a special pin to the processor. Unless interrupts are disabled in the processor (which can also happen), the processor immediately stops what it is doing, disables the interrupt system, and jumps to a predefined location in memory and executes the code located there. This predefined point is set up by the kernel and is the *entry point* for interrupt handlers.

The interrupt's journey in the kernel begins at this predefined entry point, just as system calls enter the kernel through a predefined exception handler. For each interrupt line, the processor jumps to a unique location in memory and executes the code located there. In this manner, the kernel knows the IRQ number of the incoming interrupt. The initial entry point simply saves this value and stores the current register values (which belong to the interrupted task) on the stack; then the kernel calls do_IRQ(). From here onward, most of the interrupt handling code is written in C; however, it is still architecture-dependent.

The do_IRQ() function is declared as

```
unsigned int do_IRQ(struct pt_regs regs)
```

Because the C calling convention places function arguments at the top of the stack, the pt_regs structure contains the initial register values that were previously saved in the assembly entry routine. Because the interrupt value was also saved, do_IRQ() can extract it. After the interrupt line is calculated, do_IRQ() acknowledges the receipt of the interrupt and disables interrupt delivery on the line. On normal PC machines, these operations are handled by mask_and_ack_8259A().

Next, do_IRQ() ensures that a valid handler is registered on the line and that it is enabled and not currently executing. If so, it calls handle_IRQ_event(), defined in kernel/irq/handler.c, to run the installed interrupt handlers for the line.

```
/**
 * handle_IRQ_event - irq action chain handler
 * @irq:        the interrupt number
 * @action:     the interrupt action chain for this irq
 *
 * Handles the action chain of an irq event
 */
irqreturn_t handle_IRQ_event(unsigned int irq, struct irqaction *action)
{
        irqreturn_t ret, retval = IRQ_NONE;
        unsigned int status = 0;

        if (!(action->flags & IRQF_DISABLED))
                local_irq_enable_in_hardirq();

        do {
                trace_irq_handler_entry(irq, action);
                ret = action->handler(irq, action->dev_id);
                trace_irq_handler_exit(irq, action, ret);

                switch (ret) {
                case IRQ_WAKE_THREAD:
                        /*
                         * Set result to handled so the spurious check
                         * does not trigger.
                         */
                        ret = IRQ_HANDLED;

                        /*
                         * Catch drivers which return WAKE_THREAD but
                         * did not set up a thread function
                         */
                        if (unlikely(!action->thread_fn)) {
```

```
                                warn_no_thread(irq, action);
                                break;
                }

                /*
                 * Wake up the handler thread for this
                 * action. In case the thread crashed and was
                 * killed we just pretend that we handled the
                 * interrupt. The hardirq handler above has
                 * disabled the device interrupt, so no irq
                 * storm is lurking.
                 */
                if (likely(!test_bit(IRQTF_DIED,
                                        &action->thread_flags))) {
                        set_bit(IRQTF_RUNTHREAD, &action->thread_flags);
                        wake_up_process(action->thread);
                }

                /* Fall through to add to randomness */
        case IRQ_HANDLED:
                status |= action->flags;
                break;

        default:
                break;
        }

        retval |= ret;
        action = action->next;
    } while (action);

    if (status & IRQF_SAMPLE_RANDOM)
        add_interrupt_randomness(irq);
    local_irq_disable();

    return retval;
}
```

First, because the processor disabled interrupts, they are turned back on unless
IRQF_DISABLED was specified during the handler's registration. Recall that
IRQF_DISABLED specifies that the handler must be run with interrupts disabled. Next,
each potential handler is executed in a loop. If this line is not shared, the loop terminates
after the first iteration. Otherwise, all handlers are executed. After that,
add_interrupt_randomness() is called if IRQF_SAMPLE_RANDOM was specified during
registration. This function uses the timing of the interrupt to generate entropy for the random number generator. Finally, interrupts are again disabled (do_IRQ() expects them still

to be off) and the function returns. Back in do_IRQ(), the function cleans up and returns to the initial entry point, which then jumps to ret_from_intr().

The routine ret_from_intr() is, as with the initial entry code, written in assembly. This routine checks whether a reschedule is pending. (Recall from Chapter 4, "Process Scheduling," that this implies that need_resched is set). If a reschedule is pending, and the kernel is returning to user-space (that is, the interrupt interrupted a user process), schedule() is called. If the kernel is returning to kernel-space (that is, the interrupt interrupted the kernel itself), schedule() is called only if the preempt_count is zero. Otherwise it is not safe to preempt the kernel. After schedule() returns, or if there is no work pending, the initial registers are restored and the kernel resumes whatever was interrupted.

On x86, the initial assembly routines are located in arch/x86/kernel/entry_64.S (entry_32.S for 32-bit x86) and the C methods are located in arch/x86/kernel/irq.c. Other supported architectures are similar.

/proc/interrupts

Procfs is a virtual filesystem that exists only in kernel memory and is typically mounted at /proc. Reading or writing files in procfs invokes kernel functions that simulate reading or writing from a real file. A relevant example is the /proc/interrupts file, which is populated with statistics related to interrupts on the system. Here is sample output from a uniprocessor PC:

```
       CPU0
  0:  3602371    XT-PIC    timer
  1:  3048       XT-PIC    i8042
  2:  0          XT-PIC    cascade
  4:  2689466    XT-PIC    uhci-hcd, eth0
  5:  0          XT-PIC    EMU10K1
 12:  85077      XT-PIC    uhci-hcd
 15:  24571      XT-PIC    aic7xxx
NMI:  0
LOC:  3602236
ERR:  0
```

The first column is the interrupt line. On this system, interrupts numbered 0–2, 4, 5, 12, and 15 are present. Handlers are not installed on lines not displayed. The second column is a counter of the number of interrupts received. A column is present for each processor on the system, but this machine has only one processor. As you can see, the timer interrupt has received 3,602,371 interrupts,[2] whereas the sound card (EMU10K1) has received none (which is an indication that it has not been used since the machine booted). The third column is the interrupt controller handling this interrupt. XT-PIC corresponds to the standard

---

[2] As an exercise, after reading Chapter 11 can you tell how long the system has been up (in terms of HZ), knowing the number of timer interrupts that have occurred?

PC programmable interrupt controller. On systems with an I/O APIC, most interrupts would list `IO-APIC-level` or `IO-APIC-edge` as their interrupt controller. Finally, the last column is the device associated with this interrupt. This name is supplied by the `devname` parameter to `request_irq()`, as discussed previously. If the interrupt is shared, as is the case with interrupt number 4 in this example, all the devices registered on the interrupt line are listed.

For the curious, procfs code is located primarily in `fs/proc`. The function that provides `/proc/interrupts` is, not surprisingly, architecture-dependent and named `show_interrupts()`.

Interrupt Control

The Linux kernel implements a family of interfaces for manipulating the state of interrupts on a machine. These interfaces enable you to disable the interrupt system for the current processor or mask out an interrupt line for the entire machine. These routines are all architecture-dependent and can be found in `<asm/system.h>` and `<asm/irq.h>`. See Table 7.2, later in this chapter, for a complete listing of the interfaces.

Reasons to control the interrupt system generally boil down to needing to provide synchronization. By disabling interrupts, you can guarantee that an interrupt handler will not preempt your current code. Moreover, disabling interrupts also disables kernel preemption. Neither disabling interrupt delivery nor disabling kernel preemption provides any protection from concurrent access from another processor, however. Because Linux supports multiple processors, kernel code more generally needs to obtain some sort of lock to prevent another processor from accessing shared data simultaneously. These locks are often obtained in conjunction with disabling local interrupts. The lock provides protection against concurrent access from another processor, whereas disabling interrupts provides protection against concurrent access from a possible interrupt handler. Chapters 9 and 10 discuss the various problems of synchronization and their solutions. Nevertheless, understanding the kernel interrupt control interfaces is important.

Disabling and Enabling Interrupts

To disable interrupts locally for the current processor (and *only* the current processor) and then later reenable them, do the following:

```
local_irq_disable();
/* interrupts are disabled .. */
local_irq_enable();
```

These functions are usually implemented as a single assembly operation. (Of course, this depends on the architecture.) Indeed, on x86, `local_irq_disable()` is a simple `cli` and `local_irq_enable()` is a simple `sti` instruction. `cli` and `sti` are the assembly calls to *clear* and *set* the *allow interrupts* flag, respectively. In other words, they disable and enable interrupt delivery on the issuing processor.

The `local_irq_disable()` routine is dangerous if interrupts were already disabled *prior* to its invocation. The corresponding call to `local_irq_enable()` unconditionally enables interrupts, despite the fact that they were off to begin with. Instead, a mechanism is needed to restore interrupts to a previous state. This is a common concern because a given code path in the kernel can be reached both with and without interrupts enabled, depending on the call chain. For example, imagine the previous code snippet is part of a larger function. Imagine that this function is called by two other functions, one that disables interrupts and one that does not. Because it is becoming harder as the kernel grows in size and complexity to know all the code paths leading up to a function, it is much safer to save the state of the interrupt system before disabling it. Then, when you are ready to reenable interrupts, you simply restore them to their original state:

```
unsigned long flags;

local_irq_save(flags);    /* interrupts are now disabled */
/* ... */
local_irq_restore(flags); /* interrupts are restored to their previous state */
```

Note that these methods are implemented at least in part as macros, so the `flags` parameter (which must be defined as an `unsigned long`) is seemingly passed by value. This parameter contains architecture-specific data containing the state of the interrupt systems. Because at least one supported architecture incorporates stack information into the value (ahem, SPARC), `flags` *cannot* be passed to another function (specifically, it must remain on the same stack frame). For this reason, the call to save and the call to restore interrupts must occur in the same function.

All the previous functions can be called from both interrupt and process context.

No More Global `cli()`

The kernel formerly provided a method to disable interrupts on *all* processors in the system. Furthermore, if another processor called this method, it would have to wait until interrupts were enabled before continuing. This function was named `cli()` and the corresponding enable call was named `sti()`—very x86-centric, despite existing for all architectures. These interfaces were deprecated during 2.5, and consequently all interrupt synchronization must now use a combination of local interrupt control and spin locks (discussed in Chapter 9, "An Introduction to Kernel Synchronization"). This means that code that previously only had to disable interrupts globally to ensure mutual-exclusive access to shared data now needs to do a bit more work.

Previously, driver writers could assume a `cli()` used in their interrupt handlers and anywhere else the shared data was accessed would provide mutual exclusion. The `cli()` call would ensure that no other interrupt handlers (and thus their specific handler) would run. Furthermore, if another processor entered a `cli()` protected region, it would not continue until the original processor exited its `cli()` protected region with a call to `sti()`.

Removing the global `cli()` has a handful of advantages. First, it forces driver writers to implement real locking. A fine-grained lock with a specific purpose is faster than a global lock, which is effectively what `cli()` is. Second, the removal streamlined a lot of code in the interrupt system and removed a bunch more. The result is simpler and easier to comprehend.

Disabling a Specific Interrupt Line

In the previous section, we looked at functions that disable all interrupt delivery for an entire processor. In some cases, it is useful to disable only a *specific* interrupt line for the *entire* system. This is called *masking out* an interrupt line. As an example, you might want to disable delivery of a device's interrupts before manipulating its state. Linux provides four interfaces for this task:

```
void disable_irq(unsigned int irq);
void disable_irq_nosync(unsigned int irq);
void enable_irq(unsigned int irq);
void synchronize_irq(unsigned int irq);
```

The first two functions disable a given interrupt line in the interrupt controller. This disables delivery of the given interrupt to *all* processors in the system. Additionally, the disable_irq() function does not return until any currently executing handler completes. Thus, callers are assured not only that new interrupts will not be delivered on the given line, but also that any already executing handlers have exited. The function disable_irq_nosync() does not wait for current handlers to complete.

The function synchronize_irq() waits for a specific interrupt handler to exit, if it is executing, before returning.

Calls to these functions nest. For each call to disable_irq() or disable_irq_nosync() on a given interrupt line, a corresponding call to enable_irq() is required. Only on the last call to enable_irq() is the interrupt line actually enabled. For example, if disable_irq() is called twice, the interrupt line is not actually reenabled until the second call to enable_irq().

All three of these functions can be called from interrupt or process context and do not sleep. If calling from interrupt context, be careful! You do not want, for example, to enable an interrupt line while you are handling it. (Recall that the interrupt line of a handler is masked out while it is serviced.)

It would be rather rude to disable an interrupt line shared among multiple interrupt handlers. Disabling the line disables interrupt delivery for *all* devices on the line. Therefore, drivers for newer devices tend not to use these interfaces.[3] Because PCI devices have to support interrupt line sharing by specification, they should not use these interfaces at all. Thus, disable_irq() and friends are found more often in drivers for older legacy devices, such as the PC parallel port.

---

[3] *Many older devices, particularly ISA devices, do not provide a method of obtaining whether they generated an interrupt. Therefore, often interrupt lines for ISA devices cannot be shared. Because the PCI specification mandates the sharing of interrupts, modern PCI-based devices support interrupt sharing. In contemporary computers, nearly all interrupt lines can be shared.*

Status of the Interrupt System

It is often useful to know the state of the interrupt system (for example, whether interrupts are enabled or disabled) or whether you are currently executing in interrupt context.

The macro `irqs_disabled()`, defined in `<asm/system.h>`, returns nonzero if the interrupt system on the local processor is disabled. Otherwise, it returns zero.

Two macros, defined in `<linux/hardirq.h>`, provide an interface to check the kernel's current context. They are

```
in_interrupt()
in_irq()
```

The most useful is the first: It returns nonzero if the kernel is performing any type of interrupt handling. This includes either executing an interrupt handler or a bottom half handler. The macro `in_irq()` returns nonzero only if the kernel is specifically executing an interrupt handler.

More often, you want to check whether you are in process context. That is, you want to ensure you are *not* in interrupt context. This is often the case because code wants to do something that can only be done from process context, such as sleep. If `in_interrupt()` returns zero, the kernel is in process context.

Yes, the names are confusing and do little to impart their meaning. Table 7.2 is a summary of the interrupt control methods and their description.

Table 7.2   **Interrupt Control Methods**

Function	Description
`local_irq_disable()`	Disables local interrupt delivery
`local_irq_enable()`	Enables local interrupt delivery
`local_irq_save()`	Saves the current state of local interrupt delivery and then disables it
`local_irq_restore()`	Restores local interrupt delivery to the given state
`disable_irq()`	Disables the given interrupt line and ensures no handler on the line is executing before returning
`disable_irq_nosync()`	Disables the given interrupt line
`enable_irq()`	Enables the given interrupt line
`irqs_disabled()`	Returns nonzero if local interrupt delivery is disabled; otherwise returns zero
`in_interrupt()`	Returns nonzero if in interrupt context and zero if in process context
`in_irq()`	Returns nonzero if currently executing an interrupt handler and zero otherwise

Conclusion

This chapter looked at interrupts, a hardware resource used by devices to asynchronously signal the processor. Interrupts, in effect, are used by hardware to *interrupt* the operating system.

Most modern hardware uses interrupts to communicate with operating systems. The device driver that manages a given piece of hardware registers an interrupt handler to respond to and process interrupts issued from their associated hardware. Work performed in interrupts includes acknowledging and resetting hardware, copying data from the device to main memory and vice versa, processing hardware requests, and sending out new hardware requests.

The kernel provides interfaces for registering and unregistering interrupt handlers, disabling interrupts, masking out interrupt lines, and checking the status of the interrupt system. Table 7.2 provided an overview of many of these functions.

Because interrupts interrupt other executing code (processes, the kernel itself, and even other interrupt handlers), they must execute quickly. Often, however, there is a lot of work to do. To balance the large amount of work with the need for quick execution, the kernel divides the work of processing interrupts into two halves. The interrupt handler, the top half, was discussed in this chapter. The next chapter looks at the bottom half.

8

Bottom Halves and Deferring Work

The previous chapter discussed interrupt handlers, the kernel mechanism for dealing with hardware interrupts. Interrupt handlers are an important—indeed, required—part of any operating system. Due to various limitations, however, interrupt handlers can form only the first half of any interrupt processing solution. These limitations include

- Interrupt handlers run asynchronously and thus interrupt other, potentially important, code, including other interrupt handlers. Therefore, to avoid stalling the interrupted code for too long, interrupt handlers need to run as quickly as possible.
- Interrupt handlers run with the current interrupt level disabled at best (if `IRQF_DISABLED` is unset), and at worst (if `IRQF_DISABLED` is set) with all interrupts on the current processor disabled. As disabling interrupts prevents hardware from communicating with the operating systems, interrupt handlers need to run as quickly as possible.
- Interrupt handlers are often timing-critical because they deal with hardware.
- Interrupt handlers do not run in process context; therefore, they cannot block. This limits what they can do.

It should now be evident that interrupt handlers are only a piece of the solution to managing hardware interrupts. Operating systems certainly need a quick, asynchronous, simple mechanism for immediately responding to hardware and performing any time-critical actions. Interrupt handlers serve this function well; but other, less critical work can and should be deferred to a later point when interrupts are enabled.

Consequently, managing interrupts is divided into two parts, or *halves*. The first part, interrupt handlers (*top halves*), are executed by the kernel asynchronously in immediate response to a hardware interrupt, as discussed in the previous chapter. This chapter looks at the second part of the interrupt solution, *bottom halves*.

Bottom Halves

The job of bottom halves is to perform any interrupt-related work not performed by the interrupt handler. In an ideal world, this is nearly all the work because you want the interrupt handler to perform as little work (and in turn be as fast) as possible. By offloading as much work as possible to the bottom half, the interrupt handler can return control of the system to whatever it interrupted as quickly as possible.

Nonetheless, the interrupt handler must perform *some* of the work. For example, the interrupt handler almost assuredly needs to acknowledge to the hardware the receipt of the interrupt. It may need to copy data to or from the hardware. This work is timing-sensitive, so it makes sense to perform it in the interrupt handler.

Almost anything else is fair game for performing in the bottom half. For example, if you copy data from the hardware into memory in the top half, it certainly makes sense to process it in the bottom half. Unfortunately, no hard and fast rules exist about what work to perform where—the decision is left entirely up to the device-driver author. Although no arrangement is *illegal*, an arrangement can certainly be *suboptimal*. Remember, interrupt handlers run asynchronously, with at least the current interrupt line disabled. Minimizing their duration is important. Although it is not always clear how to divide the work between the top and bottom half, a couple of useful tips help:

- If the work is time sensitive, perform it in the interrupt handler.
- If the work is related to the hardware, perform it in the interrupt handler.
- If the work needs to ensure that another interrupt (particularly the same interrupt) does not interrupt it, perform it in the interrupt handler.
- For everything else, consider performing the work in the bottom half.

When attempting to write your own device driver, looking at other interrupt handlers and their corresponding bottom halves can help. When deciding how to divide your interrupt processing work between the top and bottom half, ask yourself what *must* be in the top half and what *can* be in the bottom half. Generally, the quicker the interrupt handler executes, the better.

Why Bottom Halves?

It is crucial to understand why to defer work, and when exactly to defer it. You want to limit the amount of work you perform in an interrupt handler because interrupt handlers run with the current interrupt line disabled on all processors. Worse, handlers that register with `IRQF_DISABLED` run with *all* interrupt lines disabled on the local processor, plus the current interrupt line disabled on all processors. Minimizing the time spent with interrupts disabled is important for system response and performance. Add to this the fact that interrupt handlers run asynchronously with respect to other code—even other interrupt handlers—and it is clear that you should work to minimize how long interrupt handlers run. Processing incoming network traffic should not prevent the kernel's receipt of keystrokes. The solution is to defer some of the work until later.

But when is "later?" The important thing to realize is that *later* is often simply *not now*. The point of a bottom half is *not* to do work at some specific point in the future, but simply to defer work until *any* point in the future when the system is less busy and interrupts are again enabled. Often, bottom halves run immediately after the interrupt returns. The key is that they run with all interrupts enabled.

Linux is not alone in separating the processing of hardware interrupts into two parts; most operating systems do so. The top half is quick and simple and runs with some or all interrupts disabled. The bottom half (however it is implemented) runs later with all interrupts enabled. This design keeps system latency low by running with interrupts disabled for as little time as necessary.

A World of Bottom Halves

Unlike the top half, which is implemented entirely via the interrupt handler, multiple mechanisms are available for implementing a bottom half. These mechanisms are different interfaces and subsystems that enable you to implement bottom halves. Whereas the previous chapter looked at just a single way of implementing interrupt handlers, this chapter looks at multiple methods of implementing bottom halves. Over the course of Linux's history, there have been many bottom-half mechanisms. Confusingly, some of these mechanisms have similar or even dumb names. It requires a special type of programmer to name bottom halves.

This chapter discusses both the design and implementation of the bottom-half mechanisms that exist in 2.6. We also discuss how to use them in the kernel code you write. The old, but long since removed, bottom-half mechanisms are historically significant, and so they are mentioned when relevant.

The Original "Bottom Half"

In the beginning, Linux provided only the "bottom half" for implementing bottom halves. This name was logical because at the time that was the only means available for deferring work. The infrastructure was also known as *BH*, which is what we will call it to avoid confusion with the generic term *bottom half*. The BH interface was simple, like most things in those good old days. It provided a statically created list of 32 bottom halves for the entire system. The top half could mark whether the bottom half would run by setting a bit in a 32-bit integer. Each BH was globally synchronized. No two could run at the same time, even on different processors. This was easy to use, yet inflexible; a simple approach, yet a bottleneck.

Task Queues

Later on, the kernel developers introduced *task queues* both as a method of deferring work and as a replacement for the BH mechanism. The kernel defined a family of queues. Each queue contained a linked list of functions to call. The queued functions were run at certain times, depending on which queue they were in. Drivers could register their bottom halves in the appropriate queue. This worked fairly well, but it was still too inflexible to replace the BH interface entirely. It also was not lightweight enough for performance-critical subsystems, such as networking.

Softirqs and Tasklets

During the 2.3 development series, the kernel developers introduced *softirqs* and *tasklets*. With the exception of compatibility with existing drivers, softirqs and tasklets could completely replace the BH interface.[1] Softirqs are a set of statically defined bottom halves that can run simultaneously on any processor; even two of the same type can run concurrently. Tasklets, which have an awful and confusing name,[2] are flexible, dynamically created bottom halves built on top of softirqs. Two different tasklets can run concurrently on different processors, but two of the same type of tasklet cannot run simultaneously. Thus, tasklets are a good trade-off between performance and ease of use. For most bottom-half processing, the tasklet is sufficient. Softirqs are useful when performance is critical, such as with networking. Using softirqs requires more care, however, because two of the same softirq can run at the same time. In addition, softirqs must be registered statically at compile time. Conversely, code can dynamically register tasklets.

To further confound the issue, some people refer to all bottom halves as software interrupts or softirqs. In other words, they call both the softirq mechanism and bottom halves in general softirqs. Ignore those people. They run with the same crowd that named the BH and tasklet mechanisms.

While developing the 2.5 kernel, the BH interface was finally tossed to the curb because all BH users were converted to the other bottom-half interfaces. Additionally, the task queue interface was replaced by the work queue interface. Work queues are a simple yet useful method of queuing work to later be performed in process context. We get to them later.

Consequently, today 2.6 has three bottom-half mechanisms in the kernel: softirqs, tasklets, and work queues. The old BH and task queue interfaces are but mere memories.

Kernel Timers

Another mechanism for deferring work is *kernel timers*. Unlike the mechanisms discussed in the chapter thus far, timers defer work for a specified amount of time. That is, although the tools discussed in this chapter are useful to defer work to *any time but now*, you use timers to defer work until at least a specific time has elapsed.

Therefore, timers have different uses than the general mechanisms discussed in this chapter. A full discussion of timers is given in Chapter 11, "Timers and Time Management."

---

[1] It is nontrivial to convert BHs to softirqs or tasklets because BHs are globally synchronized and, therefore, assume that no other BH is running during their execution. The conversion did eventually happen, however, in 2.5.

[2] They have nothing to do with tasks. Think of a tasklet as a simple and easy-to-use softirq.

Dispelling the Confusion

This is some seriously confusing stuff, but actually it involves just naming issues. Let's go over it again.

Bottom half is a generic operating system term referring to the deferred portion of interrupt processing, so named because it represents the second, or bottom, half of the interrupt processing solution. In Linux, the term currently has this meaning, too. All the kernel's mechanisms for deferring work are "bottom halves." Some people also confusingly call all bottom halves "softirqs."

Bottom half also refers to the original deferred work mechanism in Linux. This mechanism is also known as a BH, so we call it by that name now and leave the former as a generic description. The BH mechanism was deprecated a while back and fully removed in the 2.5 development kernel series.

Currently, three methods exist for deferring work: softirqs, tasklets, and work queues. Tasklets are built on softirqs and work queues are their own subsystem. Table 8.1 presents a history of bottom halves.

Table 8.1   **Bottom Half Status**

Bottom Half	Status
BH	Removed in 2.5
Task queues	Removed in 2.5
Softirq	Available since 2.3
Tasklet	Available since 2.3
Work queues	Available since 2.5

With this naming confusion settled, let's look at the individual mechanisms.

Softirqs

The place to start this discussion of the actual bottom half methods is with softirqs. Softirqs are rarely used directly; tasklets are a much more common form of bottom half. Nonetheless, because tasklets are built on softirqs, we cover them first. The softirq code lives in the file `kernel/softirq.c` in the kernel source tree.

Implementing Softirqs

Softirqs are statically allocated at compile time. Unlike tasklets, you cannot dynamically register and destroy softirqs. Softirqs are represented by the `softirq_action` structure, which is defined in `<linux/interrupt.h>`:

```
struct softirq_action {
        void (*action)(struct softirq_action *);
};
```

A 32-entry array of this structure is declared in `kernel/softirq.c`:

```
static struct softirq_action softirq_vec[NR_SOFTIRQS];
```

Each registered softirq consumes one entry in the array. Consequently, there are `NR_SOFTIRQS` registered softirqs. The number of registered softirqs is statically determined at compile time and cannot be changed dynamically. The kernel enforces a limit of 32 registered softirqs; in the current kernel, however, only nine exist.[3]

The Softirq Handler

The prototype of a softirq handler, `action`, looks like

```
void softirq_handler(struct softirq_action *)
```

When the kernel runs a softirq handler, it executes this `action` function with a pointer to the corresponding `softirq_action` structure as its lone argument. For example, if `my_softirq` pointed to an entry in the `softirq_vec` array, the kernel would invoke the softirq handler function as

```
my_softirq->action(my_softirq);
```

It seems a bit odd that the kernel passes the entire structure to the softirq handler. This trick enables future additions to the structure without requiring a change in every softirq handler.

A softirq never preempts another softirq. The only event that can preempt a softirq is an interrupt handler. Another softirq—even the same one—can run on another processor, however.

Executing Softirqs

A registered softirq must be marked before it will execute. This is called *raising the softirq*. Usually, an interrupt handler marks its softirq for execution before returning. Then, at a suitable time, the softirq runs. Pending softirqs are checked for and executed in the following places:

- In the return from hardware interrupt code path
- In the `ksoftirqd` kernel thread
- In any code that explicitly checks for and executes pending softirqs, such as the networking subsystem

Regardless of the method of invocation, softirq execution occurs in `__do_softirq()`, which is invoked by `do_softirq()`. The function is quite simple. If there are pending

---

[3] *Most drivers use tasklets or work queues for their bottom half. Tasklets are built off softirqs, as the next section explains.*

softirqs, __do_softirq() loops over each one, invoking its handler. Let's look at a simplified variant of the important part of __do_softirq():

```
u32 pending;

pending = local_softirq_pending();
if (pending) {
    struct softirq_action *h;

    /* reset the pending bitmask */
    set_softirq_pending(0);

    h = softirq_vec;
    do {
        if (pending & 1)
            h->action(h);
        h++;
        pending >>= 1;
    } while (pending);
}
```

This snippet is the heart of softirq processing. It checks for, and executes, any pending softirqs. Specifically

1. It sets the pending local variable to the value returned by the local_softirq_pending() macro. This is a 32-bit mask of pending softirqs—if bit n is set, the nth softirq is pending.

2. Now that the pending bitmask of softirqs is saved, it clears the actual bitmask.[4]

3. The pointer h is set to the first entry in the softirq_vec.

4. If the first bit in pending is set, h->action(h) is called.

5. The pointer h is incremented by one so that it now points to the second entry in the softirq_vec array.

6. The bitmask pending is right-shifted by one. This tosses the first bit away and moves all other bits one place to the right. Consequently, the second bit is now the first (and so on).

7. The pointer h now points to the second entry in the array, and the pending bitmask now has the second bit as the first. Repeat the previous steps.

---

[4] *This actually occurs with local interrupts disabled, but that is omitted in this simplified example. If interrupts were not disabled, a softirq could have been raised (and thus be pending) in the intervening time between saving the mask and clearing it. This would result in incorrectly clearing a pending bit.*

8. Continue repeating until `pending` is zero, at which point there are no more pending softirqs and the work is done. Note, this check is sufficient to ensure `h` always points to a valid entry in `softirq_vec` because `pending` has at most 32 set bits and thus this loop executes at most 32 times.

Using Softirqs

Softirqs are reserved for the most timing-critical and important bottom-half processing on the system. Currently, only two subsystems—networking and block devices—directly use softirqs. Additionally, kernel timers and tasklets are built on top of softirqs. If you add a new softirq, you normally want to ask yourself why using a tasklet is insufficient. Tasklets are dynamically created and are simpler to use because of their weaker locking requirements, and they still perform quite well. Nonetheless, for timing-critical applications that can do their own locking in an efficient way, softirqs might be the correct solution.

Assigning an Index

You declare softirqs statically at compile time via an `enum` in `<linux/interrupt.h>`. The kernel uses this index, which starts at zero, as a relative priority. Softirqs with the lowest numerical priority execute before those with a higher numerical priority.

Creating a new softirq includes adding a new entry to this `enum`. When adding a new softirq, you might not want to simply add your entry to the end of the list, as you would elsewhere. Instead, you need to insert the new entry depending on the priority you want to give it. By convention, `HI_SOFTIRQ` is always the first and `RCU_SOFTIRQ` is always the last entry. A new entry likely belongs in between `BLOCK_SOFTIRQ` and `TASKLET_SOFTIRQ`. Table 8.2 contains a list of the existing tasklet types.

Table 8.2 **Softirq Types**

Tasklet	Priority	Softirq Description
HI_SOFTIRQ	0	High-priority tasklets
TIMER_SOFTIRQ	1	Timers
NET_TX_SOFTIRQ	2	Send network packets
NET_RX_SOFTIRQ	3	Receive network packets
BLOCK_SOFTIRQ	4	Block devices
TASKLET_SOFTIRQ	5	Normal priority tasklets
SCHED_SOFTIRQ	6	Scheduler
HRTIMER_SOFTIRQ	7	High-resolution timers
RCU_SOFTIRQ	8	RCU locking

Registering Your Handler

Next, the softirq handler is registered at run-time via `open_softirq()`, which takes two parameters: the softirq's index and its handler function. The networking subsystem, for example, registers its softirqs like this, in `net/core/dev.c`:

```
open_softirq(NET_TX_SOFTIRQ, net_tx_action);
open_softirq(NET_RX_SOFTIRQ, net_rx_action);
```

The softirq handlers run with interrupts enabled and cannot sleep. While a handler runs, softirqs on the current processor are disabled. Another processor, however, can execute other softirqs. If the same softirq is raised again while it is executing, another processor can run it simultaneously. This means that any shared data—even global data used only within the softirq handler—needs proper locking (as discussed in the next two chapters). This is an important point, and it is the reason tasklets are usually preferred. Simply preventing your softirqs from running concurrently is not ideal. If a softirq obtained a lock to prevent another instance of itself from running simultaneously, there would be no reason to use a softirq. Consequently, most softirq handlers resort to per-processor data (data unique to each processor and thus not requiring locking) and other tricks to avoid explicit locking and provide excellent scalability.

The *raison d'être* to softirqs is scalability. If you do not need to scale to infinitely many processors, then use a tasklet. Tasklets are essentially softirqs in which multiple instances of the same handler cannot run concurrently on multiple processors.

Raising Your Softirq

After a handler is added to the `enum` list and registered via `open_softirq()`, it is ready to run. To mark it pending, so it is run at the next invocation of `do_softirq()`, call `raise_softirq()`. For example, the networking subsystem would call,

```
raise_softirq(NET_TX_SOFTIRQ);
```

This raises the `NET_TX_SOFTIRQ` softirq. Its handler, `net_tx_action()`, runs the next time the kernel executes softirqs. This function disables interrupts prior to actually raising the softirq and then restores them to their previous state. If interrupts are already off, the function `raise_softirq_irqoff()` can be used as a small optimization. For example

```
/*
 * interrupts must already be off!
 */
raise_softirq_irqoff(NET_TX_SOFTIRQ);
```

Softirqs are most often raised from within interrupt handlers. In the case of interrupt handlers, the interrupt handler performs the basic hardware-related work, raises the softirq, and then exits. When processing interrupts, the kernel invokes `do_softirq()`. The softirq then runs and picks up where the interrupt handler left off. In this example, the "top half" and "bottom half" naming should make sense.

Tasklets

Tasklets are a bottom-half mechanism built on top of softirqs. As mentioned, they have nothing to do with tasks. Tasklets are similar in nature and behavior to softirqs; however, they have a simpler interface and relaxed locking rules.

As a device driver author, the decision whether to use softirqs versus tasklets is simple: You almost always want to use tasklets. As we saw in the previous section, you can (almost) count on one hand the users of softirqs. Softirqs are required only for high-frequency and highly threaded uses. Tasklets, on the other hand, see much greater use. Tasklets work just fine for the vast majority of cases and are very easy to use.

Implementing Tasklets

Because tasklets are implemented on top of softirqs, they *are* softirqs. As discussed, tasklets are represented by two softirqs: HI_SOFTIRQ and TASKLET_SOFTIRQ. The only difference in these types is that the HI_SOFTIRQ-based tasklets run prior to the TASKLET_SOFTIRQ-based tasklets.

The Tasklet Structure

Tasklets are represented by the `tasklet_struct` structure. Each structure represents a unique tasklet. The structure is declared in `<linux/interrupt.h>`:

```
struct tasklet_struct {
        struct tasklet_struct *next;   /* next tasklet in the list */
        unsigned long state;           /* state of the tasklet */
        atomic_t count;                /* reference counter */
        void (*func)(unsigned long);   /* tasklet handler function */
        unsigned long data;            /* argument to the tasklet function */
};
```

The `func` member is the tasklet handler (the equivalent of `action` to a softirq) and receives `data` as its sole argument.

The `state` member is exactly zero, TASKLET_STATE_SCHED, or TASKLET_STATE_RUN. TASKLET_STATE_SCHED denotes a tasklet that is scheduled to run, and TASKLET_STATE_RUN denotes a tasklet that is running. As an optimization, TASKLET_STATE_RUN is used only on multiprocessor machines because a uniprocessor machine always knows whether the tasklet is running. (It is either the currently executing code, or not.)

The `count` field is used as a reference count for the tasklet. If it is nonzero, the tasklet is disabled and cannot run; if it is zero, the tasklet is enabled and can run if marked pending.

Scheduling Tasklets

Scheduled tasklets (the equivalent of raised softirqs)[5] are stored in two per-processor structures: `tasklet_vec` (for regular tasklets) and `tasklet_hi_vec` (for high-priority tasklets). Both of these structures are linked lists of `tasklet_struct` structures. Each `tasklet_struct` structure in the list represents a different tasklet.

Tasklets are scheduled via the `tasklet_schedule()` and `tasklet_hi_schedule()` functions, which receive a pointer to the tasklet's `tasklet_struct` as their lone argument. Each function ensures that the provided tasklet is not yet scheduled and then calls `__tasklet_schedule()` and `__tasklet_hi_schedule()` as appropriate. The two functions are similar. (The difference is that one uses `TASKLET_SOFTIRQ` and one uses `HI_SOFTIRQ`.) Writing and using tasklets is covered in the next section. Now, let's look at the steps `tasklet_schedule()` undertakes:

1. Check whether the tasklet's `state` is `TASKLET_STATE_SCHED`. If it is, the tasklet is already scheduled to run and the function can immediately return.

2. Call `__tasklet_schedule()`.

3. Save the state of the interrupt system, and then disable local interrupts. This ensures that nothing on this processor will mess with the tasklet code while `tasklet_schedule()` is manipulating the tasklets.

4. Add the tasklet to be scheduled to the head of the `tasklet_vec` or `tasklet_hi_vec` linked list, which is unique to each processor in the system.

5. Raise the `TASKLET_SOFTIRQ` or `HI_SOFTIRQ` softirq, so `do_softirq()` executes this tasklet in the near future.

6. Restore interrupts to their previous state and return.

At the next earliest convenience, `do_softirq()` is run as discussed in the previous section. Because most tasklets and softirqs are marked pending in interrupt handlers, `do_softirq()` most likely runs when the last interrupt returns. Because `TASKLET_SOFTIRQ` or `HI_SOFTIRQ` is now raised, `do_softirq()` executes the associated handlers. These handlers, `tasklet_action()` and `tasklet_hi_action()`, are the heart of tasklet processing. Let's look at the steps these handlers perform:

1. Disable local interrupt delivery (there is no need to first save their state because the code here is always called as a softirq handler and interrupts are always enabled) and retrieve the `tasklet_vec` or `tasklet_hi_vec` list for this processor.

2. Clear the list for this processor by setting it equal to NULL.

---

[5] *Yet another example of the confusing naming schemes at work here. Why are softirqs raised but tasklets scheduled? Who knows? Both terms mean to mark that bottom half pending so that it is executed soon.*

3. Enable local interrupt delivery. Again, there is no need to restore them to their previous state because this function knows that they were always originally enabled.

4. Loop over each pending tasklet in the retrieved list.

5. If this is a multiprocessing machine, check whether the tasklet is running on another processor by checking the `TASKLET_STATE_RUN` flag. If it is currently running, do not execute it now and skip to the next pending tasklet. (Recall that only one tasklet of a given type may run concurrently.)

6. If the tasklet is not currently running, set the `TASKLET_STATE_RUN` flag, so another processor will not run it.

7. Check for a zero `count` value, to ensure that the tasklet is not disabled. If the tasklet is disabled, skip it and go to the next pending tasklet.

8. We now know that the tasklet is not running elsewhere, is marked as running so it will not start running elsewhere, and has a zero `count` value. Run the tasklet handler.

9. After the tasklet runs, clear the `TASKLET_STATE_RUN` flag in the tasklet's `state` field.

10. Repeat for the next pending tasklet, until there are no more scheduled tasklets waiting to run.

The implementation of tasklets is simple, but rather clever. As you saw, all tasklets are multiplexed on top of two softirqs, `HI_SOFTIRQ` and `TASKLET_SOFTIRQ`. When a tasklet is scheduled, the kernel raises one of these softirqs. These softirqs, in turn, are handled by special functions that then run any scheduled tasklets. The special functions ensure that only one tasklet of a given type runs at the same time. (But other tasklets can run simultaneously.) All this complexity is then hidden behind a clean and simple interface.

Using Tasklets

In most cases, tasklets are the preferred mechanism with which to implement your bottom half for a normal hardware device. Tasklets are dynamically created, easy to use, and quick. Moreover, although their name is mind-numbingly confusing, it grows on you: It is cute.

Declaring Your Tasklet

You can create tasklets statically or dynamically. What option you choose depends on whether you have (or want) a direct or indirect reference to the tasklet. If you are going to statically create the tasklet (and thus have a direct reference to it), use one of two macros in `<linux/interrupt.h>`:

```
DECLARE_TASKLET(name, func, data)
DECLARE_TASKLET_DISABLED(name, func, data);
```

Both these macros statically create a `struct tasklet_struct` with the given name. When the tasklet is scheduled, the given function `func` is executed and passed the argument `data`. The difference between the two macros is the initial reference count. The first macro creates the tasklet with a `count` of zero, and the tasklet is enabled. The second macro sets `count` to one, and the tasklet is disabled. Here is an example:

```
DECLARE_TASKLET(my_tasklet, my_tasklet_handler, dev);
```

This line is equivalent to

```
struct tasklet_struct my_tasklet = { NULL, 0, ATOMIC_INIT(0),
                                     my_tasklet_handler, dev };
```

This creates a tasklet named `my_tasklet` enabled with `tasklet_handler` as its handler. The value of `dev` is passed to the handler when it is executed.

To initialize a tasklet given an indirect reference (a pointer) to a dynamically created `struct tasklet_struct`, t, call `tasklet_init()`:

```
tasklet_init(t, tasklet_handler, dev);   /* dynamically as opposed to statically */
```

Writing Your Tasklet Handler

The tasklet handler must match the correct prototype:

```
void tasklet_handler(unsigned long data)
```

As with softirqs, tasklets cannot sleep. This means you cannot use semaphores or other blocking functions in a tasklet. Tasklets also run with all interrupts enabled, so you must take precautions (for example, disable interrupts and obtain a lock) if your tasklet shares data with an interrupt handler. Unlike softirqs, however, two of the same tasklets never run concurrently—although two different tasklets can run at the same time on two different processors. If your tasklet shares data with another tasklet or softirq, you need to use proper locking (see Chapter 9, "An Introduction to Kernel Synchronization," and Chapter 10, "Kernel Synchronization Methods").

Scheduling Your Tasklet

To schedule a tasklet for execution, `tasklet_schedule()` is called and passed a pointer to the relevant `tasklet_struct`:

```
tasklet_schedule(&my_tasklet);    /* mark my_tasklet as pending */
```

After a tasklet is scheduled, it runs once at some time in the near future. If the same tasklet is scheduled again, before it has had a chance to run, it still runs only once. If it is already running, for example on another processor, the tasklet is rescheduled and runs again. As an optimization, a tasklet always runs on the processor that scheduled it—making better use of the processor's cache, you hope.

You can disable a tasklet via a call to `tasklet_disable()`, which disables the given tasklet. If the tasklet is currently running, the function will not return until it finishes executing. Alternatively, you can use `tasklet_disable_nosync()`, which disables the given tasklet but does not wait for the tasklet to complete prior to returning. This is usually not safe because you cannot assume the tasklet is not still running. A call to `tasklet_enable()` enables the tasklet. This function also must be called before a tasklet created with `DECLARE_TASKLET_DISABLED()` is usable. For example:

```
tasklet_disable(&my_tasklet);    /* tasklet is now disabled */

/* we can now do stuff knowing that the tasklet cannot run .. */

tasklet_enable(&my_tasklet);     /* tasklet is now enabled */
```

You can remove a tasklet from the pending queue via `tasklet_kill()`. This function receives a pointer as a lone argument to the tasklet's `tasklet_struct`. Removing a scheduled tasklet from the queue is useful when dealing with a tasklet that often reschedules itself. This function first waits for the tasklet to finish executing and then it removes the tasklet from the queue. Nothing stops some other code from rescheduling the tasklet, of course. This function must not be used from interrupt context because it sleeps.

ksoftirqd

Softirq (and thus tasklet) processing is aided by a set of per-processor kernel threads. These kernel threads help in the processing of softirqs when the system is overwhelmed with softirqs. Because tasklets are implemented using softirqs, the following discussion applies equally to softirqs and tasklets. For brevity, we will refer mainly to softirqs.

As already described, the kernel processes softirqs in a number of places, most commonly on return from handling an interrupt. Softirqs might be raised at high rates (such as during heavy network traffic). Further, softirq functions can reactivate themselves. That is, while running, a softirq can raise itself so that it runs again (for example, the networking subsystem's softirq raises itself). The possibility of a high frequency of softirqs in conjunction with their capability to remark themselves active can result in user-space programs being starved of processor time. Not processing the reactivated softirqs in a timely manner, however, is unacceptable. When softirqs were first designed, this caused a dilemma that needed fixing, and neither obvious solution was a good one. First, let's look at each of the two obvious solutions.

The first solution is simply to keep processing softirqs as they come in and to recheck and reprocess any pending softirqs before returning. This ensures that the kernel processes softirqs in a timely manner and, most important, that any reactivated softirqs are also immediately processed. The problem lies in high load environments, in which many softirqs occur, that continually reactivate themselves. The kernel might continually service softirqs without accomplishing much else. User-space is neglected—indeed, nothing but softirqs and interrupt handlers run and, in turn, the system's users get mad. This approach might work fine if the system is never under intense load; if the system experiences moderate interrupt levels, this solution is not acceptable. User-space cannot be starved for significant periods.

The second solution is *not* to handle reactivated softirqs. On return from interrupt, the kernel merely looks at all pending softirqs and executes them as normal. If any softirqs reactivate themselves, however, they will not run until the *next* time the kernel handles pending softirqs. This is most likely not until the next interrupt occurs, which can equate to a lengthy amount of time before any new (or reactivated) softirqs are executed. Worse, on an otherwise idle system, it is beneficial to process the softirqs right away. Unfortunately, this approach is oblivious to which processes are runnable. Therefore, although this method prevents starving user-space, it does starve the softirqs and does not take good advantage of an idle system.

In designing softirqs, the kernel developers realized that some sort of compromise was needed. The solution ultimately implemented in the kernel is to *not* immediately process reactivated softirqs. Instead, if the number of softirqs grows excessive, the kernel wakes up a family of kernel threads to handle the load. The kernel threads run with the lowest possible priority (nice value of 19), which ensures they do not run in lieu of anything important. This concession prevents heavy softirq activity from completely starving user-space of processor time. Conversely, it also ensures that "excess" softirqs do run eventually. Finally, this solution has the added property that on an idle system the softirqs are handled rather quickly because the kernel threads will schedule immediately.

There is one thread per processor. The threads are each named `ksoftirqd/n` where n is the processor number. On a two-processor system, you would have `ksoftirqd/0` and `ksoftirqd/1`. Having a thread on each processor ensures an idle processor, if available, can always service softirqs. After the threads are initialized, they run a tight loop similar to this:

```
for (;;) {
        if (!softirq_pending(cpu))
                schedule();

        set_current_state(TASK_RUNNING);

        while (softirq_pending(cpu)) {
                do_softirq();
                if (need_resched())
                    schedule();
        }

        set_current_state(TASK_INTERRUPTIBLE);
}
```

If any softirqs are pending (as reported by `softirq_pending()`), `ksoftirqd` calls `do_softirq()` to handle them. Note that it does this repeatedly to handle any reactivated softirqs, too. After each iteration, `schedule()` is called if needed, to enable more important processes to run. After all processing is complete, the kernel thread sets itself `TASK_INTERRUPTIBLE` and invokes the scheduler to select a new runnable process.

The softirq kernel threads are awakened whenever `do_softirq()` detects an executed kernel thread reactivating itself.

The Old BH Mechanism

Although the old BH interface, thankfully, is no longer present in 2.6, it was around for a *long* time—since the earliest versions of the kernel. Because it had immense staying power, it certainly carries some historical significance that requires more than a passing look. Nothing in this brief section actually pertains to 2.6, but the history is important.

The BH interface is ancient, and it showed. Each BH must be statically defined, and there are a maximum of 32. Because the handlers must all be defined at compile-time, modules could not directly use the BH interface. They could piggyback off an existing BH, however. Over time, this static requirement and the maximum of 32 bottom halves became a major hindrance to their use.

All BH handlers are strictly serialized—no two BH handlers, even of different types, can run concurrently. This made synchronization easy, but it wasn't beneficial to multi-processor scalability. Performance on large SMP machines was sub par. A driver using the BH interface did not scale well to multiple processors. The networking layer, in particular, suffered.

Other than these attributes, the BH mechanism is similar to tasklets. In fact, the BH interface was implemented on top of tasklets in 2.4. The 32 possible bottom halves were represented by constants defined in `<linux/interrupt.h>`. To mark a BH as pending, the function `mark_bh()` was called and passed the number of the BH. In 2.4, this in turn scheduled the BH tasklet, `bh_action()`, to run. Before the 2.4 kernel, the BH mechanism was independently implemented and did not rely on any lower-level bottom-half mechanism, much as softirqs are implemented today.

Because of the shortcomings of this form of bottom half, kernel developers introduced task queues to replace bottom halves. Task queues never accomplished this goal, although they did win many new users. In 2.3, the softirq and tasklet mechanisms were introduced to put an end to the BH. The BH mechanism was reimplemented on top of tasklets. Unfortunately, it was complicated to port bottom halves from the BH interface to tasklets or softirqs because of the weaker inherent serialization of the new interfaces.[6] During 2.5, however, the conversion did occur when timers and SCSI—the remaining BH users—finally moved over to softirqs. The kernel developers summarily removed the BH interface. Good riddance, BH!

---

[6] That is, the weaker serialization was beneficial to performance but also harder to program. Converting a BH to a tasklet, for example, required careful thinking: Is this code safe running at the same time as any other tasklet? When finally converted, however, the performance was worth it.

Work Queues

Work queues are a different form of deferring work from what we have looked at so far. Work queues defer work into a kernel thread—this bottom half always runs in process context. Thus, code deferred to a work queue has all the usual benefits of process context. Most important, work queues are schedulable and can therefore sleep.

Normally, it is easy to decide between using work queues and softirqs/tasklets. If the deferred work needs to sleep, work queues are used. If the deferred work need not sleep, softirqs or tasklets are used. Indeed, the usual alternative to work queues is kernel threads. Because the kernel developers frown upon creating a new kernel thread (and, in some locales, it is a punishable offense), work queues are strongly preferred. They are *really* easy to use, too.

If you need a schedulable entity to perform your bottom-half processing, you need work queues. They are the only bottom-half mechanisms that run in process context, and thus, the only ones that can sleep. This means they are useful for situations in which you need to allocate a lot of memory, obtain a semaphore, or perform block I/O. If you do not need a kernel thread to handle your deferred work, consider a tasklet instead.

Implementing Work Queues

In its most basic form, the work queue subsystem is an interface for creating kernel threads to handle work queued from elsewhere. These kernel threads are called *worker threads*. Work queues let your driver create a special worker thread to handle deferred work. The work queue subsystem, however, implements and provides a default worker thread for handling work. Therefore, in its most common form, a work queue is a simple interface for deferring work to a generic kernel thread.

The default worker threads are called events/n where n is the processor number; there is one per processor. For example, on a uniprocessor system there is one thread, events/0. A dual processor system would additionally have an events/1 thread. The default worker thread handles deferred work from multiple locations. Many drivers in the kernel defer their bottom-half work to the default thread. Unless a driver or subsystem has a strong requirement for creating its own thread, the default thread is preferred.

Nothing stops code from creating its own worker thread, however. This might be advantageous if you perform large amounts of processing in the worker thread. Processor-intense and performance-critical work might benefit from its own thread. This also lightens the load on the default threads, which prevents starving the rest of the queued work.

Data Structures Representing the Threads

The worker threads are represented by the workqueue_struct structure:

```
/*
 * The externally visible workqueue abstraction is an array of
 * per-CPU workqueues:
 */
```

```
struct workqueue_struct {
        struct cpu_workqueue_struct cpu_wq[NR_CPUS];
        struct list_head list;
        const char *name;
        int singlethread;
        int freezeable;
        int rt;
};
```

This structure, defined in `kernel/workqueue.c`, contains an array of `struct cpu_workqueue_struct`, one per possible processor on the system. Because the worker threads exist on each processor in the system, there is one of these structures per worker thread, per processor, on a given machine. The `cpu_workqueue_struct` is the core data structure and is also defined in `kernel/workqueue.c`:

```
struct cpu_workqueue_struct {
        spinlock_t lock;                    /* lock protecting this structure */

        struct list_head worklist;     /* list of work */
        wait_queue_head_t more_work;
        struct work_struct *current_struct;

        struct workqueue_struct *wq; /* associated workqueue_struct */
        task_t *thread;                     /* associated thread */
};
```

Note that each *type* of worker thread has one `workqueue_struct` associated to it. Inside, there is one `cpu_workqueue_struct` for every thread and, thus, every processor, because there is one worker thread on each processor.

Data Structures Representing the Work

All worker threads are implemented as normal kernel threads running the `worker_thread()` function. After initial setup, this function enters an infinite loop and goes to sleep. When work is queued, the thread is awakened and processes the work. When there is no work left to process, it goes back to sleep.

The work is represented by the `work_struct` structure, defined in `<linux/workqueue.h>`:

```
struct work_struct {
        atomic_long_t data;
        struct list_head entry;
        work_func_t func;
};
```

These structures are strung into a linked list, one for each type of queue on each processor. For example, there is one list of deferred work for the generic thread, per processor. When a worker thread wakes up, it runs any work in its list. As it completes work, it removes the corresponding `work_struct` entries from the linked list. When the list is empty, it goes back to sleep.

Let's look at the heart of `worker_thread()`, simplified:

```
for (;;) {
        prepare_to_wait(&cwq->more_work, &wait, TASK_INTERRUPTIBLE);
        if (list_empty(&cwq->worklist))
                schedule();
        finish_wait(&cwq->more_work, &wait);
        run_workqueue(cwq);
}
```

This function performs the following functions, in an infinite loop:

1. The thread marks itself sleeping (the task's state is set to `TASK_INTERRUPTIBLE`) and adds itself to a wait queue.

2. If the linked list of work is empty, the thread calls `schedule()` and goes to sleep.

3. If the list is not empty, the thread does not go to sleep. Instead, it marks itself `TASK_RUNNING` and removes itself from the wait queue.

4. If the list is nonempty, the thread calls `run_workqueue()` to perform the deferred work.

The function `run_workqueue()`, in turn, actually performs the deferred work:

```
while (!list_empty(&cwq->worklist)) {
        struct work_struct *work;
        work_func_t f;
        void *data;

        work = list_entry(cwq->worklist.next, struct work_struct, entry);
        f = work->func;
        list_del_init(cwq->worklist.next);
        work_clear_pending(work);
        f(work);
}
```

This function loops over each entry in the linked list of pending work and executes the `func` member of the `workqueue_struct` for each entry in the linked list:

1. While the list is not empty, it grabs the next entry in the list.

2. It retrieves the function that should be called, `func`, and its argument, `data`.

3. It removes this entry from the list and clears the pending bit in the structure itself.

4. It invokes the function.

5. Repeat.

Work Queue Implementation Summary

The relationship between the different data structures is admittedly a bit convoluted. Figure 8.1 provides a graphical example, which should bring it all together.

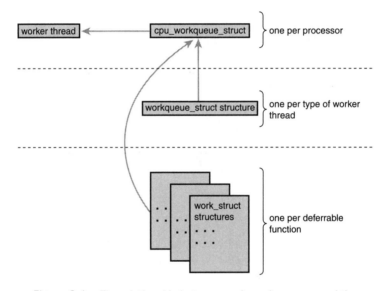

Figure 8.1   The relationship between work, work queues, and the worker threads.

At the highest level, there are worker threads. There can be multiple types of worker threads; there is one worker thread per processor of a given type. Parts of the kernel can create worker threads as needed. By default, there is the *events* worker thread. Each worker thread is represented by the `cpu_workqueue_struct` structure. The `workqueue_struct` structure represents all the worker threads of a given type.

For example, assume that in addition to the generic *events* worker type, you also create a *falcon* worker type. Also, assume you have a four-processor computer. Then there are four *events* threads (and thus four `cpu_workqueue_struct` structures) and four *falcon* threads (and thus another four `cpu_workqueue_struct` structures). There is one `workqueue_struct` for the *events* type and one for the *falcon* type.

Now, let's approach from the lowest level, which starts with work. Your driver creates work, which it wants to defer to later. The `work_struct` structure represents this work. Among other things, this structure contains a pointer to the function that handles the deferred work. The work is submitted to a *specific* worker thread—in this case, a specific falcon thread. The worker thread then wakes up and performs the queued work.

Most drivers use the existing default worker threads, named *events*. They are easy and simple. Some more serious situations, however, demand their own worker threads. The XFS filesystem, for example, creates two new types of worker threads.

Using Work Queues

Using work queues is easy. We cover the default *events* queue first and then look at creating new worker threads.

Creating Work

The first step is actually creating some work to defer. To create the structure statically at runtime, use `DECLARE_WORK`:

```
DECLARE_WORK(name, void (*func)(void *), void *data);
```

This statically creates a `work_struct` structure named `name` with handler function `func` and argument `data`.

Alternatively, you can create work at runtime via a pointer:

```
INIT_WORK(struct work_struct *work, void (*func)(void *), void *data);
```

This dynamically initializes the work queue pointed to by `work` with handler function `func` and argument `data`.

Your Work Queue Handler

The prototype for the work queue handler is

```
void work_handler(void *data)
```

A worker thread executes this function, and thus, the function runs in process context. By default, interrupts are enabled and no locks are held. If needed, the function can sleep. Note that, despite running in process context, the work handlers cannot access user-space memory because there is no associated user-space memory map for kernel threads. The kernel can access user memory only when running on behalf of a user-space process, such as when executing a system call. Only then is user memory mapped in.

Locking between work queues or other parts of the kernel is handled just as with any other process context code. This makes writing work handlers much easier. The next two chapters cover locking.

Scheduling Work

Now that the work is created, we can schedule it. To queue a given work's handler function with the default *events* worker threads, simply call

```
schedule_work(&work);
```

The work is scheduled immediately and is run as soon as the *events* worker thread on the current processor wakes up.

Sometimes you do not want the work to execute immediately, but instead after some delay. In those cases, you can schedule work to execute at a given time in the future:

```
schedule_delayed_work(&work, delay);
```

In this case, the `work_struct` represented by `&work` will not execute for at least `delay` timer ticks into the future. Using ticks as a unit of time is covered in Chapter 10.

Flushing Work

Queued work is executed when the worker thread next wakes up. Sometimes, you need to ensure that a given batch of work has completed before continuing. This is especially important for modules, which almost certainly want to call this function before unloading. Other places in the kernel also might need to make certain no work is pending, to prevent race conditions.

For these needs, there is a function to flush a given work queue:

```
void flush_scheduled_work(void);
```

This function waits until all entries in the queue are executed before returning. While waiting for any pending work to execute, the function sleeps. Therefore, you can call it only from process context.

Note that this function does not cancel any delayed work. That is, any work that was scheduled via `schedule_delayed_work()`, and whose delay is not yet up, is not flushed via `flush_scheduled_work()`. To cancel delayed work, call

```
int cancel_delayed_work(struct work_struct *work);
```

This function cancels the pending work, if any, associated with the given `work_struct`.

Creating New Work Queues

If the default queue is insufficient for your needs, you can create a new work queue and corresponding worker threads. Because this creates one worker thread per processor, you should create unique work queues only if your code needs the performance of a unique set of threads.

You create a new work queue and the associated worker threads via a simple function:

```
struct workqueue_struct *create_workqueue(const char *name);
```

The parameter `name` is used to name the kernel threads. For example, the default *events* queue is created via

```
struct workqueue_struct *keventd_wq;
keventd_wq = create_workqueue("events");
```

This function creates *all* the worker threads (one for each processor in the system) and prepares them to handle work.

Creating work is handled in the same manner regardless of the queue type. After the work is created, the following functions are analogous to `schedule_work()` and `schedule_delayed_work()`, except that they work on the given work queue and not the default *events* queue.

```
int queue_work(struct workqueue_struct *wq, struct work_struct *work)
```

```
int queue_delayed_work(struct workqueue_struct *wq,
                       struct work_struct *work,
                       unsigned long delay)
```

Finally, you can flush a wait queue via a call to the function

```
flush_workqueue(struct workqueue_struct *wq)
```

As previously discussed, this function works identically to `flush_scheduled_work()`, except that it waits for the given queue to empty before returning.

The Old Task Queue Mechanism

Like the BH interface, which gave way to softirqs and tasklets, the work queue interface grew out of shortcomings in the task queue interface. The task queue interface (often called simply *tq* in the kernel), like tasklets, also has nothing to do with tasks in the process sense.[7] The users of the task queue interface were ripped in half during the 2.5 development kernel. Half of the users were converted to tasklets, whereas the other half continued using the task queue interface. What was left of the task queue interface then became the work queue interface. Briefly looking at task queues, which were around for some time, is a useful historical exercise.

Task queues work by defining a bunch of queues. The queues have names, such as the scheduler queue, the immediate queue, or the timer queue. Each queue is run at a specific point in the kernel. A kernel thread, *keventd*, ran the work associated with the scheduler queue. This was the precursor to the full work queue interface. The timer queue was run at each tick of the system timer, and the immediate queue was run in a handful of different places to ensure it was run "immediately" (*hack!*). There were other queues, too. Additionally, you could dynamically create new queues.

All this might sound useful, but the reality is that the task queue interface was a mess. All the queues were essentially arbitrary abstractions, scattered about the kernel as if thrown in the air and kept where they landed. The only meaningful queue was the scheduler queue, which provided the only way to defer work to process context.

The other good thing about task queues was the brain-dead simple interface. Despite the myriad of queues and the arbitrary rules about when they ran, the interface was as simple as possible. But that's about it—the rest of task queues needed to go.

---

[7] *Bottom-half names are apparently a conspiracy to confuse new kernel developers. Seriously, these names are awful.*

The various task queue users were converted to other bottom-half mechanisms. Most of them switched to tasklets. The scheduler queue users stuck around. Finally, the `keventd` code was generalized into the excellent work queue mechanism we have today, and task queues were finally ripped out of the kernel.

Which Bottom Half Should I Use?

The decision over which bottom half to use is important. In the current 2.6 kernel, you have three choices: softirqs, tasklets, and work queues. Tasklets are built on softirqs and, therefore, both are similar. The work queue mechanism is an entirely different creature and is built on kernel threads.

Softirqs, by design, provide the least serialization. This requires softirq handlers to go through extra steps to ensure that shared data is safe because two or more softirqs of the same type may run concurrently on different processors. If the code in question is already highly threaded, such as in a networking subsystem that is chest-deep in per-processor variables, softirqs make a good choice. They are certainly the fastest alternative for timing-critical and high-frequency uses.

Tasklets make more sense if the code is not finely threaded. They have a simpler interface and, because two tasklets of the same type might not run concurrently, they are easier to implement. Tasklets are effectively softirqs that do not run concurrently. A driver developer should always choose tasklets over softirqs, unless prepared to utilize per-processor variables or similar magic to ensure that the softirq can safely run concurrently on multiple processors.

If your deferred work needs to run in process context, your only choice of the three is work queues. If process context is not a requirement—specifically, if you have no need to sleep—softirqs or tasklets are perhaps better suited. Work queues involve the highest overhead because they involve kernel threads and, therefore, context switching. This is not to say that they are inefficient, but in light of thousands of interrupts hitting per second (as the networking subsystem might experience), other methods make more sense. For most situations, however, work queues are sufficient.

In terms of ease of use, work queues take the crown. Using the default *events* queue is child's play. Next come tasklets, which also have a simple interface. Coming in last are softirqs, which need to be statically created and require careful thinking with their implementation.

Table 8.3 is a comparison between the three bottom-half interfaces.

Table 8.3   **Bottom Half Comparison**

Bottom Half	Context	Inherent Serialization
Softirq	Interrupt	None
Tasklet	Interrupt	Against the same tasklet
Work queues	Process	None (scheduled as process context)

In short, normal driver writers have two choices. First, do you need a schedulable entity to perform your deferred work—fundamentally, do you need to sleep for any reason? Then work queues are your only option. Otherwise, tasklets are preferred. Only if scalability becomes a concern do you investigate softirqs.

Locking Between the Bottom Halves

We have not discussed locking yet, which is such a fun and expansive topic that we devote the next two chapters to it. Nonetheless, you need to understand that it is crucial to protect shared data from concurrent access while using bottom halves, even on a single processor machine. Remember, a bottom half can run at virtually any moment. You might want to come back to this section after reading the next two chapters if the concept of locking is foreign to you.

One of the benefits of tasklets is that they are serialized with respect to themselves: The same tasklet will not run concurrently, even on two different processors. This means you do not have to worry about intra-tasklet concurrency issues. Inter-tasklet concurrency (that is, when two different tasklets share the same data) requires proper locking.

Because softirqs provide no serialization, (even two instances of the same softirq might run simultaneously), all shared data needs an appropriate lock.

If process context code and a bottom half share data, you need to disable bottom-half processing and obtain a lock before accessing the data. Doing both ensures local and SMP protection and prevents a deadlock.

If interrupt context code and a bottom half share data, you need to disable interrupts and obtain a lock before accessing the data. This also ensures both local and SMP protection and prevents a deadlock.

Any shared data in a work queue requires locking, too. The locking issues are no different from normal kernel code because work queues run in process context.

Chapter 9, "An Introduction to Kernel Synchronization," provides a background on the issues surrounding concurrency, and Chapter 10 covers the kernel locking primitives. These chapters cover how to protect data that bottom halves use.

Disabling Bottom Halves

Normally, it is not sufficient to only disable bottom halves. More often, to safely protect shared data, you need to obtain a lock *and* disable bottom halves. Such methods, which you might use in a driver, are covered in Chapter 10. If you are writing core kernel code, however, you might need to disable just the bottom halves.

To disable all bottom-half processing (specifically, all softirqs and thus all tasklets), call `local_bh_disable()`. To enable bottom-half processing, call `local_bh_enable()`. Yes, the function is misnamed; no one bothered to change the name when the BH interface gave way to softirqs. Table 8.4 is a summary of these functions.

Table 8.4   **Bottom Half Control Methods**

Method	Description
`void local_bh_disable()`	Disables softirq and tasklet processing on the local processor
`void local_bh_enable()`	Enables softirq and tasklet processing on the local processor

The calls can be nested—only the final call to `local_bh_enable()` actually enables bottom halves. For example, the first time `local_bh_disable()` is called, local softirq processing is disabled. If `local_bh_disable()` is called three more times, local processing remains disabled. Processing is not reenabled until the fourth call to `local_bh_enable()`.

The functions accomplish this by maintaining a per-task counter via the `preempt_count` (interestingly, the same counter used by kernel preemption).[8] When the counter reaches zero, bottom-half processing is possible. Because bottom halves were disabled, `local_bh_enable()` also checks for any pending bottom halves and executes them.

The functions are unique to each supported architecture and are usually written as complicated macros in `<asm/softirq.h>`. The following are close C representations for the curious:

```
/*
 * disable local bottom halves by incrementing the preempt_count
 */
void local_bh_disable(void)
{
        struct thread_info *t = current_thread_info();

        t->preempt_count += SOFTIRQ_OFFSET;
}

/*
 * decrement the preempt_count - this will 'automatically' enable
 * bottom halves if the count returns to zero
 *
 * optionally run any bottom halves that are pending
 */
void local_bh_enable(void)
{
```

---

[8] *This counter is used both by the interrupt and bottom-half subsystems. Thus, in Linux, a single per-task counter represents the atomicity of a task. This has proven useful for work such as debugging sleeping-while-atomic bugs.*

```
    struct thread_info *t = current_thread_info();

    t->preempt_count -= SOFTIRQ_OFFSET;

    /*
     * is preempt_count zero and are any bottom halves pending?
     * if so, run them
     */
    if (unlikely(!t->preempt_count && softirq_pending(smp_processor_id())))
            do_softirq();
}
```

These calls do not disable the execution of work queues. Because work queues run in process context, there are no issues with asynchronous execution, and thus, there is no need to disable them. Because softirqs and tasklets can occur asynchronously (say, on return from handling an interrupt), however, kernel code may need to disable them. With work queues, on the other hand, protecting shared data is the same as in any process context. Chapters 8 and 9 give the details.

Conclusion

In this chapter, we covered the three mechanisms used to defer work in the Linux kernel: softirqs, tasklets, and work queues. We went over their design and implementation. We discussed how to use them in your own code and we insulted their poorly conceived names. For historical completeness, we also looked at the bottom-half mechanisms that existed in previous versions of the Linux kernel: BH's and task queues.

We talked a lot in this chapter about synchronization and concurrency because such topics apply quite a bit to bottom halves. We even wrapped up the chapter with a discussion on disabling bottom halves for reasons of concurrency protection. It is now time to dive head first into these topics. Chapter 9 discusses kernel synchronization and concurrency in the abstract, providing a foundation for understanding the issues at the heart of the problem. Chapter 10 discusses the specific interfaces provided by our beloved kernel to solve these problems. Armed with the next two chapters, the world is your oyster.

9

An Introduction to Kernel Synchronization

In a shared memory application, developers must ensure that shared resources are protected from concurrent access. The kernel is no exception. Shared resources require protection from concurrent access because if multiple threads of execution[1] access and manipulate the data at the same time, the threads may overwrite each other's changes or access data while it is in an inconsistent state. Concurrent access of shared data is a recipe for instability that often proves hard to track down and debug—getting it right at the start is important.

Properly protecting shared resources can be tough. Years ago, before Linux supported symmetrical multiprocessing, preventing concurrent access of data was simple. Because only a single processor was supported, the only way data could be concurrently accessed was if an interrupt occurred or if kernel code explicitly rescheduled and enabled another task to run. With earlier kernels, development was simple.

Those halcyon days are over. Symmetrical multiprocessing support was introduced in the 2.0 kernel and has been continually enhanced ever since. Multiprocessing support implies that kernel code can simultaneously run on two or more processors. Consequently, without protection, code in the kernel, running on two different processors, can simultaneously access shared data at exactly the same time. With the introduction of the 2.6 kernel, the Linux kernel is preemptive. This implies that (again, in the absence of protection) the scheduler can preempt kernel code at virtually any point and reschedule another task. Today, a number of scenarios enable for concurrency inside the kernel, and they all require protection.

---

[1] The term threads of execution implies any instance of executing code. This includes, for example, a task in the kernel, an interrupt handler, a bottom half, or a kernel thread. This chapter may shorten threads of execution to simply threads. Keep in mind that this term describes any executing code.

This chapter discusses the issues of concurrency and synchronization in the abstract, as they exist in any operating system kernel. The next chapter details the specific mechanisms and interfaces that the Linux kernel provides to solve synchronization issues and prevent race conditions.

Critical Regions and Race Conditions

Code paths that access and manipulate shared data are called *critical regions* (also called *critical sections*). It is usually unsafe for multiple threads of execution to access the same resource simultaneously. To prevent concurrent access during critical regions, the programmer must ensure that code executes *atomically*—that is, operations complete without interruption as if the entire critical region were one indivisible instruction. It is a bug if it is possible for two threads of execution to be simultaneously executing within the same critical region. When this does occur, we call it a *race condition*, so-named because the threads *raced* to get there first. Note how rare a race condition in your code might manifest itself—debugging race conditions is often difficult because they are not easily reproducible. Ensuring that unsafe concurrency is prevented and that race conditions do not occur is called *synchronization*.

Why Do We Need Protection?

To best understand the need for synchronization, let's look at the ubiquity of race conditions. For a first example, let's consider a real-world case: an ATM (Automated Teller Machine, called a cash machine, cashpoint, or ABM outside of the United States).

One of the most common functions performed by cash machines is withdrawing money from an individual's personal bank account. A person walks up to the machine, inserts an ATM card, types in a PIN, selects *Withdrawal*, inputs a pecuniary amount, hits OK, takes the money, and mails it to me.

After the user has asked for a specific amount of money, the cash machine needs to ensure that the money actually exists in that user's account. If the money exists, it then needs to deduct the withdrawal from the total funds available. The code to implement this would look something like

```
int total = get_total_from_account();     /* total funds in account */
int withdrawal = get_withdrawal_amount();  /* amount user asked to withdrawal */

/* check whether the user has enough funds in her account */
if (total < withdrawal) {
        error("You do not have that much money!")
        return -1;
}

/* OK, the user has enough money: deduct the withdrawal amount from her total */
total -= withdrawal;
update_total_funds(total);
```

```
/* give the user their money */
spit_out_money(withdrawal);
```

Now, let's presume that another deduction in the user's funds is happening at the same time. It does not matter *how* the simultaneous deduction is happening: Assume that the user's spouse is initiating another withdrawal at another ATM, a payee is electronically transferring funds out of the account, or the bank is deducting a fee from the account (as banks these days are so wont to do). Any of these scenarios fits our example.

Both systems performing the withdrawal would have code similar to what we just looked at: First check whether the deduction is possible, then compute the new total funds, and finally execute the physical deduction. Now let's make up some numbers. Presume that the first deduction is a withdrawal from an ATM for $100 and that the second deduction is the bank applying a fee of $10 because the customer walked into the bank. Assume the customer has a total of $105 in the bank. Obviously, one of these transactions *cannot* correctly complete without sending the account into the red.

What you would expect is something like this: The fee transaction happens first. Ten dollars is less than $105, so 10 is subtracted from 105 to get a new total of 95, and $10 is pocketed by the bank. Then the ATM withdrawal comes along and fails because $95 is less than $100.

With race conditions, life can be much more interesting. Assume that the two transactions are initiated at roughly the same time. Both transactions verify that sufficient funds exist: $105 is more than both $100 and $10, so all is good. Then the withdrawal process subtracts $100 from $105, yielding $5. The fee transaction then does the same, subtracting $10 from $105 and getting $95. The withdrawal process then updates the user's new total available funds to $5. Now the fee transaction also updates the new total, resulting in $95. Free money!

Clearly, financial institutions must ensure that this can never happen. They must lock the account during certain operations, making each transaction atomic with respect to any other transaction. Such transactions must occur in their entirety, without interruption, or not occur at all.

The Single Variable

Now, let's look at a specific computing example. Consider a simple shared resource, a single global integer, and a simple critical region, the operation of merely incrementing it:

```
i++;
```

This might translate into machine instructions to the computer's processor that resemble the following:

```
get the current value of i and copy it into a register
add one to the value stored in the register
write back to memory the new value of i
```

Now, assume that there are two threads of execution, both enter this critical region, and the initial value of i is 7. The desired outcome is then similar to the following (with each row representing a unit of time):

Thread 1	Thread 2
get i (7)	—
increment i (7 -> 8)	—
write back i (8)	—
—	get i (8)
—	increment i (8 -> 9)
—	write back i (9)

As expected, 7 incremented twice is 9. A possible outcome, however, is the following:

Thread 1	Thread 2
get i (7)	get i (7)
increment i (7 -> 8)	—
—	increment i (7 -> 8)
write back i (8)	—
—	write back i (8)

If both threads of execution read the initial value of i before it is incremented, both threads increment and save the same value. As a result, the variable i contains the value 8 when, in fact, it should now contain 9. This is one of the simplest examples of a critical region. Thankfully, the solution is equally as simple: We merely need a way to perform these operations in one indivisible step. Most processors provide an instruction to atomically read, increment, and write back a single variable. Using this *atomic instruction*, the only possible outcome is

Thread 1	Thread 2
increment & store i (7 -> 8)	—
—	increment & store i (8 -> 9)

Or conversely

Thread 1	Thread 2
—	increment & store (7 -> 8)
increment & store (8 -> 9)	—

It would never be possible for the two atomic operations to interleave. The processor would physically ensure that it was impossible. Using such an instruction would alleviate the problem. The kernel provides a set of interfaces that implement these atomic instructions; they are discussed in the next chapter.

Locking

Now, let's consider a more complicated race condition that requires a more complicated solution. Assume you have a queue of requests that needs to be serviced. For this exercise, let's assume the implementation is a linked list, in which each node represents a request. Two functions manipulate the queue. One function adds a new request to the tail of the queue. Another function removes a request from the head of the queue and does something useful with the request. Various parts of the kernel invoke these two functions; thus, requests are continually being added, removed, and serviced. Manipulating the request queues certainly requires multiple instructions. If one thread attempts to read from the queue while another is in the middle of manipulating it, the reading thread will find the queue in an inconsistent state. It should be apparent the sort of damage that could occur if access to the queue could occur concurrently. Often, when the shared resource is a complex data structure, the result of a race condition is corruption of the data structure.

The previous scenario, at first, might not have a clear solution. How can you prevent one processor from reading from the queue while another processor is updating it? Although it is feasible for a particular architecture to implement simple instructions, such as arithmetic and comparison, atomically it is ludicrous for architectures to provide instructions to support the indefinitely sized critical regions that would exist in the previous example. What is needed is a way of making sure that only one thread manipulates the data structure at a time—a mechanism for preventing access to a resource while another thread of execution is in the marked region.

A *lock* provides such a mechanism; it works much like a lock on a door. Imagine the room beyond the door as the critical region. Inside the room, only one thread of execution can be present at a given time. When a thread enters the room, it locks the door behind it. When the thread is finished manipulating the shared data, it leaves the room and unlocks the door. If another thread reaches the door while it is locked, it must wait for the thread inside to exit the room and unlock the door before it can enter. Threads hold locks; locks protect data.

In the previous request queue example, a single lock could have been used to protect the queue. Whenever there was a new request to add to the queue, the thread would first obtain the lock. Then it could safely add the request to the queue and ultimately release the lock. When a thread wanted to remove a request from the queue, it too would obtain the lock. Then it could read the request and remove it from the queue. Finally, it would release the lock. Any other access to the queue would similarly need to obtain the lock. Because the lock can be held by only one thread at a time, only a single thread can manipulate the queue at a time. If a thread comes along while another thread is already updating it, the second thread has to wait for the first to release the lock before it can continue. The lock prevents concurrency and protects the queue from race conditions.

Any code that accesses the queue first needs to obtain the relevant lock. If another thread of execution comes along, the lock prevents concurrency:

Thread 1	Thread 2
try to lock the queue	try to lock the queue
succeeded: acquired lock	failed: waiting...
access queue...	waiting...
unlock the queue	waiting...
...	succeeded: acquired lock
	access queue...
	unlock the queue

Notice that locks are *advisory* and *voluntary*. Locks are entirely a programming construct that the programmer must take advantage of. Nothing prevents you from writing code that manipulates the fictional queue without the appropriate lock. Such a practice, of course, would eventually result in a race condition and corruption.

Locks come in various shapes and sizes—Linux alone implements a handful of different locking mechanisms. The most significant difference between the various mechanisms is the behavior when the lock is unavailable because another thread already holds it— some lock variants *busy wait*,[2] whereas other locks put the current task to sleep until the lock becomes available. The next chapter discusses the behavior of the different locks in Linux and their interfaces.

Astute readers are now screaming. The lock does not solve the problem; it simply shrinks the critical region down to just the lock and unlock code: probably much smaller, sure, but still a potential race! Fortunately, locks are implemented using atomic operations that ensure no race exists. A single instruction can verify whether the key is taken and, if not, seize it. How this is done is architecture-specific, but almost all processors implement an atomic *test and set* instruction that tests the value of an integer and sets it to a new value only if it is zero. A value of zero means unlocked. On the popular x86 architecture, locks are implemented using such a similar instruction called *compare and exchange*.

---

[2] *That is, spin in a tight loop, checking the status of the lock over and over, waiting for the lock to become available.*

Causes of Concurrency

In user-space, the need for synchronization stems from the fact that programs are scheduled preemptively at the will of the scheduler. Because a process can be preempted at any time and another process can be scheduled onto the processor, a process can be involuntarily preempted in the middle of accessing a critical region. If the newly scheduled process then enters the same critical region (say, if the two processes manipulate the same shared memory or write to the same file descriptor), a race can occur. The same problem can occur with multiple single-threaded processes sharing files, or within a single program with signals, because signals can occur asynchronously. This type of concurrency—in which two things do not actually happen at the same time but interleave with each other such that they might as well—is called *pseudo-concurrency*.

If you have a symmetrical multiprocessing machine, two processes can actually be executed in a critical region at the exact same time. That is called *true concurrency*. Although the causes and semantics of true versus pseudo concurrency are different, they both result in the same race conditions and require the same sort of protection.

The kernel has similar causes of concurrency:

- **Interrupts**— An interrupt can occur asynchronously at almost any time, interrupting the currently executing code.

- **Softirqs and tasklets**— The kernel can raise or schedule a softirq or tasklet at almost any time, interrupting the currently executing code.

- **Kernel preemption**— Because the kernel is preemptive, one task in the kernel can preempt another.

- **Sleeping and synchronization with user-space**— A task in the kernel can sleep and thus invoke the scheduler, resulting in the running of a new process.

- **Symmetrical multiprocessing**— Two or more processors can execute kernel code at exactly the same time.

Kernel developers need to understand and prepare for these causes of concurrency. It is a major bug if an interrupt occurs in the middle of code that is manipulating a resource and the interrupt handler can access the same resource. Similarly, it is a bug if kernel code is preemptive while it is accessing a shared resource. Likewise, it is a bug if code in the kernel sleeps while in the middle of a critical section. Finally, two processors should never simultaneously access the same piece of data. With a clear picture of what data needs protection, it is not hard to provide the locking to keep the system stable. Rather, the hard part is identifying these conditions and realizing that to prevent concurrency, you need some form of protection.

Let us reiterate this point, because it is important. Implementing the actual locking in your code to protect shared data is not difficult, especially when done early on during the design phase of development. The tricky part is identifying the actual shared data and the corresponding critical sections. This is why designing locking into your code from the get-go, and not as an afterthought, is of paramount importance. It can be difficult to go in, *ex post*, and identify critical regions and retrofit locking into the existing code. The resulting code is often not pretty, either. The takeaway from this is to *always* design proper locking into your code from the beginning.

Code that is safe from concurrent access from an interrupt handler is said to be *interrupt-safe*. Code that is safe from concurrency on symmetrical multiprocessing machines is *SMP-safe*. Code that is safe from concurrency with kernel preemption is *preempt-safe*.[3] The actual mechanisms used to provide synchronization and protect against race conditions in all these cases is covered in the next chapter.

Knowing What to Protect

Identifying what data specifically needs protection is vital. Because any data that can be accessed concurrently almost assuredly needs protection, it is often easier to identify what data does *not* need protection and work from there. Obviously, any data that is local to one particular thread of execution does not need protection, because only that thread can access the data. For example, local automatic variables (and dynamically allocated data structures whose address is stored only on the stack) do not need any sort of locking because they exist solely on the stack of the executing thread. Likewise, data that is accessed by only a specific task does not require locking (because a process can execute on only one processor at a time).

What *does* need locking? Most global kernel data structures do. A good rule of thumb is that if another thread of execution can access the data, the data needs some sort of locking; if anyone else can see it, lock it. Remember to lock *data*, not *code*.

> ### CONFIG Options: SMP Versus UP
>
> Because the Linux kernel is configurable at compile time, it makes sense that you can tailor the kernel specifically for a given machine. Most important, the `CONFIG_SMP` configure option controls whether the kernel supports SMP. Many locking issues disappear on uniprocessor machines; consequently, when `CONFIG_SMP` is unset, unnecessary code is not compiled into the kernel image. For example, such configuration enables uniprocessor machines to forego the overhead of spin locks. The same trick applies to `CONFIG_PREEMPT` (the configure option enabling kernel preemption). This was an excellent design decision— the kernel maintains one clean source base, and the various locking mechanisms are used as needed. Different combinations of `CONFIG_SMP` and `CONFIG_PREEMPT` on different architectures compile in varying lock support.
>
> In your code, provide appropriate protection for the most pessimistic case, SMP with kernel preemption, and all scenarios will be covered.

---

[3] *You will also see that, barring a few exceptions, being SMP-safe implies being preempt-safe.*

Whenever you write kernel code, you should ask yourself these questions:

- Is the data global? Can a thread of execution other than the current one access it?
- Is the data shared between process context and interrupt context? Is it shared between two different interrupt handlers?
- If a process is preempted while accessing this data, can the newly scheduled process access the same data?
- Can the current process sleep (block) on anything? If it does, in what state does that leave any shared data?
- What prevents the data from being freed out from under me?
- What happens if this function is called again on another processor?
- Given the proceeding points, how am I going to ensure that my code is safe from concurrency?

In short, nearly all global and shared data in the kernel requires some form of the synchronization methods, discussed in the next chapter.

Deadlocks

A *deadlock* is a condition involving one or more threads of execution and one or more resources, such that each thread waits for one of the resources, but all the resources are already held. The threads all wait for each other, but they never make any progress toward releasing the resources that they already hold. Therefore, none of the threads can continue, which results in a deadlock.

A good analogy is a four-way traffic stop. If each car at the stop decides to wait for the other cars before going, no car will ever proceed, and we have a traffic deadlock.

The simplest example of a deadlock is the self-deadlock:[4] If a thread of execution attempts to acquire a lock it already holds, it has to wait for the lock to be released. But it will never release the lock, because it is busy waiting for the lock, and the result is deadlock:

```
acquire lock
acquire lock, again
wait for lock to become available
...
```

---

[4] Some kernels prevent this type of deadlock by providing recursive locks. These are locks that a single thread of execution may acquire multiple times. Linux, thankfully, does not provide recursive locks. This is widely considered a good thing. Although recursive locks might alleviate the self-deadlock problem, they very readily lead to sloppy locking semantics.

Similarly, consider *n* threads and *n* locks. If each thread holds a lock that the other thread wants, all threads block while waiting for their respective locks to become available. The most common example is with two threads and two locks, which is often called the *deadly embrace* or the *ABBA deadlock*:

Thread 1	Thread 2
acquire lock A	acquire lock B
try to acquire lock B	try to acquire lock A
wait for lock B	wait for lock A

Each thread is waiting for the other, and neither thread will ever release its original lock; therefore, neither lock will become available.

Prevention of deadlock scenarios is important. Although it is difficult to prove that code is free of deadlocks, you *can* write deadlock-free code. A few simple rules go a long way:

- Implement lock ordering. Nested locks must *always* be obtained in the same order. This prevents the deadly embrace deadlock. Document the lock ordering so others will follow it.
- Prevent starvation. Ask yourself, *does this code always finish? If* foo *does not occur, will* bar *wait forever?*
- Do not double acquire the same lock.
- Design for simplicity. Complexity in your locking scheme invites deadlocks.

The first point is most important and worth stressing. If two or more locks are acquired at the same time, they must *always* be acquired in the same order. Let's assume you have the *cat*, *dog*, and *fox* locks that protect data structures of the same name. Now assume you have a function that needs to work on all three of these data structures simultaneously—perhaps to copy data between them. Whatever the case, the data structures require locking to ensure safe access. If one function acquires the locks in the order *cat*, *dog*, and then *fox*, then *every* other function must obtain these locks (or a subset of them) in this same order. For example, it is a potential deadlock (and hence a bug) to first obtain the *fox* lock and then obtain the *dog* lock because the *dog* lock must always be acquired prior to the *fox* lock. Here is an example in which this would cause a deadlock:

Thread 1	Thread 2
acquire lock cat	acquire lock fox
acquire lock dog	try to acquire lock dog
try to acquire lock fox	wait for lock dog
wait for lock fox	—

Thread one is waiting for the fox lock, which thread two holds, while thread two is waiting for the dog lock, which thread one holds. Neither ever releases its lock and hence both wait forever—bam, deadlock. If the locks were always obtained in the same order, a deadlock in this manner would not be possible.

Whenever locks are nested within other locks, a specific ordering must be obeyed. It is good practice to place the ordering in a comment above the lock. Something like the following is a good idea:

```
/*
 * cat_lock — locks access to the cat structure
 * always obtain before the dog lock!
 */
```

The order of *unlock* does not matter with respect to deadlock, although it is common practice to release the locks in an order inverse to that in which they were acquired.

Preventing deadlocks is important. The Linux kernel has some basic debugging facilities for detecting deadlock scenarios in a running kernel. These features are discussed in the next chapter.

Contention and Scalability

The term *lock contention*, or simply *contention*, describes a lock currently in use but that another thread is trying to acquire. A lock that is *highly contended* often has threads waiting to acquire it. High contention can occur because a lock is frequently obtained, held for a long time after it is obtained, or both. Because a lock's job is to serialize access to a resource, it comes as no surprise that locks can slow down a system's performance. A highly contended lock can become a bottleneck in the system, quickly limiting its performance. Of course, the locks are also required to prevent the system from tearing itself to shreds, so a solution to high contention must continue to provide the necessary concurrency protection.

Scalability is a measurement of how well a system can be expanded. In operating systems, we talk of the scalability with a large number of processes, a large number of processors, or large amounts of memory. We can discuss scalability in relation to virtually any component of a computer to which we can attach a quantity. Ideally, doubling the number of processors should result in a doubling of the system's processor performance. This, of course, is never the case.

The scalability of Linux on a large number of processors has increased dramatically in the time since multiprocessing support was introduced in the 2.0 kernel. In the early days of Linux multiprocessing support, only one task could execute in the kernel at a time. During 2.2, this limitation was removed as the locking mechanisms grew more fine-grained. Through 2.4 and onward, kernel locking became even finer grained. Today, in the 2.6 Linux kernel, kernel locking is very fine-grained and scalability is good.

The granularity of locking is a description of the size or amount of data that a lock protects. A very coarse lock protects a large amount of data—for example, an entire subsystem's set of data structures. On the other hand, a very fine-grained lock protects a small amount of data—say, only a single element in a larger structure. In reality, most locks fall somewhere in between these two extremes, protecting neither an entire subsystem nor an individual element, but perhaps a single structure or list of structures. Most locks start off fairly coarse and are made more fine-grained as lock contention proves to be a problem.

One example of evolving to finer-grained locking is the scheduler runqueues, discussed in Chapter 4, "Process Scheduling." In 2.4 and prior kernels, the scheduler had a single runqueue. (Recall that a runqueue is the list of runnable processes.) Early in the 2.6 series, the O(1) scheduler introduced per-processor runqueues, each with a unique lock. The locking evolved from a single global lock to separate locks for each processor. This was an important optimization, because the runqueue lock was highly contended on large machines, essentially serializing the entire scheduling process down to a single processor executing in the scheduler at a time. Later in the 2.6 series, the *CFS Scheduler* improved scalability further.

Generally, this scalability improvement is a good thing because it improves Linux's performance on larger and more powerful systems. Rampant scalability "improvements" can lead to a decrease in performance on smaller SMP and UP machines, however, because smaller machines may not need such fine-grained locking but will nonetheless need to put up with the increased complexity and overhead. Consider a linked list. An initial locking scheme would provide a single lock for the entire list. In time, this single lock might prove to be a scalability bottleneck on large multiprocessor machines that frequently access this linked list. In response, the single lock could be broken up into one lock per node in the linked list. For each node that you wanted to read or write, you obtained the node's unique lock. Now there is only lock contention when multiple processors are accessing the same exact node. What if there is still lock contention, however? Do you provide a lock for each element in each node? Each bit of each element? The answer is *no*. Even though this fine-grained locking might ensure excellent scalability on large SMP machines, how does it perform on dual processor machines? The overhead of all those extra locks is wasted if a dual processor machine does not see significant lock contention to begin with.

Nonetheless, scalability is an important consideration. Designing your locking from the beginning to scale well is important. Coarse locking of major resources can easily become a bottleneck on even small machines. There is a thin line between too-coarse locking and too-fine locking. Locking that is too coarse results in poor scalability if there is high lock contention, whereas locking that is too fine results in wasteful overhead if there is little lock contention. Both scenarios equate to poor performance. *Start simple and grow in complexity only as needed. Simplicity is key.*

Conclusion

Making your code SMP-safe is not something that can be added as an afterthought. Proper synchronization—locking that is free of deadlocks, scalable, and clean—requires design decisions from start through finish. Whenever you write kernel code, whether it is a new system call or a rewritten driver, protecting data from concurrent access needs to be a primary concern.

Provide sufficient protection for every scenario—SMP, kernel preemption, and so on—and rest assured the data will be safe on any given machine and configuration. The next chapter discusses just how to do this.

With the fundamentals and the theories of synchronization, concurrency, and locking behind us, let's now dive into the actual tools that the Linux kernel provides to ensure that your code is race- and deadlock-free.

10

Kernel Synchronization Methods

The previous chapter discussed the sources of and solutions to race conditions. Thankfully, the Linux kernel provides a family of synchronization methods. The Linux kernel's synchronization methods enable developers to write efficient and race-free code. This chapter discusses these methods and their interfaces, behavior, and use.

Atomic Operations

We start our discussion of synchronization methods with atomic operations because they are the foundation on which other synchronization methods are built. *Atomic operations* provide instructions that execute *atomically*—without interruption. Just as the atom was originally thought to be an indivisible particle, atomic operators are indivisible instructions. For example, as discussed in the previous chapter, an atomic increment can read and increment a variable by one in a single indivisible and uninterruptible step. Recall the simple race in incrementing an integer that we discussed in the previous chapter:

Thread 1	Thread 2
get i (7)	get i (7)
increment i (7 -> 8)	
—	increment i (7 -> 8)
write back i (8)	—
—	write back i (8)

With atomic operators, this race does not—indeed, cannot—occur. Instead, the outcome is always one of the following:

Thread 1	Thread 2
get, increment, and store i (7 -> 8)	—
—	get, increment, and store i (8 -> 9)

Or

Thread 1	Thread 2
—	get, increment, and store i (7 -> 8)
get, increment, and store i (8 -> 9)	—

The ultimate value, always nine, is correct. It is never possible for the two atomic operations to occur on the same variable concurrently. Therefore, it is not possible for the increments to race.

The kernel provides two sets of interfaces for atomic operations—one that operates on integers and another that operates on individual bits. These interfaces are implemented on every architecture that Linux supports. Most architectures contain instructions that provide atomic versions of simple arithmetic operations. Other architectures, lacking direct atomic operations, provide an operation to lock the memory bus for a single operation, thus guaranteeing that another memory-affecting operation cannot occur simultaneously.

Atomic Integer Operations

The atomic integer methods operate on a special data type, `atomic_t`. This special type is used, as opposed to having the functions work directly on the C `int` type, for several reasons. First, having the atomic functions accept only the `atomic_t` type ensures that the atomic operations are used only with these special types. Likewise, it also ensures that the data types are not passed to any nonatomic functions. Indeed, what good would atomic operations be if they were not consistently used on the data? Next, the use of `atomic_t` ensures the compiler does not (erroneously but cleverly) optimize access to the value—it is important the atomic operations receive the correct memory address and not an alias. Finally, use of `atomic_t` can hide any architecture-specific differences in its implementation. The `atomic_t` type is defined in `<linux/types.h>`:

```
typedef struct {
        volatile int counter;
} atomic_t;
```

Despite being an integer, and thus 32 bits on all the machines that Linux supports, developers and their code once had to assume that an `atomic_t` was no larger than 24 bits in size. The SPARC port in Linux has an odd implementation of atomic operations: A lock was embedded in the lower 8 bits of the 32-bit `int` (it looked like Figure 10.1). The lock was used to protect concurrent access to the atomic type because the SPARC architecture lacks appropriate support at the instruction level. Consequently, only 24 usable bits were available on SPARC machines. Although code that assumed that the full 32-bit range existed would work on other machines; it would have failed in strange and subtle ways on SPARC machines—and that is just rude. Recently, clever hacks have allowed SPARC to provide a fully usable 32-bit `atomic_t`, and this limitation is no more.

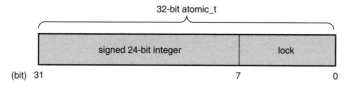

Figure 10.1   Old layout of the 32-bit `atomic_t` on SPARC.

The declarations needed to use the atomic integer operations are in `<asm/atomic.h>`. Some architectures provide additional methods that are unique to that architecture, but all architectures provide at least a minimum set of operations that are used throughout the kernel. When you write kernel code, you can ensure that these operations are correctly implemented on all architectures.

Defining an `atomic_t` is done in the usual manner. Optionally, you can set it to an initial value:

```
atomic_t v;                     /* define v */
atomic_t u = ATOMIC_INIT(0);    /* define u and initialize it to zero */
```

Operations are all simple:

```
atomic_set(&v, 4);      /* v = 4 (atomically) */
atomic_add(2, &v);      /* v = v + 2 = 6 (atomically) */
atomic_inc(&v);         /* v = v + 1 = 7 (atomically) */
```

If you ever need to convert an `atomic_t` to an int, use `atomic_read()`:

```
printk("%d\n", atomic_read(&v));    /* will print "7" */
```

A common use of the atomic integer operations is to implement counters. Protecting a sole counter with a complex locking scheme is overkill, so instead developers use `atomic_inc()` and `atomic_dec()`, which are much lighter in weight.

Another use of the atomic integer operators is atomically performing an operation and testing the result. A common example is the atomic decrement and test:

```
int atomic_dec_and_test(atomic_t *v)
```

This function decrements by one the given atomic value. If the result is zero, it returns true; otherwise, it returns false. A full listing of the standard atomic integer operations (those found on all architectures) is in Table 10.1. All the operations implemented on a specific architecture can be found in `<asm/atomic.h>`.

Table 10.1   **Atomic Integer Methods**

Atomic Integer Operation	Description
`ATOMIC_INIT(int i)`	At declaration, initialize to `i`.
`int atomic_read(atomic_t *v)`	Atomically read the integer value of `v`.
`void atomic_set(atomic_t *v, int i)`	Atomically set `v` equal to `i`.
`void atomic_add(int i, atomic_t *v)`	Atomically add `i` to `v`.
`void atomic_sub(int i, atomic_t *v)`	Atomically subtract `i` from `v`.
`void atomic_inc(atomic_t *v)`	Atomically add one to `v`.
`void atomic_dec(atomic_t *v)`	Atomically subtract one from `v`.
`int atomic_sub_and_test(int i, atomic_t *v)`	Atomically subtract `i` from `v` and return true if the result is zero; otherwise false.
`int atomic_add_negative(int i, atomic_t *v)`	Atomically add `i` to `v` and return true if the result is negative; otherwise false.
`int atomic_add_return(int i, atomic_t *v)`	Atomically add `i` to `v` and return the result.
`int atomic_sub_return(int i, atomic_t *v)`	Atomically subtract `i` from `v` and return the result.
`int atomic_inc_return(int i, atomic_t *v)`	Atomically increment `v` by one and return the result.
`int atomic_dec_return(int i, atomic_t *v)`	Atomically decrement `v` by one and return the result.
`int atomic_dec_and_test(atomic_t *v)`	Atomically decrement `v` by one and return true if zero; false otherwise.
`int atomic_inc_and_test(atomic_t *v)`	Atomically increment `v` by one and return true if the result is zero; false otherwise.

The atomic operations are typically implemented as inline functions with inline assembly. In the case where a specific function is inherently atomic, the given function is usually just a macro. For example, on most architectures, a word-sized read is always atomic. That is, a read of a single word cannot complete in the middle of a write to that word. The read always returns the word in a consistent state, either before or after the write completes, but never in the middle. Consequently, `atomic_read()` is usually just a macro returning the integer value of the `atomic_t`:

```
/**
 * atomic_read - read atomic variable
 * @v: pointer of type atomic_t
 *
 * Atomically reads the value of @v.
 */
static inline int atomic_read(const atomic_t *v)
{
        return v->counter;
}
```

Atomicity Versus Ordering

The preceding discussion on atomic reading begs a discussion on the differences between atomicity and ordering. As discussed, a word-sized read always occurs atomically. It never interleaves with a write to the same word; the read always returns the word in a consistent state—perhaps before the write completes, perhaps after, but never during. For example, if an integer is initially 42 and then set to 365, a read on the integer always returns 42 or 365 and never some commingling of the two values. We call this *atomicity*.

Your code, however, might have more stringent requirements than this: Perhaps you require that the read always occurs *before* the pending write. This type of requirement is *not* atomicity, but *ordering*. Atomicity ensures that instructions occur without interruption and that they complete either in their entirety or not at all. Ordering, on the other hand, ensures that the desired, relative ordering of two or more instructions—even if they are to occur in separate threads of execution or even separate processors—is preserved.

The atomic operations discussed in this section guarantee only atomicity. Ordering is enforced via *barrier operations*, which we discuss later in this chapter.

In your code, it is usually preferred to choose atomic operations over more complicated locking mechanisms. On most architectures, one or two atomic operations incur less overhead and less cache-line thrashing than a more complicated synchronization method. As with any performance-sensitive code, however, testing multiple approaches is always smart.

64-Bit Atomic Operations

With the rising prevalence of 64-bit architectures, it is no surprise that the Linux kernel developers augmented the 32-bit `atomic_t` type with a 64-bit variant, `atomic64_t`. For portability, the size of `atomic_t` cannot change between architectures, so `atomic_t` is 32-bit even on 64-bit architectures. Instead, the `atomic64_t` type provides a 64-bit atomic integer that functions otherwise identical to its 32-bit brother. Usage is exactly the same, except that the usable range of the integer is 64, rather than 32, bits. Nearly all the classic 32-bit atomic operations are implemented in 64-bit variants; they are prefixed with *atomic64* in lieu of *atomic*. Table 10.2 is a full listing of the standard operations; some architectures implement more, but they are not portable. As with `atomic_t`, the `atomic64_t` type is just a simple wrapper around an integer, this type a `long`:

```
typedef struct {
        volatile long counter;
} atomic64_t;
```

Table 10.2   **Atomic Integer Methods**

Atomic Integer Operation	Description
`ATOMIC64_INIT(long i)`	At declaration, initialize to `i`.
`long atomic64_read(atomic64_t *v)`	Atomically read the integer value of `v`.
`void atomic64_set(atomic64_t *v, int i)`	Atomically set `v` equal to `i`.
`void atomic64_add(int i, atomic64_t *v)`	Atomically add `i` to `v`.
`void atomic64_sub(int i, atomic64_t *v)`	Atomically subtract `i` from `v`.
`void atomic64_inc(atomic64_t *v)`	Atomically add one to `v`.
`void atomic64_dec(atomic64_t *v)`	Atomically subtract one from `v`.
`int atomic64_sub_and_test(int i, atomic64_t *v)`	Atomically subtract `i` from `v` and return true if the result is zero; otherwise false.
`int atomic64_add_negative(int i, atomic64_t *v)`	Atomically add `i` to `v` and return true if the result is negative; otherwise false.
`long atomic64_add_return(int i, atomic64_t *v)`	Atomically add `i` to `v` and return the result.
`long atomic64_sub_return(int i, atomic64_t *v)`	Atomically subtract `i` from `v` and return the result.
`long atomic64_inc_return(int i, atomic64_t *v)`	Atomically increment `v` by one and return the result.
`long atomic64_dec_return(int i, atomic64_t *v)`	Atomically decrement `v` by one and return the result.
`int atomic64_dec_and_test(atomic64_t *v)`	Atomically decrement `v` by one and return true if zero; false otherwise.
`int atomic64_inc_and_test(atomic64_t *v)`	Atomically increment `v` by one and return true if the result is zero; false otherwise.

All 64-bit architectures provide `atomic64_t` and a family of arithmetic functions to operate on it. Most 32-bit architectures do not, however, support `atomic64_t`—x86-32 is a notable exception. For portability between all Linux's supported architectures, developers should use the 32-bit `atomic_t` type. The 64-bit `atomic64_t` is reserved for code that is both architecture-specific and that requires 64-bits.

Atomic Bitwise Operations

In addition to atomic integer operations, the kernel also provides a family of functions that operate at the bit level. Not surprisingly, they are architecture-specific and defined in `<asm/bitops.h>`.

What might be surprising is that the bitwise functions operate on generic memory addresses. The arguments are a pointer and a bit number. Bit zero is the least significant bit of the given address. On 32-bit machines, bit 31 is the most significant bit, and bit 32 is the least significant bit of the following word. There are no limitations on the bit number supplied; although, most uses of the functions provide a word and, consequently, a bit number between 0 and 31 on 32-bit machines and 0 and 63 on 64-bit machines.

Because the functions operate on a generic pointer, there is no equivalent of the atomic integer's `atomic_t` type. Instead, you can work with a pointer to whatever data you want. Consider an example:

```
unsigned long word = 0;

set_bit(0, &word);       /* bit zero is now set (atomically) */
set_bit(1, &word);       /* bit one is now set (atomically) */
printk("%ul\n", word);   /* will print "3" */
clear_bit(1, &word);     /* bit one is now unset (atomically) */
change_bit(0, &word);    /* bit zero is flipped; now it is unset (atomically) */

/* atomically sets bit zero and returns the previous value (zero) */
if (test_and_set_bit(0, &word)) {
        /* never true ... */
}

/* the following is legal; you can mix atomic bit instructions with normal C */
word = 7;
```

A listing of the standard atomic bit operations is in Table 10.3.

Table 10.3   **Atomic Bitwise Methods**

Atomic Bitwise Operation	Description
`void set_bit(int nr, void *addr)`	Atomically set the nr-*th* bit starting from `addr`.
`void clear_bit(int nr, void *addr)`	Atomically clear the nr-*th* bit starting from `addr`.
`void change_bit(int nr, void *addr)`	Atomically flip the value of the nr-*th* bit starting from `addr`.
`int test_and_set_bit(int nr, void *addr)`	Atomically set the nr-*th* bit starting from `addr` and return the previous value.
`int test_and_clear_bit(int nr, void *addr)`	Atomically clear the nr-*th* bit starting from `addr` and return the previous value.
`int test_and_change_bit(int nr, void *addr)`	Atomically flip the nr-*th* bit starting from `addr` and return the previous value.
`int test_bit(int nr, void *addr)`	Atomically return the value of the nr-*th* bit starting from `addr`.

Conveniently, nonatomic versions of all the bitwise functions are also provided. They behave identically to their atomic siblings, except they do not guarantee atomicity, and their names are prefixed with double underscores. For example, the nonatomic form of `test_bit()` is `__test_bit()`. If you do not require atomicity (say, for example, because a lock already protects your data), these variants of the bitwise functions might be faster.

> ### What the Heck Is a Nonatomic Bit Operation?
>
> On first glance, the concept of a nonatomic bit operation might not make any sense. Only a single bit is involved; thus, there is no possibility of inconsistency. If one of the operations succeeds, what else could matter? Sure, *ordering* might be important, but we are talking about *atomicity* here. At the end of the day, if the bit has a value provided by any of the instructions, we should be good to go, right?
>
> Let's jump back to just what atomicity means. Atomicity requires that either instructions succeed in their entirety, uninterrupted, or instructions fail to execute at all. Therefore, if you issue two atomic bit operations, you expect two operations to succeed. After both operations complete, the bit needs to have the value as specified by the second operation. More-over, however, at some point in time prior to the final operation, the bit needs to hold the value as specified by the first operation. Put more generally, real atomicity requires that all intermediate states be correctly realized.
>
> For example, assume you issue two atomic bit operations: Initially set the bit and then clear the bit. Without atomic operations, the bit might end up cleared, but it might *never* have been set. The set operation could occur simultaneously with the clear operation and fail. The clear operation would succeed, and the bit would emerge cleared as intended. With atomic operations, however, the set would actually occur—there would be a moment in time when a read would show the bit as set—and then the clear would execute and the bit would be zero.
>
> This behavior can be important, especially when ordering comes into play or when dealing with hardware registers.

The kernel also provides routines to find the first set (or unset) bit starting at a given address:

```
int find_first_bit(unsigned long *addr, unsigned int size)
int find_first_zero_bit(unsigned long *addr, unsigned int size)
```

Both functions take a pointer as their first argument and the number of bits in total to search as their second. They return the bit number of the first set or first unset bit, respectively. If your code is searching only a word, the routines `__ffs()` and `ffz()`, which take a single parameter of the word in which to search, are optimal.

Unlike the atomic integer operations, code typically has no choice whether to use the bitwise operations—they are the only portable way to set a specific bit. The only question is whether to use the atomic or nonatomic variants. If your code is inherently safe from race conditions, you can use the nonatomic versions, which might be faster depending on the architecture.

Spin Locks

Although it would be nice if every critical region consisted of code that did nothing more complicated than incrementing a variable, reality is much crueler. In real life, critical regions can span multiple functions. For example, it is often the case that data must be removed from one structure, formatted and parsed, and added to another structure. This entire operation must occur atomically; it must not be possible for other code to read from or write to either structure before the update is completed. Because simple atomic operations are clearly incapable of providing the needed protection in such a complex scenario, a more general method of synchronization is needed: *locks*.

The most common lock in the Linux kernel is the *spin lock*. A spin lock is a lock that can be held by at most one thread of execution. If a thread of execution attempts to acquire a spin lock while it is already held, which is called *contended*, the thread busy loops—*spins*—waiting for the lock to become available. If the lock is not contended, the thread can immediately acquire the lock and continue. The spinning prevents more than one thread of execution from entering the critical region at any one time. The same lock can be used in multiple locations, so all access to a given data structure, for example, can be protected and synchronized.

Going back to the door and key analogy from the last chapter, spin locks are akin to sitting outside the door, waiting for the fellow inside to come out and hand you the key. If you reach the door and no one is inside, you can grab the key and enter the room. If you reach the door and someone is currently inside, you must wait outside for the key, effectively checking for its presence repeatedly. When the room is vacated, you can grab the key and go inside. Thanks to the key (read: spin lock), only one person (read: thread of execution) is allowed inside the room (read: critical region) at the same time.

The fact that a contended spin lock causes threads to spin (essentially wasting processor time) while waiting for the lock to become available is salient. This behavior is the point of the spin lock. It is not wise to hold a spin lock for a long time. This is the nature of the spin lock: a lightweight single-holder lock that should be held for short durations. An alternative behavior when the lock is contended is to put the current thread to sleep and wake it up when it becomes available. Then the processor can go off and execute other code. This incurs a bit of overhead—most notably the two context switches required to switch out of and back into the blocking thread, which is certainly a lot more code than the handful of lines used to implement a spin lock. Therefore, it is wise to hold spin locks for less than the duration of two context switches. Because most of us have better things to do than measure context switches, just try to hold the lock for as little time as possible.[1] Later in this chapter we discuss *semaphores*, which provide a lock that makes the waiting thread sleep, rather than spin, when contended.

Spin Lock Methods

Spin locks are architecture-dependent and implemented in assembly. The architecture-dependent code is defined in `<asm/spinlock.h>`. The actual usable interfaces are defined in `<linux/spinlock.h>`. The basic use of a spin lock is

```
DEFINE_SPINLOCK(mr_lock);
```

---

[1] *This is especially important now that the kernel is preemptive. The duration that locks are held is equivalent to the scheduling latency of the system.*

```
spin_lock(&mr_lock);
/* critical region ... */
spin_unlock(&mr_lock);
```

The lock can be held simultaneously by at most only one thread of execution. Consequently, only one thread is allowed in the critical region at a time. This provides the needed protection from concurrency on multiprocessing machines. On uniprocessor machines, the locks compile away and do not exist; they simply act as markers to disable and enable kernel preemption. If kernel preempt is turned off, the locks compile away entirely.

Warning: Spin Locks Are Not Recursive!

Unlike spin lock implementations in other operating systems and threading libraries, the Linux kernel's spin locks are not recursive. This means that if you attempt to acquire a lock you already hold, you will spin, waiting for yourself to release the lock. But because you are busy spinning, you will never release the lock and you will deadlock. Be careful!

Spin locks can be used in interrupt handlers, whereas semaphores cannot be used because they sleep. If a lock is used in an interrupt handler, you must also disable local interrupts (interrupt requests on the current processor) before obtaining the lock. Otherwise, it is possible for an interrupt handler to interrupt kernel code while the lock is held and attempt to reacquire the lock. The interrupt handler spins, waiting for the lock to become available. The lock holder, however, does not run until the interrupt handler completes. This is an example of the double-acquire deadlock discussed in the previous chapter. Note that you need to disable interrupts only on the *current* processor. If an interrupt occurs on a different processor, and it spins on the same lock, it does not prevent the lock holder (which is on a different processor) from eventually releasing the lock.

The kernel provides an interface that conveniently disables interrupts and acquires the lock. Usage is

```
DEFINE_SPINLOCK(mr_lock);
unsigned long flags;

spin_lock_irqsave(&mr_lock, flags);
/* critical region ... */
spin_unlock_irqrestore(&mr_lock, flags);
```

The routine `spin_lock_irqsave()`saves the current state of interrupts, disables them locally, and then obtains the given lock. Conversely, `spin_unlock_irqrestore()`unlocks the given lock and returns interrupts to their previous state. This way, if interrupts were initially disabled, your code would not erroneously enable them, but instead keep them disabled. Note that the `flags` variable is seemingly passed by value. This is because the lock routines are implemented partially as macros.

On uniprocessor systems, the previous example must still disable interrupts to prevent an interrupt handler from accessing the shared data, but the lock mechanism is compiled away. The lock and unlock also disable and enable kernel preemption, respectively.

What Do I Lock?

It is important that each lock is clearly associated with what it is locking. More important, you should protect *data* and not *code*. Despite the examples in this chapter explaining the importance of protecting the critical sections, it is the actual data inside that needs protection and not the code.

Big Fat Rule: Locks that simply wrap code regions are hard to understand and prone to race conditions. Lock data, not code.

Rather than lock code, always associate your shared data with a specific lock. For example, *"the* `struct foo` *is locked by* `foo_lock`." Whenever you access shared data, make sure it is safe. Most likely, this means obtaining the appropriate lock before manipulating the data and releasing the lock when finished.

If you always know before the fact that interrupts are initially enabled, there is no need to restore their previous state. You can unconditionally enable them on unlock. In those cases, `spin_lock_irq()` and `spin_unlock_irq()` are optimal:

```
DEFINE_SPINLOCK(mr_lock);


spin_lock_irq(&mr_lock);
/* critical section ... */
spin_unlock_irq(&mr_lock);
```

As the kernel grows in size and complexity, it is increasingly hard to ensure that interrupts are always enabled in any given code path in the kernel. Use of `spin_lock_irq()`therefore is not recommended. If you do use it, you had better be positive that interrupts were originally on or people will be upset when they expect interrupts to be off but find them on!

Debugging Spin Locks

The configure option `CONFIG_DEBUG_SPINLOCK` enables a handful of debugging checks in the spin lock code. For example, with this option the spin lock code checks for the use of uninitialized spin locks and unlocking a lock that is not yet locked. When testing your code, you should always run with spin lock debugging enabled. For additional debugging of lock lifecycles, enable `CONFIG_DEBUG_LOCK_ALLOC`.

Other Spin Lock Methods

You can use the method `spin_lock_init()` to initialize a dynamically created spin lock (a `spinlock_t` that you do not have a direct reference to, just a pointer).

The method `spin_trylock()` attempts to obtain the given spin lock. If the lock is contended, rather than spin and wait for the lock to be released, the function immediately returns zero. If it succeeds in obtaining the lock, it returns nonzero. Similarly, `spin_is_locked()` returns nonzero if the given lock is currently acquired. Otherwise, it returns zero. In neither case does `spin_is_locked()` actually obtain the lock.[2]

Table 10.4 shows a complete list of the standard spin lock methods.

Table 10.4   **Spin Lock Methods**

Method	Description
`spin_lock()`	Acquires given lock
`spin_lock_irq()`	Disables local interrupts and acquires given lock
`spin_lock_irqsave()`	Saves current state of local interrupts, disables local interrupts, and acquires given lock
`spin_unlock()`	Releases given lock
`spin_unlock_irq()`	Releases given lock and enables local interrupts
`spin_unlock_irqrestore()`	Releases given lock and restores local interrupts to given previous state
`spin_lock_init()`	Dynamically initializes given `spinlock_t`
`spin_trylock()`	Tries to acquire given lock; if unavailable, returns nonzero
`spin_is_locked()`	Returns nonzero if the given lock is currently acquired, otherwise it returns zero

Spin Locks and Bottom Halves

As discussed in Chapter 8, "Bottom Halves and Deferring Work," certain locking precautions must be taken when working with bottom halves. The function `spin_lock_bh()` obtains the given lock and disables all bottom halves. The function `spin_unlock_bh()` performs the inverse.

Because a bottom half might preempt process context code, if data is shared between a bottom-half process context, you must protect the data in process context with both a lock and the disabling of bottom halves. Likewise, because an interrupt handler might preempt a bottom half, if data is shared between an interrupt handler and a bottom half, you must both obtain the appropriate lock and disable interrupts.

---

[2] *Use of these two functions can lead to convoluted code. You should not frequently have to check the values of spin locks—your code should either always acquire the lock itself or always be called while the lock is already held. Some legitimate uses do exist, however, so these interfaces are provided.*

Recall that two tasklets of the same type do not ever run simultaneously. Thus, there is no need to protect data used only within a single type of tasklet. If the data is shared between two different tasklets, however, you must obtain a normal spin lock before accessing the data in the bottom half. You do not need to disable bottom halves because a tasklet never preempts another running tasklet on the same processor.

With softirqs, regardless of whether it is the same softirq type, if data is shared by softirqs, it must be protected with a lock. Recall that softirqs, even two of the same type, might run simultaneously on multiple processors in the system. A softirq never preempts another softirq running on the same processor, however, so disabling bottom halves is not needed.

Reader-Writer Spin Locks

Sometimes, lock usage can be clearly divided into reader and writer paths. For example, consider a list that is both updated and searched. When the list is updated (written to), it is important that no other threads of execution concurrently write to *or* read from the list. Writing demands mutual exclusion. On the other hand, when the list is searched (read from), it is only important that nothing else writes to the list. Multiple concurrent readers are safe so long as there are no writers. The task list's access patterns (discussed in Chapter 3, "Process Management") fit this description. Not surprisingly, a *reader-writer spin lock* protects the task list.

When a data structure is neatly split into reader/writer or consumer/producer usage patterns, it makes sense to use a locking mechanism that provides similar semantics. To satisfy this use, the Linux kernel provides reader-writer spin locks. Reader-writer spin locks provide separate reader and writer variants of the lock. One or more readers can concurrently hold the reader lock. The writer lock, conversely, can be held by at most one writer with no concurrent readers. Reader/writer locks are sometimes called *shared/exclusive* or *concurrent/exclusive locks* because the lock is available in a shared (for readers) and an exclusive (for writers) form.

Usage is similar to spin locks. The reader-writer spin lock is initialized via

```
DEFINE_RWLOCK(mr_rwlock);
```

Then, in the reader code path:

```
read_lock(&mr_rwlock);
/* critical section (read only) ... */
read_unlock(&mr_rwlock);
```

Finally, in the writer code path:

```
write_lock(&mr_rwlock);
/* critical section (read and write) ... */
write_unlock(&mr_rwlock);
```

Normally, the readers and writers are in entirely separate code paths, such as in this example.

Note that you cannot "upgrade" a read lock to a write lock. For example, consider this code snippet:

```
read_lock(&mr_rwlock);
write_lock(&mr_rwlock);
```

Executing these two functions as shown will deadlock, as the write lock spins, waiting for all readers to release the shared lock—including yourself. If you ever need to write, obtain the write lock from the start. If the line between your readers and writers is muddled, it might be an indication that you do not need to use reader-writer locks. In that case, a normal spin lock is optimal.

It is safe for multiple readers to obtain the same lock. In fact, it is safe for the same thread to recursively obtain the same read lock. This lends itself to a useful and common optimization. If you have only readers in interrupt handlers but no writers, you can mix the use of the "interrupt disabling" locks. You can use `read_lock()` instead of `read_lock_irqsave()` for reader protection. You still need to disable interrupts for write access, à la `write_lock_irqsave()`, otherwise a reader in an interrupt could deadlock on the held write lock. See Table 10.5 for a full listing of the reader-writer spin lock methods.

Table 10.5   **Reader-Writer Spin Lock Methods**

Method	Description
`read_lock()`	Acquires given lock for reading
`read_lock_irq()`	Disables local interrupts and acquires given lock for reading
`read_lock_irqsave()`	Saves the current state of local interrupts, disables local interrupts, and acquires the given lock for reading
`read_unlock()`	Releases given lock for reading
`read_unlock_irq()`	Releases given lock and enables local interrupts
`read_unlock_irqrestore()`	Releases given lock and restores local interrupts to the given previous state
`write_lock()`	Acquires given lock for writing
`write_lock_irq()`	Disables local interrupts and acquires the given lock for writing
`write_lock_irqsave()`	Saves current state of local interrupts, disables local interrupts, and acquires the given lock for writing
`write_unlock()`	Releases given lock
`write_unlock_irq()`	Releases given lock and enables local interrupts

Table 10.5   **Reader-Writer Spin Lock Methods**   (continued)

Method	Description
`write_unlock_irqrestore()`	Releases given lock and restores local interrupts to given previous state
`write_trylock()`	Tries to acquire given lock for writing; if unavailable, returns nonzero
`rwlock_init()`	Initializes given `rwlock_t`

A final important consideration in using the Linux reader-writer spin locks is that they favor readers over writers. If the read lock is held and a writer is waiting for exclusive access, readers that attempt to acquire the lock continue to succeed. The spinning writer does not acquire the lock until all readers release the lock. Therefore, a sufficient number of readers can starve pending writers. This is important to keep in mind when designing your locking. Sometimes this behavior is beneficial; sometimes it is catastrophic.

Spin locks provide a quick and simple lock. The spinning behavior is optimal for short hold times and code that cannot sleep (interrupt handlers, for example). In cases where the sleep time might be long or you potentially need to sleep *while* holding the lock, the semaphore is a solution.

Semaphores

Semaphores in Linux are sleeping locks. When a task attempts to acquire a semaphore that is unavailable, the semaphore places the task onto a wait queue and puts the task to sleep. The processor is then free to execute other code. When the semaphore becomes available, one of the tasks on the wait queue is awakened so that it can then acquire the semaphore.

Let's jump back to the door and key analogy. When a person reaches the door, he can grab the key and enter the room. The big difference lies in what happens when another dude reaches the door and the key is not available. In this case, instead of spinning, the fellow puts his name on a list and takes a number. When the person inside the room leaves, he checks the list at the door. If anyone's name is on the list, he goes over to the first name and gives him a playful jab in the chest, waking him up and allowing him to enter the room. In this manner, the key (read: semaphore) continues to ensure that there is only one person (read: thread of execution) inside the room (read: critical region) at one time. This provides better processor utilization than spin locks because there is no time spent busy looping, but semaphores have much greater overhead than spin locks. Life is always a trade-off.

You can draw some interesting conclusions from the sleeping behavior of semaphores:

- Because the contending tasks sleep while waiting for the lock to become available, semaphores are well suited to locks that are held for a long time.

- Conversely, semaphores are not optimal for locks that are held for short periods because the overhead of sleeping, maintaining the wait queue, and waking back up can easily outweigh the total lock hold time.

- Because a thread of execution sleeps on lock contention, semaphores must be obtained only in process context because interrupt context is not schedulable.

- You can (although you might not want to) sleep while holding a semaphore because you will not deadlock when another process acquires the same semaphore. (It will just go to sleep and eventually let you continue.)

- You cannot hold a spin lock while you acquire a semaphore, because you might have to sleep while waiting for the semaphore, and you cannot sleep while holding a spin lock.

These facts highlight the uses of semaphores versus spin locks. In most uses of semaphores, there is little choice as to what lock to use. If your code needs to sleep, which is often the case when synchronizing with user-space, semaphores are the sole solution. It is often easier, if not necessary, to use semaphores because they allow you the flexibility of sleeping. When you do have a choice, the decision between semaphore and spin lock should be based on lock hold time. Ideally, all your locks should be held as briefly as possible. With semaphores, however, longer lock hold times are more acceptable. Additionally, unlike spin locks, semaphores do not disable kernel preemption and, consequently, code holding a semaphore can be preempted. This means semaphores do not adversely affect scheduling latency.

Counting and Binary Semaphores

A final useful feature of semaphores is that they can allow for an arbitrary number of simultaneous lock holders. Whereas spin locks permit at most one task to hold the lock at a time, the number of permissible simultaneous holders of semaphores can be set at declaration time. This value is called the *usage count* or simply the *count*. The most common value is to allow, like spin locks, only one lock holder at a time. In this case, the count is equal to one, and the semaphore is called either a *binary semaphore* (because it is either held by one task or not held at all) or a *mutex* (because it enforces mutual exclusion). Alternatively, the count can be initialized to a nonzero value greater than one. In this case, the semaphore is called a *counting semaphore,* and it enables at most *count* holders of the lock at a time. Counting semaphores are not used to enforce mutual exclusion because they enable multiple threads of execution in the critical region at once. Instead, they are used to enforce limits in certain code. They are not used much in the kernel. If you use a semaphore, you almost assuredly want to use a mutex (a semaphore with a count of one).

Semaphores were formalized by Edsger Wybe Dijkstra[3] in 1968 as a generalized locking mechanism. A semaphore supports two atomic operations, P() and V(), named after the Dutch word *Proberen*, to test (literally, to probe), and the Dutch word *Verhogen*, to increment. Later systems called these methods down() and up(), respectively, and so does Linux. The down() method is used to acquire a semaphore by decrementing the count by one. If the new count is zero or greater, the lock is acquired and the task can enter the critical region. If the count is negative, the task is placed on a wait queue, and the processor moves on to something else. These names are used as verbs: You *down* a semaphore to acquire it. The up() method is used to release a semaphore upon completion of a critical region. This is called *upping* the semaphore. The method increments the count value; if the semaphore's wait queue is not empty, one of the waiting tasks is awakened and allowed to acquire the semaphore.

Creating and Initializing Semaphores

The semaphore implementation is architecture-dependent and defined in <asm/semaphore.h>. The struct semaphore type represents semaphores. Statically declared semaphores are created via the following, where name is the variable's name and count is the usage count of the semaphore:

```
struct semaphore name;
sema_init(&name, count);
```

As a shortcut to create the more common mutex, use the following, where, again, name is the variable name of the binary semaphore:

```
static DECLARE_MUTEX(name);
```

More frequently, semaphores are created dynamically, often as part of a larger structure. In this case, to initialize a dynamically created semaphore to which you have only an indirect pointer reference, just call sema_init(), where sem is a pointer and count is the usage count of the semaphore:

```
sema_init(sem, count);
```

Similarly, to initialize a dynamically created mutex, you can use

```
init_MUTEX(sem);
```

---

[3] *Dr. Dijkstra (1930–2002) is one of the most accomplished computer scientists in the (admittedly brief) history of computer scientists. His numerous contributions include work in OS design, algorithm theory, and the concept of semaphores. He was born in Rotterdam, The Netherlands, and taught at the University of Texas for 15 years. He would probably not be happy with the large number of GOTO statements in the Linux kernel, however.*

I do not know why the "mutex" in `init_MUTEX()` is capitalized or why the "init" comes first here but second in `sema_init()`. I suspect that after you read Chapter 8, the inconsistency is not surprising.

Using Semaphores

The function `down_interruptible()` attempts to acquire the given semaphore. If the semaphore is unavailable, it places the calling process to sleep in the `TASK_INTERRUPTIBLE` state. Recall from Chapter 3 that this process state implies that a task can be awakened with a signal, which is generally a good thing. If the task receives a signal while waiting for the semaphore, it is awakened and `down_interruptible()` returns `-EINTR`. Alternatively, the function `down()` places the task in the `TASK_UNINTERRUPTIBLE` state when it sleeps. You most likely do not want this because the process waiting for the semaphore does not respond to signals. Therefore, use of `down_interruptible()` is much more common (and correct) than `down()`. Yes, again, the naming is not ideal.

You can use `down_trylock()` to try to acquire the given semaphore without blocking. If the semaphore is already held, the function immediately returns nonzero. Otherwise, it returns zero and you successfully hold the lock.

To release a given semaphore, call `up()`. Consider an example:

```
/* define and declare a semaphore, named mr_sem, with a count of one */
static DECLARE_MUTEX(mr_sem);

/* attempt to acquire the semaphore ... */
if (down_interruptible(&mr_sem)) {
        /* signal received, semaphore not acquired ... */
}

/* critical region ... */

/* release the given semaphore */
up(&mr_sem);
```

A complete listing of the semaphore methods is in Table 10.6.

Table 10.6 **Semaphore Methods**

Method	Description
`sema_init(struct semaphore *, int)`	Initializes the dynamically created semaphore to the given count
`init_MUTEX(struct semaphore *)`	Initializes the dynamically created semaphore with a count of one
`init_MUTEX_LOCKED(struct semaphore *)`	Initializes the dynamically created semaphore with a count of zero (so it is initially locked)

Table 10.6   **Semaphore Methods**   (continued)

Method	Description
down_interruptible (struct semaphore *)	Tries to acquire the given semaphore and enter interruptible sleep if it is contended
down(struct semaphore *)	Tries to acquire the given semaphore and enter uninterruptible sleep if it is contended
down_trylock(struct semaphore *)	Tries to acquire the given semaphore and immediately return nonzero if it is contended
up(struct semaphore *)	Releases the given semaphore and wakes a waiting task, if any

Reader-Writer Semaphores

Semaphores, like spin locks, also come in a reader-writer flavor. The situations where reader-writer semaphores are preferred over standard semaphores are the same as with reader-writer spin locks versus standard spin locks.

Reader-writer semaphores are represented by the `struct rw_semaphore` type, which is declared in `<linux/rwsem.h>`. Statically declared reader-writer semaphores are created via the following, where `name` is the declared name of the new semaphore:

```
static DECLARE_RWSEM(name);
```

Reader-writer semaphores created dynamically are initialized via

```
init_rwsem(struct rw_semaphore *sem)
```

All reader-writer semaphores are mutexes—that is, their usage count is one—although they enforce mutual exclusion only for writers, not readers. Any number of readers can concurrently hold the read lock, so long as there are no writers. Conversely, only a sole writer (with no readers) can acquire the write variant of the lock. All reader-writer locks use uninterruptible sleep, so there is only one version of each `down()`. For example:

```
static DECLARE_RWSEM(mr_rwsem);

/* attempt to acquire the semaphore for reading ... */
down_read(&mr_rwsem);

/* critical region (read only) ... */

/* release the semaphore */
up_read(&mr_rwsem);
```

```
/* ... */

/* attempt to acquire the semaphore for writing ... */
down_write(&mr_rwsem);

/* critical region (read and write) ... */

/* release the semaphore */
up_write(&mr_sem);
```

As with semaphores, implementations of `down_read_trylock()` and `down_write_trylock()` are provided. Each has one parameter: a pointer to a reader-writer semaphore. They both return nonzero if the lock is successfully acquired and zero if it is currently contended. Be careful: For admittedly no good reason, this is the opposite of normal semaphore behavior!

Reader-writer semaphores have a unique method that their reader-writer spin lock cousins do not have: `downgrade_write()`. This function atomically converts an acquired write lock to a read lock.

Reader-writer semaphores, as spin locks of the same nature, should not be used unless a clear separation exists between write paths and read paths in your code. Supporting the reader-writer mechanisms has a cost, and it is worthwhile only if your code naturally splits along a reader/writer boundary.

Mutexes

Until recently, the only sleeping lock in the kernel was the semaphore. Most users of semaphores instantiated a semaphore with a *count* of one and treated them as a *mutual exclusion lock*—a sleeping version of the spin lock. Unfortunately, semaphores are rather generic and do not impose many usage constraints. This makes them useful for managing exclusive access in obscure situations, such as complicated dances between the kernel and userspace. But it also means that simpler locking is harder to do, and the lack of enforced rules makes any sort of automated debugging or constraint enforcement impossible. Seeking a simpler sleeping lock, the kernel developers introduced the *mutex*. Yes, as you are now accustomed to, that is a confusing name. Let's clarify. The term "mutex" is a generic name to refer to any sleeping lock that enforces mutual exclusion, such as a semaphore with a usage count of one. In recent Linux kernels, the proper noun "mutex" is now also a specific type of sleeping lock that implements mutual exclusion. That is, a mutex is a mutex.

The mutex is represented by `struct mutex`. It behaves similar to a semaphore with a count of one, but it has a simpler interface, more efficient performance, and additional constraints on its use. To statically define a mutex, you do:

```
DEFINE_MUTEX(name);
```

To dynamically initialize a mutex, you call

```
mutex_init(&mutex);
```

Locking and unlocking the mutex is easy:

```
mutex_lock(&mutex);
/* critical region ... */
mutex_unlock(&mutex);
```

That is it! Simpler than a semaphore and without the need to manage usage counts. Table 10.7 is a listing of the basic mutex methods.

Table 10.7 **Mutex Methods**

Method	Description
mutex_lock(struct mutex *)	Locks the given mutex; sleeps if the lock is unavailable
mutex_unlock(struct mutex *)	Unlocks the given mutex
mutex_trylock(struct mutex *)	Tries to acquire the given mutex; returns one if successful and the lock is acquired and zero otherwise
mutex_is_locked (struct mutex *)	Returns one if the lock is locked and zero otherwise

The simplicity and efficiency of the mutex comes from the additional constraints it imposes on its users over and above what the semaphore requires. Unlike a semaphore, which implements the most basic of behavior in accordance with Dijkstra's original design, the mutex has a stricter, narrower use case:

- Only one task can hold the mutex at a time. That is, the usage count on a mutex is always one.
- Whoever locked a mutex must unlock it. That is, you cannot lock a mutex in one context and then unlock it in another. This means that the mutex isn't suitable for more complicated synchronizations between kernel and user-space. Most use cases, however, cleanly lock and unlock from the same context.
- Recursive locks and unlocks are not allowed. That is, you cannot recursively acquire the same mutex, and you cannot unlock an unlocked mutex.
- A process cannot exit while holding a mutex.
- A mutex cannot be acquired by an interrupt handler or bottom half, even with `mutex_trylock()`.
- A mutex can be managed only via the official API: It must be initialized via the methods described in this section and cannot be copied, hand initialized, or reinitialized.

Perhaps the most useful aspect of the new struct mutex is that, via a special debugging mode, the kernel can programmatically check for and warn about violations of these constraints. When the kernel configuration option CONFIG_DEBUG_MUTEXES is enabled, a multitude of debugging checks ensure that these (and other) constraints are always upheld. This enables you and other users of the mutex to guarantee a regimented, simple usage pattern.

Semaphores Versus Mutexes

Mutexes and semaphores are similar. Having both in the kernel is confusing. Thankfully, the formula dictating which to use is quite simple: Unless one of mutex's additional constraints prevent you from using them, prefer the new mutex type to semaphores. When writing new code, only specific, often low-level, uses need a semaphore. Start with a mutex and move to a semaphore only if you run into one of their constraints and have no other alternative.

Spin Locks Versus Mutexes

Knowing when to use a spin lock versus a mutex (or semaphore) is important to writing optimal code. In many cases, however, there is little choice. Only a spin lock can be used in interrupt context, whereas only a mutex can be held while a task sleeps. Table 10.8 reviews the requirements that dictate which lock to use.

Table 10.8   **What to Use: Spin Locks Versus Semaphores**

Requirement	Recommended Lock
Low overhead locking	Spin lock is preferred.
Short lock hold time	Spin lock is preferred.
Long lock hold time	Mutex is preferred.
Need to lock from interrupt context	Spin lock is required.
Need to sleep while holding lock	Mutex is required.

Completion Variables

Using *completion variables* is an easy way to synchronize between two tasks in the kernel when one task needs to signal to the other that an event has occurred. One task waits on the completion variable while another task performs some work. When the other task has completed the work, it uses the completion variable to wake up any waiting tasks. If you think this sounds like a semaphore, you are right—the idea is much the same. In fact, completion variables merely provide a simple solution to a problem whose answer is otherwise semaphores. For example, the `vfork()` system call uses completion variables to wake up the parent process when the child process execs or exits.

Completion variables are represented by the `struct completion` type, which is defined in `<linux/completion.h>`. A statically created completion variable is created and initialized via

```
DECLARE_COMPLETION(mr_comp);
```

A dynamically created completion variable is initialized via `init_completion()`. On a given completion variable, the tasks that want to wait call `wait_for_completion()`. After the event has occurred, calling `complete()` signals all waiting tasks to wake up. Table 10.9 has a listing of the completion variable methods.

Table 10.9   **Completion Variable Methods**

Method	Description
`init_completion(struct completion *)`	Initializes the given dynamically created completion variable
`wait_for_completion(struct completion *)`	Waits for the given completion variable to be signaled
`complete(struct completion *)`	Signals any waiting tasks to wake up

For sample usages of completion variables, see `kernel/sched.c` and `kernel/fork.c`. A common usage is to have a completion variable dynamically created as a member of a data structure. Kernel code waiting for the initialization of the data structure calls `wait_for_completion()`. When the initialization is complete, the waiting tasks are awakened via a call to `completion()`.

BKL: The Big Kernel Lock

Welcome to the redheaded stepchild of the kernel. The Big Kernel Lock (BKL) is a global spin lock that was created to ease the transition from Linux's original SMP implementation to fine-grained locking. The BKL has some interesting properties:

- You can sleep while holding the BKL. The lock is automatically dropped when the task is unscheduled and reacquired when the task is rescheduled. Of course, this does not mean it is *always safe* to sleep while holding the BKL, merely that you *can* and you will not deadlock.

- The BKL is a recursive lock. A single process can acquire the lock multiple times and not deadlock, as it would with a spin lock.

- You can use the BKL only in process context. Unlike spin locks, you cannot acquire the BKL in interrupt context.

- New users of the BKL are forbidden. With every kernel release, fewer and fewer drivers and subsystems rely on the BKL.

These features helped ease the transition from kernel version 2.0 to 2.2. When SMP support was introduced in kernel version 2.0, only one task could be in the kernel at a time. Of course, now the kernel is quite finely threaded, we have come a long way. A goal of 2.2 was to allow multiple processors to execute in the kernel concurrently. The BKL was introduced to help ease the transition to finer-grained locking. It was a great aid then; now it is a scalability burden.

Use of the BKL is discouraged. In fact, new code should never introduce locking that uses the BKL. The lock is still fairly well used in parts of the kernel, however. Therefore, understanding the BKL and its interfaces is important. The BKL behaves like a spin lock, with the additions previously discussed. The function `lock_kernel()` acquires the lock and the function `unlock_kernel()` releases the lock. A single thread of execution might acquire the lock recursively but must then call `unlock_kernel()` an equal number of times to release the lock. On the last unlock call, the lock will be released. The function `kernel_locked()` returns nonzero if the lock is currently held; otherwise, it returns zero. These interfaces are declared in `<linux/smp_lock.h>`. Here is sample usage:

```
lock_kernel();

/*
 * Critical section, synchronized against all other BKL users...
 * Note, you can safely sleep here and the lock will be transparently
 * released. When you reschedule, the lock will be transparently
 * reacquired. This implies you will not deadlock, but you still do
 * not want to sleep if you need the lock to protect data here!
 */

unlock_kernel();
```

The BKL also disables kernel preemption while it is held. On UP kernels, the BKL code does not actually perform any physical locking. Table 10.10 has a complete list of the BKL functions.

Table 10.10   **BKL Methods**

Function	Description
lock_kernel()	Acquires the BKL.
unlock_kernel()	Releases the BKL.
kernel_locked()	Returns nonzero if the lock is held and zero otherwise. (UP always returns nonzero.)

One of the major issues concerning the BKL is determining what the lock is protecting. Too often, the BKL is seemingly associated with code (for example, "it synchronizes callers to `foo()`") instead of data ("it protects the `foo` structure"). This makes replacing BKL uses with a spin lock difficult because it is not easy to determine just what is being locked. The replacement is made even harder in that the relationship between all BKL users needs to be determined.

Sequential Locks

The *sequential lock*, generally shortened to *seq lock*, is a newer type of lock introduced in the 2.6 kernel. It provides a simple mechanism for reading and writing shared data. It works by maintaining a sequence counter. Whenever the data in question is written to, a lock is obtained and a sequence number is incremented. Prior to and after reading the data, the sequence number is read. If the values are the same, a write did not begin in the middle of the read. Further, if the values are even, a write is not underway. (Grabbing the write lock makes the value odd, whereas releasing it makes it even because the lock starts at zero.)

To define a seq lock:

```
seqlock_t mr_seq_lock = DEFINE_SEQLOCK(mr_seq_lock);
```

The write path is then

```
write_seqlock(&mr_seq_lock);
/* write lock is obtained... */
write_sequnlock(&mr_seq_lock);
```

This looks like normal spin lock code. The oddness comes in with the read path, which is quite a bit different:

```
unsigned long seq;


do {
        seq = read_seqbegin(&mr_seq_lock);
        /* read data here ... */
} while (read_seqretry(&mr_seq_lock, seq));
```

Seq locks are useful to provide a lightweight and scalable lock for use with many readers and a few writers. Seq locks, however, favor writers over readers. An acquisition of the write lock always succeeds as long as there are no other writers. Readers do not affect the write lock, as is the case with reader-writer spin locks and semaphores. Furthermore, pending writers continually cause the read loop (the previous example) to repeat, until there are no longer any writers holding the lock.

Seq locks are ideal when your locking needs meet most or all these requirements:

- Your data has a lot of readers.
- Your data has few writers.
- Although few in number, you want to favor writers over readers and never allow readers to starve writers.
- Your data is simple, such as a simple structure or even a single integer that, for whatever reason, cannot be made atomic.

A prominent user of the seq lock is *jiffies*, the variable that stores a Linux machine's uptime (see Chapter 11, "Timers and Time Management"). Jiffies holds a 64-bit count of the number of clock ticks since the machine booted. On machines that cannot atomically read the full 64-bit `jiffies_64` variable, `get_jiffies_64()` is implemented using seq locks:

```
u64 get_jiffies_64(void)
{
        unsigned long seq;
        u64 ret;

        do {
                seq = read_seqbegin(&xtime_lock);
                ret = jiffies_64;
        } while (read_seqretry(&xtime_lock, seq));
        return ret;
}
```

Updating jiffies during the timer interrupt, in turns, grabs the write variant of the seq lock:

```
write_seqlock(&xtime_lock);
jiffies_64 += 1;
write_sequnlock(&xtime_lock);
```

For a deeper discussion on jiffies and kernel time keeping, see Chapter 11 and the files `kernel/timer.c` and `kernel/time/tick-common.c` in the kernel source tree.

Preemption Disabling

Because the kernel is preemptive, a process in the kernel can stop running at any instant to enable a process of higher priority to run. This means a task can begin running in the same critical region as a task that was preempted. To prevent this, the kernel preemption code uses spin locks as markers of nonpreemptive regions. If a spin lock is held, the kernel is not preemptive. Because the concurrency issues with kernel preemption and SMP are the same, and the kernel is already SMP-safe; this simple change makes the kernel preempt-safe, too.

Or so we hope. In reality, some situations do not require a spin lock, but do need kernel preemption disabled. The most frequent of these situations is per-processor data. If the data is unique to each processor, there might be no need to protect it with a lock because only that one processor can access the data. If no spin locks are held, the kernel is preemptive, and it would be possible for a newly scheduled task to access this same variable, as shown here:

```
task A manipulates per-processor variable foo, which is not protected by a lock
task A is preempted
task B is scheduled
task B manipulates variable foo
task B completes
```

```
task A is rescheduled
task A continues manipulating variable foo
```

Consequently, even if this were a uniprocessor computer, the variable could be accessed pseudo-concurrently by multiple processes. Normally, this variable would require a spin lock (to prevent true concurrency on multiprocessing machines). If this were a per-processor variable, however, it might not require a lock.

To solve this, kernel preemption can be disabled via `preempt_disable()`. The call is nestable; you can call it any number of times. For each call, a corresponding call to `preempt_enable()` is required. The final corresponding call to `preempt_enable()` reenables preemption. For example:

```
preempt_disable();
/* preemption is disabled ... */
preempt_enable();
```

The preemption count stores the number of held locks and `preempt_disable()` calls. If the number is zero, the kernel is preemptive. If the value is one or greater, the kernel is not preemptive. This count is incredibly useful—it is a great way to do atomicity and sleep debugging. The function `preempt_count()` returns this value. See Table 10.11 for a listing of kernel preemption-related functions.

Table 10.11   **Kernel Preemption-Related Methods**

Function	Description
`preempt_disable()`	Disables kernel preemption by incrementing the preemption counter
`preempt_enable()`	Decrements the preemption counter and checks and services any pending reschedules if the count is now zero
`preempt_enable_no_resched()`	Enables kernel preemption but does not check for any pending reschedules
`preempt_count()`	Returns the preemption count

As a cleaner solution to per-processor data issues, you can obtain the processor number (which presumably is used to index into the per-processor data) via `get_cpu()`. This function disables kernel preemption prior to returning the current processor number:

```
int cpu;

/* disable kernel preemption and set "cpu" to the current processor */
cpu = get_cpu();


/* manipulate per-processor data ... */
```

```
/* reenable kernel preemption, "cpu" can change and so is no longer valid */
put_cpu();
```

Ordering and Barriers

When dealing with synchronization between multiple processors or with hardware devices, it is sometimes a requirement that memory-reads (loads) and memory-writes (stores) issue in the order specified in your program code. When talking with hardware, you often need to ensure that a given read occurs before another read or write. Additionally, on symmetrical multiprocessing systems, it might be important for writes to appear in the order that your code issues them (usually to ensure subsequent reads see the data in the same order). Complicating these issues is the fact that both the compiler and the processor can reorder reads and writes[4] for performance reasons. Thankfully, all processors that do reorder reads or writes provide machine instructions to enforce ordering requirements. It is also possible to instruct the compiler not to reorder instructions around a given point. These instructions are called *barriers*.

Essentially, on some processors the following code may allow the processor to store the new value in b *before* it stores the new value in a:

```
a = 1;
b = 2;
```

Both the compiler and processor see no relation between a and b. The compiler would perform this reordering at compile time; the reordering would be static, and the resulting object code would simply set b before a. The processor, however, could perform the reordering dynamically during execution by fetching and dispatching seemingly unrelated instructions in whatever order it feels is best. The vast majority of the time, such reordering is optimal because there is no apparent relation between a and b. Sometimes the programmer knows best, though.

Although the previous example might be reordered, the processor would never reorder writes such as the following because there is clearly a data dependency between a and b:

```
a = 1;
b = a;
```

Neither the compiler nor the processor, however, knows about code in other contexts. Occasionally, it is important that writes are seen by other code and the outside world in the specific order you intend. This is often the case with hardware devices but is also common on multiprocessing machines.

---

[4] *Intel x86 processors do not ever reorder writes. That is, they do not do out-of-order stores. But other processors do.*

The rmb() method provides a read memory barrier. It ensures that no loads are re-ordered across the rmb() call. That is, no loads prior to the call will be reordered to after the call, and no loads after the call will be reordered to before the call.

The wmb() method provides a write barrier. It functions in the same manner as rmb(), but with respect to stores instead of loads—it ensures no stores are reordered across the barrier.

The mb() call provides both a read barrier and a write barrier. No loads *or* stores will be reordered across a call to mb(). It is provided because a single instruction (often the same instruction used by rmb()) can provide both the load and store barrier.

A variant of rmb(), read_barrier_depends(), provides a read barrier but *only for loads on which subsequent loads depend*. All reads prior to the barrier are guaranteed to complete before any reads after the barrier that depend on the reads prior to the barrier. Got it? Basically, it enforces a read barrier, similar to rmb(), but only for certain reads—those that depend on each other. On some architectures, read_barrier_depends() is much quicker than rmb() because it is not needed and is, thus, a *noop*.

Let's consider an example using mb() and rmb(). The initial value of a is one, and the initial value of b is two.

Thread 1	Thread 2
a = 3;	—
mb();	—
b = 4;	c = b;
—	rmb();
—	d = a;

Without using the memory barriers, on some processors it is possible for c to receive the *new* value of b, whereas d receives the *old* value of a. For example, c could equal four (what you'd expect), yet d could equal one (not what you'd expect). Using the mb() ensured that a and b were written in the intended order, whereas the rmb() insured c and d were read in the intended order.

This sort of reordering occurs because modern processors dispatch and commit instructions out of order, to optimize use of their pipelines. What can end up happening in the previous example is that the instructions associated with the loads of b and a occur out of order. The rmb() and wmb() functions correspond to instructions that tell the processor to commit any pending load or store instructions, respectively, before continuing.

Let's look at a similar example, but one that uses read_barrier_depends() instead of rmb(). In this example, initially a is one, b is two, and p is &b.

Thread 1	Thread 2
a = 3;	—
mb();	—
p = &a;	pp = p;
—	read_barrier_depends();
—	b = *pp;

Again, without memory barriers, it would be possible for b to be set to pp before pp was set to p. The read_barrier_depends(), however, provides a sufficient barrier because the load of *pp depends on the load of p. It would also be sufficient to use rmb() here, but because the reads are data dependent, we can use the potentially faster read_barrier_depends(). Note that in either case, the mb() is required to enforce the intended load/store ordering in the left thread.

The macros smp_rmb(), smp_wmb(), smp_mb(), and smp_read_barrier_depends() provide a useful optimization. On SMP kernels they are defined as the usual memory barriers, whereas on UP kernels they are defined only as a compiler barrier. You can use these SMP variants when the ordering constraints are specific to SMP systems.

The barrier() method prevents the compiler from optimizing loads or stores across the call. The compiler knows not to rearrange stores and loads in ways that would change the effect of the C code and existing data dependencies. It does not have knowledge, however, of events that can occur outside the current context. For example, the compiler cannot know about interrupts that might read the same data you are writing. For this reason, you might want to ensure a store is issued before a load, for example. The previous memory barriers also function as compiler barriers, but a compiler barrier is much lighter in weight than a memory barrier. Indeed, a compiler barrier is practically free, because it simply prevents the compiler from *possibly* rearranging things.

Table 10.12 has a full listing of the memory and compiler barrier methods provided by all architectures in the Linux kernel.

Table 10.12 **Memory and Compiler Barrier Methods**

Barrier	Description
rmb()	Prevents loads from being reordered across the barrier
read_barrier_depends()	Prevents data-dependent loads from being reordered across the barrier
wmb()	Prevents stores from being reordered across the barrier
mb()	Prevents load or stores from being reordered across the barrier

Table 10.12   **Memory and Compiler Barrier Methods**

Barrier	Description
smp_rmb()	Provides an rmb() on SMP, and on UP provides a barrier()
smp_read_barrier_depends()	Provides a read_barrier_depends() on SMP, and provides a barrier() on UP
smp_wmb()	Provides a wmb() on SMP, and provides a barrier() on UP
smp_mb()	Provides an mb() on SMP, and provides a barrier() on UP
barrier()	Prevents the compiler from optimizing stores or loads across the barrier

Note that the actual effects of the barriers vary for each architecture. For example, if a machine does not perform out-of-order stores (for example, Intel x86 processors do not), wmb() does nothing. You can use the appropriate memory barrier for the worst case (that is, the weakest ordering processor) and your code will compile optimally for your architecture.

Conclusion

This chapter applied the concepts and theories of the last chapter to help you understand the actual methods provided by the Linux kernel for enforcing synchronization and concurrency. We started with the simplest method of ensuring synchronization, atomic operations. We then looked at spin locks, the most common lock in the kernel, which provide a lightweight single-holder lock that busy waits while contended. Next, we discussed semaphores, a sleeping lock, and its more general (and used) cousin, the mutex. Following mutexes, we studied less common, more specialized locking primitives such as completion variables and seq locks. We poked fun at the BKL, looked at preemption disabling, and tackled barriers. It has been a wild ride.

Armed with this chapter's arsenal of synchronization methods, you can now write kernel code that prevents race conditions, ensures the correct synchronization, and correctly runs on machines with multiple processors.

11

Timers and Time Management

The passing of time is important to the kernel. A large number of kernel functions are time-driven, as opposed to event-driven.[1] Some of these functions are periodic, such as balancing the scheduler runqueues or refreshing the screen. They occur on a fixed schedule, such as 100 times per second. The kernel schedules other functions, such as delayed disk I/O, at a relative time in the future. For example, the kernel might schedule work for 500 milliseconds from now. Finally, the kernel must also manage the system uptime and the current date and time.

Note the differences between relative and absolute time. Scheduling an event for 5 seconds in the future requires no concept of the *absolute* time—only the *relative* time (for example, 5 seconds from now). Conversely, managing the current time of day requires the kernel to understand not just the passing of time but also some absolute measurement of it. Both of these concepts are crucial to the management of time.

Moreover, the implementation differs between how events that occur periodically and events the kernel schedules for a fixed point in the future are handled. Events that occur periodically—say, every 10 milliseconds—are driven by the *system timer*. The system timer is a programmable piece of hardware that issues an interrupt at a fixed frequency. The interrupt handler for this timer—called the *timer interrupt*—updates the system time and performs periodic work. The system timer and its timer interrupt are central to Linux and a large focus of this chapter.

The other focus of this chapter is *dynamic timers*, the facility used to schedule events that run once after a specified time has elapsed. For example, the floppy device driver uses a timer to shut off the floppy drive motor after a specified period of inactivity. The kernel can create and destroy timers dynamically. This chapter covers the kernel implementation of dynamic timers, and the interface available for their use in your code.

---

[1] More accurately, time-driven events are also event-driven—the event being the passing of time. In this chapter, however, we single out time-driven events because of their frequency in and importance to the kernel.

Kernel Notion of Time

Certainly, the concept of *time* to a computer is a bit obscure. Indeed, the kernel must work with the system's hardware to comprehend and manage time. The hardware provides a system timer that the kernel uses to gauge the passing of time. This system timer works off of an electronic time source, such as a digital clock or the frequency of the processor. The system timer goes off (often called *hitting* or *popping*) at a preprogrammed frequency, called the *tick rate*. When the system timer goes off, it issues an interrupt that the kernel handles via a special interrupt handler.

Because the kernel knows the preprogrammed tick rate, it knows the time between any two successive timer interrupts. This period is called a *tick* and is equal to 1/(tick rate) seconds. This is how the kernel keeps track of both wall time and system uptime. Wall time—the actual time of day—is important to user-space applications. The kernel keeps track of it simply because the kernel controls the timer interrupt. A family of system calls provides the date and time of day to user-space. The system uptime—the relative time since the system booted—is useful to both kernel-space and user-space. A lot of code must be aware of the *passing* of time. The difference between two uptime readings—now and then—is a simple measure of this relativity.

The timer interrupt is important to the management of the operating system. A large number of kernel functions live and die by the passing of time. Some of the work executed periodically by the timer interrupt includes

- Updating the system uptime
- Updating the time of day
- On an SMP system, ensuring that the scheduler runqueues are balanced and, if not, balancing them (as discussed in Chapter 4, "Process Scheduling")
- Running any dynamic timers that have expired
- Updating resource usage and processor time statistics

Some of this work occurs on *every* timer interrupt—that is, the work is carried out with the frequency of the tick rate. Other functions execute periodically but only every *n* timer interrupts. That is, these functions occur at some fraction of the tick rate. The section "The Timer Interrupt Handler" looks at the timer interrupt handler.

The Tick Rate: HZ

The frequency of the system timer (the tick rate) is programmed on system boot based on a static preprocessor define, HZ. The value of HZ differs for each supported architecture. On some supported architectures, it even differs between machine types.

The kernel defines the value in <asm/param.h>. The tick rate has a frequency of HZ hertz and a period of 1/HZ seconds. For example, by default the x86 architecture defines HZ to be 100. Therefore, the timer interrupt on i386 has a frequency of 100HZ and occurs 100 times per second (every one-hundredth of a second, which is every

10 milliseconds). Other common values for HZ are 250 and 1000, corresponding to periods of 4ms and 1ms, respectively. Table 11.1 is a complete listing of the supported architectures and their defined tick rates.

Table 11.1 **Frequency of the Timer Interrupt**

Architecture	Frequency (in Hertz)
Alpha	1024
Arm	100
avr32	100
Blackfin	100
Cris	100
h8300	100
ia64	1024
m32r	100
m68k	100
m68knommu	50, 100, or 1000
Microblaze	100
Mips	100
mn10300	100
parisc	100
powerpc	100
Score	100
s390	100
Sh	100
sparc	100
Um	100
x86	100

When writing kernel code, never assume that HZ has any given value. This is not a common mistake these days because so many architectures have varying tick rates. In the past, however, Alpha was the only architecture with a tick rate not equal to 100Hz, and it was common to see code incorrectly hard-code the value 100 when the HZ value should have been used. Examples of using HZ in kernel code are shown later.

The frequency of the timer interrupt is important. As you already saw, the timer interrupt performs a lot of work. Indeed, the kernel's entire notion of time derives from the periodicity of the system timer. Picking the right value, like a successful relationship, is all about compromise.

The Ideal HZ Value

Starting with the initial version of Linux, the i386 architecture has had a timer interrupt frequency of 100 Hz. During the 2.5 development series, however, the frequency was raised to 1000 Hz and was (as such things are) controversial. Although the frequency is again 100 Hz, it is now a configuration option, allowing users to compile a kernel with a custom HZ value. Because so much of the system is dependent on the timer interrupt, changing its frequency has a reasonable impact on the system. Of course, there are pros and cons to larger versus smaller HZ values.

Increasing the tick rate means the timer interrupt runs more frequently. Consequently, the work it performs occurs more often. This has the following benefits:

- The timer interrupt has a higher resolution and, consequently, all timed events have a higher resolution.
- The accuracy of timed events improves.

The resolution increases by the same factor as the tick rate increases. For example, the granularity of timers with HZ=100 is 10 milliseconds. In other words, all periodic events occur along the timer interrupt's 10 millisecond period and no finer *precision*[2] is guaranteed. With HZ=1000, however, resolution is 1 millisecond—10 times finer. Although kernel code can create timers with 1-millisecond resolution, there is no guarantee the precision afforded with HZ=100 is sufficient to execute the timer on anything better than 10-millisecond intervals.

Likewise, accuracy improves in the same manner. Assuming the kernel starts timers at random times, the average timer is off by half the period of the timer interrupt because timers might expire at any time, but are executed only on occurrences of the timer interrupt. For example, with HZ=100, the average event occurs +/− 5 milliseconds off from the desired time. Thus, error is 5 milliseconds on average. With HZ=1000, the average error drops to 0.5 milliseconds—a tenfold improvement.

Advantages with a Larger HZ

This higher resolution and greater accuracy provides multiple advantages:

- Kernel timers execute with finer resolution and increased accuracy. (This provides a large number of improvements, one of which is the following.)

---

[2] *We use precision here in the computer sense, not the scientific. Precision in science is a statistical measurement of repeatability. In computers, precision is the number of significant figures used to represent a value.*

- System calls such as `poll()` and `select()` that optionally employ a timeout value execute with improved precision.

- Measurements, such as resource usage or the system uptime, are recorded with a finer resolution.

- Process preemption occurs more accurately.

Some of the most readily noticeable performance benefits come from the improved precision of `poll()` and `select()` timeouts. The improvement might be quite large; an application that makes heavy use of these system calls might waste a great deal of time waiting for the timer interrupt, when, in fact, the timeout has actually expired. Remember, the average error (that is, potentially wasted time) is half the period of the timer interrupt.

Another benefit of a higher tick rate is the greater accuracy in process preemption, which results in decreased scheduling latency. Recall from Chapter 4 that the timer interrupt is responsible for decrementing the running process's timeslice count. When the count reaches zero, `need_resched` is set and the kernel runs the scheduler as soon as possible. Now assume a given process is running and has 2 milliseconds of its timeslice remaining. In 2 milliseconds, the scheduler *should* preempt the running process and begin executing a new process. Unfortunately, this event does not occur until the next timer interrupt, which might not be in 2 milliseconds. At worst the next timer interrupt might be $1/HZ$ of a second away! With `HZ=100`, a process can get nearly 10 extra milliseconds to run. Of course, this all balances out and fairness is preserved, because all tasks receive the same imprecision in scheduling—but that is not the issue. The problem stems from the latency created by the delayed preemption. If the to-be-scheduled task had something time-sensitive to do, such as refill an audio buffer, the delay might not be acceptable. Increasing the tick rate to 1000Hz lowers the worst-case scheduling overrun to just 1 millisecond, and the average-case overrun to just 0.5 milliseconds.

Disadvantages with a Larger HZ

Now, there must be *some* downside to increasing the tick rate, or it would have been 1000Hz (or even higher) to start. Indeed, there is one large issue: A higher tick rate implies more frequent timer interrupts, which implies higher overhead, because the processor must spend more time executing the timer interrupt handler. The higher the tick rate, the more time the processor spends executing the timer interrupt. This adds up to not just less processor time available for other work, but also a more frequent thrashing of the processor's cache and increase in power consumption. The issue of the overhead's impact is debatable. A move from `HZ=100` to `HZ=1000` clearly brings with it ten times greater overhead. However, how substantial is the overhead to begin with? The final agreement is that, at least on modern systems, `HZ=1000` does not create unacceptable overhead and the move to a 1000Hz timer has not hurt performance too much. Nevertheless, it is possible in 2.6 to compile the kernel with a different value for HZ.[3]

> ## A Tickless OS
>
> You might wonder whether an operating system even needs a fixed timer interrupt. Although that has been the norm for 40 years, with nearly all general-purpose operating systems employing a timer interrupt similar to the system described in this chapter, the Linux kernel supports an option known as a *tickless operation*. When a kernel is built with the CONFIG_HZ configuration option set, the system dynamically schedules the timer interrupt in accordance with pending timers. Instead of firing the timer interrupt every, say, 1ms, the interrupt is dynamically scheduled and rescheduled as needed. If the next timer is set to go off in 3ms, the timer interrupt fires in 3ms. After that, if there is no work for 50ms, the kernel reschedules the interrupt to go off in 50ms.
>
> The reduction in overhead is welcome, but the real gain is in power savings, particular on an idle system. On a standard tick-based system, the kernel needs to service timer interrupts, even during idle periods. With a tickless system, moments of idleness are not interrupted by unnecessary time interrupts, reducing system power consumption. Whether the idle period is 200 milliseconds or 200 seconds, over time the gains add up to tangible power savings.

Jiffies

The global variable jiffies holds the number of ticks that have occurred since the system booted. On boot, the kernel initializes the variable to zero, and it is incremented by one during each timer interrupt. Thus, because there are HZ timer interrupts in a second, there are HZ jiffies in a second. The system uptime is therefore jiffies/HZ seconds. What actually happens is slightly more complicated: The kernel initializes jiffies to a special initial value, causing the variable to overflow more often, catching bugs. When the actual value of jiffies is sought, this "offset" is first subtracted.

> ## The Etymology of the Jiffy
>
> The origin of the term *jiffy* is unknown. Phrases such as *in a jiffy* are thought to originate from 18th-century England. In lay terms, *jiffy* refers to an indeterminate but brief period of time.
>
> In scientific applications, *jiffy* represents various intervals of time, most commonly 10ms. In physics, a jiffy is sometimes used to refer to the time it takes for light to travel some specific distance (usually a foot or a centimeter or across a nucleon).
>
> In computer engineering, a jiffy is often the time between two successive clock cycles. In electrical engineering, a jiffy is the time to complete one AC (alternating current) cycle. In the United States, this is 1/60 of a second.

---

[3] *Because of architectural and NTP-related issues, however, not just any value is acceptable for* HZ. *On x86, 100, 500, and 1000 all work fine.*

> In operating systems, especially Unix, a jiffy is the time between two successive clock ticks. Historically, this has been 10ms. As we have seen in this chapter, however, a jiffy in Linux can have various values.

The `jiffies` variable is declared in `<linux/jiffies.h>` as

```
extern unsigned long volatile jiffies;
```

In the next section, we look at its actual definition, which is a bit peculiar. For now, let's look at some sample kernel code. The following expression converts from seconds to a unit of `jiffies`:

```
(seconds * HZ)
```

Likewise, this expression converts from `jiffies` to seconds:

```
(jiffies / HZ)
```

The former, converting from seconds to ticks, is more common. For example, code often needs to set a value for some time in the future, for example:

```
unsigned long time_stamp = jiffies;        /* now */
unsigned long next_tick = jiffies + 1;     /* one tick from now */
unsigned long later = jiffies + 5*HZ;      /* five seconds from now */
unsigned long fraction = jiffies + HZ / 10; /* a tenth of a second from now */
```

Converting from ticks to seconds is typically reserved for communicating with userspace, as the kernel itself rarely cares about any sort of absolute time.

Note that the `jiffies` variable is prototyped as `unsigned long` and that storing it in anything else is incorrect.

Internal Representation of Jiffies

The `jiffies` variable has always been an `unsigned long`, and therefore 32 bits in size on 32-bit architectures and 64-bits on 64-bit architectures. With a tick rate of 100, a 32-bit `jiffies` variable would overflow in about 497 days. With HZ increased to 1000, however, that overflow now occurs in just 49.7 days! If `jiffies` were stored in a 64-bit variable on all architectures, then for any reasonable HZ value the `jiffies` variable would never overflow in anyone's lifetime.

For performance and historical reasons—mainly compatibility with existing kernel code—the kernel developers wanted to keep `jiffies` an `unsigned long`. Some smart thinking and a little linker magic saved that day.

As you previously saw, `jiffies` is defined as an `unsigned long`:

```
extern unsigned long volatile jiffies;
```

A second variable is also defined in `<linux/jiffies.h>`:

```
extern u64 jiffies_64;
```

The `ld(1)` script used to link the main kernel image (`arch/x86/kernel/vmlinux.lds.S` on x86) then *overlays* the `jiffies` variable over the start of the `jiffies_64` variable:

```
jiffies = jiffies_64;
```

Thus, `jiffies` is the lower 32 bits of the full 64-bit `jiffies_64` variable. Code can continue to access the `jiffies` variable exactly as before. Because most code uses `jiffies` simply to measure elapses in time, most code cares about only the lower 32 bits. The time management code uses the entire 64 bits, however, and thus prevents overflow of the full 64-bit value. Figure 11.1 shows the layout of `jiffies` and `jiffies_64`.

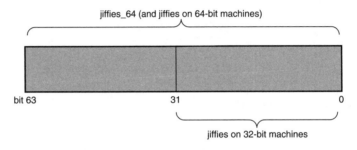

Figure 11.1   Layout of `jiffies` and `jiffies_64`.

Code that accesses `jiffies` simply reads the lower 32 bits of `jiffies_64`. The function `get_jiffies_64()` can be used to read the full 64-bit value.[4] Such a need is rare; consequently, most code simply continues to read the lower 32 bits directly via the `jiffies` variable.

On 64-bit architectures, `jiffies_64` and `jiffies` refer to the same thing. Code can either read `jiffies` or call `get_jiffies_64()` as both actions have the same effect.

Jiffies Wraparound

The `jiffies` variable, like any C integer, experiences *overflow* when its value is increased beyond its maximum storage limit. For a 32-bit unsigned integer, the maximum value is $2^{32} - 1$. Thus, a possible 4294967295 timer ticks can occur before the tick count overflows. When the tick count is equal to this maximum and it is incremented, it wraps around to zero.

Look at an example of a wraparound:

```
unsigned long timeout = jiffies + HZ/2;       /* timeout in 0.5s */
```

---

[4] *A special function is needed because 32-bit architectures cannot atomically access both 32-bit words in a 64-bit value. The special function locks the jiffies count via the* `xtime_lock` *lock before reading.*

```
/* do some work ... */

/* then see whether we took too long */
if (timeout > jiffies) {
        /* we did not time out, good ... */
} else {
        /* we timed out, error ... */
}
```

The intention of this code snippet is to set a timeout for some time in the future—for one half second from now, in this example. The code then proceeds to perform some work, presumably poking hardware and waiting for a response. When done, if the whole ordeal took longer than the timeout, the code handles the error as appropriate.

Multiple potential overflow issues are here, but let's study one of them: Consider what happens if `jiffies` wrapped back to zero after setting `timeout`. Then the first conditional would fail because the `jiffies` value would be smaller than `timeout` despite logically being larger. Conceptually, the `jiffies` value should be a large number—larger than `timeout`. Because it overflowed its maximum value, however, it is now a small value—perhaps only a handful of ticks over zero. Because of the wraparound, the results of the `if` statement are switched. Whoops!

Thankfully, the kernel provides four macros for comparing tick counts that correctly handle wraparound in the tick count. They are in `<linux/jiffies.h>`. Listed here are simplified versions of the macros:

```
#define time_after(unknown, known) ((long)(known) - (long)(unknown) < 0)
#define time_before(unknown, known) ((long)(unknown) - (long)(known) < 0)
#define time_after_eq(unknown, known) ((long)(unknown) - (long)(known) >= 0)
#define time_before_eq(unknown, known) ((long)(known) - (long)(unknown) >= 0)
```

The unknown parameter is typically `jiffies` and the known parameter is the value against which you want to compare.

The `time_after(unknown, known)` macro returns true if time unknown is after time known; otherwise, it returns false. The `time_before(unknown, known)` macro returns true if time unknown is before time known; otherwise, it returns false. The final two macros perform identically to the first two, except they also return true if the parameters are equal.

The timer-wraparound-safe version of the previous example would look like this:

```
unsigned long timeout = jiffies + HZ/2;        /* timeout in 0.5s */

/* ... */
if (time_before(jiffies, timeout)) {
        /* we did not time out, good ... */
} else {
        /* we timed out, error ... */
}
```

If you are curious as to why these macros prevent errors because of wraparound, try various values for the two parameters. Then assume one parameter wrapped to zero and see what happens.

User-Space and HZ

In kernels earlier than 2.6, changing the value of HZ resulted in user-space anomalies. This happened because values were exported to user-space in units of ticks-per-second. As these interfaces became permanent, applications grew to rely on a specific value of HZ. Consequently, changing HZ would scale various exported values by some constant—without user-space knowing! Uptime would read 20 hours when it was in fact two!

To prevent such problems, the kernel needs to scale all exported jiffies values. It does this by defining USER_HZ, which is the HZ value that user-space expects. On x86, because HZ was historically 100, USER_HZ is 100. The function jiffies_to_clock_t(), defined in kernel/time.c, is then used to scale a tick count in terms of HZ to a tick count in terms of USER_HZ. The expression used depends on whether USER_HZ and HZ are integer multiples of themselves and whether USER_HZ is less than or equal to HZ. If both those conditions are true, and for most systems they usually are, the expression is rather simple:

```
return x / (HZ / USER_HZ);
```

A more complicated algorithm is used if the values are not integer multiples.

Finally, the function jiffies_64_to_clock_t() is provided to convert a 64-bit jiffies value from HZ to USER_HZ units.

These functions are used anywhere a value in ticks-per-seconds needs to be exported to user-space. Following is an example:

```
unsigned long start;
unsigned long total_time;

start = jiffies;
/* do some work ... */
total_time = jiffies - start;
printk("That took %lu ticks\n", jiffies_to_clock_t(total_time));
```

User-space expects the previous value as if HZ=USER_HZ. If they are not equivalent, the macro scales as needed and everyone is happy. Of course, this example is silly: It would make more sense to print the message in seconds, not ticks. For example:

```
printk("That took %lu seconds\n", total_time / HZ);
```

Hardware Clocks and Timers

Architectures provide two hardware devices to help with time keeping: the system timer, which we have been discussing, and the real-time clock. The actual behavior and implementation of these devices varies between different machines, but the general purpose and design is about the same for each.

Real-Time Clock

The real-time clock (RTC) provides a nonvolatile device for storing the system time. The RTC continues to keep track of time even when the system is off by way of a small battery typically included on the system board. On the PC architecture, the RTC and the CMOS are integrated, and a single battery keeps the RTC running and the BIOS settings preserved.

On boot, the kernel reads the RTC and uses it to initialize the wall time, which is stored in the `xtime` variable. The kernel does not typically read the value again; however, some supported architectures, such as x86, periodically save the current wall time back to the RTC. Nonetheless, the real time clock's primary importance is only during boot, when the `xtime` variable is initialized.

System Timer

The system timer serves a much more important (and frequent) role in the kernel's time-keeping. The idea behind the system timer, regardless of architecture, is the same—to provide a mechanism for driving an interrupt at a periodic rate. Some architectures implement this via an electronic clock that oscillates at a programmable frequency. Other systems provide a decrementer: A counter is set to some initial value and decrements at a fixed rate until the counter reaches zero. When the counter reaches zero, an interrupt is triggered. In any case, the effect is the same.

On x86, the primary system timer is the programmable interrupt timer (PIT). The PIT exists on all PC machines and has been driving interrupts since the days of DOS. The kernel programs the PIT on boot to drive the system timer interrupt (interrupt zero) at HZ frequency. It is a simple device with limited functionality, but it gets the job done. Other x86 time sources include the local APIC timer and the processor's time stamp counter (TSC).

The Timer Interrupt Handler

Now that we have an understanding of HZ, `jiffies`, and what the system timer's role is, let's look at the actual implementation of the timer interrupt handler. The timer interrupt is broken into two pieces: an architecture-dependent and an architecture-independent routine.

The architecture-dependent routine is registered as the interrupt handler for the system timer and, thus, runs when the timer interrupt hits. Its exact job depends on the given architecture, of course, but most handlers perform at least the following work:

- Obtain the `xtime_lock` lock, which protects access to `jiffies_64` and the wall time value, `xtime`.
- Acknowledge or reset the system timer as required.
- Periodically save the updated wall time to the real time clock.
- Call the architecture-independent timer routine, `tick_periodic()`.

The architecture-independent routine, `tick_periodic()`, performs much more work:

- Increment the `jiffies_64` count by one. (This is safe, even on 32-bit architectures, because the `xtime_lock` lock was previously obtained.)
- Update resource usages, such as consumed system and user time, for the currently running process.
- Run any dynamic timers that have expired (discussed in the following section).
- Execute `scheduler_tick()`, as discussed in Chapter 4.
- Update the wall time, which is stored in `xtime`.
- Calculate the infamous load average.

The routine is simple because other functions handle most of the work:

```
static void tick_periodic(int cpu)
{
        if (tick_do_timer_cpu == cpu) {
                write_seqlock(&xtime_lock);

                /* Keep track of the next tick event */
                tick_next_period = ktime_add(tick_next_period, tick_period);

                do_timer(1);
                write_sequnlock(&xtime_lock);
        }

        update_process_times(user_mode(get_irq_regs()));
        profile_tick(CPU_PROFILING);
}
```

Most of the important work is enabled in `do_timer()` and `update_process_times()`. The former is responsible for actually performing the increment to `jiffies_64`:

```
void do_timer(unsigned long ticks)
{
        jiffies_64 += ticks;
        update_wall_time();
        calc_global_load();
}
```

The function `update_wall_time()`, as its name suggests, updates the wall time in accordance with the elapsed ticks, whereas `calc_global_load()` updates the system's load average statistics.

When `do_timer()` ultimately returns, `update_process_times()` is invoked to update various statistics that a tick has elapsed, noting via `user_tick` whether it occurred in user-space or kernel-space:

```
void update_process_times(int user_tick)
{
        struct task_struct *p = current;
        int cpu = smp_processor_id();

        /* Note: this timer irq context must be accounted for as well. */
        account_process_tick(p, user_tick);
        run_local_timers();
        rcu_check_callbacks(cpu, user_tick);
        printk_tick();
        scheduler_tick();
        run_posix_cpu_timers(p);
}
```

Recall from `tick_periodic()` that the value of `user_tick` is set by looking at the system's registers:

```
update_process_times(user_mode(get_irq_regs()));
```

The `account_process_tick()` function does the actual updating of the process's times:

```
void account_process_tick(struct task_struct *p, int user_tick)
{
        cputime_t one_jiffy_scaled = cputime_to_scaled(cputime_one_jiffy);
        struct rq *rq = this_rq();

        if (user_tick)
                account_user_time(p, cputime_one_jiffy, one_jiffy_scaled);
        else if ((p != rq->idle) || (irq_count() != HARDIRQ_OFFSET))
                account_system_time(p, HARDIRQ_OFFSET, cputime_one_jiffy,
                                    one_jiffy_scaled);
        else
                account_idle_time(cputime_one_jiffy);
}
```

You might realize that this approach implies that the kernel credits a process for running the *entire* previous tick in whatever mode the processor was in when the timer interrupt occurred. In reality, the process might have entered and exited kernel mode many times during the last tick. In fact, the process might not even have been the only process running in the last tick! This granular process accounting is classic Unix, and without much more complex accounting, this is the best the kernel can provide. It is also another reason for a higher frequency tick rate.

Next, the `run_local_timers()` function marks a softirq (see Chapter 8, "Bottom Halves and Deferring Work") to handle the execution of any expired timers. Timers are covered in a following section, "Timers."

Finally, the `scheduler_tick()` function decrements the currently running process's timeslice and sets `need_resched` if needed. On SMP machines, it also balances the per-processor runqueues as needed. This is discussed in Chapter 4.

The `tick_periodic()` function returns to the original architecture-dependent interrupt handler, which performs any needed cleanup, releases the `xtime_lock` lock, and finally returns.

All this occurs every `1/HZ` of a second. That is potentially *100* or *1,000* times per second on an x86 machine!

The Time of Day

The current time of day (the wall time) is defined in `kernel/time/timekeeping.c`:

```
struct timespec xtime;
```

The `timespec` data structure is defined in `<linux/time.h>` as:

```
struct timespec {
        __kernel_time_t tv_sec;      /* seconds */
        long tv_nsec;                /* nanoseconds */
};
```

The `xtime.tv_sec` value stores the number of seconds that have elapsed since January 1, 1970 (UTC). This date is called the *epoch*. Most Unix systems base their notion of the current wall time as relative to this epoch. The `xtime.v_nsec` value stores the number of nanoseconds that have elapsed in the last second.

Reading or writing the `xtime` variable requires the `xtime_lock` lock, which is *not* a normal spinlock but a *seqlock*. Chapter 10, "Kernel Synchronization Methods," discusses seqlocks.

To update `xtime`, a write seqlock is required:

```
write_seqlock(&xtime_lock);

/* update xtime ... */

write_sequnlock(&xtime_lock);
```

Reading `xtime` requires the use of the `read_seqbegin()` and `read_seqretry()` functions:

```
unsigned long seq;

do {
        unsigned long lost;
        seq = read_seqbegin(&xtime_lock);

        usec = timer->get_offset();
        lost = jiffies - wall_jiffies;
        if (lost)
                usec += lost * (1000000 / HZ);
        sec = xtime.tv_sec;
```

```
        usec += (xtime.tv_nsec / 1000);
} while (read_seqretry(&xtime_lock, seq));
```

This loop repeats until the reader is assured that it read the data without an intervening write. If the timer interrupt occurred and updated xtime during the loop, the returned sequence number is invalid and the loop repeats.

The primary user-space interface for retrieving the wall time is gettimeofday(), which is implemented as sys_gettimeofday() in kernel/time.c:

```
asmlinkage long sys_gettimeofday(struct timeval *tv, struct timezone *tz)
{
        if (likely(tv)) {
                struct timeval ktv;
                do_gettimeofday(&ktv);
                if (copy_to_user(tv, &ktv, sizeof(ktv)))
                        return -EFAULT;
        }
        if (unlikely(tz)) {
                if (copy_to_user(tz, &sys_tz, sizeof(sys_tz)))
                        return -EFAULT;
        }
        return 0;
}
```

If the user provided a non-NULL tv value, the architecture-dependent do_gettimeofday() is called. This function primarily performs the xtime read loop previously discussed. Likewise, if tz is non-NULL, the system time zone (stored in sys_tz) is returned to the user. If there were errors copying the wall time or time zone back to user-space, the function returns -EFAULT. Otherwise, it returns zero for success.

The kernel also implements the time()[5] system call, but gettimeofday() largely supersedes it. The C library also provides other wall time–related library calls, such as ftime() and ctime().

The settimeofday() system call sets the wall time to the specified value. It requires the CAP_SYS_TIME capability.

Other than updating xtime, the kernel does not make nearly as frequent use of the current wall time as user-space does. One notable exception is in the filesystem code, which stores various timestamps (accessed, modified, and so on) in inodes.

---

[5] Some architectures, however, do not implement sys_time() and instead specify that it is emulated in the C library through the use of gettimeofday().

Timers

Timers—sometimes called *dynamic timers* or *kernel timers*—are essential for managing the flow of time in kernel code. Kernel code often needs to delay execution of some function until a later time. In previous chapters, we looked at using the bottom-half mechanisms, which are great for deferring work until later. Unfortunately, the definition of *later* is intentionally quite vague. The purpose of bottom halves is not so much to *delay work*, but simply to *not do the work now*. What we need is a tool for delaying work a specified amount of time—certainly no less, and with hope, not much longer. The solution is kernel timers.

A timer is easy to use. You perform some initial setup, specify an expiration time, specify a function to execute upon said expiration, and activate the timer. The given function runs after the timer expires. Timers are *not* cyclic. The timer is destroyed after it expires. This is one reason for the *dynamic* nomenclature: Timers are constantly created and destroyed, and there is no limit on the number of timers. Timers are popular throughout the entire kernel.

Using Timers

Timers are represented by `struct timer_list`, which is defined in `<linux/timer.h>`:

```
struct timer_list {
        struct list_head entry;          /* entry in linked list of timers */
        unsigned long expires;           /* expiration value, in jiffies */
        void (*function)(unsigned long); /* the timer handler function */
        unsigned long data;              /* lone argument to the handler */
        struct tvec_t_base_s *base;      /* internal timer field, do not touch */
};
```

Fortunately, the usage of timers requires little understanding of this data structure. Toying with it is discouraged to keep code forward compatible with changes. The kernel provides a family of timer-related interfaces to make timer management easy. Everything is declared in `<linux/timer.h>`. Most of the actual implementation is in `kernel/timer.c`.

The first step in creating a timer is defining it:

```
struct timer_list my_timer;
```

Next, the timer's internal values must be initialized. This is done via a helper function and must be done prior to calling *any* timer management functions on the timer:

```
init_timer(&my_timer);
```

Now you fill out the remaining values as required:

```
my_timer.expires = jiffies + delay;  /* timer expires in delay ticks */
my_timer.data = 0;                    /* zero is passed to the timer handler */
my_timer.function = my_function;      /* function to run when timer expires */
```

The `my_timer.expires` value specifies the timeout value in absolute ticks. When the current `jiffies` count is equal to or greater than `my_timer.expires`, the handler function `my_timer.function` is run with the lone argument of `my_timer.data`. As you can see from the `timer_list` definition, the function must match this prototype:

```
void my_timer_function(unsigned long data);
```

The `data` parameter enables you to register multiple timers with the same handler, and differentiate between them via the argument. If you do not need the argument, you can simply pass zero (or any other value).

Finally, you activate the timer:

```
add_timer(&my_timer);
```

And, voila, the timer is off and running! Note the significance of the `expired` value. The kernel runs the timer handler when the current tick count is *equal to or greater than* the specified expiration. Although the kernel guarantees to run no timer handler *prior* to the timer's expiration, there may be a delay in running the timer. Typically, timers are run fairly close to their expiration; however, they might be delayed until the first timer tick after their expiration. Consequently, timers cannot be used to implement any sort of hard real-time processing.

Sometimes you might need to modify the expiration of an already active timer. The kernel implements a function, `mod_timer()`, which changes the expiration of a given timer:

```
mod_timer(&my_timer, jiffies + new_delay);  /* new expiration */
```

The `mod_timer()` function can operate on timers that are initialized but not active, too. If the timer is inactive, `mod_timer()` activates it. The function returns zero if the timer were inactive and one if the timer were active. In either case, upon return from `mod_timer()`, the timer is activated and set to the new expiration.

If you need to deactivate a timer prior to its expiration, use the `del_timer()` function:

```
del_timer(&my_timer);
```

The function works on both active and inactive timers. If the timer is already inactive, the function returns zero; otherwise, the function returns one. Note that you do *not* need to call this for timers that have expired because they are automatically deactivated.

A potential race condition that must be guarded against exists when deleting timers. When `del_timer()` returns, it guarantees only that the timer is no longer active (that is, that it will not be executed in the future). On a multiprocessing machine, however, the timer handler might already be executing on another processor. To deactivate the timer and wait until a potentially executing handler for the timer exits, use `del_timer_sync()`:

```
del_timer_sync(&my_timer);
```

Unlike `del_timer()`, `del_timer_sync()` cannot be used from interrupt context.

Timer Race Conditions

Because timers run asynchronously with respect to the currently executing code, several potential race conditions exist. First, never do the following as a substitute for a mere mod_timer(), because this is unsafe on multiprocessing machines:

```
del_timer(my_timer)
my_timer->expires = jiffies + new_delay;
add_timer(my_timer);
```

Second, in almost all cases, you should use del_timer_sync() over del_timer(). Otherwise, you cannot assume the timer is not currently running, and that is why you made the call in the first place! Imagine if, after deleting the timer, the code went on to free or otherwise manipulate resources used by the timer handler. Therefore, the synchronous version is preferred.

Finally, you must make sure to protect any shared data used in the timer handler function. The kernel runs the function asynchronously with respect to other code. Data with a timer should be protected as discussed in Chapters 8 and 9, "An Introduction to Kernel Synchronization."

Timer Implementation

The kernel executes timers in bottom-half context, as softirqs, after the timer interrupt completes. The timer interrupt handler runs update_process_times(), which calls run_local_timers():

```
void run_local_timers(void)
{
        hrtimer_run_queues();
        raise_softirq(TIMER_SOFTIRQ);   /* raise the timer softirq */
        softlockup_tick();
}
```

The TIMER_SOFTIRQ softirq is handled by run_timer_softirq(). This function runs all the expired timers (if any) on the current processor.

Timers are stored in a linked list. However, it would be unwieldy for the kernel to either constantly traverse the entire list looking for expired timers, or keep the list sorted by expiration value; the insertion and deletion of timers would then become expensive. Instead, the kernel partitions timers into five groups based on their expiration value. Timers move down through the groups as their expiration time draws closer. The partitioning ensures that, in most executions of the timer softirq, the kernel has to do little work to find the expired timers. Consequently, the timer management code is efficient.

Delaying Execution

Often, kernel code (especially drivers) needs a way to delay execution for some time without using timers or a bottom-half mechanism. This is usually to enable hardware time to complete a given task. The time is typically quite short. For example, the specifications for a network card might list the time to change Ethernet modes as two microseconds. After setting the desired speed, the driver should wait at least the two microseconds before continuing.

The kernel provides a number of solutions, depending on the semantics of the delay. The solutions have different characteristics. Some hog the processor while delaying—effectively preventing—the accomplishment of any real work. Other solutions do not hog the processor but offer no guarantee that your code will resume in exactly the required time.[6]

Busy Looping

The simplest solution to implement (although rarely the optimal solution) is *busy waiting* or *busy looping*. This technique works only when the time you want to delay is some integer multiple of the tick rate or precision is not important.

The idea is simple: Spin in a loop until the desired number of clock ticks pass. For example

```
unsigned long timeout = jiffies + 10;        /* ten ticks */


while (time_before(jiffies, timeout))
        ;
```

The loop continues until `jiffies` is larger than `delay`, which occurs only after 10 clock ticks have passed. On x86 with `HZ` equal to 1,000, this results in a wait of 10 milliseconds. Similarly

```
unsigned long delay = jiffies + 2*HZ;        /* two seconds */


while (time_before(jiffies, delay))
        ;
```

This spins until `2*HZ` clock ticks has passed, which is always two seconds regardless of the clock rate.

This approach is not nice to the rest of the system. While your code waits, the processor is tied up spinning in a silly loop—no useful work is accomplished! You rarely want to take this brain-dead approach, and it is shown here because it is a clear and simple method for delaying execution. You might also encounter it in someone else's not-so-pretty code.

---

[6] Actually, no approach guarantees that the delay will be for exactly the time requested. Some come extremely close, however, and they all promise to wait at least as long as needed. Some just wait longer.

A better solution would be to reschedule your process to allow the processor to accomplish other work while your code waits:

```
unsigned long delay = jiffies + 5*HZ;
```

```
while (time_before(jiffies, delay))
        cond_resched();
```

The call to `cond_resched()` schedules a new process, but only if `need_resched` is set. In other words, this solution conditionally invokes the scheduler only if there is some more important task to run. Note that because this approach invokes the scheduler, you cannot make use of it from an interrupt handler—only from process context. All these approaches are best used from process context, because interrupt handlers should execute as quickly as possible. (And busy looping does not help accomplish that goal!) Furthermore, delaying execution in any manner, if at all possible, should not occur while a lock is held or interrupts are disabled.

C aficionados might wonder what guarantee is given that the previous loops even work. The C compiler is usually free to perform a given load only once. Normally, no assurance is given that the `jiffies` variable in the loop's conditional statement is even reloaded on each loop iteration. The kernel requires, however, that `jiffies` be reread on each iteration, as the value is incremented elsewhere: in the timer interrupt. Indeed, this is why the variable is marked `volatile` in `<linux/jiffies.h>`. The `volatile` keyword instructs the compiler to reload the variable on each access from main memory and never alias the variable's value in a register, guaranteeing that the previous loop completes as expected.

Small Delays

Sometimes, kernel code (again, usually drivers) requires short (smaller than a clock tick) and rather precise delays. This is often to synchronize with hardware, which again usually lists some minimum time for an activity to complete—often less than a millisecond. It would be impossible to use `jiffies`-based delays, as in the previous examples, for such a short wait. With a timer interrupt of 100Hz, the clock tick is a rather large 10 milliseconds! Even with a 1,000Hz timer interrupt, the clock tick is still one millisecond. Another solution is clearly necessary for smaller, more precise delays.

Thankfully, the kernel provides three functions for microsecond, nanosecond, and millisecond delays, defined in `<linux/delay.h>` and `<asm/delay.h>`, which do not use `jiffies`:

```
void udelay(unsigned long usecs)
void ndelay(unsigned long nsecs)
void mdelay(unsigned long msecs)
```

The former function delays execution by busy looping for the specified number of *microseconds*. The latter function delays execution for the specified number of *milliseconds*.

Recall one second equals 1,000 milliseconds, which equals 1,000,000 microseconds. Usage is trivial:

```
udelay(150);        /* delay for 150 µs */
```

The `udelay()` function is implemented as a loop that knows how many iterations can be executed in a given period of time. The `mdelay()` function is then implemented in terms of `udelay()`. Because the kernel knows how many loops the processor can complete in a second (see the sidebar on BogoMIPS), the `udelay()` function simply scales that value to the correct number of loop iterations for the given delay.

My BogoMIPS Are Bigger Than Yours!

The BogoMIPS value has always been a source of confusion and humor. In reality, the BogoMIPS calculation has little to do with the performance of your computer and is primarily used only for the `udelay()` and `mdelay()` functions. Its name is a contraction of *bogus* (that is, fake) and *MIPS* (million of instructions per second). Everyone is familiar with a boot message similar to the following (this is on a 2.4GHz 7300-series Intel Xeon):

```
Detected 2400.131 MHz processor.
Calibrating delay loop... 4799.56 BogoMIPS
```

The BogoMIPS value is the number of busy loop iterations the processor can perform in a given period. In effect, BogoMIPS are a measurement of how fast a processor can do nothing! This value is stored in the `loops_per_jiffy` variable and is readable from /proc/cpuinfo. The delay loop functions use the `loops_per_jiffy` value to figure out (fairly precisely) how many busy loop iterations they need to execute to provide the requisite delay.

The kernel computes `loops_per_jiffy` on boot via `calibrate_delay()` in init/main.c.

The `udelay()` function should be called only for small delays because larger delays on fast machines might result in overflow. As a rule, do not use `udelay()` for delays more than one millisecond in duration. For longer durations, `mdelay()` works fine. Like the other busy waiting solutions for delaying execution, neither of these functions (especially `mdelay()`, because it is used for such long delays) should be used unless absolutely needed. Remember that it is rude to busy loop with locks held or interrupts disabled because system response and performance will be adversely affected. If you require precise delays, however, these calls are your best bet. Typical uses of these busy waiting functions delay for a small amount of time, usually in the microsecond range.

schedule_timeout()

A more optimal method of delaying execution is to use `schedule_timeout()`. This call puts your task to sleep until at least the specified time has elapsed. There is no guarantee that the sleep duration will be *exactly* the specified time—only that the duration is at least as long as specified. When the specified time has elapsed, the kernel wakes the task up and places it back on the runqueue. Usage is easy:

```
/* set task's state to interruptible sleep */
set_current_state(TASK_INTERRUPTIBLE);

/* take a nap and wake up in "s" seconds */
schedule_timeout(s * HZ);
```

The lone parameter is the desired relative timeout, in jiffies. This example puts the task in interruptible sleep for s seconds. Because the task is marked TASK_INTERRUPTIBLE, it wakes up prematurely if it receives a signal. If the code does not want to process signals, you can use TASK_UNINTERRUPTIBLE instead. The task must be in one of these two states before schedule_timeout() is called or else the task will not go to sleep.

Note that because schedule_timeout() invokes the scheduler, code that calls it must be capable of sleeping. See Chapters 8 and 9 for discussions on atomicity and sleeping. In short, you must be in process context and must not hold a lock.

schedule_timeout() Implementation

The schedule_timeout() function is fairly straightforward. Indeed, it is a simple application of kernel timers, so let's take a look at it:

```
signed long schedule_timeout(signed long timeout)
{
        timer_t timer;
        unsigned long expire;


        switch (timeout)
        {
        case MAX_SCHEDULE_TIMEOUT:
                schedule();
                goto out;
        default:
                if (timeout < 0)
                {
                        printk(KERN_ERR "schedule_timeout: wrong timeout "
                            "value %lx from %p\n", timeout,
                            __builtin_return_address(0));
                        current->state = TASK_RUNNING;
                        goto out;
                }
        }

        expire = timeout + jiffies;

        init_timer(&timer);
```

```
        timer.expires = expire;
        timer.data = (unsigned long) current;
        timer.function = process_timeout;

        add_timer(&timer);
        schedule();
        del_timer_sync(&timer);


        timeout = expire - jiffies;


out:
        return timeout < 0 ? 0 : timeout;
}
```

The function creates a timer with the original name `timer` and sets it to expire in `timeout` clock ticks in the future. It sets the timer to execute the `process_timeout()` function when the timer expires. It then enables the timer and calls `schedule()`. Because the task is supposedly marked `TASK_INTERRUPTIBLE` or `TASK_UNINTERRUPTIBLE`, the scheduler does *not* run the task, but instead picks a new one.

When the timer expires, it runs `process_timeout()`:

```
void process_timeout(unsigned long data)
{
        wake_up_process((task_t *) data);
}
```

This function puts the task in the `TASK_RUNNING` state and places it back on the runqueue.

When the task reschedules, it returns to where it left off in `schedule_timeout()` (right after the call to `schedule()`). In case the task was awakened prematurely (if a signal was received), the timer is destroyed. The function then returns the time slept.

The code in the `switch()` statement is for special cases and is not part of the general usage of the function. The `MAX_SCHEDULE_TIMEOUT` check enables a task to sleep indefinitely. In that case, no timer is set (because there is no bound on the sleep duration), and the scheduler is immediately invoked. If you do this, you must have another method of waking your task up!

Sleeping on a Wait Queue, with a Timeout

Chapter 4 looked at how process context code in the kernel can place itself on a wait queue to wait for a specific event and then invoke the scheduler to select a new task. Elsewhere, when the event finally occurs, `wake_up()` is called, and the tasks sleeping on the wait queue are awakened and can continue running.

Sometimes it is desirable to wait for a specific event *or* wait for a specified time to elapse—whichever comes first. In those cases, code might simply call `schedule_timeout()` instead of `schedule()` after placing itself on a wait queue. The task wakes up when the desired event occurs or the specified time elapses. The code needs to check *why* it woke up—it might be because of the event occurring, the time elapsing, or a received signal—and continue as appropriate.

Conclusion

In this chapter, we looked at the kernel's concept of time and how both wall time and uptime are managed. We contrasted relative time with absolute time and absolute events with periodic events. We then covered time concepts such as the timer interrupt, timer ticks, `HZ`, and `jiffies`.

We looked at the implementation of timers and how you can use them in your own kernel code. We finished the chapter with an overview of other methods developers can use to pass time.

Much of the kernel code that you write will require some understanding of time and its passing. With high probability—especially if you hack on drivers—you will need to deal with kernel timers. Reading this chapter is good for more than just passing the time.

12

Memory Management

Memory allocation inside the kernel is not as easy as memory allocation outside the kernel. Simply put, the kernel lacks luxuries enjoyed by user-space. Unlike user-space, the kernel is not always afforded the capability to easily allocate memory. For example, the kernel cannot easily deal with memory allocation errors, and the kernel often cannot sleep. Because of these limitations, and the need for a lightweight memory allocation scheme, getting hold of memory in the kernel is more complicated than in user-space. This is not to say that, from a programmer's point of view, kernel memory allocations are difficult—just different.

This chapter discusses the methods used to obtain memory inside the kernel. Before you can delve into the actual allocation interfaces, however, you need to understand how the kernel handles memory.

Pages

The kernel treats physical pages as the basic unit of memory management. Although the processor's smallest addressable unit is a byte or a word, the memory management unit (MMU, the hardware that manages memory and performs virtual to physical address translations) typically deals in pages. Therefore, the MMU maintains the system's page tables with page-sized granularity (hence their name). In terms of virtual memory, pages are the smallest unit that matters.

As you can see in Chapter 19, "Portability," each architecture defines its own page size. Many architectures even support multiple page sizes. Most 32-bit architectures have 4KB pages, whereas most 64-bit architectures have 8KB pages. This implies that on a machine with 4KB pages and 1GB of memory, physical memory is divided into 262,144 distinct pages.

The kernel represents *every* physical page on the system with a `struct page` structure. This structure is defined in `<linux/mm_types.h>`. I've simplified the definition, removing two confusing unions that do not help color our discussion of the basics:

```
struct page {
        unsigned long        flags;
```

```
    atomic_t                _count;
    atomic_t                _mapcount;
    unsigned long           private;
    struct address_space    *mapping;
    pgoff_t                 index;
    struct list_head        lru;
    void                    *virtual;
};
```

Let's look at the important fields. The `flags` field stores the status of the page. Such flags include whether the page is dirty or whether it is locked in memory. Bit flags represent the various values, so at least 32 different flags are simultaneously available. The flag values are defined in `<linux/page-flags.h>`.

The `_count` field stores the usage count of the page—that is, how many references there are to this page. When this count reaches negative one, no one is using the page, and it becomes available for use in a new allocation. Kernel code should not check this field directly but instead use the function `page_count()`, which takes a `page` structure as its sole parameter. Although internally `_count` is negative one when the page is free, `page_count()` returns zero to indicate free and a positive nonzero integer when the page is in use. A page may be used by the page cache (in which case the `mapping` field points to the `address_space` object associated with this page), as private data (pointed at by `private`), or as a mapping in a process's page table.

The `virtual` field is the page's virtual address. Normally, this is simply the address of the page in virtual memory. Some memory (called high memory) is not permanently mapped in the kernel's address space. In that case, this field is `NULL`, and the page must be dynamically mapped if needed. We discuss high memory shortly.

The important point to understand is that the `page` structure is associated with physical pages, not virtual pages. Therefore, what the structure describes is transient at best. Even if the data contained in the page continues to exist, it might not always be associated with the same `page` structure because of swapping and so on. The kernel uses this data structure to describe the associated physical page. The data structure's goal is to describe physical memory, not the data contained therein.

The kernel uses this structure to keep track of all the pages in the system, because the kernel needs to know whether a page is free (that is, if the page is not allocated). If a page is not free, the kernel needs to know who owns the page. Possible owners include user-space processes, dynamically allocated kernel data, static kernel code, the page cache, and so on.

Developers are often surprised that an instance of this structure is allocated for each physical page in the system. They think, "*What a lot of memory wasted!*" Let's look at just how bad (or good) the space consumption is from all these pages. Assume struct `page` consumes 40 bytes of memory, the system has 8KB physical pages, and the system has 4GB of physical memory. In that case, there are about 524,288 pages and `page` structures on the system. The `page` structures consume 20MB: perhaps a surprisingly large number in absolute terms, but only a small fraction of a percent relative to the system's 4GB—not too high a cost for managing all the system's physical pages.

Zones

Because of hardware limitations, the kernel cannot treat all pages as identical. Some pages, because of their physical address in memory, cannot be used for certain tasks. Because of this limitation, the kernel divides pages into different *zones*. The kernel uses the zones to group pages of similar properties. In particular, Linux has to deal with two shortcomings of hardware with respect to memory addressing:

- Some hardware devices can perform DMA (direct memory access) to only certain memory addresses.
- Some architectures can physically addressing larger amounts of memory than they can virtually address. Consequently, some memory is not permanently mapped into the kernel address space.

Because of these constraints, Linux has four primary memory zones:

- ZONE_DMA—This zone contains pages that can undergo DMA.
- ZONE_DMA32—Like ZOME_DMA, this zone contains pages that can undergo DMA. Unlike ZONE_DMA, these pages are accessible only by 32-bit devices. On some architectures, this zone is a larger subset of memory.
- ZONE_NORMAL—This zone contains normal, regularly mapped, pages.
- ZONE_HIGHMEM—This zone contains "high memory," which are pages not permanently mapped into the kernel's address space.

These zones, and two other, less notable ones, are defined in <linux/mmzone.h>.

The actual use and layout of the memory zones is architecture-dependent. For example, some architectures have no problem performing DMA into any memory address. In those architectures, ZONE_DMA is empty and ZONE_NORMAL is used for allocations regardless of their use. As a counterexample, on the x86 architecture, ISA devices cannot perform DMA into the full 32-bit address space[1] because ISA devices can access only the first 16MB of physical memory. Consequently, ZONE_DMA on x86 consists of all memory in the range 0MB–16MB.

ZONE_HIGHMEM works in the same regard. What an architecture can and cannot directly map varies. On 32-bit x86 systems, ZONE_HIGHMEM is all memory above the physical 896MB mark. On other architectures, ZONE_HIGHMEM is empty because all memory is

---

[1] *Similarly, some broken PCI devices can perform DMA into only a 24-bit address space.*

directly mapped. The memory contained in ZONE_HIGHMEM is called *high memory*.[2] The rest
of the system's memory is called *low memory*.

ZONE_NORMAL tends to be whatever is left over after the previous two zones claim their
requisite shares. On x86, for example, ZONE_NORMAL is all physical memory from 16MB to
896MB. On other (more fortunate) architectures, ZONE_NORMAL is all available memory.
Table 12.1 is a listing of each zone and its consumed pages on x86-32.

Table 12.1 **Zones on x86-32**

Zone	Description	Physical Memory
ZONE_DMA	DMA-able pages	< 16MB
ZONE_NORMAL	Normally addressable pages	16–896MB
ZONE_HIGHMEM	Dynamically mapped pages	> 896MB

Linux partitions the system's pages into zones to have a pooling in place to satisfy allocations as needed. For example, having a ZONE_DMA pool gives the kernel the capability to
satisfy memory allocations needed for DMA. If such memory is needed, the kernel can
simply pull the required number of pages from ZONE_DMA. Note that the zones do not
have any physical relevance but are simply logical groupings used by the kernel to keep
track of pages.

Although some allocations may require pages from a particular zone, other allocations
may pull from multiple zones. For example, although an allocation for DMA-able memory must originate from ZONE_DMA, a normal allocation can come from ZONE_DMA or
ZONE_NORMAL but not both; allocations cannot cross zone boundaries. The kernel prefers
to satisfy normal allocations from the normal zone, of course, to save the pages in
ZONE_DMA for allocations that need it. But if push comes to shove (say, if memory should
get low), the kernel can dip its fingers in whatever zone is available and suitable.

Not all architectures define all zones. For example, a 64-bit architecture such as Intel's
x86-64 can fully map and handle 64-bits of memory. Thus, x86-64 has no ZONE_HIGHMEM
and all physical memory is contained within ZONE_DMA and ZONE_NORMAL.

Each zone is represented by struct zone, which is defined in <linux/mmzone.h>:

```
struct zone {
        unsigned long              watermark[NR_WMARK];
        unsigned long              lowmem_reserve[MAX_NR_ZONES];
        struct per_cpu_pageset     pageset[NR_CPUS];
        spinlock_t                 lock;
```

---

[2] *Linux's high memory has nothing to do with high memory in DOS, which works around limitations of
DOS and x86's "real mode" processor state.*

```
struct free_area          free_area[MAX_ORDER]
spinlock_t                lru_lock;
struct zone_lru {
        struct list_head list;
        unsigned long    nr_saved_scan;
} lru[NR_LRU_LISTS];
struct zone_reclaim_stat reclaim_stat;
unsigned long             pages_scanned;
unsigned long             flags;
atomic_long_t             vm_stat[NR_VM_ZONE_STAT_ITEMS];
int                       prev_priority;
unsigned                  int inactive_ratio;
wait_queue_head_t         *wait_table;
unsigned long             wait_table_hash_nr_entries;
unsigned long             wait_table_bits;
struct pglist_data        *zone_pgdat;
unsigned long             zone_start_pfn;
unsigned long             spanned_pages;
unsigned long             present_pages;
const char                *name;
};
```

The structure is big, but only three zones are in the system and, thus, only three of these structures. Let's look at the more important fields.

The `lock` field is a spin lock that protects the structure from concurrent access. Note that it protects just the structure and not all the pages that reside in the zone. A specific lock does not protect individual pages, although parts of the kernel may lock the data that happens to reside in said pages.

The `watermark` array holds the minimum, low, and high watermarks for this zone. The kernel uses watermarks to set benchmarks for suitable per-zone memory consumption, varying its aggressiveness as the watermarks vary vis-à-vis free memory.

The `name` field is, unsurprisingly, a `NULL`-terminated string representing the name of this zone. The kernel initializes this value during boot in `mm/page_alloc.c`, and the three zones are given the names DMA, Normal, and HighMem.

Getting Pages

Now with an understanding of how the kernel manages memory—via pages, zones, and so on—let's look at the interfaces the kernel implements to enable you to allocate and free memory within the kernel.

The kernel provides one low-level mechanism for requesting memory, along with several interfaces to access it. All these interfaces allocate memory with page-sized granularity and are declared in `<linux/gfp.h>`. The core function is

```
struct page * alloc_pages(gfp_t gfp_mask, unsigned int order)
```

This allocates 2^{order} (that is, `1 << order`) contiguous physical pages and returns a pointer to the first page's page structure; on error it returns NULL. We look at the gfp_t type and gfp_mask parameter in a later section. You can convert a given page to its logical address with the function

```
void * page_address(struct page *page)
```

This returns a pointer to the logical address where the given physical page currently resides. If you have no need for the actual struct page, you can call

```
unsigned long __get_free_pages(gfp_t gfp_mask, unsigned int order)
```

This function works the same as alloc_pages(), except that it directly returns the logical address of the first requested page. Because the pages are contiguous, the other pages simply follow from the first.

If you need only one page, two functions are implemented as wrappers to save you a bit of typing:

```
struct page * alloc_page(gfp_t gfp_mask)
unsigned long __get_free_page(gfp_t gfp_mask)
```

These functions work the same as their brethren but pass zero for the order (2^0 = one page).

Getting Zeroed Pages

If you need the returned page filled with zeros, use the function

```
unsigned long get_zeroed_page(unsigned int gfp_mask)
```

This function works the same as __get_free_page(), except that the allocated page is then zero-filled—every bit of every byte is unset. This is useful for pages given to userspace because the random garbage in an allocated page is not so random; it might contain sensitive data. All data must be zeroed or otherwise cleaned before it is returned to userspace to ensure system security is not compromised. Table 12.2 is a listing of all the low-level page allocation methods.

Table 12.2   **Low-Level Page Allocation Methods**

Flag	Description
alloc_page(gfp_mask)	Allocates a single page and returns a pointer to its
alloc_pages(gfp_mask, order)	Allocates 2^{order} pages and returns a pointer to the first page's page structure
__get_free_page(gfp_mask)	Allocates a single page and returns a pointer to its logical address
__get_free_pages(gfp_mask,	Allocates 2^{order} pages and returns a pointer to the first page's logical address

Table 12.2   **Low-Level Page Allocation Methods**

Flag	Description
get_zeroed_page(gfp_mask)	Allocates a single page, zero its contents and returns a pointer to its logical address

Freeing Pages

A family of functions enables you to free allocated pages when you no longer need them:

```
void __free_pages(struct page *page, unsigned int order)
void free_pages(unsigned long addr, unsigned int order)
void free_page(unsigned long addr)
```

You must be careful to free only pages you allocate. Passing the wrong struct page or address, or the incorrect order, can result in corruption. Remember, the kernel trusts itself. Unlike with user-space, the kernel will happily hang itself if you ask it.

Let's look at an example. Here, we want to allocate eight pages:

```
unsigned long page;

page = __get_free_pages(GFP_KERNEL, 3);
if (!page) {
        /* insufficient memory: you must handle this error! */
        return -ENOMEM;
}

/* 'page' is now the address of the first of eight contiguous pages ... */
```

And here we free the eight pages, after we are done using them:

```
free_pages(page, 3);

/*
 * our pages are now freed and we should no
 * longer access the address stored in 'page'
 */
```

The GFP_KERNEL parameter is an example of a gfp_mask flag. It is discussed shortly.

Make note of the error checking after the call to __get_free_pages(). A kernel allocation *can* fail, and your code *must* check for and handle such errors. This might mean unwinding everything you have done thus far. It therefore often makes sense to allocate your memory at the start of the routine to make handling the error easier. Otherwise, by the time you attempt to allocate memory, it may be rather hard to bail out.

These low-level page functions are useful when you need page-sized chunks of physically contiguous pages, especially if you need exactly a single page or two. For more general byte-sized allocations, the kernel provides kmalloc().

kmalloc()

The kmalloc() function's operation is similar to that of user-space's familiar malloc() routine, with the exception of the additional flags parameter. The kmalloc() function is a simple interface for obtaining kernel memory in byte-sized chunks. If you need whole pages, the previously discussed interfaces might be a better choice. For most kernel allocations, however, kmalloc() is the preferred interface.

The function is declared in <linux/slab.h>:

```
void * kmalloc(size_t size, gfp_t flags)
```

The function returns a pointer to a region of memory that is at *least* size bytes in length.[3] The region of memory allocated is physically contiguous. On error, it returns NULL. Kernel allocations always succeed, unless an insufficient amount of memory is available. Thus, you must check for NULL after all calls to kmalloc() and handle the error appropriately.

Let's look at an example. Assume you need to dynamically allocate enough room for a fictional dog structure:

```
struct dog *p;
```

```
p = kmalloc(sizeof(struct dog), GFP_KERNEL);
if (!p)
        /* handle error ... */
```

If the kmalloc() call succeeds, p now points to a block of memory that is at least the requested size. The GFP_KERNEL flag specifies the behavior of the memory allocator while trying to obtain the memory to return to the caller of kmalloc().

gfp_mask Flags

You've seen various examples of allocator flags in both the low-level page allocation functions and kmalloc(). Now it's time to discuss these flags in depth. Flags are represented by the gfp_t type, which is defined in <linux/types.h> as an unsigned int. *gfp* stands for __get_free_pages(), one of the memory allocation routines we discussed earlier.

The flags are broken up into three categories: action modifiers, zone modifiers, and types. Action modifiers specify *how* the kernel is supposed to allocate the requested memory. In certain situations, only certain methods can be employed to allocate memory. For

---

[3] *kmalloc() may allocate more than you asked, although you have no way of knowing how much more! Because at its heart the kernel allocator is page-based, some allocations may be rounded up to fit within the available memory. The kernel never returns less memory than requested. If the kernel is unable to find at least the requested amount, the allocation fails and the function returns NULL.*

example, interrupt handlers must instruct the kernel not to sleep (because interrupt handlers cannot reschedule) in the course of allocating memory. Zone modifiers specify from *where* to allocate memory. As you saw earlier in this chapter, the kernel divides physical memory into multiple zones, each of which serves a different purpose. Zone modifiers specify from which of these zones to allocate. Type flags specify a combination of action and zone modifiers as needed by a certain *type* of memory allocation. Type flags simplify the specification of multiple modifiers; instead of providing a combination of action and zone modifiers, you can specify just one type flag. The GFP_KERNEL is a type flag, which is used for code in process context inside the kernel. Let's look at the flags.

Action Modifiers

All the flags, the action modifiers included, are declared in `<linux/gfp.h>`. The file `<linux/slab.h>` includes this header, however, so you often need not include it directly. In reality, you usually use only the type modifiers, which are discussed later. Nonetheless, it is good to have an understanding of these individual flags. Table 12.3 is a list of the action modifiers.

Table 12.3   **Action Modifiers**

Flag	Description
__GFP_WAIT	The allocator can sleep.
__GFP_HIGH	The allocator can access emergency pools.
__GFP_IO	The allocator can start disk I/O.
__GFP_FS	The allocator can start filesystem I/O.
__GFP_COLD	The allocator should use cache cold pages.
__GFP_NOWARN	The allocator does not print failure warnings.
__GFP_REPEAT	The allocator repeats the allocation if it fails, but the allocation can potentially fail.
__GFP_NOFAIL	The allocator indefinitely repeats the allocation. The allocation cannot fail.
__GFP_NORETRY	The allocator never retries if the allocation fails.
__GFP_NOMEMALLOC	The allocator does not fall back on reserves.
__GFP_HARDWALL	The allocator enforces "hardwall" cpuset boundaries.
__GFP_RECLAIMABLE	The allocator marks the pages reclaimable.
__GFP_COMP	The allocator adds compound page metadata (used internally by the `hugetlb` code).

These allocations can be specified together. For example

```
ptr = kmalloc(size, __GFP_WAIT | __GFP_IO | __GFP_FS);
```

This call instructs the page allocator (ultimately `alloc_pages()`) that the allocation can block, perform I/O, and perform filesystem operations, if needed. This enables the kernel great freedom in how it can find the free memory to satisfy the allocation.

Most allocations specify these modifiers but do so indirectly by way of the type flags we discuss shortly. Don't worry—you won't have to figure out which of these weird flags to use every time you allocate memory!

Zone Modifiers

Zone modifiers specify from which memory zone the allocation should originate. Normally, allocations can be fulfilled from any zone. The kernel prefers ZONE_NORMAL, however, to ensure that the other zones have free pages when they are needed.

There are only three zone modifiers because there are only three zones other than ZONE_NORMAL (which is where, by default, allocations originate). Table 12.4 is a listing of the zone modifiers.

Table 12.4 **Zone Modifiers**

Flag	Description
__GFP_DMA	Allocates only from ZONE_DMA
__GFP_DMA32	Allocates only from ZONE_DMA32
__GFP_HIGHMEM	Allocates from ZONE_HIGHMEM or ZONE_NORMAL

Specifying one of these three flags modifies the zone from which the kernel attempts to satisfy the allocation. The __GFP_DMA flag forces the kernel to satisfy the request from ZONE_DMA. This flag says, *I absolutely must have memory into which I can perform DMA*. Conversely, the __GFP_HIGHMEM flag instructs the allocator to satisfy the request from either ZONE_NORMAL or (preferentially) ZONE_HIGHMEM. This flag says, *I can use high memory, so I can be a doll and hand you back some of that, but normal memory works, too.* If neither flag is specified, the kernel fulfills the allocation from either ZONE_DMA or ZONE_NORMAL, with a strong preference to satisfy the allocation from ZONE_NORMAL.

You cannot specify __GFP_HIGHMEM to either __get_free_pages() or kmalloc(). Because these both return a logical address, and not a page structure, it is possible that these functions would allocate memory not currently mapped in the kernel's virtual address space and, thus, does not have a logical address. Only alloc_pages() can allocate high memory. The majority of your allocations, however, will not specify a zone modifier because ZONE_NORMAL is sufficient.

Type Flags

The type flags specify the required action and zone modifiers to fulfill a particular type of transaction. Therefore, kernel code tends to use the correct type flag and not specify the myriad of other flags it might need. This is both simpler and less error-prone. Table 12.5 is a list of the type flags, and Table 12.6 shows which modifiers are associated with each type flag.

Table 12.5   **Type Flags**

Flag	Description
GFP_ATOMIC	The allocation is high priority and must not sleep. This is the flag to use in interrupt handlers, in bottom halves, while holding a spin-lock, and in other situations where you cannot sleep.
GFP_NOWAIT	Like GFP_ATOMIC, except that the call will not fallback on emergency memory pools. This increases the liklihood of the memory allocation failing.
GFP_NOIO	This allocation can block, but must not initiate disk I/O. This is the flag to use in block I/O code when you cannot cause more disk I/O, which might lead to some unpleasant recursion.
GFP_NOFS	This allocation can block and can initiate disk I/O, if it must, but it will not initiate a filesystem operation. This is the flag to use in filesystem code when you cannot start another filesystem operation.
GFP_KERNEL	This is a normal allocation and might block. This is the flag to use in process context code when it is safe to sleep. The kernel will do whatever it has to do to obtain the memory requested by the caller. This flag should be your default choice.
GFP_USER	This is a normal allocation and might block. This flag is used to allocate memory for user-space processes.
GFP_HIGHUSER	This is an allocation from ZONE_HIGHMEM and might block. This flag is used to allocate memory for user-space processes.
GFP_DMA	This is an allocation from ZONE_DMA. Device drivers that need DMA-able memory use this flag, usually in combination with one of the preceding flags.

Table 12.6   **Modifiers Behind Each Type Flag**

Flag	Modifier Flags
GFP_ATOMIC	__GFP_HIGH
GFP_NOWAIT	0
GFP_NOIO	__GFP_WAIT

Table 12.6   **Modifiers Behind Each Type Flag**   (continued)

Flag	Modifier Flags
GFP_NOFS	(__GFP_WAIT | __GFP_IO)
GFP_KERNEL	(__GFP_WAIT | __GFP_IO | __GFP_FS)
GFP_USER	(__GFP_WAIT | __GFP_IO | __GFP_FS)
GFP_HIGHUSER	(__GFP_WAIT | __GFP_IO | __GFP_FS | __GFP_HIGHMEM)
GFP_DMA	__GFP_DMA

Let's look at the frequently used flags and when and why you might need them. The vast majority of allocations in the kernel use the GFP_KERNEL flag. The resulting allocation is a normal priority allocation that might sleep. Because the call can block, this flag can be used only from process context that can safely reschedule. (That is, no locks are held and so on.) Because this flag does not make any stipulations as to how the kernel may obtain the requested memory, the memory allocation has a high probability of succeeding.

On the far other end of the spectrum is the GFP_ATOMIC flag. Because this flag specifies a memory allocation that cannot sleep, the allocation is restrictive in the memory it can obtain for the caller. If no sufficiently sized contiguous chunk of memory is available, the kernel is not likely to free memory because it cannot put the caller to sleep. Conversely, the GFP_KERNEL allocation can put the caller to sleep to swap inactive pages to disk, flush dirty pages to disk, and so on. Because GFP_ATOMIC cannot perform any of these actions, it has less of a chance of succeeding (at least when memory is low) compared to GFP_KERNEL allocations. Nonetheless, the GFP_ATOMIC flag is the only option when the current code cannot sleep, such as with interrupt handlers, softirqs, and tasklets.

In between these two flags are GFP_NOIO and GFP_NOFS. Allocations initiated with these flags might block, but they refrain from performing certain other operations. A GFP_NOIO allocation does not initiate any disk I/O whatsoever to fulfill the request. On the other hand, GFP_NOFS might initiate disk I/O, but does not initiate filesystem I/O. Why might you need these flags? They are needed for certain low-level block I/O or filesystem code, respectively. Imagine if a common path in the filesystem code allocated memory *without* the GFP_NOFS flag. The allocation could result in *more* filesystem operations, which would then beget other allocations and, thus, more filesystem operations! This could continue indefinitely. Code such as this that invokes the allocator must ensure that the allocator also does not execute it, or else the allocation can create a deadlock. Not surprisingly, the kernel uses these two flags only in a handful of places.

The GFP_DMA flag is used to specify that the allocator must satisfy the request from ZONE_DMA. This flag is used by device drivers, which need DMA-able memory for their devices. Normally, you combine this flag with the GFP_ATOMIC or GFP_KERNEL flag.

In the vast majority of the code that you write, you use either GFP_KERNEL or GFP_ATOMIC. Table 12.7 is a list of the common situations and the flags to use. Regardless of the allocation type, you must check for and handle failures.

Table 12.7   **Which Flag to Use When**

Situation	Solution
Process context, can sleep	Use GFP_KERNEL.
Process context, cannot sleep	Use GFP_ATOMIC, or perform your allocations with GFP_KERNEL at an earlier or later point when you can sleep.
Interrupt handler	Use GFP_ATOMIC.
Softirq	Use GFP_ATOMIC.
Tasklet	Use GFP_ATOMIC.
Need DMA-able memory, can sleep	Use (GFP_DMA | GFP_KERNEL).
Need DMA-able memory, cannot sleep	Use (GFP_DMA | GFP_ATOMIC), or perform your allocation at an earlier point when you can sleep.

kfree()

The counterpart to kmalloc() is kfree(), which is declared in <linux/slab.h>:

```
void kfree(const void *ptr)
```

The kfree() method frees a block of memory previously allocated with kmalloc(). Do not call this function on memory not previously allocated with kmalloc(), or on memory that has already been freed. Doing so is a bug, resulting in bad behavior such as freeing memory belonging to another part of the kernel. As in user-space, be careful to balance your allocations with your deallocations to prevent memory leaks and other bugs. Note that calling kfree(NULL) is explicitly checked for and safe.

Let's look at an example of allocating memory in an interrupt handler. In this example, an interrupt handler wants to allocate a buffer to hold incoming data. The preprocessor macro BUF_SIZE is the size in bytes of this desired buffer, which is presumably larger than just a couple of bytes.

```
char *buf;

buf = kmalloc(BUF_SIZE, GFP_ATOMIC);
if (!buf)
        /* error allocating memory ! */
```

Later, when you no longer need the memory, do not forget to free it:

```
kfree(buf);
```

vmalloc()

The vmalloc() function works in a similar fashion to kmalloc(), except it allocates
memory that is only virtually contiguous and not necessarily physically contiguous. This
is how a user-space allocation function works: The pages returned by malloc() are contiguous within the virtual address space of the processor, but there is no guarantee that
they are actually contiguous in physical RAM. The kmalloc() function guarantees that
the pages are physically contiguous (and virtually contiguous). The vmalloc() function
ensures only that the pages are contiguous within the virtual address space. It does this by
allocating potentially noncontiguous chunks of physical memory and "fixing up" the page
tables to map the memory into a contiguous chunk of the logical address space.

For the most part, only hardware devices require physically contiguous memory allocations. On many architectures, hardware devices live on the other side of the memory
management unit and, thus, do not understand virtual addresses. Consequently, any
regions of memory that hardware devices work with must exist as a physically contiguous
block and not merely a virtually contiguous one. Blocks of memory used only by software—for example, process-related buffers—are fine using memory that is only virtually
contiguous. In your programming, you never know the difference. All memory appears to
the kernel as logically contiguous.

Despite the fact that physically contiguous memory is required in only certain cases,
most kernel code uses kmalloc() and not vmalloc() to obtain memory. Primarily, this is
for performance. The vmalloc() function, to make nonphysically contiguous pages contiguous in the virtual address space, must specifically set up the page table entries. Worse,
pages obtained via vmalloc() must be mapped by their individual pages (because they
are not physically contiguous), which results in much greater TLB[4] thrashing than you see
when directly mapped memory is used. Because of these concerns, vmalloc() is used
only when absolutely necessary—typically, to obtain large regions of memory. For example, when modules are dynamically inserted into the kernel, they are loaded into memory
created via vmalloc().

The vmalloc() function is declared in <linux/vmalloc.h> and defined in
mm/vmalloc.c. Usage is identical to user-space's malloc():

```
void * vmalloc(unsigned long size)
```

---

[4] The TLB (translation lookaside buffer) is a hardware cache used by most architectures to cache the
mapping of virtual addresses to physical addresses. This greatly improves the performance of the system, because most memory access is done via virtual addressing.

The function returns a pointer to at least `size` bytes of virtually contiguous memory. On error, the function returns `NULL`. The function might sleep and thus cannot be called from interrupt context or other situations in which blocking is not permissible.

To free an allocation obtained via `vmalloc()`, use

```
void vfree(const void *addr)
```

This function frees the block of memory beginning at `addr` that was previously allocated via `vmalloc()`. The function can also sleep and, thus, cannot be called from interrupt context. It has no return value.

Usage of these functions is simple:

```
char *buf;

buf = vmalloc(16 * PAGE_SIZE); /* get 16 pages */
if (!buf)
        /* error! failed to allocate memory */

/*
 * buf now points to at least a 16*PAGE_SIZE bytes
 * of virtually contiguous block of memory
 */
```

After you finish with the memory, make sure to free it by using

```
vfree(buf);
```

Slab Layer

Allocating and freeing data structures is one of the most common operations inside any kernel. To facilitate frequent allocations and deallocations of data, programmers often introduce *free lists*. A free list contains a block of available, already allocated, data structures. When code requires a new instance of a data structure, it can grab one of the structures off the free list rather than allocate the sufficient amount of memory and set it up for the data structure. Later, when the data structure is no longer needed, it is returned to the free list instead of deallocated. In this sense, the free list acts as an object cache, caching a frequently used *type* of object.

One of the main problems with free lists in the kernel is that there exists no global control. When available memory is low, there is no way for the kernel to communicate to every free list that it should shrink the sizes of its cache to free up memory. The kernel has no understanding of the random free lists at all. To remedy this, and to consolidate code, the Linux kernel provides the slab layer (also called the slab allocator). The slab layer acts as a generic data structure-caching layer.

The concept of a slab allocator was first implemented in Sun Microsystem's SunOS 5.4 operating system.[5] The Linux data structure caching layer shares the same name and basic design.

The slab layer attempts to leverage several basic tenets:

- Frequently used data structures tend to be allocated and freed often, so cache them.

- Frequent allocation and deallocation can result in memory fragmentation (the inability to find large contiguous chunks of available memory). To prevent this, the cached free lists are arranged contiguously. Because freed data structures return to the free list, there is no resulting fragmentation.

- The free list provides improved performance during frequent allocation and deallocation because a freed object can be immediately returned to the next allocation.

- If the allocator is aware of concepts such as object size, page size, and total cache size, it can make more intelligent decisions.

- If part of the cache is made per-processor (separate and unique to each processor on the system), allocations and frees can be performed without an SMP lock.

- If the allocator is NUMA-aware, it can fulfill allocations from the same memory node as the requestor.

- Stored objects can be *colored* to prevent multiple objects from mapping to the same cache lines.

The slab layer in Linux was designed and implemented with these premises in mind.

Design of the Slab Layer

The slab layer divides different objects into groups called *caches*, each of which stores a different type of object. There is one cache per object type. For example, one cache is for process descriptors (a free list of `task_struct` structures), whereas another cache is for inode objects (`struct inode`). Interestingly, the `kmalloc()` interface is built on top of the slab layer, using a family of general purpose caches.

The caches are then divided into *slabs* (hence the name of this subsystem). The slabs are composed of one or more physically contiguous pages. Typically, slabs are composed of only a single page. Each cache may consist of multiple slabs.

Each slab contains some number of *objects*, which are the data structures being cached. Each slab is in one of three states: full, partial, or empty. A full slab has no free objects. (All objects in the slab are allocated.) An empty slab has no allocated objects. (All objects in the slab are free.) A partial slab has some allocated objects and some free objects. When some part of the kernel requests a new object, the request is satisfied from a partial slab, if one exists. Otherwise, the request is satisfied from an empty slab. If there exists no empty

---

[5] *And subsequently documented in Bonwick, J. "The Slab Allocator: An Object-Caching Kernel Memory Allocator," USENIX, 1994.*

slab, one is created. Obviously, a full slab can never satisfy a request because it does not have any free objects. This strategy reduces fragmentation.

Let's look at the inode structure as an example, which is the in-memory representation of a disk inode (see Chapter 13, "The Virtual Filesystem"). These structures are frequently created and destroyed, so it makes sense to manage them via the slab allocator. Thus, struct inode is allocated from the inode_cachep cache. (Such a naming convention is standard.) This cache is made up of one or more slabs—probably a lot of slabs because there are a lot of objects. Each slab contains as many struct inode objects as possible. When the kernel requests a new inode structure, the kernel returns a pointer to an already allocated, but unused structure from a partial slab or, if there is no partial slab, an empty slab. When the kernel is done using the inode object, the slab allocator marks the object as free. Figure 12.1 diagrams the relationship between caches, slabs, and objects.

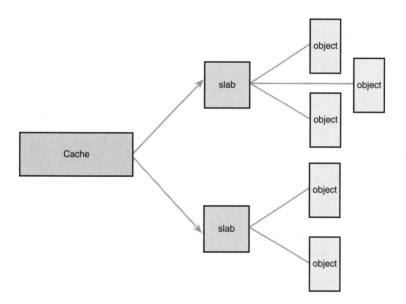

Figure 12.1   The relationship between caches, slabs, and objects.

Each cache is represented by a kmem_cache structure. This structure contains three lists—slabs_full, slabs_partial, and slabs_empty—stored inside a kmem_list3 structure, which is defined in mm/slab.c. These lists contain all the slabs associated with the cache. A slab descriptor, struct slab, represents each slab:

```
struct slab {
        struct list_head  list;      /* full, partial, or empty list */
        unsigned long     colouroff; /* offset for the slab coloring */
        void              *s_mem;    /* first object in the slab */
        unsigned int      inuse;     /* allocated objects in the slab */
```

```
        kmem_bufctl_t    free;       /* first free object, if any */
};
```

Slab descriptors are allocated either outside the slab in a general cache or inside the slab itself, at the beginning. The descriptor is stored inside the slab if the total size of the slab is sufficiently small, or if internal slack space is sufficient to hold the descriptor.

The slab allocator creates new slabs by interfacing with the low-level kernel page allocator via __get_free_pages():

```
static void *kmem_getpages(struct kmem_cache *cachep, gfp_t flags, int nodeid)
{
        struct page *page;
        void *addr;
        int i;

        flags |= cachep->gfpflags;
        if (likely(nodeid == -1)) {
                addr = (void*)__get_free_pages(flags, cachep->gfporder);
                if (!addr)
                        return NULL;
                page = virt_to_page(addr);
        } else {
                page = alloc_pages_node(nodeid, flags, cachep->gfporder);
                if (!page)
                        return NULL;
                addr = page_address(page);
        }

        i = (1 << cachep->gfporder);
        if (cachep->flags & SLAB_RECLAIM_ACCOUNT)
                atomic_add(i, &slab_reclaim_pages);
        add_page_state(nr_slab, i);
        while (i--) {
                SetPageSlab(page);
                page++;
        }
        return addr;
}
```

This function uses __get_free_pages() to allocate memory sufficient to hold the cache. The first parameter to this function points to the specific cache that needs more pages. The second parameter points to the flags given to __get_free_pages(). Note how this value is binary OR'ed against another value. This adds default flags that the cache requires to the flags parameter. The power-of-two size of the allocation is stored in cachep->gfporder. The previous function is a bit more complicated than one might expect because code that makes the allocator NUMA-aware. When nodeid is not negative one, the allocator attempts to fulfill the allocation from the same memory node that requested the allocation. This provides better performance on NUMA systems, in which accessing memory outside your node results in a performance penalty.

For educational purposes, we can ignore the NUMA-aware code and write a simple `kmem_getpages()`:

```
static inline void * kmem_getpages(struct kmem_cache *cachep, gfp_t flags)
{
        void *addr;

        flags |= cachep->gfpflags;
        addr = (void*) __get_free_pages(flags, cachep->gfporder);

        return addr;
}
```

Memory is then freed by `kmem_freepages()`, which calls `free_pages()` on the given cache's pages. Of course, the point of the slab layer is to refrain from allocating and freeing pages. In turn, the slab layer invokes the page allocation function only when there does not exist any partial or empty slabs in a given cache. The freeing function is called only when available memory grows low and the system is attempting to free memory, or when a cache is explicitly destroyed.

The slab layer is managed on a per-cache basis through a simple interface, which is exported to the entire kernel. The interface enables the creation and destruction of new caches and the allocation and freeing of objects within the caches. The sophisticated management of caches and the slabs within is entirely handled by the internals of the slab layer. After you create a cache, the slab layer works just like a specialized allocator for the specific type of object.

Slab Allocator Interface

A new cache is created via

```
struct kmem_cache * kmem_cache_create(const char *name,
                                      size_t size,
                                      size_t align,
                                      unsigned long flags,
                                      void (*ctor)(void *));
```

The first parameter is a string storing the name of the cache. The second parameter is the size of each element in the cache. The third parameter is the offset of the first object within a slab. This is done to ensure a particular alignment within the page. Normally, zero is sufficient, which results in the standard alignment. The `flags` parameter specifies optional settings controlling the cache's behavior. It can be zero, specifying no special behavior, or one or more of the following flags OR'ed together:

- `SLAB_HWCACHE_ALIGN`—This flag instructs the slab layer to align each object within a slab to a cache line. This prevents "false sharing" (two or more objects mapping to the same cache line despite existing at different addresses in memory). This improves performance but comes at a cost of increased memory footprint because the stricter alignment results in more wasted slack space. How large the increase in memory consumption is depends on the size of the objects and how they naturally align with respect to the system's cache lines. For frequently used caches in per-formance-critical code, setting this option is a good idea; otherwise, think twice.

- SLAB_POISON—This flag causes the slab layer to fill the slab with a known value (a5a5a5a5). This is called *poisoning* and is useful for catching access to uninitial-ized memory.

- SLAB_RED_ZONE—This flag causes the slab layer to insert "red zones" around the allocated memory to help detect buffer overruns.

- SLAB_PANIC—This flag causes the slab layer to panic if the allocation fails. This flag is useful when the allocation *must not fail*, as in, say, allocating the VMA structure cache (see Chapter 15, "The Process Address Space") during bootup.

- SLAB_CACHE_DMA—This flag instructs the slab layer to allocate each slab in DMA-able memory. This is needed if the allocated object is used for DMA and must reside in ZONE_DMA. Otherwise, you do not need this and you should not set it.

The final parameter, ctor, is a constructor for the cache. The constructor is called whenever new pages are added to the cache. In practice, caches in the Linux kernel do not often utilize a constructor. In fact, there once was a deconstructor parameter, too, but it was removed because no kernel code used it. You can pass NULL for this parameter.

On success, kmem_cache_create() returns a pointer to the created cache. Otherwise, it returns NULL. This function must not be called from interrupt context because it can sleep.

To destroy a cache, call

```
int kmem_cache_destroy(struct kmem_cache *cachep)
```

As the name implies, this function destroys the given cache. It is generally invoked from module shutdown code in modules that create their own caches. It must not be called from interrupt context because it may sleep. The caller of this function must ensure two conditions are true prior to invoking this function:

- All slabs in the cache are empty. Indeed, if an object in one of the slabs were still allocated and in use, how could the cache be destroyed?

- No one accesses the cache during (and obviously after) a call to kmem_cache_destroy(). The caller must ensure this synchronization.

On success, the function returns zero; it returns nonzero otherwise.

Allocating from the Cache

After a cache is created, an object is obtained from the cache via

```
void * kmem_cache_alloc(struct kmem_cache *cachep, gfp_t flags)
```

This function returns a pointer to an object from the given cache cachep. If no free objects are in any slabs in the cache, and the slab layer must obtain new pages via kmem_getpages(), the value of flags is passed to __get_free_pages(). These are the same flags we looked at earlier. You probably want GFP_KERNEL or GFP_ATOMIC.

To later free an object and return it to its originating slab, use the function

```
void kmem_cache_free(struct kmem_cache *cachep, void *objp)
```

This marks the object objp in cachep as free.

Example of Using the Slab Allocator

Let's look at a real-life example that uses the task_struct structure (the process descriptor). This code, in slightly more complicated form, is in kernel/fork.c.

First, the kernel has a global variable that stores a pointer to the task_struct cache:

```
struct kmem_cache *task_struct_cachep;
```

During kernel initialization, in fork_init(), defined in kernel/fork.c, the cache is created:

```
task_struct_cachep = kmem_cache_create("task_struct",
                                sizeof(struct task_struct),
                                ARCH_MIN_TASKALIGN,
                                SLAB_PANIC | SLAB_NOTRACK,
                                NULL);
```

This creates a cache named task_struct, which stores objects of type struct task_struct. The objects are created with an offset of ARCH_MIN_TASKALIGN bytes within the slab. This preprocessor definition is an architecture-specific value. It is usually defined as L1_CACHE_BYTES—the size in bytes of the L1 cache. There is no constructor. Note that the return value is not checked for NULL, which denotes failure, because the SLAB_PANIC flag was given. If the allocation fails, the slab allocator calls panic(). If you do not provide this flag, you must check the return! The SLAB_PANIC flag is used here because this is a requisite cache for system operation. (The machine is not much good without process descriptors.)

Each time a process calls fork(), a new process descriptor must be created (recall Chapter 3, "Process Management"). This is done in dup_task_struct(), which is called from do_fork():

```
struct task_struct *tsk;
```

```
tsk = kmem_cache_alloc(task_struct_cachep, GFP_KERNEL);
if (!tsk)
        return NULL;
```

After a task dies, if it has no children waiting on it, its process descriptor is freed and returned to the `task_struct_cachep` slab cache. This is done in `free_task_struct()` (in which `tsk` is the exiting task):

```
kmem_cache_free(task_struct_cachep, tsk);
```

Because process descriptors are part of the core kernel and always needed, the `task_struct_cachep` cache is never destroyed. If it were, however, you would destroy the cache via

```
int err;
```

```
err = kmem_cache_destroy(task_struct_cachep);
if (err)
        /* error destroying cache */
```

Easy enough? The slab layer handles all the low-level alignment, coloring, allocations, freeing, and reaping during low-memory conditions. If you frequently create many objects of the same type, consider using the slab cache. Definitely do not implement your own free list!

Statically Allocating on the Stack

In user-space, allocations such as some of the examples discussed thus far could have occurred on the stack because we knew the size of the allocation a priori. User-space is afforded the luxury of a large, dynamically growing stack, whereas the kernel has no such luxury—the kernel's stack is small and fixed. When each process is given a small, fixed stack, memory consumption is minimized, and the kernel need not burden itself with stack management code.

The size of the per-process kernel stacks depends on both the architecture and a compile-time option. Historically, the kernel stack has been two pages per process. This is usually 8KB for 32-bit architectures and 16KB for 64-bit architectures because they usually have 4KB and 8KB pages, respectively.

Single-Page Kernel Stacks

Early in the 2.6 kernel series, however, an option was introduced to move to single-page kernel stacks. When enabled, each process is given only a single page—4KB on 32-bit architectures and 8KB on 64-bit architectures. This was done for two reasons. First, it results in a page with less memory consumption per process. Second and most important is that as uptime increases, it becomes increasingly hard to find two physically contiguous unallocated pages. Physical memory becomes fragmented, and the resulting VM pressure from allocating a single new process is expensive.

There is one more complication. Keep with me: We have almost grasped the entire universe of knowledge with respect to kernel stacks. Now, each process's entire call chain has to fit in its kernel stack. Historically, however, interrupt handlers also used the kernel stack of the process they interrupted, thus they too had to fit. This was efficient and simple, but it placed even tighter constraints on the already meager kernel stack. When the stack moved to only a single page, interrupt handlers no longer fit.

To rectify this problem, the kernel developers implemented a new feature: interrupt stacks. Interrupt stacks provide a single per-processor stack used for interrupt handlers. With this option, interrupt handlers no longer share the kernel stack of the interrupted process. Instead, they use their own stacks. This consumes only a single page per processor.

To summarize, kernel stacks are either one or two pages, depending on compile-time configuration options. The stack can therefore range from 4KB to 16KB. Historically, interrupt handlers shared the stack of the interrupted process. When single page stacks are enabled, interrupt handlers are given their own stacks. In any case, unbounded recursion and `alloca()` are obviously not allowed.

Okay. Got it?

Playing Fair on the Stack

In any given function, you must keep stack usage to a minimum. There is no hard and fast rule, but you should keep the sum of all local (that is, automatic) variables in a particular function to a maximum of a couple hundred bytes. Performing a large static allocation on the stack, such as of a large array or structure, is dangerous. Otherwise, stack allocations are performed in the kernel just as in user-space. Stack overflows occur silently and will undoubtedly result in problems. Because the kernel does not make any effort to manage the stack, when the stack overflows, the excess data simply spills into whatever exists at the tail end of the stack. The first thing to eat it is the `thread_info` structure. (Recall from Chapter 3 that this structure is allocated at the end of each process's kernel stack.) Beyond the stack, any kernel data might lurk. At best, the machine will crash when the stack overflows. At worst, the overflow will silently corrupt data.

Therefore, it is wise to use a dynamic allocation scheme, such as one of those previously discussed in this chapter for any large memory allocations.

High Memory Mappings

By definition, pages in high memory might not be permanently mapped into the kernel's address space. Thus, pages obtained via `alloc_pages()` with the `__GFP_HIGHMEM` flag might not have a logical address.

On the x86 architecture, all physical memory beyond the 896MB mark is high memory and is not permanently or automatically mapped into the kernel's address space, despite x86 processors being capable of physically addressing up to 4GB (64GB with PAE[6]) of physical RAM. After they are allocated, these pages must be mapped into the

---

[6] *PAE stands for Physical Address Extension. It is a feature of x86 processors that enables them to physically address 36 bits (64GB) worth of memory, despite having only a 32-bit virtual address space.*

kernel's logical address space. On x86, pages in high memory are mapped somewhere between the 3GB and 4GB mark.

Permanent Mappings

To map a given `page` structure into the kernel's address space, use this function, declared in `<linux/highmem.h>`:

```
void *kmap(struct page *page)
```

This function works on either high or low memory. If the `page` structure belongs to a page in low memory, the page's virtual address is simply returned. If the page resides in high memory, a permanent mapping is created and the address is returned. The function may sleep, so `kmap()` works only in process context.

Because the number of permanent mappings are limited (if not, we would not be in this mess and could just permanently map all memory), high memory should be unmapped when no longer needed. This is done via the following function, which unmaps the given `page`:

```
void kunmap(struct page *page)
```

Temporary Mappings

For times when a mapping must be created but the current context cannot sleep, the kernel provides *temporary mappings* (which are also called *atomic mappings*). These are a set of reserved mappings that can hold a temporary mapping. The kernel can atomically map a high memory page into one of these reserved mappings. Consequently, a temporary mapping can be used in places that cannot sleep, such as interrupt handlers, because obtaining the mapping never blocks.

Setting up a temporary mapping is done via

```
void *kmap_atomic(struct page *page, enum km_type type)
```

The `type` parameter is one of the following enumerations, which describe the purpose of the temporary mapping. They are defined in `<asm-generic/kmap_types.h>`:

```
enum km_type {
        KM_BOUNCE_READ,
        KM_SKB_SUNRPC_DATA,
        KM_SKB_DATA_SOFTIRQ,
        KM_USER0,
        KM_USER1,
        KM_BIO_SRC_IRQ,
        KM_BIO_DST_IRQ,
        KM_PTE0,
        KM_PTE1,
        KM_PTE2,
        KM_IRQ0,
```

```
        KM_IRQ1,
        KM_SOFTIRQ0,
        KM_SOFTIRQ1,
        KM_SYNC_ICACHE,
        KM_SYNC_DCACHE,
        KM_UML_USERCOPY,
        KM_IRQ_PTE,
        KM_NMI,
        KM_NMI_PTE,
        KM_TYPE_NR
};
```

This function does not block and thus can be used in interrupt context and other places that cannot reschedule. It also disables kernel preemption, which is needed because the mappings are unique to each processor. (And a reschedule might change which task is running on which processor.)

The mapping is undone via

```
void kunmap_atomic(void *kvaddr, enum km_type type)
```

This function also does not block. In many architectures it does not do anything at all except enable kernel preemption, because a temporary mapping is valid only until the next temporary mapping. Thus, the kernel can just "forget about" the kmap_atomic() mapping, and kunmap_atomic() does not need to do anything special. The next atomic mapping then simply overwrites the previous one.

Per-CPU Allocations

Modern SMP-capable operating systems use per-CPU data—data that is unique to a given processor—extensively. Typically, per-CPU data is stored in an array. Each item in the array corresponds to a possible processor on the system. The current processor number indexes this array, which is how the 2.4 kernel handles per-CPU data. Nothing is wrong with this approach, so plenty of 2.6 kernel code still uses it. You declare the data as

```
unsigned long my_percpu[NR_CPUS];
```

Then you access it as

```
int cpu;
```

```
cpu = get_cpu();    /* get current processor and disable kernel preemption */
my_percpu[cpu]++;   /* ... or whatever */
printk("my_percpu on cpu=%d is %lu\n", cpu, my_percpu[cpu]);
put_cpu();          /* enable kernel preemption */
```

Note that no lock is required because this data is unique to the current processor. If no processor touches this data except the current, no concurrency concerns exist, and the current processor can safely access the data without lock.

Kernel preemption is the only concern with per-CPU data. Kernel preemption poses two problems, listed here:

- If your code is preempted and reschedules on another processor, the `cpu` variable is no longer valid because it points to the wrong processor. (In general, code cannot sleep after obtaining the current processor.)
- If another task preempts your code, it can concurrently access `my_percpu` on the *same* processor, which is a race condition.

Any fears are unwarranted, however, because the call `get_cpu()`, on top of returning the current processor number, also disables kernel preemption. The corresponding call to `put_cpu()` enables kernel preemption. Note that if you use a call to `smp_processor_id()` to get the current processor number, kernel preemption is not disabled; always use the aforementioned methods to remain safe.

The New `percpu` Interface

The 2.6 kernel introduced a new interface, known as *percpu*, for creating and manipulating per-CPU data. This interface generalizes the previous example. Creation and manipulation of per-CPU data is simplified with this new approach.

The previously discussed method of creating and accessing per-CPU data is still valid and accepted. This new interface, however, grew out of the needs for a simpler and more powerful method for manipulating per-CPU data on large symmetrical multiprocessing computers.

The header `<linux/percpu.h>` declares all the routines. You can find the actual definitions there, in `mm/slab.c`, and in `<asm/percpu.h>`.

Per-CPU Data at Compile-Time

Defining a per-CPU variable at compile time is quite easy:

```
DEFINE_PER_CPU(type, name);
```

This creates an instance of a variable of type `type`, named `name`, for each processor on the system. If you need a declaration of the variable elsewhere, to avoid compile warnings, the following macro is your friend:

```
DECLARE_PER_CPU(type, name);
```

You can manipulate the variables with the `get_cpu_var()` and `put_cpu_var()` routines. A call to `get_cpu_var()` returns an lvalue for the given variable on the current processor. It also disables preemption, which `put_cpu_var()` correspondingly enables.

```
get_cpu_var(name)++;    /* increment name on this processor */
put_cpu_var(name);      /* done; enable kernel preemption */
```

You can obtain the value of *another* processor's per-CPU data, too:

```
per_cpu(name, cpu)++;    /* increment name on the given processor */
```

You need to be careful with this approach because `per_cpu()` neither disables kernel preemption nor provides any sort of locking mechanism. The lockless nature of per-CPU data exists only if the current processor is the only manipulator of the data. If other processors touch other processors' data, you need locks. Be careful. Chapter 9, "An Introduction to Kernel Synchronization," and Chapter 10, "Kernel Synchronization Methods," discuss locking.

Another subtle note: These compile-time per-CPU examples do not work for modules because the linker actually creates them in a unique executable section (for the curious, `.data.percpu`). If you need to access per-CPU data from modules, or if you need to create such data dynamically, there is hope.

Per-CPU Data at Runtime

The kernel implements a dynamic allocator, similar to `kmalloc()`, for creating per-CPU data. This routine creates an instance of the requested memory for each processor on the systems. The prototypes are in `<linux/percpu.h>`:

```
void *alloc_percpu(type);  /* a macro */
void *__alloc_percpu(size_t size, size_t align);
void free_percpu(const void *);
```

The `alloc_percpu()` macro allocates one instance of an object of the given type for every processor on the system. It is a wrapper around `__alloc_percpu()`, which takes the actual number of bytes to allocate as a parameter and the number of bytes on which to align the allocation. The `alloc_percpu()` macro aligns the allocation on a byte boundary that is the natural alignment of the given type. Such alignment is the usual behavior. For example,

```
struct rabid_cheetah = alloc_percpu(struct rabid_cheetah);
```

is the same as

```
struct rabid_cheetah = __alloc_percpu(sizeof (struct rabid_cheetah),
                                __alignof__ (struct rabid_cheetah));
```

The `__alignof__` construct is a gcc feature that returns the required (or recommended, in the case of weird architectures with no alignment requirements) alignment in bytes for a given type or lvalue. Its syntax is just like that of `sizeof`. For example, the following would return four on x86:

```
__alignof__ (unsigned long)
```

When given an lvalue, the return value is the largest alignment that the lvalue might have. For example, an lvalue inside a structure could have a greater alignment requirement than if an instance of the same type were created outside of the structure, because of structure alignment requirements. Issues of alignment are further discussed in Chapter 19.

A corresponding call to `free_percpu()` frees the given data on all processors.

A call to `alloc_percpu()` or `__alloc_percpu()` returns a pointer, which is used to indirectly reference the dynamically created per-CPU data. The kernel provides two macros to make this easy:

```
get_cpu_var(ptr);    /* return a void pointer to this processor's copy of ptr */
put_cpu_var(ptr);    /* done; enable kernel preemption */
```

The `get_cpu_var()` macro returns a pointer to the specific instance of the current processor's data. It also disables kernel preemption, which a call to `put_cpu_var()` then enables.

Let's look at a full example of using these functions. Of course, this example is a bit silly because you would normally allocate the memory once (perhaps in some initialization function), use it in various places, and free it once (perhaps in some shutdown function). Nevertheless, this example should make usage quite clear:

```
void *percpu_ptr;
unsigned long *foo;

percpu_ptr = alloc_percpu(unsigned long);
if (!ptr)
        /* error allocating memory .. */

foo = get_cpu_var(percpu_ptr);
/* manipulate foo .. */
put_cpu_var(percpu_ptr);
```

Reasons for Using Per-CPU Data

There are several benefits to using per-CPU data. The first is the reduction in locking requirements. Depending on the semantics by which processors access the per-CPU data, you might not need any locking at all. Keep in mind that the *"only this processor accesses this data"* rule is only a programming convention. You need to ensure that the local processor accesses only its unique data. Nothing stops you from cheating.

Second, per-CPU data greatly reduces cache invalidation. This occurs as processors try to keep their caches in sync. If one processor manipulates data held in another processor's cache, that processor must flush or otherwise update its cache. Constant cache invalidation is called *thrashing the cache* and wreaks havoc on system performance. The use of per-CPU data keeps cache effects to a minimum because processors ideally access only their own data. The *percpu* interface cache-aligns all data to ensure that accessing one processor's data does not bring in another processor's data on the same cache line.

Consequently, the use of per-CPU data often removes (or at least minimizes) the need for locking. The only safety requirement for the use of per-CPU data is disabling kernel preemption, which is much cheaper than locking, and the interface does so automatically. Per-CPU data can safely be used from either interrupt or process context. Note, however, that you cannot sleep in the middle of accessing per-CPU data (or else you might end up on a different processor).

No one is currently required to use the new per-CPU interface. Doing things manually (with an array as originally discussed) is fine, as long as you disable kernel preemption. The new interface, however, is much easier to use and might gain additional optimizations in the future. If you do decide to use per-CPU data in your kernel code, consider the new interface. One caveat *against* its use is that it is not backward compatible with earlier kernels.

Picking an Allocation Method

With myriad allocations methods and approaches, it is not always obvious how to get at memory in the kernel—but it sure is important! If you need contiguous physical pages, use one of the low-level page allocators or `kmalloc()`. This is the standard manner of allocating memory from within the kernel, and most likely, how you will allocate most of your memory. Recall that the two most common flags given to these functions are `GFP_ATOMIC` and `GFP_KERNEL`. Specify the `GFP_ATOMIC` flag to perform a high priority allocation that will not sleep. This is a requirement of interrupt handlers and other pieces of code that cannot sleep. Code that can sleep, such as process context code that does not hold a spin lock, should use `GFP_KERNEL`. This flag specifies an allocation that can sleep, if needed, to obtain the requested memory.

If you want to allocate from high memory, use `alloc_pages()`. The `alloc_pages()` function returns a `struct page` and not a pointer to a logical address. Because high memory might not be mapped, the only way to access it might be via the corresponding `struct page` structure. To obtain an actual pointer, use `kmap()` to map the high memory into the kernel's logical address space.

If you do not need physically contiguous pages—only virtually contiguous—use `vmalloc()`, although bear in mind the slight performance hit taken with `vmalloc()` over `kmalloc()`. The `vmalloc()` function allocates kernel memory that is virtually contiguous but not, per se, physically contiguous. It performs this feat much as user-space allocations do, by mapping chunks of physical memory into a contiguous logical address space.

If you are creating and destroying many large data structures, consider setting up a slab cache. The slab layer maintains a per-processor object cache (a free list), which might greatly enhance object allocation and deallocation performance. Rather than frequently allocate and free memory, the slab layer stores a cache of already allocated objects for you. When you need a new chunk of memory to hold your data structure, the slab layer often does not need to allocate more memory and instead simply can return an object from the cache.

Conclusion

In this chapter, we studied how the Linux kernel manages memory. We looked at the various units and categorizations of memory, including bytes, pages, and zones. (Chapter 15 looks at a fourth categorization, the process address space.) We then discussed various mechanisms for obtaining memory, including the page allocator and the slab allocator. Obtaining memory inside the kernel is not always easy because you must be careful to ensure that the allocation process respects certain kernel conditions, such as an inability to block or access the filesystem. To that end, we discussed the gfp flags and the various use cases and requirements for each flag. The relative difficulty in getting hold of memory in the kernel is one of the largest differences between kernel and user-space development. While much of this chapter discussed the family of interfaces used to obtain memory, you should now also wield an understanding of *why* memory allocation in a kernel is difficult.

With this chapter under our belt, the next chapter discusses the virtual filesystem (VFS), the kernel subsystem responsible for managing filesystems and providing a unified, consistent file API to user-space applications. Onward!

13

The Virtual Filesystem

The *Virtual Filesystem* (sometimes called the *Virtual File Switch* or more commonly simply the *VFS*) is the subsystem of the kernel that implements the file and filesystem-related interfaces provided to user-space programs. All filesystems rely on the VFS to enable them not only to coexist, but also to interoperate. This enables programs to use standard Unix system calls to read and write to different filesystems, even on different media, as shown in Figure 13.1.

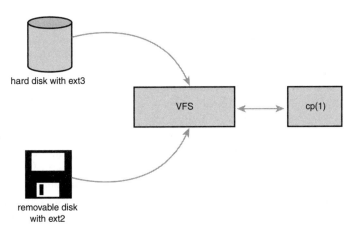

Figure 13.1   The VFS in action: Using the cp(1) utility to move data from a hard disk mounted as ext3 to a removable disk mounted as ext2. Two different filesystems, two different media, one VFS.

Common Filesystem Interface

The VFS is the glue that enables system calls such as open(), read(), and write()to work regardless of the filesystem or underlying physical medium. These days, that might not sound novel—we have long been taking such a feature for granted—but it is a nontrivial feat for such generic system calls to work across many diverse filesystems and vary-ing media. More so, the system calls work *between* these different filesystems and media—we can use standard system calls to copy or move files from one filesystem to another. In older operating systems, such as DOS, this would never have worked; any access to a non-native filesystem required special tools. It is only because modern operating systems, such as Linux, abstract access to the filesystems via a virtual interface that such interoperation and generic access is possible.

New filesystems and new varieties of storage media can find their way into Linux, and programs need not be rewritten or even recompiled. In this chapter, we will discuss the VFS, which provides the abstraction allowing myriad filesystems to behave as one. In the next chapter, we will discuss the block I/O layer, which allows various storage devices—CD to Blu-ray discs to hard drives to CompactFlash. Together, the VFS and the block I/O layer provide the abstractions, interfaces, and glue that allow user-space programs to issue generic system calls to access files via a uniform naming policy on any filesystem, which itself exists on any storage medium.

Filesystem Abstraction Layer

Such a generic interface for any type of filesystem is feasible only because the kernel implements an abstraction layer around its low-level filesystem interface. This abstraction layer enables Linux to support different filesystems, even if they differ in supported fea-tures or behavior. This is possible because the VFS provides a common file model that can represent any filesystem's general feature set and behavior. Of course, it is biased toward Unix-style filesystems. (You see what constitutes a Unix-style filesystem later in this chap-ter.) Regardless, wildly differing filesystem types are still supportable in Linux, from DOS's FAT to Windows's NTFS to many Unix-style and Linux-specific filesystems.

The abstraction layer works by defining the basic conceptual interfaces and data struc-tures that all filesystems support. The filesystems mold their view of concepts such as "*this is how I open files*" and "*this is what a directory is to me*" to match the expectations of the VFS. The actual filesystem code hides the implementation details. To the VFS layer and the rest of the kernel, however, each filesystem looks the same. They all support notions such as files and directories, and they all support operations such as creating and deleting files.

The result is a general abstraction layer that enables the kernel to support many types of filesystems easily and cleanly. The filesystems are programmed to provide the abstracted interfaces and data structures the VFS expects; in turn, the kernel easily works with any filesystem and the exported user-space interface seamlessly works on any filesystem.

In fact, nothing in the kernel needs to understand the underlying details of the filesys-tems, except the filesystems themselves. For example, consider a simple user-space pro-gram that does

```
ret = write (fd, buf, len);
```

This system call writes the `len` bytes pointed to by `buf` into the current position in the file represented by the file descriptor `fd`. This system call is first handled by a generic `sys_write()` system call that determines the actual file writing method for the filesystem on which `fd` resides. The generic write system call then invokes this method, which is part of the filesystem implementation, to write the data to the media (or whatever this filesystem does on write). Figure 13.2 shows the flow from user-space's `write()` call through the data arriving on the physical media. On one side of the system call is the generic VFS interface, providing the frontend to user-space; on the other side of the system call is the filesystem-specific backend, dealing with the implementation details. The rest of this chapter looks at how the VFS achieves this abstraction and provides its interfaces.

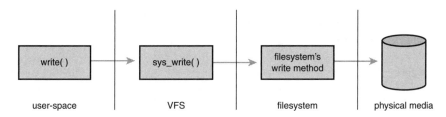

Figure 13.2   The flow of data from user-space issuing a `write()` call, through the VFS's generic system call, into the filesystem's specific write method, and finally arriving at the physical media.

Unix Filesystems

Historically, Unix has provided four basic filesystem-related abstractions: files, directory entries, inodes, and mount points.

A *filesystem* is a hierarchical storage of data adhering to a specific structure. Filesystems contain files, directories, and associated control information. Typical operations performed on filesystems are creation, deletion, and mounting. In Unix, filesystems are mounted at a specific mount point in a global hierarchy known as a *namespace*.[1] This enables all mounted filesystems to appear as entries in a single tree. Contrast this single, unified tree with the behavior of DOS and Windows, which break the file namespace up into drive letters, such as `c:`. This breaks the namespace up among device and partition boundaries, "leaking" hardware details into the filesystem abstraction. As this delineation may be arbitrary and even confusing to the user, it is inferior to Linux's unified namespace.

A *file* is an ordered string of bytes. The first byte marks the beginning of the file, and the last byte marks the end of the file. Each file is assigned a human-readable name for identification by both the system and the user. Typical file operations are read, write,

---

[1] *Recently, Linux has made this hierarchy per-process, to give a unique namespace to each process. Because each process inherits its parent's namespace (unless you specify otherwise), there is seemingly one global namespace.*

create, and delete. The Unix concept of the file is in stark contrast to record-oriented filesystems, such as OpenVMS's Files-11. Record-oriented filesystems provide a richer, more structured representation of files than Unix's simple byte-stream abstraction, at the cost of simplicity and flexibility.

Files are organized in directories. A *directory* is analogous to a folder and usually contains related files. Directories can also contain other directories, called subdirectories. In this fashion, directories may be nested to form paths. Each component of a path is called a *directory entry*. A path example is /home/wolfman/butter—the root directory /, the directories home and wolfman, and the file butter are all directory entries, called *dentries*. In Unix, directories are actually normal files that simply list the files contained therein. Because a directory is a file to the VFS, the same operations performed on files can be performed on directories.

Unix systems separate the concept of a file from any associated information about it, such as access permissions, size, owner, creation time, and so on. This information is sometimes called *file metadata* (that is, data about the file's data) and is stored in a separate data structure from the file, called the *inode*. This name is short for *index node*, although these days the term *inode* is much more ubiquitous.

All this information is tied together with the filesystem's own control information, which is stored in the *superblock*. The superblock is a data structure containing information about the filesystem as a whole. Sometimes the collective data is referred to as *filesystem metadata*. Filesystem metadata includes information about both the individual files and the filesystem as a whole.

Traditionally, Unix filesystems implement these notions as part of their physical on-disk layout. For example, file information is stored as an inode in a separate block on the disk; directories are files; control information is stored centrally in a superblock, and so on. The Unix file concepts are *physically mapped* on to the storage medium. The Linux VFS is designed to work with filesystems that understand and implement such concepts. Non-Unix filesystems, such as FAT or NTFS, still work in Linux, but their filesystem code must provide the appearance of these concepts. For example, even if a filesystem does not support distinct inodes, it must assemble the inode data structure in memory as if it did. Or if a filesystem treats directories as a special object, to the VFS they must represent directories as mere files. Often, this involves some special processing done on-the-fly by the non-Unix filesystems to cope with the Unix paradigm and the requirements of the VFS. Such filesystems still work, however, and the overhead is not unreasonable.

VFS Objects and Their Data Structures

The VFS is object-oriented.[2] A family of data structures represents the common file model. These data structures are akin to objects. Because the kernel is programmed strictly in C, without the benefit of a language directly supporting object-oriented paradigms, the data structures are represented as C structures. The structures contain both data and pointers to filesystem-implemented functions that operate on the data.

The four primary object types of the VFS are

- The *superblock* object, which represents a specific mounted filesystem.
- The *inode* object, which represents a specific file.
- The *dentry* object, which represents a directory entry, which is a single component of a path.
- The *file* object, which represents an open file as associated with a process.

Note that because the VFS treats directories as normal files, there is not a specific directory object. Recall from earlier in this chapter that a dentry represents a component in a path, which might include a regular file. In other words, a dentry is not the same as a directory, but a directory is just another kind of file. Got it?

An *operations* object is contained within each of these primary objects. These objects describe the methods that the kernel invokes against the primary objects:

- The `super_operations` object, which contains the methods that the kernel can invoke on a specific filesystem, such as `write_inode()` and `sync_fs()`
- The `inode_operations` object, which contains the methods that the kernel can invoke on a specific file, such as `create()` and `link()`
- The `dentry_operations` object, which contains the methods that the kernel can invoke on a specific directory entry, such as `d_compare()` and `d_delete()`
- The `file_operations` object, which contains the methods that a process can invoke on an open file, such as `read()` and `write()`

The operations objects are implemented as a structure of pointers to functions that operate on the parent object. For many methods, the objects can inherit a generic function if basic functionality is sufficient. Otherwise, the specific instance of the particular filesystem fills in the pointers with its own filesystem-specific methods.

---

[2] People often miss this, or even deny it, but there are many examples of object-oriented programming in the kernel. Although the kernel developers may shun C++ and other explicitly object-oriented languages, thinking in terms of objects is often useful. The VFS is a good example of how to do clean and efficient OOP in C, which is a language that lacks any OOP constructs.

Again, note that *objects* refer to structures—not explicit class types, such as those in C++ or Java. These structures, however, represent specific instances of an object, their associated data, and methods to operate on themselves. They are very much objects.

The VFS loves structures, and it is comprised of a couple more than the primary objects previously discussed. Each registered filesystem is represented by a `file_system_type` structure. This object describes the filesystem and its capabilities. Furthermore, each mount point is represented by the `vfsmount` structure. This structure contains information about the mount point, such as its location and mount flags.

Finally, two per-process structures describe the filesystem and files associated with a process. They are, respectively, the `fs_struct` structure and the `file` structure.

The rest of this chapter discusses these objects and the role they play in implementing the VFS layer.

The Superblock Object

The superblock object is implemented by each filesystem and is used to store information describing that specific filesystem. This object usually corresponds to the *filesystem superblock* or the *filesystem control block*, which is stored in a special sector on disk (hence the object's name). Filesystems that are not disk-based (a virtual memory–based filesystem, such as *sysfs*, for example) generate the superblock on-the-fly and store it in memory.

The superblock object is represented by struct `super_block` and defined in `<linux/fs.h>`. Here is what it looks like, with comments describing each entry:

```
struct super_block {
        struct list_head        s_list;             /* list of all superblocks */
        dev_t                   s_dev;              /* identifier */
        unsigned long           s_blocksize;        /* block size in bytes */
        unsigned char           s_blocksize_bits;   /* block size in bits */
        unsigned char           s_dirt;             /* dirty flag */
        unsigned long long      s_maxbytes;         /* max file size */
        struct file_system_type s_type;             /* filesystem type */
        struct super_operations s_op;               /* superblock methods */
        struct dquot_operations *dq_op;             /* quota methods */
        struct quotactl_ops     *s_qcop;            /* quota control methods */
        struct export_operations *s_export_op;      /* export methods */
        unsigned long           s_flags;            /* mount flags */
        unsigned long           s_magic;            /* filesystem's magic number */
        struct dentry           *s_root;            /* directory mount point */
        struct rw_semaphore     s_umount;           /* unmount semaphore */
        struct semaphore        s_lock;             /* superblock semaphore */
        int                     s_count;            /* superblock ref count */
        int                     s_need_sync;        /* not-yet-synced flag */
        atomic_t                s_active;           /* active reference count */
        void                    *s_security;        /* security module */
        struct xattr_handler    **s_xattr;          /* extended attribute handlers */
```

```
    struct list_head        s_inodes;         /* list of inodes */
    struct list_head        s_dirty;          /* list of dirty inodes */
    struct list_head        s_io;             /* list of writebacks */
    struct list_head        s_more_io;        /* list of more writeback */
    struct hlist_head       s_anon;           /* anonymous dentries */
    struct list_head        s_files;          /* list of assigned files */
    struct list_head        s_dentry_lru;     /* list of unused dentries */
    int                     s_nr_dentry_unused; /* number of dentries on list */
    struct block_device     *s_bdev;          /* associated block device */
    struct mtd_info         *s_mtd;           /* memory disk information */
    struct list_head        s_instances;      /* instances of this fs */
    struct quota_info       s_dquot;          /* quota-specific options */
    int                     s_frozen;         /* frozen status */
    wait_queue_head_t       s_wait_unfrozen;  /* wait queue on freeze */
    char                    s_id[32];         /* text name */
    void                    *s_fs_info;       /* filesystem-specific info */
    fmode_t                 s_mode;           /* mount permissions */
    struct semaphore        s_vfs_rename_sem; /* rename semaphore */
    u32                     s_time_gran;      /* granularity of timestamps */
    char                    *s_subtype;       /* subtype name */
    char                    *s_options;       /* saved mount options */
};
```

The code for creating, managing, and destroying superblock objects lives in fs/super.c. A superblock object is created and initialized via the alloc_super() function. When mounted, a filesystem invokes this function, reads its superblock off of the disk, and fills in its superblock object.

Superblock Operations

The most important item in the superblock object is s_op, which is a pointer to the superblock operations table. The superblock operations table is represented by struct super_operations and is defined in <linux/fs.h>. It looks like this:

```
struct super_operations {
  struct inode *(*alloc_inode)(struct super_block *sb);
  void (*destroy_inode)(struct inode *);
  void (*dirty_inode) (struct inode *);
  int (*write_inode) (struct inode *, int);
  void (*drop_inode) (struct inode *);
  void (*delete_inode) (struct inode *);
  void (*put_super) (struct super_block *);
  void (*write_super) (struct super_block *);
  int (*sync_fs)(struct super_block *sb, int wait);
  int (*freeze_fs) (struct super_block *);
  int (*unfreeze_fs) (struct super_block *);
```

```
int (*statfs) (struct dentry *, struct kstatfs *);
int (*remount_fs) (struct super_block *, int *, char *);
void (*clear_inode) (struct inode *);
void (*umount_begin) (struct super_block *);
int (*show_options)(struct seq_file *, struct vfsmount *);
int (*show_stats)(struct seq_file *, struct vfsmount *);
ssize_t (*quota_read)(struct super_block *, int, char *, size_t, loff_t);
ssize_t (*quota_write)(struct super_block *, int, const char *, size_t, loff_t);
int (*bdev_try_to_free_page)(struct super_block*, struct page*, gfp_t);
};
```

Each item in this structure is a pointer to a function that operates on a superblock object. The superblock operations perform low-level operations on the filesystem and its inodes.

When a filesystem needs to perform an operation on its superblock, it follows the pointers from its superblock object to the desired method. For example, if a filesystem wanted to write to its superblock, it would invoke

```
sb->s_op->write_super(sb);
```

In this call, `sb` is a pointer to the filesystem's superblock. Following that pointer into `s_op` yields the superblock operations table and ultimately the desired `write_super()` function, which is then invoked. Note how the `write_super()` call must be passed a superblock, despite the method being associated with one. This is because of the lack of object-oriented support in C. In C++, a call such as the following would suffice:

```
sb.write_super();
```

In C, there is no way for the method to easily obtain its parent, so you have to pass it.

Let's take a look at some of the superblock operations that are specified by `super_operations`:

- `struct inode * alloc_inode(struct super_block *sb)`

  Creates and initializes a new inode object under the given superblock.

- `void destroy_inode(struct inode *inode)`

  Deallocates the given inode.

- `void dirty_inode(struct inode *inode)`

  Invoked by the VFS when an inode is dirtied (modified). Journaling filesystems such as ext3 and ext4 use this function to perform journal updates.

- `void write_inode(struct inode *inode, int wait)`

  Writes the given inode to disk. The `wait` parameter specifies whether the operation should be synchronous.

- `void drop_inode(struct inode *inode)`

Called by the VFS when the last reference to an inode is dropped. Normal Unix filesystems do not define this function, in which case the VFS simply deletes the inode.

- **void delete_inode(struct inode *inode)**

Deletes the given inode from the disk.

- **void put_super(struct super_block *sb)**

Called by the VFS on unmount to release the given superblock object. The caller must hold the **s_lock** lock.

- **void write_super(struct super_block *sb)**

Updates the on-disk superblock with the specified superblock. The VFS uses this function to synchronize a modified in-memory superblock with the disk. The caller must hold the **s_lock** lock.

- **int sync_fs(struct super_block *sb, int wait)**

Synchronizes filesystem metadata with the on-disk filesystem. The **wait** parameter specifies whether the operation is synchronous.

- **void write_super_lockfs(struct super_block *sb)**

Prevents changes to the filesystem, and then updates the on-disk superblock with the specified superblock. It is currently used by LVM (the Logical Volume Manager).

- **void unlockfs(struct super_block *sb)**

Unlocks the filesystem against changes as done by **write_super_lockfs()**.

- **int statfs(struct super_block *sb, struct statfs *statfs)**

Called by the VFS to obtain filesystem statistics. The statistics related to the given filesystem are placed in **statfs**.

- **int remount_fs(struct super_block *sb, int *flags, char *data)**

Called by the VFS when the filesystem is remounted with new mount options. The caller must hold the **s_lock** lock.

- **void clear_inode(struct inode *inode)**

Called by the VFS to release the inode and clear any pages containing related data.

- **void umount_begin(struct super_block *sb)**

Called by the VFS to interrupt a mount operation. It is used by network filesystems, such as NFS.

All these functions are invoked by the VFS, in process context. All except **dirty_inode()** may all block if needed.

Some of these functions are optional; a specific filesystem can then set its value in the superblock operations structure to **NULL**. If the associated pointer is **NULL**, the VFS either calls a generic function or does nothing, depending on the operation.

The Inode Object

The inode object represents all the information needed by the kernel to manipulate a file or directory. For Unix-style filesystems, this information is simply read from the on-disk inode. If a filesystem does not have inodes, however, the filesystem must obtain the information from wherever it is stored on the disk. Filesystems without inodes generally store file-specific information as part of the file; unlike Unix-style filesystems, they do not separate file data from its control information. Some modern filesystems do neither and store file metadata as part of an on-disk database. Whatever the case, the inode object is constructed in memory in whatever manner is applicable to the filesystem.

The inode object is represented by `struct inode` and is defined in `<linux/fs.h>`. Here is the structure, with comments describing each entry:

```
struct inode {
        struct hlist_node       i_hash;                 /* hash list */
        struct list_head        i_list;                 /* list of inodes */
        struct list_head        i_sb_list;              /* list of superblocks */
        struct list_head        i_dentry;               /* list of dentries */
        unsigned long           i_ino;                  /* inode number */
        atomic_t                i_count;                /* reference counter */
        unsigned int            i_nlink;                /* number of hard links */
        uid_t                   i_uid;                  /* user id of owner */
        gid_t                   i_gid;                  /* group id of owner */
        kdev_t                  i_rdev;                 /* real device node */
        u64                     i_version;              /* versioning number */
        loff_t                  i_size;                 /* file size in bytes */
        seqcount_t              i_size_seqcount;        /* serializer for i_size */
        struct timespec         i_atime;                /* last access time */
        struct timespec         i_mtime;                /* last modify time */
        struct timespec         i_ctime;                /* last change time */
        unsigned int            i_blkbits;              /* block size in bits */
        blkcnt_t                i_blocks;               /* file size in blocks */
        unsigned short          i_bytes;                /* bytes consumed */
        umode_t                 i_mode;                 /* access permissions */
        spinlock_t              i_lock;                 /* spinlock */
        struct rw_semaphore     i_alloc_sem;            /* nests inside of i_sem */
        struct semaphore        i_sem;                  /* inode semaphore */
        struct inode_operations *i_op;                  /* inode ops table */
        struct file_operations  *i_fop;                 /* default inode ops */
        struct super_block      *i_sb;                  /* associated superblock */
        struct file_lock        *i_flock;               /* file lock list */
        struct address_space    *i_mapping;             /* associated mapping */
        struct address_space    i_data;                 /* mapping for device */
        struct dquot            *i_dquot[MAXQUOTAS]; /* disk quotas for inode */
        struct list_head        i_devices;              /* list of block devices */
        union {
```

```
        struct pipe_inode_info  *i_pipe;         /* pipe information */
        struct block_device     *i_bdev;         /* block device driver */
        struct cdev             *i_cdev;         /* character device driver */
    };
    unsigned long          i_dnotify_mask;   /* directory notify mask */
    struct dnotify_struct  *i_dnotify;       /* dnotify */
    struct list_head       inotify_watches;  /* inotify watches */
    struct mutex           inotify_mutex;    /* protects inotify_watches */
    unsigned long          i_state;          /* state flags */
    unsigned long          dirtied_when;     /* first dirtying time */
    unsigned int           i_flags;          /* filesystem flags */
    atomic_t               i_writecount;     /* count of writers */
    void                   *i_security;      /* security module */
    void                   *i_private;       /* fs private pointer */
};
```

An inode represents each file on a filesystem, but the inode object is constructed in memory only as files are accessed. This includes special files, such as device files or pipes. Consequently, some of the entries in `struct inode` are related to these special files. For example, the `i_pipe` entry points to a named pipe data structure, `i_bdev` points to a block device structure, and `i_cdev` points to a character device structure. These three pointers are stored in a union because a given inode can represent only one of these (or none of them) at a time.

It might occur that a given filesystem does not support a property represented in the inode object. For example, some filesystems might not record an access timestamp. In that case, the filesystem is free to implement the feature however it sees fit; it can store zero for `i_atime`, make `i_atime` equal to `i_mtime`, update `i_atime` in memory but never flush it back to disk, or whatever else the filesystem implementer decides.

Inode Operations

As with the superblock operations, the `inode_operations` member is important. It describes the filesystem's implemented functions that the VFS can invoke on an inode. As with the superblock, inode operations are invoked via

```
i->i_op->truncate(i)
```

In this call, `i` is a reference to a particular inode. In this case, the `truncate()` operation defined by the filesystem on which `i` exists is called on the given inode. The `inode_operations` structure is defined in `<linux/fs.h>`:

```
struct inode_operations {
    int (*create) (struct inode *,struct dentry *,int, struct nameidata *);
    struct dentry * (*lookup) (struct inode *,struct dentry *, struct nameidata *);
    int (*link) (struct dentry *,struct inode *,struct dentry *);
    int (*unlink) (struct inode *,struct dentry *);
    int (*symlink) (struct inode *,struct dentry *,const char *);
```

```
int (*mkdir) (struct inode *,struct dentry *,int);
int (*rmdir) (struct inode *,struct dentry *);
int (*mknod) (struct inode *,struct dentry *,int,dev_t);
int (*rename) (struct inode *, struct dentry *,
               struct inode *, struct dentry *);
int (*readlink) (struct dentry *, char __user *,int);
void * (*follow_link) (struct dentry *, struct nameidata *);
void (*put_link) (struct dentry *, struct nameidata *, void *);
void (*truncate) (struct inode *);
int (*permission) (struct inode *, int);
int (*setattr) (struct dentry *, struct iattr *);
int (*getattr) (struct vfsmount *mnt, struct dentry *, struct kstat *);
int (*setxattr) (struct dentry *, const char *,const void *,size_t,int);
ssize_t (*getxattr) (struct dentry *, const char *, void *, size_t);
ssize_t (*listxattr) (struct dentry *, char *, size_t);
int (*removexattr) (struct dentry *, const char *);
void (*truncate_range)(struct inode *, loff_t, loff_t);
long (*fallocate)(struct inode *inode, int mode, loff_t offset,
                  loff_t len);
int (*fiemap)(struct inode *, struct fiemap_extent_info *, u64 start,
              u64 len);
};
```

The following interfaces constitute the various functions that the VFS may perform, or ask a specific filesystem to perform, on a given inode:

- `int create(struct inode *dir, struct dentry *dentry, int mode)`

  The VFS calls this function from the `creat()` and `open()` system calls to create a new inode associated with the given dentry object with the specified initial access mode.

- `struct dentry * lookup(struct inode *dir, struct dentry *dentry)`

  This function searches a directory for an inode corresponding to a filename specified in the given dentry.

- `int link(struct dentry *old_dentry,`
  `        struct inode *dir,`
  `        struct dentry *dentry)`

  Invoked by the `link()` system call to create a hard link of the file `old_dentry` in the directory `dir` with the new filename `dentry`.

- `int unlink(struct inode *dir,`
  `          struct dentry *dentry)`

  Called from the `unlink()` system call to remove the inode specified by the directory entry `dentry` from the directory `dir`.

- ```
  int symlink(struct inode *dir,
              struct dentry *dentry,
              const char *symname)
  ```
  Called from the `symlink()` system call to create a symbolic link named `symname` to the file represented by `dentry` in the directory `dir`.

- ```
  int mkdir(struct inode *dir,
            struct dentry *dentry,
            int mode)
  ```
  Called from the `mkdir()` system call to create a new directory with the given initial mode.

- ```
  int rmdir(struct inode *dir,
            struct dentry *dentry)
  ```
  Called by the `rmdir()` system call to remove the directory referenced by `dentry` from the directory `dir`.

- ```
  int mknod(struct inode *dir,
            struct dentry *dentry,
            int mode, dev_t rdev)
  ```
  Called by the `mknod()` system call to create a special file (device file, named pipe, or socket). The file is referenced by the device `rdev` and the directory entry `dentry` in the directory `dir`. The initial permissions are given via `mode`.

- ```
  int rename(struct inode *old_dir,
             struct dentry *old_dentry,
             struct inode *new_dir,
             struct dentry *new_dentry)
  ```
  Called by the VFS to move the file specified by `old_dentry` from the `old_dir` directory to the directory `new_dir`, with the filename specified by `new_dentry`.

- ```
  int readlink(struct dentry *dentry,
               char *buffer, int buflen)
  ```
  Called by the `readlink()` system call to copy at most `buflen` bytes of the full path associated with the symbolic link specified by `dentry` into the specified buffer.

- ```
  int follow_link(struct dentry *dentry,
                  struct nameidata *nd)
  ```
  Called by the VFS to translate a symbolic link to the inode to which it points. The link pointed at by `dentry` is translated, and the result is stored in the `nameidata` structure pointed at by `nd`.

- ```
  int put_link(struct dentry *dentry,
               struct nameidata *nd)
  ```
  Called by the VFS to clean up after a call to `follow_link()`.

- `void truncate(struct inode *inode)`

  Called by the VFS to modify the size of the given file. Before invocation, the inode's `i_size` field must be set to the desired new size.

- `int permission(struct inode *inode, int mask)`

  Checks whether the specified access mode is allowed for the file referenced by `inode`. This function returns zero if the access is allowed and a negative error code otherwise. Most filesystems set this field to `NULL` and use the generic VFS method, which simply compares the mode bits in the inode's objects to the given mask. More complicated filesystems, such as those supporting access control lists (ACLs), have a specific `permission()` method.

- `int setattr(struct dentry *dentry,`
  `            struct iattr *attr)`

  Called from `notify_change()` to notify a "change event" after an inode has been modified.

- `int getattr(struct vfsmount *mnt,`
  `            struct dentry *dentry,`
  `            struct kstat *stat)`

  Invoked by the VFS upon noticing that an inode needs to be refreshed from disk. Extended attributes allow the association of key/values pairs with files.

- `int setxattr(struct dentry *dentry,`
  `             const char *name,`
  `             const void *value,`
  `             size_t size, int flags)`

  Used by the VFS to set the extended attribute `name` to the value `value` on the file referenced by `dentry`.

- `ssize_t getxattr(struct dentry *dentry,`
  `                 const char *name,`
  `                 void *value, size_t size)`

  Used by the VFS to copy into `value` the value of the extended attribute `name` for the specified file.

- `ssize_t listxattr(struct dentry *dentry,`
  `                  char *list, size_t size)`

  Copies the list of all attributes for the specified file into the buffer `list`.

- `int removexattr(struct dentry *dentry,`
  `                const char *name)`

  Removes the given attribute from the given file.

The Dentry Object

As discussed, the VFS treats directories as a type of file. In the path /bin/vi, both bin and
vi are files—bin being the special directory file and vi being a regular file. An inode
object represents each of these components. Despite this useful unification, the VFS often
needs to perform directory-specific operations, such as path name lookup. Path name
lookup involves translating each component of a path, ensuring it is valid, and following it
to the next component.

To facilitate this, the VFS employs the concept of a directory entry (dentry). A *dentry* is
a specific component in a path. Using the previous example, /, bin, and vi are all dentry
objects. The first two are directories and the last is a regular file. This is an important
point: Dentry objects are *all* components in a path, including files. Resolving a path and
walking its components is a nontrivial exercise, time-consuming and heavy on string
operations, which are expensive to execute and cumbersome to code. The dentry object
makes the whole process easier.

Dentries might also include mount points. In the path /mnt/cdrom/foo, the components /, mnt, cdrom, and foo are all dentry objects. The VFS constructs dentry objects on-
the-fly, as needed, when performing directory operations.

Dentry objects are represented by struct dentry and defined in <linux/dcache.h>.
Here is the structure, with comments describing each member:

```
struct dentry {
        atomic_t                d_count;    /* usage count */
        unsigned int            d_flags;    /* dentry flags */
        spinlock_t              d_lock;     /* per-dentry lock */
        int                     d_mounted;  /* is this a mount point? */
        struct inode            *d_inode;   /* associated inode */
        struct hlist_node       d_hash;     /* list of hash table entries */
        struct dentry           *d_parent;  /* dentry object of parent */
        struct qstr             d_name;     /* dentry name */
        struct list_head        d_lru;      /* unused list */
        union {
            struct list_head    d_child;    /* list of dentries within */
            struct rcu_head     d_rcu;      /* RCU locking */
        } d_u;
        struct list_head        d_subdirs;  /* subdirectories */
        struct list_head        d_alias;    /* list of alias inodes */
        unsigned long           d_time;     /* revalidate time */
        struct dentry_operations *d_op;     /* dentry operations table */
        struct super_block      *d_sb;      /* superblock of file */
        void                    *d_fsdata;  /* filesystem-specific data */
        unsigned char           d_iname[DNAME_INLINE_LEN_MIN]; /* short name */
};
```

Unlike the previous two objects, the dentry object does not correspond to any sort of
on-disk data structure. The VFS creates it on-the-fly from a string representation of a path

name. Because the dentry object is not physically stored on the disk, no flag in `struct dentry` specifies whether the object is modified (that is, whether it is dirty and needs to be written back to disk).

Dentry State

A valid dentry object can be in one of three states: used, unused, or negative.

A used dentry corresponds to a valid inode (`d_inode` points to an associated inode) and indicates that there are one or more users of the object (`d_count` is positive). A used dentry is in use by the VFS and points to valid data and, thus, cannot be discarded.

An unused dentry corresponds to a valid inode (`d_inode` points to an inode), but the VFS is not currently using the dentry object (`d_count` is zero). Because the dentry object still points to a valid object, the dentry is kept around—cached—in case it is needed again. Because the dentry has not been destroyed prematurely, the dentry need not be re-created if it is needed in the future, and path name lookups can complete quicker than if the dentry was not cached. If it is necessary to reclaim memory, however, the dentry can be discarded because it is not in active use.

A negative dentry is not associated with a valid inode (`d_inode` is `NULL`) because either the inode was deleted or the path name was never correct to begin with. The dentry is kept around, however, so that future lookups are resolved quickly. For example, consider a daemon that continually tries to open and read a config file that is not present. The `open()` system calls continually returns `ENOENT`, but not until after the kernel constructs the path, walks the on-disk directory structure, and verifies the file's inexistence. Because even this failed lookup is expensive, caching the "negative" results are worthwhile. Although a negative dentry is useful, it can be destroyed if memory is at a premium because nothing is actually using it.

A dentry object can also be freed, sitting in the slab object cache, as discussed in the previous chapter. In that case, there is no valid reference to the dentry object in any VFS or any filesystem code.

The Dentry Cache

After the VFS layer goes through the trouble of resolving each element in a path name into a dentry object and arriving at the end of the path, it would be quite wasteful to throw away all that work. Instead, the kernel caches dentry objects in the dentry cache or, simply, the *dcache*.

The dentry cache consists of three parts:

- Lists of "used" dentries linked off their associated inode via the `i_dentry` field of the inode object. Because a given inode can have multiple links, there might be multiple dentry objects; consequently, a list is used.

- A doubly linked "least recently used" list of unused and negative dentry objects. The list is inserted at the head, such that entries toward the head of the list are newer than entries toward the tail. When the kernel must remove entries to reclaim memory, the entries are removed from the tail; those are the oldest and presumably have the least chance of being used in the near future.

- A hash table and hashing function used to quickly resolve a given path into the associated dentry object.

The hash table is represented by the `dentry_hashtable` array. Each element is a pointer to a list of dentries that hash to the same value. The size of this array depends on the amount of physical RAM in the system.

The actual hash value is determined by `d_hash()`. This enables filesystems to provide a unique hashing function.

Hash table lookup is performed via `d_lookup()`. If a matching dentry object is found in the dcache, it is returned. On failure, `NULL` is returned.

As an example, assume that you are editing a source file in your home directory, `/home/dracula/src/the_sun_sucks.c`. Each time this file is accessed (for example, when you first open it, later save it, compile it, and so on), the VFS must follow each directory entry to resolve the full path: `/`, `home`, `dracula`, `src`, and finally `the_sun_sucks.c`. To avoid this time-consuming operation each time this path name is accessed, the VFS can first try to look up the path name in the dentry cache. If the lookup succeeds, the required final dentry object is obtained without serious effort. Conversely, if the dentry is not in the dentry cache, the VFS must manually resolve the path by walking the filesystem for each component of the path. After this task is completed, the kernel adds the dentry objects to the dcache to speed up any future lookups.

The dcache also provides the front end to an inode cache, the *icache*. Inode objects that are associated with dentry objects are not freed because the dentry maintains a positive usage count over the inode. This enables dentry objects to pin inodes in memory. As long as the dentry is cached, the corresponding inodes are cached, too. Consequently, when a path name lookup succeeds from cache, as in the previous example, the associated inodes are already cached in memory.

Caching dentries and inodes is beneficial because file access exhibits both spatial and temporal locality. File access is temporal in that programs tend to access and reaccess the same files over and over. Thus when a file is accessed, there is a high probability that caching the associated dentries and inodes will result in a cache hit in the near future. File access is spatial in that programs tend to access multiple files in the same directory. Thus caching directories entries for one file have a high probability of a cache hit, as a related file is likely manipulated next.

Dentry Operations

The `dentry_operations` structure specifies the methods that the VFS invokes on directory entries on a given filesystem.

The `dentry_operations` structure is defined in `<linux/dcache.h>`:

```
struct dentry_operations {
        int (*d_revalidate) (struct dentry *, struct nameidata *);
        int (*d_hash) (struct dentry *, struct qstr *);
        int (*d_compare) (struct dentry *, struct qstr *, struct qstr *);
        int (*d_delete) (struct dentry *);
        void (*d_release) (struct dentry *);
        void (*d_iput) (struct dentry *, struct inode *);
        char *(*d_dname) (struct dentry *, char *, int);
};
```

The methods are as follows:

- `int d_revalidate(struct dentry *dentry,`
                    `struct nameidata *)`

  Determines whether the given dentry object is valid. The VFS calls this function whenever it is preparing to use a dentry from the dcache. Most filesystems set this method to `NULL` because their dentry objects in the dcache are always valid.

- `int d_hash(struct dentry *dentry,`
              `struct qstr *name)`

  Creates a hash value from the given dentry. The VFS calls this function whenever it adds a dentry to the hash table.

- `int d_compare(struct dentry *dentry,`
                 `struct qstr *name1,`
                 `struct qstr *name2)`

  Called by the VFS to compare two filenames, `name1` and `name2`. Most filesystems leave this at the VFS default, which is a simple string compare. For some filesystems, such as FAT, a simple string compare is insufficient. The FAT filesystem is not case-sensitive and therefore needs to implement a comparison function that disregards case. This function requires the `dcache_lock`.

- `int d_delete (struct dentry *dentry)`

  Called by the VFS when the specified dentry object's `d_count` reaches zero. This function requires the `dcache_lock` and the dentry's `d_lock`.

- `void d_release(struct dentry *dentry)`

  Called by the VFS when the specified dentry is going to be freed. The default function does nothing.

- `void d_iput(struct dentry *dentry,`
                    `struct inode *inode)`

Called by the VFS when a dentry object loses its associated inode (say, because the entry was deleted from the disk). By default, the VFS simply calls the `iput()` function to release the inode. If a filesystem overrides this function, it must also call `iput()` in addition to performing whatever filesystem-specific work it requires.

The File Object

The final primary VFS object that we shall look at is the file object. The file object is used to represent a file opened by a process. When we think of the VFS from the perspective of user-space, the file object is what readily comes to mind. Processes deal directly with files, not superblocks, inodes, or dentries. It is not surprising that the information in the file object is the most familiar (data such as access mode and current offset) or that the file operations are familiar system calls such as `read()` and `write()`.

The file object is the in-memory representation of an open file. The object (but not the physical file) is created in response to the `open()` system call and destroyed in response to the `close()` system call. All these file-related calls are actually methods defined in the file operations table. Because multiple processes can open and manipulate a file at the same time, there can be multiple file objects in existence for the same file. The file object merely represents a process's view of an open file. The object points back to the dentry (which in turn points back to the inode) that actually represents the open file. The inode and dentry objects, of course, are unique.

The file object is represented by `struct file` and is defined in `<linux/fs.h>`. Let's look at the structure, again with comments added to describe each entry:

```
struct file {
    union {
        struct list_head    fu_list;      /* list of file objects */
        struct rcu_head     fu_rcuhead;   /* RCU list after freeing */
    } f_u;
    struct path             f_path;       /* contains the dentry */
    struct file_operations *f_op;         /* file operations table */
    spinlock_t              f_lock;       /* per-file struct lock */
    atomic_t                f_count;      /* file object's usage count */
    unsigned int            f_flags;      /* flags specified on open */
    mode_t                  f_mode;       /* file access mode */
    loff_t                  f_pos;        /* file offset (file pointer) */
    struct fown_struct      f_owner;      /* owner data for signals */
    const struct cred      *f_cred;       /* file credentials */
    struct file_ra_state    f_ra;         /* read-ahead state */
    u64                     f_version;    /* version number */
    void                   *f_security;   /* security module */
    void                   *private_data; /* tty driver hook */
```

```
        struct list_head       f_ep_links;    /* list of epoll links */
        spinlock_t             f_ep_lock;     /* epoll lock */
        struct address_space   *f_mapping;    /* page cache mapping */
        unsigned long          f_mnt_write_state; /* debugging state */
};
```

Similar to the dentry object, the file object does not actually correspond to any on-disk data. Therefore, no flag in the object represents whether the object is dirty and needs to be written back to disk. The file object does point to its associated dentry object via the f_dentry pointer. The dentry in turn points to the associated inode, which reflects whether the file itself is dirty.

File Operations

As with all the other VFS objects, the file operations table is quite important. The operations associated with struct file are the familiar system calls that form the basis of the standard Unix system calls.

The file object methods are specified in file_operations and defined in <linux/fs.h>:

```
struct file_operations {
        struct module *owner;
        loff_t (*llseek) (struct file *, loff_t, int);
        ssize_t (*read) (struct file *, char __user *, size_t, loff_t *);
        ssize_t (*write) (struct file *, const char __user *, size_t, loff_t *);
        ssize_t (*aio_read) (struct kiocb *, const struct iovec *,
                        unsigned long, loff_t);
        ssize_t (*aio_write) (struct kiocb *, const struct iovec *,
                        unsigned long, loff_t);
        int (*readdir) (struct file *, void *, filldir_t);
        unsigned int (*poll) (struct file *, struct poll_table_struct *);
        int (*ioctl) (struct inode *, struct file *, unsigned int,
                unsigned long);
        long (*unlocked_ioctl) (struct file *, unsigned int, unsigned long);
        long (*compat_ioctl) (struct file *, unsigned int, unsigned long);
        int (*mmap) (struct file *, struct vm_area_struct *);
        int (*open) (struct inode *, struct file *);
        int (*flush) (struct file *, fl_owner_t id);
        int (*release) (struct inode *, struct file *);
        int (*fsync) (struct file *, struct dentry *, int datasync);
        int (*aio_fsync) (struct kiocb *, int datasync);
        int (*fasync) (int, struct file *, int);
        int (*lock) (struct file *, int, struct file_lock *);
        ssize_t (*sendpage) (struct file *, struct page *,
                        int, size_t, loff_t *, int);
        unsigned long (*get_unmapped_area) (struct file *,
                                        unsigned long,
```

```
                                    unsigned long,
                                    unsigned long,
                                    unsigned long);
        int (*check_flags) (int);
        int (*flock) (struct file *, int, struct file_lock *);
        ssize_t (*splice_write) (struct pipe_inode_info *,
                                 struct file *,
                                 loff_t *,
                                 size_t,
                                 unsigned int);
        ssize_t (*splice_read) (struct file *,
                                loff_t *,
                                struct pipe_inode_info *,
                                size_t,
                                unsigned int);
        int (*setlease) (struct file *, long, struct file_lock **);
};
```

Filesystems can implement unique functions for each of these operations, or they can use a generic method if one exists. The generic methods tend to work fine on normal Unix-based filesystems. A filesystem is under no obligation to implement all these methods—although not implementing the basics is silly—and can simply set the method to NULL if not interested.

Here are the individual operations:

- `loff_t llseek(struct file *file,`
              `loff_t offset, int origin)`

  Updates the file pointer to the given offset. It is called via the `llseek()` system call.

- `ssize_t read(struct file *file,`
              `char *buf, size_t count,`
              `loff_t *offset)`

  Reads count bytes from the given file at position offset into buf. The file pointer is then updated. This function is called by the read() system call.

- `ssize_t aio_read(struct kiocb *iocb,`
                  `char *buf, size_t count,`
                  `loff_t offset)`

  Begins an asynchronous read of count bytes into buf of the file described in iocb. This function is called by the aio_read() system call.

- `ssize_t write(struct file *file,`
               `const char *buf, size_t count,`
               `loff_t *offset)`

  Writes count bytes from buf into the given file at position offset. The file pointer is then updated. This function is called by the write() system call.

- ```
  ssize_t aio_write(struct kiocb *iocb,
                    const char *buf,
                    size_t count, loff_t offset)
  ```

Begins an asynchronous write of `count` bytes into `buf` of the file described in `iocb`. This function is called by the `aio_write()` system call.

- ```
  int readdir(struct file *file, void *dirent,
              filldir_t filldir)
  ```

Returns the next directory in a directory listing. This function is called by the `readdir()` system call.

- ```
  unsigned int poll(struct file *file,
                    struct poll_table_struct *poll_table)
  ```

Sleeps, waiting for activity on the given file. It is called by the `poll()` system call.

- ```
  int ioctl(struct inode *inode,
            struct file *file,
            unsigned int cmd,
            unsigned long arg)
  ```

Sends a command and argument pair to a device. It is used when the file is an open device node. This function is called from the `ioctl()` system call. Callers must hold the BKL.

- ```
  int unlocked_ioctl(struct file *file,
                     unsigned int cmd,
                     unsigned long arg)
  ```

Implements the same functionality as `ioctl()` but without needing to hold the BKL. The VFS calls `unlocked_ioctl()` if it exists in lieu of `ioctl()` when userspace invokes the ioctl() system call. Thus filesystems need implement only one, preferably `unlocked_ioctl()`.

- ```
  int compat_ioctl(struct file *file,
                   unsigned int cmd,
                   unsigned long arg)
  ```

Implements a portable variant of `ioctl()` for use on 64-bit systems by 32-bit applications. This function is designed to be 32-bit safe even on 64-bit architectures, performing any necessary size conversions. New drivers should design their ioctl commands such that all are portable, and thus enable `compat_ioctl()` and `unlocked_ioctl()` to point to the same function. Like `unlocked_ioctl()`, `compat_ioctl()` does not hold the BKL.

- ```
  int mmap(struct file *file,
           struct vm_area_struct *vma)
  ```

Memory maps the given file onto the given address space and is called by the `mmap()` system call.
  ```

- `int open(struct inode *inode,`
        `struct file *file)`

Creates a new file object and links it to the corresponding inode object. It is called by the `open()` system call.

- `int flush(struct file *file)`

Called by the VFS whenever the reference count of an open file decreases. Its purpose is filesystem-dependent.

- `int release(struct inode *inode,`
        `struct file *file)`

Called by the VFS when the last remaining reference to the file is destroyed—for example, when the last process sharing a file descriptor calls `close()` or exits. Its purpose is filesystem-dependent.

- `int fsync(struct file *file,`
        `struct dentry *dentry,`
        `int datasync)`

Called by the `fsync()` system call to write all cached data for the file to disk.

- `int aio_fsync(struct kiocb *iocb,`
        `int datasync)`

Called by the `aio_fsync()` system call to write all cached data for the file associated with `iocb` to disk.

- `int fasync(int fd, struct file *file, int on)`

Enables or disables signal notification of asynchronous I/O.

- `int lock(struct file *file, int cmd,`
        `struct file_lock *lock)`

Manipulates a file lock on the given file.

- `ssize_t readv(struct file *file,`
        `const struct iovec *vector,`
        `unsigned long count,`
        `loff_t *offset)`

Called by the `readv()` system call to read from the given file and put the results into the count buffers described by `vector`. The file offset is then incremented.

- `ssize_t writev(struct file *file,`
        `const struct iovec *vector,`
        `unsigned long count,`
        `loff_t *offset)`

Called by the `writev()` system call to write from the count buffers described by `vector` into the file specified by `file`. The file offset is then incremented.

- `ssize_t sendfile(struct file *file,`
        `loff_t *offset,`

```
                        size_t size,
                        read_actor_t actor,
                        void *target)
```

Called by the `sendfile()` system call to copy data from one file to another. It performs the copy entirely in the kernel and avoids an extraneous copy to user-space.

- `ssize_t sendpage(struct file *file,`
```
                        struct page *page,
                        int offset, size_t size,
                        loff_t *pos, int more)
```

Used to send data from one file to another.

- `unsigned long get_unmapped_area(struct file *file,`
```
                                     unsigned long addr,
                                     unsigned long len,
                                     unsigned long offset,
                                     unsigned long flags)
```

Gets unused address space to map the given file.

- `int check_flags(int flags)`

Used to check the validity of the flags passed to the `fcntl()` system call when the `SETFL` command is given. As with many VFS operations, filesystems need not implement `check_flags()`; currently, only NFS does so. This function enables filesystems to restrict invalid `SETFL` flags otherwise enabled by the generic `fcntl()` function. In the case of NFS, combining `O_APPEND` and `O_DIRECT` is not enabled.

- `int flock(struct file *filp,`
```
                int cmd,
                struct file_lock *fl)
```

Used to implement the `flock()` system call, which provides advisory locking.

So Many Ioctls!

Not long ago, there existed only a single ioctl method. Today, there are three methods. `unlocked_ioctl()` is the same as `ioctl()`, except it is called without the Big Kernel Lock (BKL). It is thus up to the author of that function to ensure proper synchronization. Because the BKL is a coarse-grained, inefficient lock, drivers should implement `unlocked_ioctl()` and not `ioctl()`.

`compat_ioctl()` is also called without the BKL, but its purpose is to provide a 32-bit compatible ioctl method for 64-bit systems. How you implement it depends on your existing ioctl commands. Older drivers with implicitly sized types (such as `long`) should implement a `compat_ioctl()` method that works appropriately with 32-bit applications. This generally means translating the 32-bit values to the appropriate types for a 64-bit kernel. New drivers that have the luxury of designing their ioctl commands from scratch should ensure all their arguments and data are explicitly sized, safe for 32-bit apps on a 32-bit system, 32-bit apps on a 64-bit system, and 64-bit apps on a 64-bit system. These drivers can then point the `compat_ioctl()` function pointer at the same function as `unlocked_ioctl()`.

Data Structures Associated with Filesystems

In addition to the fundamental VFS objects, the kernel uses other standard data structures to manage data related to filesystems. The first object is used to describe a specific variant of a filesystem, such as ext3, ext4, or UDF. The second data structure describes a mounted instance of a filesystem.

Because Linux supports so many different filesystems, the kernel must have a special structure for describing the capabilities and behavior of each filesystem. The file_system_type structure, defined in <linux/fs.h>, accomplishes this:

```
struct file_system_type {
        const char              *name;      /* filesystem's name */
        int                     fs_flags;   /* filesystem type flags */


        /* the following is used to read the superblock off the disk */
        struct super_block      *(*get_sb) (struct file_system_type *, int,
                                            char *, void *);

        /* the following is used to terminate access to the superblock */
        void                    (*kill_sb) (struct super_block *);

        struct module           *owner;     /* module owning the filesystem */
        struct file_system_type *next;      /* next file_system_type in list */
        struct list_head        fs_supers;  /* list of superblock objects */

        /* the remaining fields are used for runtime lock validation */
        struct lock_class_key   s_lock_key;
        struct lock_class_key   s_umount_key;
        struct lock_class_key   i_lock_key;
        struct lock_class_key   i_mutex_key;
        struct lock_class_key   i_mutex_dir_key;
        struct lock_class_key   i_alloc_sem_key;
};
```

The get_sb() function reads the superblock from the disk and populates the superblock object when the filesystem is loaded. The remaining functions describe the filesystem's properties.

There is only one file_system_type per filesystem, regardless of how many instances of the filesystem are mounted on the system, or whether the filesystem is even mounted at all.

Things get more interesting when the filesystem is actually mounted, at which point the vfsmount structure is created. This structure represents a specific instance of a filesystem—in other words, a mount point.

The vfsmount structure is defined in <linux/mount.h>. Here it is:

```
struct vfsmount {
        struct list_head    mnt_hash;           /* hash table list */
```

```
struct vfsmount        *mnt_parent;      /* parent filesystem */
struct dentry          *mnt_mountpoint;  /* dentry of this mount point */
struct dentry          *mnt_root;        /* dentry of root of this fs */
struct super_block     *mnt_sb;          /* superblock of this filesystem */
struct list_head        mnt_mounts;      /* list of children */
struct list_head        mnt_child;       /* list of children */
int                     mnt_flags;       /* mount flags */
char                   *mnt_devname;     /* device file name */
struct list_head        mnt_list;        /* list of descriptors */
struct list_head        mnt_expire;      /* entry in expiry list */
struct list_head        mnt_share;       /* entry in shared mounts list */
struct list_head        mnt_slave_list;  /* list of slave mounts */
struct list_head        mnt_slave;       /* entry in slave list */
struct vfsmount        *mnt_master;      /* slave's master */
struct mnt_namespace   *mnt_namespace;   /* associated namespace */
int                     mnt_id;          /* mount identifier */
int                     mnt_group_id;    /* peer group identifier */
atomic_t                mnt_count;       /* usage count */
int                     mnt_expiry_mark; /* is marked for expiration */
int                     mnt_pinned;      /* pinned count */
int                     mnt_ghosts;      /* ghosts count */
atomic_t                __mnt_writers;   /* writers count */
};
```

The complicated part of maintaining the list of all mount points is the relation between the filesystem and all the other mount points. The various linked lists in vfsmount keep track of this information.

The vfsmount structure also stores the flags, if any, specified on mount in the mnt_flags field. Table 13.1 is a list of the standard mount flags.

Table 13.1   **Standard Mount Flags**

Flag	Description
MNT_NOSUID	Forbids setuid and setgid flags on binaries on this filesystem
MNT_NODEV	Forbids access to device files on this filesystem
MNT_NOEXEC	Forbids execution of binaries on this filesystem

These flags are most useful on removable devices that the administrator does not trust. They are defined in <linux/mount.h> along with other, lesser used, flags.

Data Structures Associated with a Process

Each process on the system has its own list of open files, root filesystem, current working directory, mount points, and so on. Three data structures tie together the VFS layer and the processes on the system: files_struct, fs_struct, and namespace.

The `files_struct` is defined in `<linux/fdtable.h>`. This table's address is pointed to by the `files` entry in the processor descriptor. All per-process information about open files and file descriptors is contained therein. Here it is, with comments:

```
struct files_struct {
        atomic_t                count;              /* usage count */
        struct fdtable          *fdt;               /* pointer to other fd table */
        struct fdtable          fdtab;              /* base fd table */
        spinlock_t              file_lock;          /* per-file lock */
        int                     next_fd;            /* cache of next available fd */
        struct embedded_fd_set close_on_exec_init; /* list of close-on-exec fds */
        struct embedded_fd_set open_fds_init        /* list of open fds */
        struct file             *fd_array[NR_OPEN_DEFAULT]; /* base files array */
};
```

The array `fd_array` points to the list of open file objects. Because `NR_OPEN_DEFAULT` is equal to `BITS_PER_LONG`, which is 64 on a 64-bit architecture; this includes room for 64 file objects. If a process opens more than 64 file objects, the kernel allocates a new array and points the `fdt` pointer at it. In this fashion, access to a reasonable number of file objects is quick, taking place in a static array. If a process opens an abnormal number of files, the kernel can create a new array. If the majority of processes on a system opens more than 64 files, for optimum performance the administrator can increase the `NR_OPEN_DEFAULT` preprocessor macro to match.

The second process-related structure is `fs_struct`, which contains filesystem information related to a process and is pointed at by the `fs` field in the process descriptor. The structure is defined in `<linux/fs_struct.h>`. Here it is, with comments:

```
struct fs_struct {
        int         users;    /* user count */
        rwlock_t    lock;     /* per-structure lock */
        int         umask;    /* umask */
        int         in_exec;  /* currently executing a file */
        struct path root;     /* root directory */
        struct path pwd;      /* current working directory */
};
```

This structure holds the current working directory (`pwd`) and root directory of the current process.

The third and final structure is the `namespace` structure, which is defined in `<linux/mnt_namespace.h>` and pointed at by the `mnt_namespace` field in the process descriptor. Per-process namespaces were added to the 2.4 Linux kernel. They enable each process to have a unique view of the mounted filesystems on the system—not just a unique root directory, but an entirely unique filesystem hierarchy. Here is the structure, with the usual comments:

```
struct mnt_namespace {
        atomic_t            count; /* usage count */
        struct vfsmount     *root; /* root directory */
```

```
        struct list_head    list;  /* list of mount points */
        wait_queue_head_t   poll;  /* polling waitqueue */
        int                 event; /* event count */
};
```

The `list` member specifies a doubly linked list of the mounted filesystems that make up the namespace.

These data structures are linked from each process descriptor. For most processes, the process descriptor points to unique `files_struct` and `fs_struct` structures. For processes created with the clone flag `CLONE_FILES` or `CLONE_FS`, however, these structures are shared.[3] Consequently, multiple process descriptors might point to the same `files_struct` or `fs_struct` structure. The `count` member of each structure provides a reference count to prevent destruction while a process is still using the structure.

The `namespace` structure works the other way around. By default, all processes share the same namespace. (That is, they all see the same filesystem hierarchy from the same mount table.) Only when the `CLONE_NEWNS` flag is specified during `clone()` is the process given a unique copy of the `namespace` structure. Because most processes do *not* provide this flag, all the processes inherit their parents' namespaces. Consequently, on many systems there is only one namespace, although the functionality is but a single `CLONE_NEWNS` flag away.

Conclusion

Linux supports a wide range of filesystems, from native filesystems, such as ext3 and ext4, to networked filesystems, such as NFS and Coda—more than 60 filesystems alone in the official kernel. The VFS layer provides these disparate filesystems with both a framework for their implementation and an interface for working with the standard system calls. The VFS layer, thus, both makes it clean to implement new filesystems in Linux and enables those filesystems to automatically interoperate via the standard Unix system calls.

This chapter described the purpose of the VFS and discussed its various data structures, including the all-important inode, dentry, and superblock objects. Chapter 14, "The Block I/O Layer," discusses how data physically ends up in a filesystem.

---

[3] *Threads usually specify* `CLONE_FILES` *and* `CLONE_FS` *and, thus, share a single* `files_struct` *and* `fs_struct` *among themselves. Normal processes, on the other hand, do not specify these flags and consequently have their own filesystems information and open files tables.*

The Block I/O Layer

Block devices are hardware devices distinguished by the random (that is, not necessarily sequential) access of fixed-size chunks of data. The fixed-size chunks of data are called *blocks*. The most common block device is a hard disk, but many other block devices exist, such as floppy drives, Blu-ray readers, and flash memory. Notice how these are all devices on which you mount a filesystem—filesystems are the lingua franca of block devices.

The other basic type of device is a *character device*. Character devices, or *char* devices, are accessed as a stream of sequential data, one byte after another. Example character devices are serial ports and keyboards. If the hardware device is accessed as a stream of data, it is implemented as a character device. On the other hand, if the device is accessed randomly (nonsequentially), it is a block device.

The difference comes down to whether the device accesses data randomly—in other words, whether the device can *seek* to one position from another. As an example, consider the keyboard. As a driver, the keyboard provides a stream of data. If you type *wolf*, the keyboard driver returns a stream with those four letters in exactly that order. Reading the letters out of order, or reading any letter but the next one in the stream, makes little sense. The keyboard driver is thus a char device; the device provides a stream of characters that the user types onto the keyboard. Reading from the keyboard returns a stream first with *w*, then *o*, then *l*, and ultimately *f*. When no keystrokes are waiting, the stream is empty. A hard drive, conversely, is quite different. The hard drive's driver might ask to read the contents of one arbitrary block and then read the contents of a different block; the blocks need not be consecutive. The hard disk's data is accessed randomly, and not as a stream; therefore, the hard disk is a block device.

Managing block devices in the kernel requires more care, preparation, and work than managing character devices. Character devices have only one position—the current one—whereas block devices must be able to navigate back and forth between any location on the media. Indeed, the kernel does not have to provide an entire subsystem dedicated to the management of character devices, but block devices receive exactly that. Such a subsystem is a necessity partly because of the complexity of block devices. A large reason, however, for such extensive support is that block devices are quite performance sensitive; getting every last drop out of your hard disk is much more important than squeezing an extra percent of speed out of your keyboard. Furthermore, as you will see, the complexity of block devices provides a lot of room for such optimizations. The topic of this chapter is how the kernel manages block devices and their requests. This part of the kernel is known as the *block I/O layer*. Interestingly, revamping the block I/O layer was the primary goal for the 2.5 development kernel. This chapter covers the all-new block I/O layer in the 2.6 kernel.

Anatomy of a Block Device

The smallest addressable unit on a block device is a *sector*. Sectors come in various powers of two, but 512 bytes is the most common size. The sector size is a physical property of the device, and the sector is the fundamental unit of all block devices—the device cannot address or operate on a unit smaller than the sector, although many block devices can operate on multiple sectors at one time. Most block devices have 512-byte sectors, although other sizes are common. For example, many CD-ROM discs have 2-kilobyte sectors.

Software has different goals and therefore imposes its own smallest logically addressable unit, which is the *block*. The block is an abstraction of the filesystem—filesystems can be accessed only in multiples of a block. Although the physical device is addressable at the sector level, the kernel performs all disk operations in terms of blocks. Because the device's smallest addressable unit is the sector, the block size can be no smaller than the sector and must be a multiple of a sector. Furthermore, the kernel (as with hardware and the sector) needs the block to be a power of two. The kernel also requires that a block be no larger than the page size (see Chapter 12, "Memory Management," and Chapter 19, "Portability").[1] Therefore, block sizes are a power-of-two multiple of the sector size and are not greater than the page size. Common block sizes are 512 bytes, 1 kilobyte, and 4 kilobytes.

Somewhat confusingly, some people refer to sectors and blocks with different names. Sectors, the smallest addressable unit to the device, are sometimes called "hard sectors" or "device blocks." Meanwhile, blocks, the smallest addressable unit to the filesystem, are sometimes referred to as "filesystem blocks" or "I/O blocks." This chapter continues to call the two notions *sectors* and *blocks*, but you should keep these other terms in mind. Figure 14.1 is a diagram of the relationship between sectors and buffers.

Other terminology, at least with respect to hard disks, is common—terms such as *clusters*, *cylinders*, and *heads*. Those notions are specific only to certain block devices and, for the most part, are invisible to user-space software. The reason that the sector is important

---

[1] *This is an artificial constraint that could go away in the future. Forcing the block to remain equal to or smaller than the page size, however, simplifies the kernel.*

to the kernel is because all device I/O must be done in units of sectors. In turn, the higher-level concept used by the kernel—blocks—is built on top of sectors.

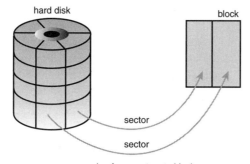

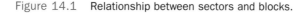

mapping from sectors to blocks

Figure 14.1   Relationship between sectors and blocks.

Buffers and Buffer Heads

When a block is stored in memory—say, after a read or pending a write—it is stored in a *buffer*. Each buffer is associated with exactly one block. The buffer serves as the object that represents a disk block in memory. Recall that a block is composed of one or more sectors but is no more than a page in size. Therefore, a single page can hold one or more blocks in memory. Because the kernel requires some associated control information to accompany the data (such as from which block device and which specific block the buffer is), each buffer is associated with a descriptor. The descriptor is called a *buffer head* and is of type struct `buffer_head`. The `buffer_head` structure holds all the information that the kernel needs to manipulate buffers and is defined in <linux/buffer_head.h>.

Take a look at this structure, with comments describing each field:

```
struct buffer_head {
        unsigned long b_state;       /* buffer state flags */
        struct buffer_head *b_this_page; /* list of page's buffers */
        struct page *b_page;         /* associated page */
        sector_t b_blocknr;          /* starting block number */
        size_t b_size;               /* size of mapping */
        char *b_data;                /* pointer to data within the page */
        struct block_device *b_bdev; /* associated block device */
        bh_end_io_t *b_end_io;       /* I/O completion */
        void *b_private;             /* reserved for b_end_io */
        struct list_head b_assoc_buffers;  /* associated mappings */
        struct address_space *b_assoc_map; /* associated address space */
        atomic_t b_count;            /* use count */
};
```

The `b_state` field specifies the state of this particular buffer. It can be one or more of the flags in Table 14.1. The legal flags are stored in the `bh_state_bits` enumeration, which is defined in `<linux/buffer_head.h>`.

Table 14.1 **bh_state Flags**

Status Flag	Meaning
BH_Uptodate	Buffer contains valid data.
BH_Dirty	Buffer is dirty. (The contents of the buffer are newer than the contents of the block on disk and therefore the buffer must eventually be written back to disk.)
BH_Lock	Buffer is undergoing disk I/O and is locked to prevent concurrent access.
BH_Req	Buffer is involved in an I/O request.
BH_Mapped	Buffer is a valid buffer mapped to an on-disk block.
BH_New	Buffer is newly mapped via `get_block()` and not yet accessed.
BH_Async_Read	Buffer is undergoing asynchronous read I/O via `end_buffer_async_read()`.
BH_Async_Write	Buffer is undergoing asynchronous write I/O via `end_buffer_async_write()`.
BH_Delay	Buffer does not yet have an associated on-disk block (delayed allocation).
BH_Boundary	Buffer forms the boundary of contiguous blocks—the next block is discontinuous.
BH_Write_EIO	Buffer incurred an I/O error on write.
BH_Ordered	Ordered write.
BH_Eopnotsupp	Buffer incurred a "not supported" error.
BH_Unwritten	Space for the buffer has been allocated on disk but the actual data has not yet been written out.
BH_Quiet	Suppress errors for this buffer.

The `bh_state_bits` enumeration also contains as the last value in the list a `BH_PrivateStart` flag. This is not a valid state flag but instead corresponds to the first usable bit of which other code can make use. All bit values equal to and greater than `BH_PrivateStart` are not used by the block I/O layer proper, so these bits are safe to use by individual drivers who want to store information in the `b_state` field. Drivers can base the bit values of their internal flags off this flag and rest assured that they are not encroaching on an official bit used by the block I/O layer.

The `b_count` field is the buffer's usage count. The value is incremented and decremented by two inline functions, both of which are defined in `<linux/buffer_head.h>`:

```
static inline void get_bh(struct buffer_head *bh)
{
        atomic_inc(&bh->b_count);
}

static inline void put_bh(struct buffer_head *bh)
{
        atomic_dec(&bh->b_count);
}
```

Before manipulating a buffer head, you must increment its reference count via `get_bh()` to ensure that the buffer head is not deallocated out from under you. When finished with the buffer head, decrement the reference count via `put_bh()`.

The physical block on disk to which a given buffer corresponds is the `b_blocknr`-th logical block on the block device described by `b_bdev`.

The physical page in memory to which a given buffer corresponds is the page pointed to by `b_page`. More specifically, `b_data` is a pointer directly to the block (that exists somewhere in `b_page`), which is `b_size` bytes in length. Therefore, the block is located in memory starting at address `b_data` and ending at address `(b_data + b_size)`.

The purpose of a buffer head is to describe this mapping between the on-disk block and the physical in-memory buffer (which is a sequence of bytes on a specific page). Acting as a descriptor of this buffer-to-block mapping is the data structure's only role in the kernel.

Before the 2.6 kernel, the buffer head was a much more important data structure: It was *the* unit of I/O in the kernel. Not only did the buffer head describe the disk-block-to-physical-page mapping, but it also acted as the container used for all block I/O. This had two primary problems. First, the buffer head was a large and unwieldy data structure (it has shrunken a bit nowadays), and it was neither clean nor simple to manipulate data in terms of buffer heads. Instead, the kernel prefers to work in terms of pages, which are simple and enable for greater performance. A large buffer head describing each individual buffer (which might be smaller than a page) was inefficient. Consequently, in the 2.6 kernel, much work has gone into making the kernel work directly with pages and address spaces instead of buffers. Some of this work is discussed in Chapter 16, "The Page Cache and Page Writeback," where the `address_space` structure and the *pdflush* daemons are discussed.

The second issue with buffer heads is that they describe only a single buffer. When used as the container for all I/O operations, the buffer head forces the kernel to break up potentially large block I/O operations (say, a write) into multiple `buffer_head` structures.

This results in needless overhead and space consumption. As a result, the primary goal of the 2.5 development kernel was to introduce a new, flexible, and lightweight container for block I/O operations. The result is the `bio` structure, which is discussed in the next section.

The `bio` Structure

The basic container for block I/O within the kernel is the `bio` structure, which is defined in `<linux/bio.h>`. This structure represents block I/O operations that are in flight (active) as a list of *segments*. A segment is a chunk of a buffer that is contiguous in memory. Thus, individual buffers need not be contiguous in memory. By allowing the buffers to be described in chunks, the `bio` structure provides the capability for the kernel to perform block I/O operations of even a single buffer from multiple locations in memory. Vector I/O such as this is called *scatter-gather I/O*.

Here is `struct bio`, defined in `<linux/bio.h>`, with comments added for each field:

```
struct bio {
        sector_t           bi_sector;         /* associated sector on disk */
        struct bio         *bi_next;          /* list of requests */
        struct block_device *bi_bdev;         /* associated block device */
        unsigned long      bi_flags;          /* status and command flags */
        unsigned long      bi_rw;             /* read or write? */
        unsigned short     bi_vcnt;           /* number of bio_vecs off */
        unsigned short     bi_idx;            /* current index in bi_io_vec */
        unsigned short     bi_phys_segments;  /* number of segments */
        unsigned int       bi_size;           /* I/O count */
        unsigned int       bi_seg_front_size; /* size of first segment */
        unsigned int       bi_seg_back_size;  /* size of last segment */
        unsigned int       bi_max_vecs;       /* maximum bio_vecs possible */
        unsigned int       bi_comp_cpu;       /* completion CPU */
        atomic_t           bi_cnt;            /* usage counter */
        struct bio_vec     *bi_io_vec;        /* bio_vec list */
        bio_end_io_t       *bi_end_io;        /* I/O completion method */
        void               *bi_private;       /* owner-private method */
        bio_destructor_t   *bi_destructor;    /* destructor method */
        struct bio_vec     bi_inline_vecs[0]; /* inline bio vectors */
};
```

The primary purpose of a `bio` structure is to represent an in-flight block I/O operation. To this end, the majority of the fields in the structure are housekeeping related. The most important fields are `bi_io_vec`, `bi_vcnt`, and `bi_idx`. Figure 14.2 shows the relationship between the `bio` structure and its friends.

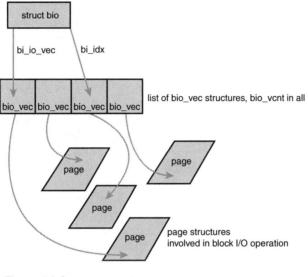

Figure 14.2   Relationship between **struct bio**, **struct bio_vec**, and **struct page**.

I/O vectors

The `bi_io_vec` field points to an array of `bio_vec` structures. These structures are used as lists of individual segments in this specific block I/O operation. Each `bio_vec` is treated as a vector of the form `<page, offset, len>`, which describes a specific segment: the physical page on which it lies, the location of the block as an offset into the page, and the length of the block starting from the given offset. The full array of these vectors describes the entire buffer. The `bio_vec` structure is defined in `<linux/bio.h>`:

```
struct bio_vec {
        /* pointer to the physical page on which this buffer resides */
        struct page      *bv_page;

        /* the length in bytes of this buffer */
        unsigned int     bv_len;

        /* the byte offset within the page where the buffer resides */
        unsigned int     bv_offset;
};
```

In each given block I/O operation, there are `bi_vcnt` vectors in the `bio_vec` array starting with `bi_io_vec`. As the block I/O operation is carried out, the `bi_idx` field is used to point to the current index into the array.

In summary, each block I/O request is represented by a `bio` structure. Each request is composed of one or more blocks, which are stored in an array of `bio_vec` structures.

These structures act as vectors and describe each segment's location in a physical page in memory. The first segment in the I/O operation is pointed to by b_io_vec. Each additional segment follows after the first, for a total of bi_vcnt segments in the list. As the block I/O layer submits segments in the request, the bi_idx field is updated to point to the current segment.

The bi_idx field is used to point to the current bio_vec in the list, which helps the block I/O layer keep track of partially completed block I/O operations. A more important usage, however, is to allow the splitting of bio structures. With this feature, drivers implementing a Redundant Array of Inexpensive Disks (RAID, a hard disk setup that enables single volumes to span multiple disks for performance and reliability purposes) can take a single bio structure, initially intended for a single device and split it among the multiple hard drives in the RAID array. All the RAID driver needs to do is copy the bio structure and update the bi_idx field to point to where the individual drive should start its operation.

The bio structure maintains a usage count in the bi_cnt field. When this field reaches zero, the structure is destroyed and the backing memory is freed. The following two functions manage the usage counters for you.

```
void bio_get(struct bio *bio)
void bio_put(struct bio *bio)
```

The former increments the usage count, whereas the latter decrements the usage count (and, if the count reaches zero, destroys the bio structure). Before manipulating an in-flight bio structure, be sure to increment its usage count to make sure it does not complete and deallocate out from under you. When you finish, decrement the usage count in turn.

Finally, the bi_private field is a private field for the owner (that is, creator) of the structure. As a rule, you can read or write this field only if you allocated the bio structure.

The Old Versus the New

The difference between buffer heads and the new bio structure is important. The bio structure represents an I/O operation, which may include one or more pages in memory. On the other hand, the buffer_head structure represents a single buffer, which describes a single block on the disk. Because buffer heads are tied to a single disk block in a single page, buffer heads result in the unnecessary dividing of requests into block-sized chunks, only to later reassemble them. Because the bio structure is lightweight, it can describe discontiguous blocks and does not unnecessarily split I/O operations.

Switching from struct buffer_head to struct bio provided other benefits, as well:

- The bio structure can easily represent high memory, because struct bio deals with only physical pages and not direct pointers.
- The bio structure can represent both normal page I/O and direct I/O (I/O operations that do not go through the page cache—see Chapter 16, "The Page Cache and Page Writeback," for a discussion on the page cache).

- The `bio` structure makes it easy to perform scatter-gather (vectored) block I/O operations, with the data involved in the operation originating from multiple physical pages.

- The `bio` structure is much more lightweight than a buffer head because it contains only the minimum information needed to represent a block I/O operation and not unnecessary information related to the buffer itself.

The concept of buffer heads is still required, however; buffer heads function as descriptors, mapping disk blocks to pages. The `bio` structure does not contain any information about the state of a buffer—it is simply an array of vectors describing one or more segments of data for a single block I/O operation, plus related information. In the current setup, the `buffer_head` structure is still needed to contain information about buffers while the `bio` structure describes in-flight I/O. Keeping the two structures separate enables each to remain as small as possible.

Request Queues

Block devices maintain *request queues* to store their pending block I/O requests. The request queue is represented by the `request_queue` structure and is defined in `<linux/blkdev.h>`. The request queue contains a doubly linked list of requests and associated control information. Requests are added to the queue by higher-level code in the kernel, such as filesystems. As long as the request queue is nonempty, the block device driver associated with the queue grabs the request from the head of the queue and submits it to its associated block device. Each item in the queue's request list is a single request, of type `struct request`.

Individual requests on the queue are represented by `struct request`, which is also defined in `<linux/blkdev.h>`. Each request can be composed of more than one `bio` structure because individual requests can operate on multiple consecutive disk blocks. Note that although the blocks on the disk must be adjacent, the blocks in memory need not be; each `bio` structure can describe multiple segments (recall, segments are contiguous chunks of a block in memory) and the request can be composed of multiple `bio` structures.

I/O Schedulers

Simply sending out requests to the block devices in the order that the kernel issues them, as soon as it issues them, results in poor performance. One of the slowest operations in a modern computer is disk seeks. Each seek—positioning the hard disk's head at the location of a specific block—takes many milliseconds. Minimizing seeks is absolutely crucial to the system's performance.

Therefore, the kernel does not issue block I/O requests to the disk in the order they are received or as soon as they are received. Instead, it performs operations called *merging* and *sorting* to greatly improve the performance of the system as a whole.[2] The subsystem of the kernel that performs these operations is called the *I/O scheduler.*

The I/O scheduler divides the resource of disk I/O among the pending block I/O requests in the system. It does this through the merging and sorting of pending requests in the request queue. The I/O scheduler is not to be confused with the process scheduler (see Chapter 4, "Process Scheduling"), which divides the resource of the processor among the processes on the system. The two subsystems are similar in nature but not the same. Both the process scheduler and the I/O scheduler virtualize a resource among multiple objects. In the case of the process scheduler, the processor is virtualized and shared among the processes on the system. This provides the illusion of virtualization inherent in a multitasking and timesharing operating system, such as any Unix. On the other hand, the I/O scheduler virtualizes block devices among multiple outstanding block requests. This is done to minimize disk seeks and ensure optimum disk performance.

The Job of an I/O Scheduler

An I/O scheduler works by managing a block device's request queue. It decides the order of requests in the queue and at what time each request is dispatched to the block device. It manages the request queue with the goal of reducing seeks, which results in greater *global throughput.* The modifier "global" here is important. An I/O scheduler, very openly, is unfair to some requests at the expense of improving the *overall* performance of the system.

I/O schedulers perform two primary actions to minimize seeks: merging and sorting. Merging is the coalescing of two or more requests into one. Consider an example request that is submitted to the queue by a filesystem—say, to read a chunk of data from a file. (At this point, of course, everything occurs in terms of sectors and blocks and not files but presume that the requested blocks originate from a chunk of a file.) If a request is already in the queue to read from an adjacent sector on the disk (for example, an earlier chunk of the same file), the two requests can be merged into a single request operating on one or more adjacent on-disk sectors. By merging requests, the I/O scheduler reduces the overhead of multiple requests down to a single request. More important only a single command needs to be issued to the disk and servicing the multiple requests can be done without seeking. Consequently, merging requests reduces overhead and minimizes seeks.

Now, assume your fictional read request is submitted to the request queue, but there is no read request to an adjacent sector. You therefore cannot merge this request with any other request. Now, you could simply stick this request onto the tail of the queue. But, what if there are other requests to a similar location on the disk? Would it not make sense to insert this new request into the queue at a spot near other requests operating on physi-

---

[2] *This point must be stressed. A system without these features, or wherein these features are poorly implemented, would perform poorly even with only a modest number of block I/O operations.*

cally near sectors? In fact, I/O schedulers do exactly this. The entire request queue is kept sorted, sectorwise, so that all seeking activity along the queue moves (as much as possible) sequentially over the sectors of the hard disk. The goal is not just to minimize each individual seek but to minimize all seeking by keeping the disk head moving in a straight line. This is similar to the algorithm employed in elevators—elevators do not jump all over, wildly, from floor to floor. Instead, they try to move gracefully in a single direction. When the final floor is reached in one direction, the elevator can reverse course and move in the other direction. Because of this similarity, I/O schedulers (or sometimes just their sorting algorithm) are called *elevators*.

The Linus Elevator

Now let's look at some real-life I/O schedulers. The first I/O scheduler is called the *Linus Elevator*. (Yes, Linus has an elevator named after him!) It was the default I/O scheduler in 2.4. In 2.6, it was replaced by the following I/O schedulers that we will look at—however, because this elevator is simpler than the subsequent ones, while performing many of the same functions, it serves as an excellent introduction.

The Linus Elevator performs both merging and sorting. When a request is added to the queue, it is first checked against every other pending request to see whether it is a possible candidate for merging. The Linus Elevator I/O scheduler performs both *front* and *back merging*. The type of merging performed depends on the location of the existing adjacent request. If the new request immediately proceeds an existing request, it is front merged. Conversely, if the new request immediately precedes an existing request, it is back merged. Because of the way files are laid out (usually by increasing sector number) and the I/O operations performed in a typical workload (data is normally read from start to finish and not in reverse), front merging is rare compared to back merging. Nonetheless, the Linus Elevator checks for and performs both types of merge.

If the merge attempt fails, a possible insertion point in the queue (a location in the queue where the new request fits sectorwise between the existing requests) is then sought. If one is found, the new request is inserted there. If a suitable location is not found, the request is added to the tail of the queue. Additionally, if an existing request is found in the queue that is older than a predefined threshold, the new request is added to the tail of the queue even if it can be insertion sorted elsewhere. This prevents many requests to nearby on-disk locations from indefinitely starving requests to other locations on the disk. Unfortunately, this "age" check is not efficient. It does not provide any real attempt to service requests in a given timeframe; it merely stops insertion-sorting requests after a suitable delay. This improves latency but can still lead to request starvation, which was the big must-fix of the 2.4 I/O scheduler.

In summary, when a request is added to the queue, four operations are possible. In order, they are

1. If a request to an adjacent on-disk sector is in the queue, the existing request and the new request merge into a single request.

2. If a request in the queue is sufficiently old, the new request is inserted at the tail of the queue to prevent starvation of the other, older, requests.

3. If a suitable location sector-wise is in the queue, the new request is inserted there. This keeps the queue sorted by physical location on disk.

4. Finally, if no such suitable insertion point exists, the request is inserted at the tail of the queue.

The Linus elevator is implemented in `block/elevator.c`.

The Deadline I/O Scheduler

The Deadline I/O scheduler sought to prevent the starvation caused by the Linus Elevator. In the interest of minimizing seeks, heavy disk I/O operations to one area of the disk can indefinitely starve request operations to another part of the disk. Indeed, a stream of requests to the same area of the disk can result in other far-off requests never being serviced. This starvation is unfair.

Worse, the general issue of request starvation introduces a specific instance of the problem known as *writes starving reads*. Write operations can usually be committed to disk whenever the kernel gets around to them, entirely asynchronous with respect to the submitting application. Read operations are quite different. Normally, when an application submits a read request, the application blocks until the request is fulfilled. That is, read requests occur synchronously with respect to the submitting application. Although system response is largely unaffected by write latency (the time required to commit a write request), read latency (the time required to commit a read request) is important. Write latency has little bearing on application performance,[3] but an application must wait, twiddling its thumbs, for the completion of each read request. Consequently, read latency is important to the performance of the system.

Compounding the problem, read requests tend to be dependent on each other. For example, consider the reading of a large number of files. Each read occurs in small buffered chunks. The application does not start reading the next chunk (or the next file, for that matter) until the previous chunk is read from disk and returned to the application. Worse, both read and write operations require the reading of various metadata, such as inodes. Reading these blocks off the disk further serializes I/O. Consequently, if each read request is individually starved, the total delay to such applications compounds and can grow enormous. Recognizing that the asynchrony and interdependency of read requests results in a much stronger bearing of read latency on the performance of the system, the Deadline I/O scheduler implements several features to ensure that request starvation in general, and read starvation in specific, is minimized.

---

[3] *We still do not want to delay write requests indefinitely, however, because the kernel wants to ensure that data is eventually written to disk to prevent in-memory buffers from growing too large or too old.*

Note that reducing request starvation comes at a cost to global throughput. Even the
Linus Elevator makes this compromise, albeit in a much milder manner. The Linus Elevator could provide better overall throughput (via a greater minimization of seeks) if it
always inserted requests into the queue sectorwise and never checked for old requests and
reverted to insertion at the tail of the queue. Although minimizing seeks is important,
indefinite starvation is not good either. The Deadline I/O scheduler, therefore, works
harder to limit starvation while still providing good global throughput. Make no mistake:
It is a tough act to provide request fairness, yet maximize global throughput.

In the Deadline I/O scheduler, each request is associated with an expiration time. By
default, the expiration time is 500 milliseconds in the future for read requests and 5 seconds in the future for write requests. The Deadline I/O scheduler operates similarly to
the Linus Elevator in that it maintains a request queue sorted by physical location on disk.
It calls this queue the *sorted queue*. When a new request is submitted to the sorted queue,
the Deadline I/O scheduler performs merging and insertion like the Linus Elevator.[4] The
Deadline I/O scheduler also, however, inserts the request into a second queue that
depends on the type of request. Read requests are sorted into a special read FIFO queue,
and write requests are inserted into a special write FIFO queue. Although the normal
queue is sorted by on-disk sector, these queues are kept FIFO. (Effectively, they are sorted
by time.) Consequently, new requests are always added to the tail of the queue. Under
normal operation, the Deadline I/O scheduler pulls requests from the head of the sorted
queue into the dispatch queue. The dispatch queue is then fed to the disk drive. This
results in minimal seeks.

If the request at the head of either the write FIFO queue or the read FIFO queue
expires (that is, if the current time becomes greater than the expiration time associated
with the request), the Deadline I/O scheduler then begins servicing requests from the
FIFO queue. In this manner, the Deadline I/O scheduler attempts to ensure that no
request is outstanding longer than its expiration time. See Figure 14.3.

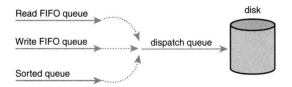

Figure 14.3   The three queues of the Deadline I/O scheduler.

Note that the Deadline I/O scheduler does not make any strict guarantees over
request latency. It is capable, however, of generally committing requests on or before their

---

[4] *Performing front merging is optional in the Deadline I/O scheduler, however. It is not always worth
the trouble because many workloads have few requests that can be front merged.*

expiration. This prevents request starvation. Because read requests are given a substantially smaller expiration value than write requests, the Deadline I/O scheduler also works to ensure that write requests do not starve read requests. This preference toward read requests provides minimized read latency.

The Deadline I/O scheduler lives in `block/deadline-iosched.c`.

The Anticipatory I/O Scheduler

Although the Deadline I/O scheduler does a great job minimizing read latency, it does so at the expense of global throughput. Consider a system undergoing heavy write activity. Every time a read request is submitted, the I/O scheduler quickly rushes to handle the read request. This results in the disk seeking over to where the read is, performing the read operation, and then seeking back to continue the ongoing write operation, repeating this little charade for each read request. The preference toward read requests is a good thing, but the resulting pair of seeks (one to the location of the read request and another back to the ongoing write) is detrimental to global disk throughput. The Anticipatory I/O scheduler aims to continue to provide excellent read latency, but also provide excellent global throughput.

First, the Anticipatory I/O scheduler starts with the Deadline I/O scheduler as its base. Therefore, it is not entirely different. The Anticipatory I/O scheduler implements three queues (plus the dispatch queue) and expirations for each request, just like the Deadline I/O scheduler. The major change is the addition of an *anticipation heuristic*.

The Anticipatory I/O scheduler attempts to minimize the seek storm that accompanies read requests issued during other disk I/O activity. When a read request is issued, it is handled as usual, within its usual expiration period. After the request is submitted, however, the Anticipatory I/O scheduler does not immediately seek back and return to handling other requests. Instead, it does absolutely nothing for a few milliseconds. (The actual value is configurable; by default it is six milliseconds.) In those few milliseconds, there is a good chance that the application will submit another read request. Any requests issued to an adjacent area of the disk are immediately handled. After the waiting period elapses, the Anticipatory I/O scheduler seeks back to where it left off and continues handling the previous requests.

It is important to note that the few milliseconds spent in *anticipation* for more requests are well worth it if they minimize even a modest percentage of the back-and-forth seeking that results from the servicing of read requests during other heavy requests. If an adjacent I/O request is issued within the waiting period, the I/O scheduler just saved a pair of seeks. As more and more reads are issued to the same area of disk, many more seeks are prevented.

Of course, if no activity occurs within the waiting period, the Anticipatory I/O scheduler loses, and a few milliseconds are wasted. The key to reaping maximum benefit from the Anticipatory I/O scheduler is correctly anticipating the actions of applications and filesystems. This is done via a set of statistics and associated heuristics. The Anticipatory I/O scheduler keeps track of per-process statistics pertaining to block I/O habits in hopes of correctly anticipating the actions of applications. With a sufficiently high percentage of correct anticipations, the Anticipatory I/O scheduler can greatly reduce the penalty of seeking to service read requests, while still providing the attention to such requests that system response requires. This enables the Anticipatory I/O scheduler to minimize read latency, while also minimizing the number and duration of seeks. This results in low system latency and high system throughput.

The Anticipatory I/O scheduler lives in the file `block/as-iosched.c` in the kernel source tree. It performs well across most workloads. It is ideal for servers, although it performs poorly on certain uncommon but critical workloads involving seek-happy databases.

The Complete Fair Queuing I/O Scheduler

The Complete Fair Queuing (CFQ) I/O scheduler is an I/O scheduler designed for specialized workloads, but that in practice actually provides good performance across multiple workloads. It is fundamentally different from the previous I/O schedulers that have been covered, however.

The CFQ I/O scheduler assigns incoming I/O requests to specific queues based on the process originating the I/O request. For example, I/O requests from process foo go in foo's queues, and I/O requests from process bar go in bar's queue. Within each queue, requests are coalesced with adjacent requests and insertion sorted. The queues are thus kept sorted sectorwise, as with the other I/O scheduler's queues. The difference with the CFQ I/O scheduler is that there is one queue for each process submitting I/O.

The CFQ I/O scheduler then services the queues round robin, plucking a configurable number of requests (by default, four) from each queue before continuing on to the next. This provides fairness at a per-process level, assuring that each process receives a fair slice of the disk's bandwidth. The intended workload is multimedia, in which such a fair algorithm can guarantee that, for example, an audio player can always refill its audio buffers from disk in time. In practice, however, the CFQ I/O scheduler performs well in many scenarios.

The Complete Fair Queuing I/O scheduler lives in `block/cfq-iosched.c`. It is recommended for desktop workloads, although it performs reasonably well in nearly all workloads without any pathological corner cases. It is now the default I/O scheduler in Linux.

The Noop I/O Scheduler

A fourth and final I/O scheduler is the Noop I/O scheduler, so named because it is basically a noop—it does not do much. The Noop I/O scheduler does not perform sorting or any other form of seek-prevention whatsoever. In turn, it has no need to implement anything akin to the slick algorithms to minimize request latency that you saw in the previous three I/O schedulers.

The Noop I/O scheduler does perform merging, however, as its lone chore. When a new request is submitted to the queue, it is coalesced with any adjacent requests. Other than this operation, the Noop I/O Scheduler truly is a noop, merely maintaining the request queue in near-FIFO order, from which the block device driver can pluck requests.

The Noop I/O scheduler's lack of hard work is with reason. It is intended for block devices that are truly random-access, such as flash memory cards. If a block device has little or no overhead associated with "seeking," then there is no need for insertion sorting of incoming requests, and the Noop I/O scheduler is the ideal candidate.

The Noop I/O scheduler lives in `block/noop-iosched.c`. It is intended only for random-access devices.

I/O Scheduler Selection

You have now seen four different I/O schedulers in the 2.6 kernel. Each of these I/O schedulers can be enabled and built into the kernel. By default, block devices use the Complete Fair Queuing I/O scheduler. This can be overridden via the boot-time option `elevator=foo` on the kernel command line, where `foo` is a valid and enabled I/O Scheduler. See Table 14.2.

Table 14.2   **Parameters Given to `elevator` Option**

Parameter	I/O Scheduler
`as`	Anticipatory
`cfq`	Complete Fair Queuing
`deadline`	Deadline
`noop`	Noop

For example, the kernel command line option `elevator=as` would enable use of the Anticipatory I/O scheduler for all block devices, overriding the default Complete Fair Queuing scheduler.

Conclusion

In this chapter, we discussed the fundamentals of block devices, and we looked at the data structures used by the block I/O layer: the `bio`, representing in-flight I/O; the `buffer_head`, representing a block-to-page mapping; and the `request` structure, representing a specific I/O request. We followed the I/O request on its brief but important life, culminating in the I/O scheduler. We discussed the dilemmas involved in scheduling I/O and went over the four I/O schedulers currently in the Linux kernel, and the old Linus Elevator from 2.4.

Next up, we tackle the process address space.

The Process Address Space

Chapter 12, "Memory Management," looked at how the kernel manages physical memory. In addition to managing its own memory, the kernel also has to manage the memory of user-space processes. This memory is called the *process address space*, which is the representation of memory given to each user-space process on the system. Linux is a virtual memory operating system, and thus the resource of memory is virtualized among the processes on the system. An individual process's view of memory is as if it alone has full access to the system's physical memory. More important, the address space of even a single process can be much larger than physical memory. This chapter discusses how the kernel manages the process address space.

Address Spaces

The process address space consists of the virtual memory addressable by a process and the addresses within the virtual memory that the process is allowed to use. Each process is given a *flat* 32- or 64-bit address space, with the size depending on the architecture. The term *flat* denotes that the address space exists in a single range. (For example, a 32-bit address space extends from the address 0 to 4294967295.) Some operating systems provide a *segmented address space*, with addresses existing not in a single linear range, but instead in multiple segments. Modern virtual memory operating systems generally have a flat memory model and not a segmented one. Normally, this flat address space is unique to each process. A memory address in one process's address space is completely unrelated to that same memory address in another process's address space. Both processes can have different data at the same address in their respective address spaces. Alternatively, processes can elect to share their address space with other processes. We know these processes as *threads*.

A memory address is a given value within the address space, such as `4021f000`. This particular value identifies a specific byte in a process's 32-bit address space. Although a process can address up to 4GB of memory (with a 32-bit address space), it doesn't have permission to access all of it. The interesting part of the address space is the intervals of memory addresses, such as `08048000-0804c000`, that the process has permission to access.

These intervals of legal addresses are called *memory areas*. The process, through the kernel, can dynamically add and remove memory areas to its address space.

The process can access a memory address only in a valid memory area. Memory areas have associated permissions, such as readable, writable, and executable, that the associated process must respect. If a process accesses a memory address not in a valid memory area, or if it accesses a valid area in an invalid manner, the kernel kills the process with the dreaded "Segmentation Fault" message.

Memory areas can contain all sorts of goodies, such as

- A memory map of the executable file's code, called the *text section*.
- A memory map of the executable file's initialized global variables, called the *data section*.
- A memory map of the zero page (a page consisting of all zeros, used for purposes such as this) containing uninitialized global variables, called the *bss section*.[1]
- A memory map of the zero page used for the process's user-space stack. (Do not confuse this with the process's kernel stack, which is separate and maintained and used by the kernel.)
- An additional text, data, and bss section for each shared library, such as the C library and dynamic linker, loaded into the process's address space.
- Any memory mapped files.
- Any shared memory segments.
- Any anonymous memory mappings, such as those associated with `malloc()`.[2]

All valid addresses in the process address space exist in exactly one area; memory areas do not overlap. As you can see, there is a separate memory area for each different chunk of memory in a running process: the stack, object code, global variables, mapped file, and so on.

The Memory Descriptor

The kernel represents a process's address space with a data structure called the *memory descriptor*. This structure contains all the information related to the process address space. The memory descriptor is represented by `struct mm_struct` and defined in

---

[1] The term "BSS" is historical. It stands for block started by symbol. *Uninitialized variables are not stored in the executable object because they do not have any associated value. But the C standard decrees that uninitialized global variables are assigned certain default values (basically, all zeros), so the kernel loads the variables (without value) from the executable into memory and maps the zero page over the area, thereby giving the variables the value zero, without having to waste space in the object file with explicit initializations.*

[2] *Newer versions of glibc implement* `malloc()` *via* `mmap()`, *in addition to* `brk()`.

`<linux/mm_types.h>`. Let's look at the memory descriptor, with comments added describing each field:

```
struct mm_struct {
        struct vm_area_struct   *mmap;              /* list of memory areas */
        struct rb_root          mm_rb;             /* red-black tree of VMAs */
        struct vm_area_struct   *mmap_cache;        /* last used memory area */
        unsigned long           free_area_cache;    /* 1st address space hole */
        pgd_t                   *pgd;               /* page global directory */
        atomic_t                mm_users;           /* address space users */
        atomic_t                mm_count;           /* primary usage counter */
        int                     map_count;          /* number of memory areas */
        struct rw_semaphore     mmap_sem;           /* memory area semaphore */
        spinlock_t              page_table_lock;    /* page table lock */
        struct list_head        mmlist;             /* list of all mm_structs */
        unsigned long           start_code;         /* start address of code */
        unsigned long           end_code;           /* final address of code */
        unsigned long           start_data;         /* start address of data */
        unsigned long           end_data;           /* final address of data */
        unsigned long           start_brk;          /* start address of heap */
        unsigned long           brk;                /* final address of heap */
        unsigned long           start_stack;        /* start address of stack */
        unsigned long           arg_start;          /* start of arguments */
        unsigned long           arg_end;            /* end of arguments */
        unsigned long           env_start;          /* start of environment */
        unsigned long           env_end;            /* end of environment */
        unsigned long           rss;                /* pages allocated */
        unsigned long           total_vm;           /* total number of pages */
        unsigned long           locked_vm;          /* number of locked pages */
        unsigned long           saved_auxv[AT_VECTOR_SIZE]; /* saved auxv */
        cpumask_t               cpu_vm_mask;        /* lazy TLB switch mask */
        mm_context_t            context;            /* arch-specific data */
        unsigned long           flags;              /* status flags */
        int                     core_waiters;       /* thread core dump waiters */
        struct core_state       *core_state;        /* core dump support */
        spinlock_t              ioctx_lock;         /* AIO I/O list lock */
        struct hlist_head       ioctx_list;         /* AIO I/O list */
};
```

The mm_users field is the number of processes using this address space. For example, if two threads share this address space, mm_users is equal to two. The mm_count field is the primary reference count for the mm_struct. All mm_users equate to one increment of mm_count. Thus, in the previous example, mm_count is only one. If nine threads shared an address space, mm_users would be nine, but again mm_count would be only one. Only when mm_users reaches zero (when all threads using an address space exit) is mm_count decremented. When mm_count finally reaches zero, there are no remaining references to this `mm_struct`, and it is freed. When the kernel operates on an address space and needs to bump its associated reference count, the kernel increments `mm_count`. Having two counters enables the kernel to differentiate between the main usage counter (`mm_count`) and the number of processes using the address space (`mm_users`).

The `mmap` and `mm_rb` fields are different data structures that contain the same thing: all the memory areas in this address space. The former stores them in a linked list, whereas the latter stores them in a red-black tree. A red-black tree is a type of binary tree; like all binary trees, searching for a given element is an `O(log n)` operation. For further discussion on red-black trees, see "Lists and Trees of Memory Areas," later in this chapter.

Although the kernel would normally avoid the extra baggage of using two data structures to organize the same data, the redundancy comes in handy here. The `mmap` data structure, as a linked list, allows for simple and efficient traversing of all elements. On the other hand, the `mm_rb` data structure, as a red-black tree, is more suitable to searching for a given element. Memory areas are discussed in more detail later in this chapter. The kernel isn't duplicating the `mm_struct` structures; just the containing objects. Overlaying a linked list onto a tree, and using both to access the same set of data, is sometimes called a *threaded tree*.

All of the `mm_struct` structures are strung together in a doubly linked list via the `mmlist` field. The initial element in the list is the `init_mm` memory descriptor, which describes the address space of the init process. The list is protected from concurrent access via the `mmlist_lock`, which is defined in `kernel/fork.c`.

Allocating a Memory Descriptor

The memory descriptor associated with a given task is stored in the `mm` field of the task's process descriptor. (The process descriptor is represented by the `task_struct` structure, defined in `<linux/sched.h>`.) Thus, `current->mm` is the current process's memory descriptor. The `copy_mm()` function copies a parent's memory descriptor to its child during `fork()`. The `mm_struct` structure is allocated from the `mm_cachep` slab cache via the `allocate_mm()` macro in `kernel/fork.c`. Normally, each process receives a unique `mm_struct` and thus a unique process address space.

Processes may elect to share their address spaces with their children by means of the `CLONE_VM` flag to `clone()`. The process is then called a *thread*. Recall from Chapter 3, "Process Management," that this is essentially the *only* difference between normal processes and so-called threads in Linux; the Linux kernel does not otherwise differentiate between them. Threads are regular processes to the kernel that merely share certain resources.

In the case that `CLONE_VM` is specified, `allocate_mm()` is *not* called, and the process's `mm` field is set to point to the memory descriptor of its parent via this logic in `copy_mm()`:

```
if (clone_flags & CLONE_VM) {
        /*
         * current is the parent process and
         * tsk is the child process during a fork()
```

```
    */
    atomic_inc(&current->mm->mm_users);
    tsk->mm = current->mm;
}
```

Destroying a Memory Descriptor

When the process associated with a specific address space exits, the `exit_mm()`, defined in `kernel/exit.c`, function is invoked. This function performs some housekeeping and updates some statistics. It then calls `mmput()`, which decrements the memory descriptor's `mm_users` user counter. If the user count reaches zero, `mmdrop()` is called to decrement the `mm_count` usage counter. If *that* counter is finally zero, the `free_mm()` macro is invoked to return the `mm_struct` to the `mm_cachep` slab cache via `kmem_cache_free()`, because the memory descriptor does not have any users.

The `mm_struct` and Kernel Threads

Kernel threads do not have a process address space and therefore do not have an associated memory descriptor. Thus, the `mm` field of a kernel thread's process descriptor is NULL. This is the *definition* of a kernel thread—processes that have no user context.

This lack of an address space is fine because kernel threads do not ever access any user-space memory. (Whose would they access?) Because kernel threads do not have any pages in user-space, they do not deserve their own memory descriptor and page tables. (Page tables are discussed later in the chapter.) Despite this, kernel threads need some of the data, such as the page tables, even to access kernel memory. To provide kernel threads the needed data, without wasting memory on a memory descriptor and page tables, or wasting processor cycles to switch to a new address space whenever a kernel thread begins running, kernel threads use the memory descriptor of whatever task ran previously.

Whenever a process is scheduled, the process address space referenced by the process's `mm` field is loaded. The `active_mm` field in the process descriptor is then updated to refer to the new address space. Kernel threads do not have an address space and `mm` is NULL. Therefore, when a kernel thread is scheduled, the kernel notices that `mm` is NULL and keeps the previous process's address space loaded. The kernel then updates the `active_mm` field of the kernel thread's process descriptor to refer to the previous process's memory descriptor. The kernel thread can then use the previous process's page tables as needed. Because kernel threads do not access user-space memory, they make use of only the information in the address space pertaining to kernel memory, which is the same for all processes.

Virtual Memory Areas

The memory area structure, `vm_area_struct`, represents memory areas. It is defined in `<linux/mm_types.h>`. In the Linux kernel, memory areas are often called *virtual memory areas* (abbreviated *VMAs*).

The vm_area_struct structure describes a single memory area over a contiguous interval in a given address space. The kernel treats each memory area as a unique memory object. Each memory area possesses certain properties, such as permissions and a set of associated operations. In this manner, each VMA structure can represent different types of memory areas—for example, memory-mapped files or the process's user-space stack. This is similar to the object-oriented approach taken by the VFS layer (see Chapter 13). Here's the structure, with comments added describing each field:

```
struct vm_area_struct {
        struct mm_struct                *vm_mm;         /* associated mm_struct */
        unsigned long                   vm_start;       /* VMA start, inclusive */
        unsigned long                   vm_end;         /* VMA end , exclusive */
        struct vm_area_struct           *vm_next;       /* list of VMA's */
        pgprot_t                        vm_page_prot;   /* access permissions */
        unsigned long                   vm_flags;       /* flags */
        struct rb_node                  vm_rb;          /* VMA's node in the tree */
        union {         /* links to address_space->i_mmap or i_mmap_nonlinear */
                struct {
                        struct list_head        list;
                        void                    *parent;
                        struct vm_area_struct   *head;
                } vm_set;
                struct prio_tree_node prio_tree_node;
        } shared;
        struct list_head                anon_vma_node;  /* anon_vma entry */
        struct anon_vma                 *anon_vma;      /* anonymous VMA object */
        struct vm_operations_struct     *vm_ops;        /* associated ops */
        unsigned long                   vm_pgoff;       /* offset within file */
        struct file                     *vm_file;       /* mapped file, if any */
        void                            *vm_private_data; /* private data */
};
```

Recall that each memory descriptor is associated with a unique interval in the process's address space. The vm_start field is the initial (lowest) address in the interval, and the vm_end field is the first byte after the final (highest) address in the interval. That is, vm_start is the inclusive start, and vm_end is the exclusive end of the memory interval. Thus, vm_end - vm_start is the length in bytes of the memory area, which exists over the interval [vm_start, vm_end). Intervals in different memory areas in the same address space cannot overlap.

The vm_mm field points to this VMA's associated mm_struct. Note that each VMA is unique to the mm_struct with which it is associated. Therefore, even if two separate processes map the same file into their respective address spaces, each has a unique vm_area_struct to identify its unique memory area. Conversely, two threads that share an address space also share all the vm_area_struct structures therein.

VMA Flags

The vm_flags field contains bit flags, defined in <linux/mm.h>, that specify the behavior of and provide information about the pages contained in the memory area. Unlike permissions associated with a specific physical page, the VMA flags specify behavior for which the kernel is responsible, not the hardware. Furthermore, vm_flags contains information that relates to each page in the memory area, or the memory area as a whole, and not specific individual pages. Table 15.1 is a listing of the possible vm_flags values.

Table 15.1 **vm_flags**

Flag	Effect on the VMA and Its Pages
VM_READ	Pages can be read from.
VM_WRITE	Pages can be written to.
VM_EXEC	Pages can be executed.
VM_SHARED	Pages are shared.
VM_MAYREAD	The VM_READ flag can be set.
VM_MAYWRITE	The VM_WRITE flag can be set.
VM_MAYEXEC	The VM_EXEC flag can be set.
VM_MAYSHARE	The VM_SHARE flag can be set.
VM_GROWSDOWN	The area can grow downward.
VM_GROWSUP	The area can grow upward.
VM_SHM	The area is used for shared memory.
VM_DENYWRITE	The area maps an unwritable file.
VM_EXECUTABLE	The area maps an executable file.
VM_LOCKED	The pages in this area are locked.
VM_IO	The area maps a device's I/O space.
VM_SEQ_READ	The pages seem to be accessed sequentially.
VM_RAND_READ	The pages seem to be accessed randomly.
VM_DONTCOPY	This area must not be copied on fork().
VM_DONTEXPAND	This area cannot grow via mremap().
VM_RESERVED	This area must not be swapped out.
VM_ACCOUNT	This area is an accounted VM object.
VM_HUGETLB	This area uses hugetlb pages.
VM_NONLINEAR	This area is a nonlinear mapping.

Let's look at some of the more important and interesting flags in depth. The VM_READ, VM_WRITE, and VM_EXEC flags specify the usual read, write, and execute permissions for the pages *in this particular memory area*. They are combined as needed to form the appropriate access permissions that a process accessing this VMA must respect. For example, the object code for a process might be mapped with VM_READ and VM_EXEC but not VM_WRITE. On the other hand, the data section from an executable object would be mapped VM_READ and VM_WRITE, but VM_EXEC would make little sense. Meanwhile, a read-only memory mapped data file would be mapped with only the VM_READ flag.

The VM_SHARED flag specifies whether the memory area contains a mapping that is shared among multiple processes. If the flag is set, it is intuitively called a *shared mapping*. If the flag is not set, only a single process can view this particular mapping, and it is called a *private mapping*.

The VM_IO flag specifies that this memory area is a mapping of a device's I/O space. This field is typically set by device drivers when mmap() is called on their I/O space. It specifies, among other things, that the memory area must not be included in any process's core dump. The VM_RESERVED flag specifies that the memory region must not be swapped out. It is also used by device driver mappings.

The VM_SEQ_READ flag provides a hint to the kernel that the application is performing sequential (that is, linear and contiguous) reads in this mapping. The kernel can then opt to increase the read-ahead performed on the backing file. The VM_RAND_READ flag specifies the exact opposite: that the application is performing relatively random (that is, not sequential) reads in this mapping. The kernel can then opt to decrease or altogether disable read-ahead on the backing file. These flags are set via the madvise() system call with the MADV_SEQUENTIAL and MADV_RANDOM flags, respectively. Read-ahead is the act of reading sequentially ahead of requested data, in hopes that the additional data will be needed soon. Such behavior is beneficial if applications are reading data sequentially. If data access patterns are random, however, read-ahead is not effective.

VMA Operations

The vm_ops field in the vm_area_struct structure points to the table of operations associated with a given memory area, which the kernel can invoke to manipulate the VMA. The vm_area_struct acts as a generic object for representing any type of memory area, and the operations table describes the specific methods that can operate on this particular instance of the object.

The operations table is represented by struct vm_operations_struct and is defined in <linux/mm.h>:

```
struct vm_operations_struct {
        void (*open) (struct vm_area_struct *);
        void (*close) (struct vm_area_struct *);
        int (*fault) (struct vm_area_struct *, struct vm_fault *);
        int (*page_mkwrite) (struct vm_area_struct *vma, struct vm_fault *vmf);
        int (*access) (struct vm_area_struct *, unsigned long ,
                        void *, int, int);
};
```

Here's a description for each individual method:

- void open(struct vm_area_struct *area)

  This function is invoked when the given memory area is added to an address space.

- void close(struct vm_area_struct *area)

  This function is invoked when the given memory area is removed from an address space.

- int fault(struct vm_area_sruct *area, struct vm_fault *vmf)

  This function is invoked by the page fault handler when a page that is not present in physical memory is accessed.

- int page_mkwrite(struct vm_area_sruct *area, struct vm_fault *vmf)

  This function is invoked by the page fault handler when a page that was read-only is being made writable.

- int access(struct vm_area_struct *vma, unsigned long address, void *buf, int len, int write)

  This function is invoked by access_process_vm() when get_user_pages() fails.

Lists and Trees of Memory Areas

As discussed, memory areas are accessed via both the mmap and the mm_rb fields of the memory descriptor. These two data structures independently point to all the memory area objects associated with the memory descriptor. In fact, they both contain pointers to the same vm_area_struct structures, merely represented in different ways.

The first field, mmap, links together all the memory area objects in a singly linked list. Each vm_area_struct structure is linked into the list via its vm_next field. The areas are sorted by ascending address. The first memory area is the vm_area_struct structure to which mmap points. The last structure points to NULL.

The second field, mm_rb, links together all the memory area objects in a red-black tree. The root of the red-black tree is mm_rb, and each vm_area_struct structure in this address space is linked to the tree via its vm_rb field.

A *red-black tree* is a type of balanced binary tree. Each element in a red-black tree is called a *node*. The initial node is called the *root* of the tree. Most nodes have two children: a left child and a right child. Some nodes have only one child, and the final nodes, called *leaves*, have no children. For any node, the elements to the left are smaller in value, whereas the elements to the right are larger in value. Furthermore, each node is assigned a color (red or black, hence the name of this tree) according to two rules: The children of a red node are black, and every path through the tree from a node to a leaf must contain the same number of black nodes. The root node is always red. Searching of, insertion to, and deletion from the tree is an O(log(n)) operation.

The linked list is used when every node needs to be traversed. The red-black tree is used when locating a specific memory area in the address space. In this manner, the kernel uses the redundant data structures to provide optimal performance regardless of the operation performed on the memory areas.

Memory Areas in Real Life

Let's look at a particular process's address space and the memory areas inside. This task uses the useful /proc filesystem and the pmap(1) utility. The example is a simple user-space program, which does absolutely nothing of value, except act as an example:

```
int main(int argc, char *argv[])
{
        return 0;
}
```

Take note of a few of the memory areas in this process's address space. First, you know there is the text section, data section, and bss. Assuming this process is dynamically linked with the C library, these three memory areas also exist for libc.so and again for ld.so. Finally, there is also the process's stack.

The output from /proc/<pid>/maps lists the memory areas in this process's address space:

```
rlove@wolf:~$ cat /proc/1426/maps
00e80000-00faf000 r-xp 00000000 03:01 208530    /lib/tls/libc-2.5.1.so
00faf000-00fb2000 rw-p 0012f000 03:01 208530    /lib/tls/libc-2.5.1.so
00fb2000-00fb4000 rw-p 00000000 00:00 0
08048000-08049000 r-xp 00000000 03:03 439029    /home/rlove/src/example
08049000-0804a000 rw-p 00000000 03:03 439029    /home/rlove/src/example
40000000-40015000 r-xp 00000000 03:01 80276     /lib/ld-2.5.1.so
40015000-40016000 rw-p 00015000 03:01 80276     /lib/ld-2.5.1.so
4001e000-4001f000 rw-p 00000000 00:00 0
bfffe000-c0000000 rwxp fffff000 00:00 0
```

The data is in the form

```
start-end permission   offset   major:minor   inode   file
```

The pmap(1) utility[3] formats this information in a bit more readable manner:

```
rlove@wolf:~$ pmap 1426
example[1426]
00e80000 (1212 KB)    r-xp (03:01 208530)    /lib/tls/libc-2.5.1.so
00faf000 (12 KB)      rw-p (03:01 208530)    /lib/tls/libc-2.5.1.so
00fb2000 (8 KB)       rw-p (00:00 0)
08048000 (4 KB)       r-xp (03:03 439029)    /home/rlove/src/example
```

---

[3] The pmap(1) utility displays a formatted listing of a process's memory areas. It is a bit more readable than the /proc output, but it is the same information. It is found in newer versions of the procps package.

```
08049000 (4 KB)      rw-p (03:03 439029)     /home/rlove/src/example
40000000 (84 KB)     r-xp (03:01 80276)      /lib/ld-2.5.1.so
40015000 (4 KB)      rw-p (03:01 80276)      /lib/ld-2.5.1.so
4001e000 (4 KB)      rw-p (00:00 0)
bfffe000 (8 KB)      rwxp (00:00 0)          [ stack ]
mapped: 1340 KB      writable/private: 40 KB     shared: 0 KB
```

The first three rows are the text section, data section, and bss of `libc.so`, the C library. The next two rows are the text and data section of our executable object. The following three rows are the text section, data section, and bss for `ld.so`, the dynamic linker. The last row is the process's stack.

Note how the text sections are all readable and executable, which is what you expect for object code. On the other hand, the data section and bss (which both contain global variables) are marked readable and writable, but not executable. The stack is, naturally, readable, writable, and executable—not of much use otherwise.

The entire address space takes up about 1340KB, but only 40KB are writable and private. If a memory region is shared or nonwritable, the kernel keeps only one copy of the backing file in memory. This might seem like common sense for shared mappings, but the nonwritable case can come as a bit of a surprise. If you consider that a nonwritable mapping can never be changed (the mapping is only read from), it is clear that it is safe to load the image only once into memory. Therefore, the C library needs to occupy only 1212KB in physical memory and not 1212KB multiplied by every process using the library. Because this process has access to about 1340KB worth of data and code, yet consumes only about 40KB of physical memory, the space savings from such sharing is substantial.

Note the memory areas without a mapped file on device `00:00` and inode zero. This is the zero page, which is a mapping that consists of all zeros. By mapping the zero page over a writable memory area, the area is in effect "initialized" to all zeros. This is important in that it provides a zeroed memory area, which is expected by the bss. Because the mapping is not shared, as soon as the process writes to this data, a copy is made (à la copy-on-write) and the value updated from zero.

Each of the memory areas associated with the process corresponds to a `vm_area_struct` structure. Because the process was not a thread, it has a unique `mm_struct` structure referenced from its `task_struct`.

Manipulating Memory Areas

The kernel often has to perform operations on a memory area, such as whether a given address exists in a given VMA. These operations are frequent and form the basis of the `mmap()` routine, which is covered in the next section. A handful of helper functions are defined to assist these jobs.

These functions are all declared in `<linux/mm.h>`.

find_vma()

The kernel provides a function, find_vma(), for searching for the VMA in which a given memory address resides. It is defined in mm/mmap.c:

```
struct vm_area_struct * find_vma(struct mm_struct *mm, unsigned long addr);
```

This function searches the given address space for the first memory area whose vm_end field is greater than addr. In other words, this function finds the first memory area that contains addr or begins at an address greater than addr. If no such memory area exists, the function returns NULL. Otherwise, a pointer to the vm_area_struct structure is returned. Note that because the returned VMA may start at an address greater than addr, the given address does not necessarily lie *inside* the returned VMA. The result of the find_vma() function is cached in the mmap_cache field of the memory descriptor. Because of the probability of an operation on one VMA being followed by more operations on that same VMA, the cached results have a decent hit rate (about 30–40% in practice). Checking the cached result is quick. If the given address is *not* in the cache, you must search the memory areas associated with this memory descriptor for a match. This is done via the red–black tree:

```
struct vm_area_struct * find_vma(struct mm_struct *mm, unsigned long addr)
{
        struct vm_area_struct *vma = NULL;

        if (mm) {
                vma = mm->mmap_cache;
                if (!(vma && vma->vm_end > addr && vma->vm_start <= addr)) {
                        struct rb_node *rb_node;

                        rb_node = mm->mm_rb.rb_node;
                        vma = NULL;
                        while (rb_node) {
                                struct vm_area_struct * vma_tmp;

                                vma_tmp = rb_entry(rb_node,
                                                struct vm_area_struct, vm_rb);
                                if (vma_tmp->vm_end > addr) {
                                        vma = vma_tmp;
                                        if (vma_tmp->vm_start <= addr)
                                                break;
                                        rb_node = rb_node->rb_left;
                                } else
                                        rb_node = rb_node->rb_right;
                        }
                        if (vma)
                                mm->mmap_cache = vma;
                }
```

```
        }

        return vma;
}
```

The initial check of `mmap_cache` tests whether the cached VMA contains the desired address. Note that simply checking whether the VMA's `vm_end` field is bigger than `addr` would not ensure that this is the first such VMA that is larger than `addr`. Thus, for the cache to be useful here, the given `addr` must lie in the VMA—thankfully, this is just the sort of scenario in which consecutive operations on the same VMA would occur.

If the cache does not contain the desired VMA, the function must search the red-black tree. If the current VMA's `vm_end` is larger than `addr`, the function follows the left child; otherwise, it follows the right child. The function terminates as soon as a VMA is found that contains `addr`. If such a VMA is not found, the function continues traversing the tree and returns the first VMA it found that starts after `addr`. If no VMA is ever found, `NULL` is returned.

find_vma_prev()

The `find_vma_prev()` function works the same as `find_vma()`, but it also returns the last VMA *before* `addr`. The function is also defined in `mm/mmap.c` and declared in `<linux/mm.h>`:

```
struct vm_area_struct * find_vma_prev(struct mm_struct *mm, unsigned long addr,
                                struct vm_area_struct **pprev)
```

The `pprev` argument stores a pointer to the VMA preceding `addr`.

find_vma_intersection()

The `find_vma_intersection()` function returns the first VMA that overlaps a given address interval. The function is defined in `<linux/mm.h>` because it is inline:

```
static inline struct vm_area_struct *
find_vma_intersection(struct mm_struct *mm,
                        unsigned long start_addr,
                        unsigned long end_addr)
{
        struct vm_area_struct *vma;

        vma = find_vma(mm, start_addr);
        if (vma && end_addr <= vma->vm_start)
                vma = NULL;
        return vma;
}
```

The first parameter is the address space to search, `start_addr` is the start of the interval, and `end_addr` is the end of the interval.

Obviously, if find_vma() returns NULL, so would find_vma_intersection(). If find_vma() returns a valid VMA, however, find_vma_intersection() returns the same VMA only if it does *not* start after the end of the given address range. If the returned memory area does start after the end of the given address range, the function returns NULL.

mmap() and do_mmap(): Creating an Address Interval

The do_mmap() function is used by the kernel to create a new linear address interval. Saying that this function creates a new VMA is not technically correct, because if the created address interval is adjacent to an existing address interval, and if they share the same permissions, the two intervals are merged into one. If this is not possible, a new VMA is created. In any case, do_mmap() is the function used to add an address interval to a process's address space—whether that means expanding an existing memory area or creating a new one.

The do_mmap() function is declared in <linux/mm.h>:

```
unsigned long do_mmap(struct file *file, unsigned long addr,
                      unsigned long len, unsigned long prot,
                      unsigned long flag, unsigned long offset)
```

This function maps the file specified by file at offset offset for length len. The file parameter can be NULL and offset can be zero, in which case the mapping will not be backed by a file. In that case, this is called an *anonymous mapping*. If a file and offset are provided, the mapping is called a *file-backed mapping*.

The addr function optionally specifies the initial address from which to start the search for a free interval.

The prot parameter specifies the access permissions for pages in the memory area. The possible permission flags are defined in <asm/mman.h> and are unique to each supported architecture, although in practice each architecture defines the flags listed in Table 15.2.

Table 15.2 **Page Protection Flags**

Flag	Effect on the Pages in the New Interval
PROT_READ	Corresponds to VM_READ
PROT_WRITE	Corresponds to VM_WRITE
PROT_EXEC	Corresponds to VM_EXEC
PROT_NONE	Cannot access page

The `flags` parameter specifies flags that correspond to the remaining VMA flags. These flags specify the type and change the behavior of the mapping. They are also defined in `<asm/mman.h>`. See Table 15.3.

Table 15.3   **Map Type Flags**

Flag	Effect on the New Interval
MAP_SHARED	The mapping can be shared.
MAP_PRIVATE	The mapping cannot be shared.
MAP_FIXED	The new interval *must* start at the given address `addr`.
MAP_ANONYMOUS	The mapping is not file-backed, but is anonymous.
MAP_GROWSDOWN	Corresponds to VM_GROWSDOWN.
MAP_DENYWRITE	Corresponds to VM_DENYWRITE.
MAP_EXECUTABLE	Corresponds to VM_EXECUTABLE.
MAP_LOCKED	Corresponds to VM_LOCKED.
MAP_NORESERVE	No need to reserve space for the mapping.
MAP_POPULATE	Populate (prefault) page tables.
MAP_NONBLOCK	Do not block on I/O.

If any of the parameters are invalid, `do_mmap()` returns a negative value. Otherwise, a suitable interval in virtual memory is located. If possible, the interval is merged with an adjacent memory area. Otherwise, a new `vm_area_struct` structure is allocated from the `vm_area_cachep` slab cache, and the new memory area is added to the address space's linked list and red-black tree of memory areas via the `vma_link()` function. Next, the `total_vm` field in the memory descriptor is updated. Finally, the function returns the initial address of the newly created address interval.

The `do_mmap()` functionality is exported to user-space via the `mmap()` system call. The `mmap()` system call is defined as

```
void  * mmap2(void *start,
            size_t length,
            int prot,
            int flags,
            int fd,
            off_t pgoff)
```

This system call is named `mmap2()` because it is the second variant of `mmap()`. The original `mmap()` took an offset in bytes as the last parameter; the current `mmap2()` receives the offset in pages. This enables larger files with larger offsets to be mapped. The original mmap(), as specified by POSIX, is available from the C library as mmap(), but is no longer implemented in the kernel proper, whereas the new version is available as mmap2(). Both library calls use the mmap2() system call, with the original mmap() converting the offset from bytes to pages.

munmap() and do_munmap(): Removing an Address Interval

The do_munmap() function removes an address interval from a specified process address space. The function is declared in <linux/mm.h>:

```
int do_munmap(struct mm_struct *mm, unsigned long start, size_t len)
```

The first parameter specifies the address space from which the interval starting at address start of length len bytes is removed. On success, zero is returned. Otherwise, a negative error code is returned.

The munmap() system call is exported to user-space as a means to enable processes to remove address intervals from their address space; it is the complement of the mmap() system call:

```
int munmap(void *start, size_t length)
```

The system call is defined in mm/mmap.c and acts as a simple wrapper to do_munmap():

```
asmlinkage long sys_munmap(unsigned long addr, size_t len)
{
        int ret;
        struct mm_struct *mm;

        mm = current->mm;
        down_write(&mm->mmap_sem);
        ret = do_munmap(mm, addr, len);
        up_write(&mm->mmap_sem);
        return ret;
}
```

Page Tables

Although applications operate on virtual memory mapped to physical addresses, processors operate directly on those physical addresses. Consequently, when an application accesses a virtual memory address, it must first be converted to a physical address before the processor can resolve the request. Performing this lookup is done via page tables. Page tables work by splitting the virtual address into chunks. Each chunk is used as an index into a table. The table points to either another table or the associated physical page.

In Linux, the page tables consist of three levels. The multiple levels enable a sparsely populated address space, even on 64-bit machines. If the page tables were implemented as a single static array, their size on even 32-bit architectures would be enormous. Linux uses three levels of page tables even on architectures that do not support three levels in hardware. (For example, some hardware uses only two levels or implements a hash in hardware.) Using three levels is a sort of "greatest common denominator"—architectures with a less complicated implementation can simplify the kernel page tables as needed with compiler optimizations.

The top-level page table is the page global directory (PGD), which consists of an array of `pgd_t` types. On most architectures, the `pgd_t` type is an `unsigned long`. The entries in the PGD point to entries in the second-level directory, the PMD.

The second-level page table is the page middle directory (PMD), which is an array of `pmd_t` types. The entries in the PMD point to entries in the PTE.

The final level is called simply the page table and consists of page table entries of type `pte_t`. Page table entries point to physical pages.

In most architectures, page table lookups are handled (at least to some degree) by hardware. In normal operation, hardware can handle much of the responsibility of using the page tables. The kernel must set things up, however, in such a way that the hardware is happy and can do its thing. Figure 15.1 diagrams the flow of a virtual to physical address lookup using page tables.

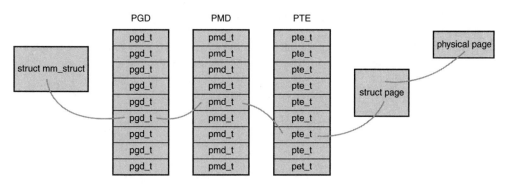

Figure 15.1   Virtual-to-physical address lookup.

Each process has its own page tables (threads share them, of course). The `pgd` field of the memory descriptor points to the process's page global directory. Manipulating and traversing page tables requires the `page_table_lock`, which is located inside the associated memory descriptor.

Page table data structures are quite architecture-dependent and thus are defined in `<asm/page.h>`.

Because nearly every access of a page in virtual memory must be resolved to its corresponding address in physical memory, the performance of the page tables is very critical. Unfortunately, looking up all these addresses in memory can be done only so quickly. To facilitate this, most processors implement a *translation lookaside buffer*, or simply *TLB*, which acts as a hardware cache of virtual-to-physical mappings. When accessing a virtual address, the processor first checks whether the mapping is cached in the TLB. If there is a hit, the physical address is immediately returned. Otherwise, if there is a miss, the page tables are consulted for the corresponding physical address.

Nonetheless, page table management is still a critical—and evolving—part of the kernel. Changes to this area in 2.6 include allocating parts of the page table out of high memory. Future possibilities include shared page tables with copy-on-write semantics. In that scheme, page tables would be shared between parent and child across a fork(). When the parent or the child attempted to modify a particular page table entry, a copy would be created, and the two processes would no longer share that entry. Sharing page tables would remove the overhead of copying the page table entries on fork().

Conclusion

In this suspense-laden chapter, we looked at the abstraction of virtual memory provided to each process. We looked at how the kernel represents the process address space (via struct mm_struct) and how the kernel represents regions of memory within that space (struct vm_area_struct). We covered how the kernel creates (via mmap()) and destroys (via munmap()) these memory regions. Finally, we covered page tables. Because Linux is a virtual memory–based operating system, these concepts are essential to its operation and process model.

The next chapter covers the page cache, a general in-memory data cache used to fulfill all page I/O, and how the kernel performs page-based data writeback.

16

The Page Cache and Page Writeback

The Linux kernel implements a disk cache called the *page cache*. The goal of this cache is to minimize disk I/O by storing data in physical memory that would otherwise require disk access. This chapter deals with the page cache and the process by which changes to the page cache are propagated back to disk, which is called *page writeback*.

Two factors comingle to make disk caches a critical component of any modern operating system. First, disk access is several orders of magnitude slower than memory access—milliseconds versus nanoseconds. Accessing data from memory rather than the disk is much faster, and accessing data from the processor's L1 or L2 cache is faster still. Second, data accessed once will, with a high likelihood, find itself accessed again in the near future. This principle—that access to a particular piece of data tends to be clustered in time—is called *temporal locality*, which ensures that if data is cached on its first access, there is a high probability of a cache hit (access to data in the cache) in the near future. Given that memory is so much faster than disk, coupled with the fact that once-used is likely twice-used data, an in-memory cache of the disk is a large performance win.

Approaches to Caching

The page cache consists of physical pages in RAM, the contents of which correspond to physical blocks on a disk. The size of the page cache is dynamic; it can grow to consume any free memory and shrink to relieve memory pressure. We call the storage device being cached the *backing store* because the disk stands behind the cache as the source of the canonical version of any cached data. Whenever the kernel begins a read operation—for example, when a process issues the read() system call—it first checks if the requisite data is in the page cache. If it is, the kernel can forgo accessing the disk and read the data directly out of RAM. This is called a *cache hit*. If the data is not in the cache, called a *cache miss*, the kernel must schedule block I/O operations to read the data off the disk. After the data is read off the disk, the kernel populates the page cache with the data so that any subsequent reads can occur out of the cache. Entire files need not be cached; the page cache can hold some files in their entirety while storing only a page or two of other files. What is cached depends on what has been accessed.

Write Caching

This explains how data ends up in the page cache via read operations, but what happens when a process writes to disk, for example via the `write()` system call? Generally speaking, caches can implement one of three different strategies. In the first strategy, called *no-write*, the cache simply does not cache write operations. A write operation against a piece of data stored in the cache would be written directly to disk, invalidating the cached data and requiring it to be read from disk again on any subsequent read. Caches rarely employ this strategy because it not only fails to cache write operations, but it also makes them costly by invalidating the cache.

In the second strategy, a write operation would automatically update both the in-memory cache and the on-disk file. This approach is called a *write-through cache* because write operations immediately go *through* the cache to the disk. This approach has the benefit of keeping the cache *coherent*—synchronized and valid for the backing store—without needing to *invalidate* it. It is also simple.

The third strategy, employed by Linux, is called *write-back*.[1] In a write-back cache, processes perform write operations directly into the page cache. The backing store is not immediately or directly updated. Instead, the written-to pages in the page cache are marked as *dirty* and are added to a *dirty list*. Periodically, pages in the dirty list are written back to disk in a process called *writeback*, bringing the on-disk copy in line with the in-memory cache. The pages are then marked as no longer dirty. The term "dirty" can be confusing because what is actually dirty is not the data in the page cache (which is up to date) but the data on disk (which is out of date). A better term would be *unsynchronized*. Nonetheless, we say the cache contents, not the invalid disk contents, are dirty. A write-back is generally considered superior to a write-through strategy because by deferring the writes to disk, they can be coalesced and performed in bulk at a later time. The downside is complexity.

Cache Eviction

The final piece to caching is the process by which data is removed from the cache, either to make room for more relevant cache entries or to shrink the cache to make available more RAM for other uses. This process, and the strategy that decides what to remove, is called *cache eviction*. Linux's cache eviction works by selecting *clean* (not dirty) pages and

---

[1] *Some books or operating systems call such a strategy a* copy-back *or* write-behind *cache. All three names are synonyms. Linux and other Unix systems use the noun "write-back" to refer to the caching strategy and the verb "writeback" to refer to the action of writing cached data back to the backing store. This book follows that usage.*

simply replacing them with something else. If insufficient clean pages are in the cache, the kernel forces a writeback to make more clean pages available. The hard part is deciding *what* to evict. The ideal eviction strategy evicts the pages least likely to be used in the future. Of course, knowing what pages are least likely to be accessed requires knowing the future, which is why this hopeful strategy is often referred to as the *clairvoyant algorithm*. Such a strategy is ideal, but impossible to implement.

Least Recently Used

Cache eviction strategies attempt to approximate the clairvoyant algorithm with what information they have access to. One of the more successful algorithms, particularly for general-purpose page caches, is called *least recently used*, or *LRU*. An LRU eviction strategy requires keeping track of when each page is accessed (or at least sorting a list of pages by access time) and evicting the pages with the oldest timestamp (or at the start of the sorted list). This strategy works well because the longer a piece of cached data sits idle, the less likely it is to be accessed in the near future. Least recently used is a great approximation of most likely to be used. However, one particular failure of the LRU strategy is that many files are accessed once and then never again. Putting them at the top of the LRU list is thus not optimal. Of course, as before, the kernel has no way of knowing that a file is going to be accessed only once. But it does know how many times it has been accessed in the past.

The Two-List Strategy

Linux, therefore, implements a modified version of LRU, called the *two-list strategy*. Instead of maintaining one list, the LRU list, Linux keeps two lists: the *active list* and the *inactive list*. Pages on the active list are considered "hot" and are not available for eviction. Pages on the inactive list are available for cache eviction. Pages are placed on the active list only when they are accessed *while already residing* on the inactive list. Both lists are maintained in a pseudo-LRU manner: Items are added to the tail and removed from the head, as with a queue. The lists are kept in balance: If the active list becomes much larger than the inactive list, items from the active list's head are moved back to the inactive list, making them available for eviction. The two-list strategy solves the only-used-once failure in a classic LRU and also enables simpler, pseudo-LRU semantics to perform well. This two-list approach is also known as *LRU/2*; it can be generalized to n-lists, called *LRU/n*.

We now know how the page cache is populated (via reads and writes), how it is synchronized in the face of writes (via writeback), and how old data is evicted to make way for new data (via a two-list strategy). Let's now consider a real-world scenario to see how the page cache benefits the system. Assume you are working on a large software project—the Linux kernel, perhaps—and have many source files open. As you open and read source code, the files are stored in the page cache. Jumping around from file to file is instantaneous as the data is cached. As you edit the files, saving them appears instantaneous as well because the writes only need to go to memory, not the disk. When you compile the project, the cached files enable the compilation to proceed with far fewer disk accesses, and thus much more quickly. If the entire source tree is too big to fit in memory, some of it must be evicted—and thanks to the two-list strategy, any evicted files will be on the inactive list and likely not one of the source files you are directly editing. Later, hopefully when you are not compiling, the kernel will perform page writeback and update the on-disk copies of the source files with any changes you made. This caching results in a dramatic increase in system performance. To see the difference, compare how long it takes to compile your large software project when "cache cold"—say, fresh off a reboot—versus "cache warm."

The Linux Page Cache

The page cache, as its name suggests, is a cache of pages in RAM. The pages originate from reads and writes of regular filesystem files, block device files, and memory-mapped files. In this manner, the page cache contains chunks of recently accessed files. During a page I/O operation, such as read(),[2] the kernel checks whether the data resides in the page cache. If the data is in the page cache, the kernel can quickly return the requested page from memory rather than read the data off the comparatively slow disk. In the rest of this chapter, we explore the data structures and kernel facilities that maintain Linux's page cache.

The address_space Object

A page in the page cache can consist of multiple noncontiguous physical disk blocks.[3] Checking the page cache to see whether certain data has been cached is made difficult because of this noncontiguous layout of the blocks that constitute each page. Therefore, it is not possible to index the data in the page cache using only a device name and block number, which would otherwise be the simplest solution.

Furthermore, the Linux page cache is quite general in what pages it can cache. Indeed, the original page cache introduced in System V Release 4 cached only filesystem data. Consequently, the SVR4 page cache used its equivalent of the inode object, called struct vnode, to manage the page cache. The Linux page cache aims to cache *any* page-based object, which includes many forms of files and memory mappings.

Although the Linux page cache could work by extending the inode structure (discussed in Chapter 13, "The Virtual Filesystem") to support page I/O operations, such a

---

[2] *As you saw in Chapter 13, "The Virtual Filesystem," it is not the* read() *and* write() *system calls that perform the actual page I/O operation, but the filesystem-specific methods specified by* file->f_op->read() *and* file->f_op->write().

[3] *For example, a physical page is 4KB in size on the x86 architecture, whereas a disk block on many filesystems can be as small as 512 bytes. Therefore, 8 blocks might fit in a single page. The blocks need not be contiguous because the files might be laid out all over the disk.*

choice would confine the page cache to files. To maintain a generic page cache—one not tied to physical files or the `inode` structure—the Linux page cache uses a new object to manage entries in the cache and page I/O operations. That object is the `address_space` structure. Think of `address_space` as the physical analogue to the virtual `vm_area_struct` introduced in Chapter 15, "The Process Address Space." While a single file may be represented by 10 `vm_area_struct` structures (if, say, five processes each `mmap()` it twice), the file has only one `address_space` structure—just as the file may have many virtual addresses but exist only once in physical memory. Like much else in the Linux kernel, `address_space` is misnamed. A better name is perhaps `page_cache_entity` or `physical_pages_of_a_file`.

The `address_space` structure is defined in `<linux/fs.h>`:

```
struct address_space {
        struct inode           *host;             /* owning inode */
        struct radix_tree_root page_tree;         /* radix tree of all pages */
        spinlock_t             tree_lock;         /* page_tree lock */
        unsigned int           i_mmap_writable;   /* VM_SHARED ma count */
        struct prio_tree_root  i_mmap;            /* list of all mappings */
        struct list_head       i_mmap_nonlinear;  /* VM_NONLINEAR ma list */
        spinlock_t             i_mmap_lock;       /* i_mmap lock */
        atomic_t               truncate_count;    /* truncate re count */
        unsigned long          nrpages;           /* total number of pages */
        pgoff_t                writeback_index;   /* writeback start offset */
        struct address_space_operations   *a_ops; /* operations table */
        unsigned long          flags;             /* gfp_mask and error flags */
        struct backing_dev_info *backing_dev_info; /* read-ahead information */
        spinlock_t             private_lock;      /* private lock */
        struct list_head       private_list;      /* private list */
        struct address_space   *assoc_mapping;    /* associated buffers */
};
```

The `i_mmap` field is a priority search tree of all shared and private mappings in this address space. A priority search tree is a clever mix of heaps and radix trees.[4] Recall from earlier that while a cached file is associated with one `address_space` structure, it can have many `vm_area_struct` structures—a one-to-many mapping from the physical pages to many virtual pages. The `i_mmap` field allows the kernel to efficiently find the mappings associated with this cached file.

There are a total of `nrpages` in the address space.

The `address_space` is associated with some kernel object. Normally, this is an inode. If so, the `host` field points to the associated inode. The `host` field is NULL if the associated

---

[4] The kernel implementation is based on the radix priority search tree proposed by Edward M. McCreight in SIAM Journal of Computing, volume 14, number 2, pages 257–276, May 1985.

object is not an inode—for example, if the address_space is associated with the swapper.

address_space Operations

The a_ops field points to the address space operations table, in the same manner as the VFS objects and their operations tables. The operations table is represented by struct address_space_operations and is also defined in <linux/fs.h>:

```
struct address_space_operations {
        int (*writepage)(struct page *, struct writeback_control *);
        int (*readpage) (struct file *, struct page *);
        int (*sync_page) (struct page *);
        int (*writepages) (struct address_space *,
                        struct writeback_control *);
        int (*set_page_dirty) (struct page *);
        int (*readpages) (struct file *, struct address_space *,
                        struct list_head *, unsigned);
        int (*write_begin)(struct file *, struct address_space *mapping,
                        loff_t pos, unsigned len, unsigned flags,
                        struct page **pagep, void **fsdata);
        int (*write_end)(struct file *, struct address_space *mapping,
                        loff_t pos, unsigned len, unsigned copied,
                        struct page *page, void *fsdata);
        sector_t (*bmap) (struct address_space *, sector_t);
        int (*invalidatepage) (struct page *, unsigned long);
        int (*releasepage) (struct page *, int);
        int (*direct_IO) (int, struct kiocb *, const struct iovec *,
                        loff_t, unsigned long);
        int (*get_xip_mem) (struct address_space *, pgoff_t, int,
                        void **, unsigned long *);
        int (*migratepage) (struct address_space *,
                        struct page *, struct page *);
        int (*launder_page) (struct page *);
        int (*is_partially_uptodate) (struct page *,
                        read_descriptor_t *,
                        unsigned long);
        int (*error_remove_page) (struct address_space *,
                        struct page *);
};
```

These function pointers point at the functions that implement page I/O for this cached object. Each backing store describes how it interacts with the page cache via its own address_space_operations. For example, the ext3 filesystem defines its operations in fs/ext3/inode.c. Thus, these are the functions that manage the page cache, including the most common: reading pages into the cache and updated data in the cache. Thus, the readpage() and writepage() methods are most important. Let's look at the steps involved in each, starting with a page read operation. First, the Linux kernel attempts to find the request data in the page cache. The `find_get_page()` method is used to perform this check; it is passed an `address_space` and page offset. These values search the page cache for the desired data:

```
page = find_get_page(mapping, index);
```

Here, `mapping` is the given `address_space` and `index` is the desired offset into the file, in pages. (Yes, calling the `address_space` structure `mapping` just furthers the naming confusion. I'm replicating the kernel's naming for consistency, but I do not condone it.) If the page does not exist in the cache, `find_get_page()` returns NULL and a new page is allocated and added to the page cache:

```
struct page *page;
int error;

/* allocate the page ... */
page = page_cache_alloc_cold(mapping);
if (!page)
        /* error allocating memory */

/* ... and then add it to the page cache */
error = add_to_page_cache_lru(page, mapping, index, GFP_KERNEL);
if (error)
        /* error adding page to page cache */
```

Finally, the requested data can be read from disk, added to the page cache, and returned to the user:

```
error = mapping->a_ops->readpage(file, page);
```

Write operations are a bit different. For file mappings, whenever a page is modified, the VM simply calls

```
SetPageDirty(page);
```

The kernel later writes the page out via the `writepage()` method. Write operations on specific files are more complicated. The generic write path in `mm/filemap.c` performs the following steps:

```
page = __grab_cache_page(mapping, index, &cached_page, &lru_pvec);
status = a_ops->prepare_write(file, page, offset, offset+bytes);
page_fault = filemap_copy_from_user(page, offset, buf, bytes);
status = a_ops->commit_write(file, page, offset, offset+bytes);
```

First, the page cache is searched for the desired page. If it is not in the cache, an entry is allocated and added. Next, the kernel sets up the write request and the data is copied from user-space into a kernel buffer. Finally, the data is written to disk.

Because the previous steps are performed during all page I/O operations, all page I/O is guaranteed to go through the page cache. Consequently, the kernel attempts to satisfy all read requests from the page cache. If this fails, the page is read in from disk and added to the page cache. For write operations, the page cache acts as a staging ground for the writes. Therefore, all written pages are also added to the page cache.

Radix Tree

Because the kernel must check for the existence of a page in the page cache before initiating any page I/O, such a check must be quick. Otherwise, the overhead of searching and checking the page cache could nullify any benefits the cache might provide. (At least if the cache hit rate is low—the overhead would have to be awful to cancel out the benefit of retrieving the data from memory in lieu of disk.)

As you saw in the previous section, the page cache is searched via the `address_space` object plus an offset value. Each `address_space` has a unique radix tree stored as `page_tree`. A radix tree is a type of binary tree. The radix tree enables quick searching for the desired page, given only the file offset. Page cache searching functions such as `find_get_page()` call `radix_tree_lookup()`, which performs a search on the given tree for the given object.

The core radix tree code is available in generic form in `lib/radix-tree.c`. Users of the radix tree need to include `<linux/radix-tree.h>`.

The Old Page Hash Table

Prior to the 2.6 kernel, the page cache was not searched via the radix tree. Instead, a global hash was maintained over all the pages in the system. The hash returned a doubly linked list of entries that hash to the same given value. If the desired page were in the cache, one of the items in the list was the corresponding page. Otherwise, the page was not in the page cache and the hash function returned NULL.

The global hash had four primary problems:

- A single global lock protected the hash. Lock contention was quite high on even moderately sized machines, and performance suffered as a result.
- The hash was larger than necessary because it contained all the pages in the page cache, whereas only pages pertaining to the current file were relevant.
- Performance when the hash lookup failed (that is, the given page was not in the page cache) was slower than desired, particularly because it was necessary to walk the chains off of a given hash value.
- The hash consumed more memory than other possible solutions.

The introduction of the radix tree-based page cache in 2.6 solved these issues.

The Buffer Cache

Individual disk blocks also tie into the page cache, by way of block I/O buffers. Recall from Chapter 14, "The Block I/O Layer," that a buffer is the in-memory representation of a single physical disk block. Buffers act as descriptors that map pages in memory to disk blocks; thus, the page cache also reduces disk access during block I/O operations by both caching disk blocks and buffering block I/O operations until later. This caching is often referred to as the *buffer cache*, although as implemented it is not a separate cache but is part of the page cache.

Block I/O operations manipulate a single disk block at a time. A common block I/O operation is reading and writing inodes. The kernel provides the `bread()` function to perform a low-level read of a single block from disk. Via buffers, disk blocks are mapped to their associated in-memory pages and cached in the page cache.

The buffer and page caches were not always unified; doing so was a major feature of the 2.4 Linux kernel. In earlier kernels, there were two separate disk caches: the page cache and the buffer cache. The former cached pages; the latter cached buffers. The two caches were not unified: A disk block could exist in both caches simultaneously. This led to wasted effort synchronizing the two cached copies and memory wasted in duplicating cached items. Today, we have one disk cache: the page cache. The kernel still needs to use buffers, however, to represent disk blocks in memory. Conveniently, the buffers describe the mapping of a block onto a page, which is in the page cache.

The Flusher Threads

Write operations are deferred in the page cache. When data in the page cache is newer than the data on the backing store, we call that data *dirty*. Dirty pages that accumulate in memory eventually need to be written back to disk. Dirty page writeback occurs in three situations:

- When free memory shrinks below a specified threshold, the kernel writes dirty data back to disk to free memory because only clean (nondirty) memory is available for eviction. When clean, the kernel can evict the data from the cache and then shrink the cache, freeing up more memory.

- When dirty data grows older than a specific threshold, sufficiently old data is written back to disk to ensure that dirty data does not remain dirty indefinitely.

- When a user process invokes the `sync()` and `fsync()` system calls, the kernel performs writeback on demand.

These three jobs have rather different goals. In fact, two separate kernel threads performed the work in older kernels (see the following section). In 2.6, however, a gang[5] of kernel threads, the *flusher threads*, performs all three jobs.

First, the flusher threads need to flush dirty data back to disk when the amount of free memory in the system shrinks below a specified level. The goal of this background writeback is to regain memory consumed by dirty pages when available physical memory is

---

[5] *The term "gang" is commonly used in computer science to denote a group of things that can operate in parallel.*

low. The memory level at which this process begins is configured by the
`dirty_background_ratio` sysctl. When free memory drops below this threshold, the kernel invokes the `wakeup_flusher_threads()` call to wake up one or more flusher threads
and have them run the `bdi_writeback_all ()` function to begin writeback of dirty
pages. This function takes as a parameter the number of pages to attempt to write back.
The function continues writing out data until two conditions are true:

- The specified minimum number of pages has been written out.

- The amount of free memory is above the `dirty_background_ratio` threshold.

These conditions ensure that the flusher threads do their part to relieve low-memory
conditions. Writeback stops prior to these conditions only if the flusher threads write
back *all* the dirty pages and there is nothing left to do.

For its second goal, a flusher thread periodically wakes up (unrelated to low-memory
conditions) and writes out old dirty pages. This is performed to ensure that no dirty pages
remain in memory indefinitely. During a system failure, because memory is volatile, dirty
pages in memory that have not been written to disk are lost. Consequently, periodically
synchronizing the page cache with the disk is important. On system boot, a timer is initialized to wake up a flusher thread and have it run the `wb_writeback()` function. This
function then writes back all data that was modified longer than `dirty_expire_interval`
milliseconds ago. The timer is then reinitialized to expire again in `dirty_writeback_`
`interval` milliseconds. In this manner, the flusher threads periodically wake up and write
to disk all dirty pages older than a specified limit.

The system administrator can set these values either in `/proc/sys/vm` or via sysctl.
Table 16.1 lists the variables.

Table 16.1   **Page Writeback Settings**

Variable	Description
`dirty_background_ratio`	As a percentage of total memory, the number of pages at which the flusher threads begin writeback of dirty data.
`dirty_expire_interval`	In milliseconds, how old data must be to be written out the next time a flusher thread wakes to perform periodic writeback.
`dirty_ratio`	As a percentage of total memory, the number of pages a process generates before it begins writeback of dirty data.
`dirty_writeback_interval`	In milliseconds, how often a flusher thread should wake up to write data back out to disk.
`laptop_mode`	A Boolean value controlling *laptop mode*. See the following section.

The flusher code lives in `mm/page-writeback.c` and `mm/backing-dev.c` and the writeback mechanism lives in `fs/fs-writeback.c`.

Laptop Mode

Laptop mode is a special page writeback strategy intended to optimize battery life by minimizing hard disk activity and enabling hard drives to remain spun down as long as possible. It is configurable via `/proc/sys/vm/laptop_mode`. By default, this file contains a zero and laptop mode is disabled. Writing a one to this file enables laptop mode.

Laptop mode makes a single change to page writeback behavior. In addition to performing writeback of dirty pages when they grow too old, the flusher threads also piggyback off any other physical disk I/O, flushing *all* dirty buffers to disk. In this manner, page writeback takes advantage that the disk was just spun up, ensuring that it will not cause the disk to spin up later.

This behavioral change makes the most sense when `dirty_expire_interval` and `dirty_writeback_interval` are set to large values—say, 10 minutes. With writeback so delayed, the disk is spun up infrequently, and when it does spin up, laptop mode ensures that the opportunity is well utilized. Because shutting off the disk drive is a significant source of power savings, laptop mode can greatly improve how long a laptop lasts on battery. The downside is that a system crash or other failure can lose a lot of data.

Many Linux distributions automatically enable and disable laptop mode, and modify other writeback tunables, when going on and off battery. This enables a machine to benefit from laptop mode when on battery power and then automatically return to normal page writeback behavior when plugged into AC.

History: bdflush, kupdated, and pdflush

Prior to the 2.6 kernel, the job of the flusher threads was met by two other kernel threads, *bdflush* and *kupdated*.

The bdflush kernel thread performed background writeback of dirty pages when available memory was low. A set of thresholds was maintained, similar to the flusher threads', and bdflush was awakened via `wakeup_bdflush()` whenever free memory dropped below those thresholds.

Two main differences distinguish bdflush and the current flusher threads. The first, which is discussed in the next section, is that there was always only one bdflush daemon, whereas the number of flusher threads is a function of the number of disk spindles. The second difference is that bdflush was buffer-based; it wrote back dirty buffers. Conversely, the flusher threads are page-based; they write back whole pages. Of course, the pages can correspond to buffers, but the actual I/O unit is a full page and not a single buffer. This is beneficial as managing pages is easier than managing buffers because pages are a more general and common unit.

Because bdflush flushes buffers only when memory is low or the number of buffers is too large, the kupdated thread was introduced to periodically write back dirty pages. It served an identical purpose to the `wb_writeback()` function.

In the 2.6 kernel, bdflush and kupdated gave way to the *pdflush threads*. Short for *page dirty flush* (more of those confusing names), the pdflush threads performed similar to the flusher threads of today. The main difference is that the number of pdflush threads is dynamic, by default between two and eight, depending on the I/O load of the system. The pdflush threads are not associated with any specific disk; instead, they are global to all disks in the system. This allows for a simple implementation. The downside is that pdflush can easily trip up on congested disks, and congestion is easy to cause with modern hardware. Moving to per-spindle flushing enables the I/O to perform synchronously, simplifying the congestion logic and improving performance. The flusher threads replaced the pdflush threads in the 2.6.32 kernel. The per-spindle flushing is the main difference; the rest of this section is also applicable to pdflush and thus any 2.6 kernel.

Avoiding Congestion with Multiple Threads

One of the major flaws in the bdflush solution was that bdflush consisted of one thread. This led to possible congestion during heavy page writeback where the single bdflush thread would block on a single congested device queue (the list of I/O requests waiting to submit to disk), whereas other device queues would sit relatively idle. If the system has multiple disks and the associated processing power, the kernel should keep each disk busy. Unfortunately, even with plenty of data needing writeback, bdflush can become stuck handling a single queue and fail to keep all disks saturated. This occurs because the throughput of disks is a finite—and unfortunately comparatively small—number. If only a single thread is performing page writeback, that single thread can easily spend a long time waiting for a single disk because disk throughput is such a limiting quantity. To mitigate this, the kernel needs to multithread page writeback. In this manner, no single device queue can become a bottleneck.

The 2.6 kernel solves this problem by enabling multiple flusher threads to exist. Each thread individually flushes dirty pages to disk, allowing different flusher threads to concentrate on different device queues. With the pdflush threads, the number of threads was dynamic, and each thread tried to stay busy grabbing data from the per-superblock dirty list and writing it back to disk. The pdflush approach prevents a single busy disk from starving other disks. This is all good, but what if each pdflush thread were to get hung up writing to the same, congested, queue? In that case, the performance of multiple pdflush threads would not be an improvement over a single thread. The memory consumed, however, would be significantly greater. To mitigate this effect, the pdflush threads employ congestion avoidance: They actively try to write back pages whose queues are not congested. As a result, the pdflush threads spread out their work and refrain from merely hammering on the same busy device.

This approach worked fairly well, but the congestion avoidance was not perfect. On modern systems, congestion is easy to cause because I/O bus technology improves at a slower rate than the rest of the computer—processors keep getting faster according to Moore's Law, but hard drives are only marginally quicker than they were two decades ago. Moreover, aside from pdflush, no other part of the I/O system employs congestion avoidance. Thus, in certain cases pdflush can avoid writing back on a specific disk far longer than desired. With the current flusher threads model, available since 2.6.32, the threads are associated with a block device, so each thread grabs data from its per-block device dirty list and writes it back to its disk. Writeback is thus synchronous and the threads, because there is one per disk, do not need to employ complicated congestion avoidance. This approach improves fairness and decreases the risk of starvation.

Because of the improvements in page writeback, starting with the introduction of pdflush and continuing with the flusher threads, the 2.6 kernel can keep many more disks saturated than any earlier kernel. In the face of heavy activity, the flusher threads can maintain high throughput across multiple disks.

Conclusion

This chapter looked at Linux's page cache and page writeback. We saw how the kernel performs all page I/O through the page cache and how this page cache, by storing data in memory, significantly improves the performance of the system by reducing the amount of disk I/O. We discussed how writes are maintained in the page cache through a process called write-back caching, which keeps pages "dirty" in memory and defers writing the data back to disk. The flusher "gang" of kernel threads handles this eventual page writeback.

Over the last few chapters, we have built a solid understanding of memory and filesystem management. Now let's segue over to the topic of device drivers and modules to see how the Linux kernel provides a modular and dynamic infrastructure for the run-time insertion and removal of kernel code.

17

Devices and Modules

In this chapter, we discuss four kernel components related to device drivers and device management:

- **Device types**—Classifications used in all Unix systems to unify behavior of common devices
- **Modules**—The mechanism by which the Linux kernel can load and unload object code on demand
- **Kernel objects**—Support for adding simple object-oriented behavior and a parent/child relationship to kernel data structures
- **Sysfs**—A filesystem representation of the system's device tree

Device Types

In Linux, as with all Unix systems, devices are classified into one of three types:

- Block devices
- Character devices
- Network devices

Often abbreviated *blkdevs*, *block devices* are addressable in device-specified chunks called *blocks* and generally support *seeking*, the random access of data. Example block devices include hard drives, Blu-ray discs, and memory devices such as flash. Block devices are accessed via a special file called a *block device node* and generally mounted as a filesystem. We discuss filesystems in Chapter 13, "The Virtual Filesystem," and block devices in Chapter 14, "The Block I/O Layer."

Often abbreviated *cdevs*, character devices are generally not addressable, providing access to data only as a stream, generally of characters (bytes). Example character devices include keyboards, mice, printers, and most pseudo-devices. Character devices are accessed via a special file called a *character device node*. Unlike with block devices, applications interact with character devices directly through their device node.

Sometimes called *Ethernet devices* after the most common type of network devices, *network devices* provide access to a network (such as the Internet) via a physical adapter (such as your laptop's 802.11 card) and a specific protocol (such as IP). Breaking Unix's "everything is a file" design principle, network devices are not accessed via a device node but with a special interface called the *socket API*.

Linux provides a handful of other device types, but they are specialized to a single task and not common. One exception is *miscellaneous devices*, often abbreviated *miscdevs*, which are actually a simplified form of character devices. Miscellaneous devices enable a device driver author to represent simple devices easily, trading functionality for common infrastructure.

Not all device drivers represent physical devices. Some device drivers are *virtual*, providing access to kernel functionality. We call these *pseudo devices*; some of the most common are the *kernel random number generator* (accessible at /dev/random and /dev/urandom), the *null device* (accessible at /dev/null), the *zero device* (accessible at /dev/zero), the *full device* (accessible at /dev/full), and the *memory device* (accessible at /dev/mem). Most device drivers, however, represent physical hardware.

Modules

Despite being "monolithic," in the sense that the whole kernel runs in a single address space, the Linux kernel is modular, supporting the dynamic insertion and removal of code from itself at runtime. Related subroutines, data, and entry and exit points are grouped together in a single binary image, a loadable kernel object, called a *module*. Support for modules allows systems to have only a minimal base kernel image, with optional features and drivers supplied via loadable, separate objects. Modules also enable the removal and reloading of kernel code, facilitate debugging, and allow for the loading of new drivers on demand in response to the hot plugging of new devices.

This chapter looks at the magic behind modules in the kernel and how you can write your own module.

Hello, World!

Unlike development on core subsystems of the kernel—which is much of the material discussed thus far—module development is more like writing a new application, at least in the sense that modules have entry points and exit points and live in their own files.

It might be cliché, but it would be a travesty to have the opportunity to write a *Hello, World!* and not capitalize on the occasion. Here is a *Hello, World!* kernel module:

```
/*
 * hello.c - The Hello, World! Kernel Module
 */

#include <linux/init.h>
#include <linux/module.h>
#include <linux/kernel.h>
```

```
/*
 * hello_init - the init function, called when the module is loaded.
 * Returns zero if successfully loaded, nonzero otherwise.
 */
static int hello_init(void)
{
        printk(KERN_ALERT "I bear a charmed life.\n");
        return 0;
}

/*
 * hello_exit - the exit function, called when the module is removed.
 */
static void hello_exit(void)
{
        printk(KERN_ALERT "Out, out, brief candle!\n");
}

module_init(hello_init);
module_exit(hello_exit);

MODULE_LICENSE("GPL");
MODULE_AUTHOR("Shakespeare");
MODULE_DESCRIPTION("A Hello, World Module");
```

This is as simple a kernel module as one can get. The `hello_init()` function is registered as this module's entry point via `module_init()`. The kernel invokes `hello_init()` when the module is loaded. The call to `module_init()` is not actually a function call but a macro that assigns its sole parameter as the initialization function for this module. All `init` functions must have the form,

```
int my_init(void);
```

Because `init` functions are typically not directly invoked by external code, you don't need to export the function beyond file-level scope, and it can be marked as `static`.

Init functions return an `int`. If initialization (or whatever your init function does) was successful, the function must return zero. On failure, the function must unwind any initialization and return nonzero.

This init function merely prints a simple message and returns zero. In actual modules, init functions register resources, initialize hardware, allocate data structures, and so on. If this file were compiled statically into the kernel image, the init function would be stored in the kernel image and run on kernel boot.

The `module_exit()` function registers a module's exit point. In this example, we register the function `hello_exit()`. The kernel invokes the exit point when the module is removed from memory. Exit functions might free resources, shutdown and reset hardware, and perform other cleanup before returning. Simply put, exit functions are responsible for undoing whatever the init function and lifetime of the module did—essentially cleaning up after the module. After the exit function returns, the module is unloaded.

Exit functions must have the form

```
void my_exit(void);
```

As with the init function, you probably want to mark it static.

If this file were compiled into the static kernel image, the exit function would *not* be included, and it would *never* be invoked because if it were not a module, the code could never be removed from memory.

The MODULE_LICENSE() macro specifies the copyright license for this file. Loading a non-GPL module into memory results in the tainted flag being set in the kernel. The copyright license serves two purposes. First, it is for informational purposes; many kernel developers give bug reports less credence when the tainted flag is set in an oops, because they presume a binary-only module (that is, a module that they cannot debug) was loaded into the kernel. Second, non-GPL modules cannot invoke GPL-only symbols. We cover GPL-only symbols in the section "Exported Symbols" later in this chapter.

Finally, the MODULE_AUTHOR() and MODULE_DESCRIPTION() macros provide, respectively, the module's author and a brief description of the module. The value of these macros is entirely informational.

Building Modules

In the 2.6 kernel, building modules is easier than in previous versions, thanks to the new *kbuild* build system. The first decision in building modules is deciding where the module source is to live. You can add the module source to the kernel source proper, either as a patch or by eventually merging your code into the official tree. Alternatively, you can maintain and build your module source outside the source tree.

Living in the Source Tree

Ideally, your module is an official part of Linux and thus lives in the kernel source tree. Getting your work into the kernel proper might require more work at first, but it is the preferred path because when your code is in the Linux kernel, the entire kernel community can help maintain and debug it.

When you decide to place your module in the kernel source tree, the next step is deciding *where* in the tree your module is to live. Drivers are stored in subdirectories of the drivers/ directory in the root of the kernel source tree. Inside drivers/, class, type, and specific device further organize drivers. For example, drivers for character devices live in drivers/char/, block devices live in drivers/block/, and USB devices live in drivers/usb/. The rules are flexible because many devices belong in multiple categories—for instance, many USB devices are character devices, but they reside in drivers/usb/ not drivers/char/. Despite such complications, when you get the hang of it, the organization is understandable and descriptive.

Let's assume you have a character device and want to store it in `drivers/char/`. Inside this directory are numerous C source files and a handful of other directories. Drivers with only one or two source files might simply stick their source in this directory. Drivers with multiple source files or other accompanying data might create a new subdirectory. There is no hard and fast rule. Presume that you want to create your own subdirectory. Let's further assume that your driver is for a fishing pole with a computer interface, the Fish Master XL 3000, so you need to create a `fishing` subdirectory inside `drivers/char/`.

Next, you need to add a line to the Makefile in `drivers/char/`. So you edit `drivers/char/Makefile` and add

```
obj-m += fishing/
```

This causes the build system to descend into the `fishing/` subdirectory whenever it compiles modules. More likely, your driver's compilation is contingent on a specific configuration option; for example, perhaps `CONFIG_FISHING_POLE` (see the section "Managing Configuration Options" later in this chapter for how to add a new configuration option). In that case, you would instead add the line

```
obj-$(CONFIG_FISHING_POLE) += fishing/
```

Finally, inside `drivers/char/fishing/`, you add a new Makefile with the following line:

```
obj-m += fishing.o
```

The build system now descends into `fishing/` and builds the module `fishing.ko` from `fishing.c`. Yes, confusingly, you write an extension of `.o` but the module is compiled as `.ko`. As before, more likely your fishing pole driver's compilation is conditional on a configuration option. So you probably want to write the following:

```
obj-$(CONFIG_FISHING_POLE) += fishing.o
```

One day, your fishing pole driver might get so complicated—autodetection of fishing line test is just the latest "must have!"—that it grows to occupy more than one source file. No problem, anglers! You simply make your Makefile read the following:

```
obj-$(CONFIG_FISHING_POLE) += fishing.o
fishing-objs := fishing-main.o fishing-line.o
```

Now, `fishing-main.c` and `fishing-line.c` will be compiled and linked into `fishing.ko` whenever `CONFIG_FISHING_POLE` is set.

Finally, you might need to pass to the C compiler additional compile flags during the build process solely for your file. To do so, simply add a line such as the following to your Makefile:

```
EXTRA_CFLAGS += -DTITANIUM_POLE
```

If you opted to place your source file(s) in `drivers/char/` and not create a new subdirectory, you would merely place the preceding lines (that you placed in your Makefile in `drivers/char/fishing/`) into `drivers/char/Makefile`.

To compile, run the kernel build process as usual. If your module's build was conditioned on a configuration option, as it was with `CONFIG_FISHING_POLE`, make sure that the option is enabled before beginning.

Living Externally

If you prefer to maintain and build your module outside the kernel source tree, to live the life of an outsider, simply create a Makefile in your own source directory with this single line:

```
obj-m := fishing.o
```

This compiles `fishing.c` into `fishing.ko`. If your source spans multiple files, two lines will suffice:

```
obj-m := fishing.o
fishing-objs := fishing-main.o fishing-line.o
```

This example compiles `fishing-main.c` and `fishing-line.c` into `fishing.ko`.

The main difference in living externally is the build process. Because your module lives outside the kernel tree, you need to instruct `make` on how to find the kernel source files and base Makefile. This is also easy:

```
make -C /kernel/source/location SUBDIRS=$PWD modules
```

In this example, `/kernel/source/location` is the location of your configured kernel source tree. Recall that you should *not* store your working copy of the kernel source tree in `/usr/src/linux` but somewhere else, easily accessible, in your home directory.

Installing Modules

Compiled modules are installed into `/lib/modules/`*version*`/kernel/`, where each directory under `kernel/` corresponds to the module's location in the kernel source tree. For example, with a kernel version of 2.6.34, the compiled fishing pole module would live at `/lib/modules/2.6.34/kernel/drivers/char/fishing.ko` if you stuck it directly in `drivers/char/`.

The following build command is used to install compiled modules into the correct location:

```
make modules_install
```

This needs to be run as root.

Generating Module Dependencies

The Linux module utilities understand dependencies. This means that module `chum` can depend on module `bait`, and when you load the `chum` module, the module loader automatically loads the `bait` module. This dependency information must be generated. Most

Linux distributions generate the mapping automatically and keep it up to date on each boot. To build the module dependency information, as root simply run

```
depmod
```

To perform a quick update, rebuilding only the information for modules newer than the dependency information, run as root

```
depmod -A
```

The module dependency information is stored in the file `/lib/modules/`*version*`/modules.dep`.

Loading Modules

The simplest way to load a module is via `insmod`. This utility is basic. It simply asks the kernel to load the module you specify. The `insmod` program does not perform any dependency resolution or advanced error checking. Usage is trivial. As root, simply run this command:

```
insmod module.ko
```

Here, `module.ko` is the filename of the module that you want to load. To load the fishing pole module, you would run this command as root:

```
insmod fishing.ko
```

In a similar fashion, to remove a module, you use the `rmmod` utility. As root, simply run the following, where `module` is the name of an already-loaded module:

```
rmmod module
```

For example, this command removes the fishing pole module:

```
rmmod fishing
```

These utilities, however, are unintelligent. The utility `modprobe` provides dependency resolution, error checking and reporting, configurable behavior, and more advanced features. Its use is highly encouraged.

To insert a module into the kernel via `modprobe`, run as root:

```
modprobe module [ module parameters ]
```

Here, `module` is the name of the module to load. Any following arguments are taken as parameters to pass to the module on load. See the section "Module Parameters" for a discussion on module parameters.

The `modprobe` command attempts to load not only the requested module, but also any modules on which it depends. Consequently, it is the preferred mechanism for loading kernel modules.

The `modprobe` command can also be used to remove modules from the kernel. To remove a module, as root, run

```
modprobe -r modules
```

Here, *modules* specifies one or more modules to remove. Unlike `rmmod`, `modprobe` also removes any modules on which the given module depends, if they are unused. Section 8 of the Linux manual pages provides a reference on its other, less used, options.

Managing Configuration Options

An earlier section in this chapter looked at compiling the fishing pole module only if the `CONFIG_FISHING_POLE` configuration option was set. Configuration options have been discussed in earlier chapters, too, but now let's look at actually adding a new one, continuing with the fishing pole device driver example.

Thanks to the new "kbuild" system in the 2.6 kernel, adding new configuration options is easy. All you have to do is add an entry to the `Kconfig` file responsible for the applicable branch of the kernel source tree. For drivers, this is usually the directory in which the source lives. If the fishing pole driver lives in `drivers/char/`, you use `drivers/char/Kconfig`.

If you *created* a new subdirectory and want a new `Kconfig` file to live there, you need to source it from an existing `Kconfig`. You do this by adding a line such as the following to an existing `Kconfig` file:

```
source "drivers/char/fishing/Kconfig"
```

In this example, you would add this line to `drivers/char/Kconfig`.

Entries in `Kconfig` are easy to add. Our fishing pole module would look like this:

```
config FISHING_POLE
        tristate "Fish Master 3000 support"
        default n
        help
          If you say Y here, support for the Fish Master 3000 with computer
          interface will be compiled into the kernel and accessible via a
          device node. You can also say M here and the driver will be built as a
          module named fishing.ko.

          If unsure, say N.
```

The first line defines what configuration option this entry represents. Note that the `CONFIG_` prefix is assumed and *not* written.

The second line states that this option is a *tristate*, meaning that it can be built into the kernel (Y), built as a module (M), or not built at all (N). To remove the option of building as a module—say, if this option represented a feature and not a device driver—use the directive `bool` instead of `tristate`. The quoted text following the directive provides the name of this option in the various configuration utilities.

The third line specifies the default for this option, which is not built (n). You can also specify the default as built into the kernel (y) or built as a module (m). For device drivers, the default is usually to not build it (n).

The `help` directive signifies that the rest of the test, indented as it is, is the help text for this entry. The various configuration tools can display this text when requested. Because this text is for developers building their own kernels, it can be succinct and technical. End users do not typically build kernels and, if they did, they could presumably understand the configuration help.

There are other options, too. The `depends` directive specifies options that must be set before this option can be set. If the dependencies are not met, the option is disabled. For example, if you added the following directive to the `Kconfig` entry, the device driver could not be enabled (y or m) until the `CONFIG_FISH_TANK` option is enabled:

```
depends on FISH_TANK
```

The `select` directive is like `depends`, except that it forces the given option if our option is selected. The `select` directive should not be used as frequently as `depends` because it automatically enables other configuration options. The following line enables `CONFIG_BAIT` whenever `CONFIG_FISHING_POLE` is enabled:

```
select BAIT
```

For both `select` and `depends`, you can request multiple options via `&&`. With `depends`, you can also specify that an option *not* be enabled by prefixing the option with an exclamation mark. For example

```
depends on EXAMPLE_DRIVERS && !NO_FISHING_ALLOWED
```

This line specifies that the driver depends on `CONFIG_EXAMPLE_DRIVERS` being set and `CONFIG_NO_FISHING_ALLOWED` being unset.

The `tristate` and `bool` options can be followed by the directive `if`, which makes the entire option conditional on another configuration option. If the condition is not met, the configuration option is not only disabled but also does not appear in the configuration utilities. For example, this directive instructs the configuration system to display an option only if `CONFIG_OCEAN` is set. Here, *deep sea mode* is available only if `CONFIG_OCEAN` is enabled:

```
bool "Deep Sea Mode" if OCEAN
```

The `if` directive can also follow the `default` directive, enforcing the default only if the conditional is met.

The configuration system exports several meta-options to help make configuration easier. The option `CONFIG_EMBEDDED` is enabled only if the users specified that they want to see options designed for disabling key features (presumably to save precious memory on embedded systems). The option `CONFIG_BROKEN_ON_SMP` is used to specify a driver that is not SMP-safe. Normally this option is not set, forcing the user to explicitly acknowledge the brokenness. New drivers, of course, should not use this flag. The option `CONFIG_DEBUG_KERNEL` enables the selection of debugging-related options. Finally, the `CONFIG_EXPERIMENTAL` option is used to flag options that are experimental or otherwise of beta quality. The option defaults to off, again forcing users to explicitly acknowledge the risk before they enable your driver.

Module Parameters

The Linux kernel provides a simple framework, enabling drivers to declare parameters that the user can specify on either boot or module load and then have these parameters exposed in your driver as global variables. These module parameters also show up in sysfs (see later in this chapter). Consequently, creating and managing module parameters that can be specified in a myriad of convenient ways is trivial.

Defining a module parameter is done via the macro `module_param()`:

```
module_param(name, type, perm);
```

Here, *name* is the name of both the parameter exposed to the user and the variable holding the parameter inside your module. The *type* argument holds the parameter's data type; it is one of `byte`, `short`, `ushort`, `int`, `uint`, `long`, `ulong`, `charp`, `bool`, or `invbool`. These types are, respectively, a byte, a short integer, an unsigned short integer, an integer, an unsigned integer, a long integer, an unsigned long integer, a pointer to a `char`, a Boolean, and a Boolean whose value is inverted from what the user specifies. The `byte` type is stored in a single `char` and the Boolean types are stored in variables of type `int`. The rest are stored in the corresponding primitive C types. Finally, the `perm` argument specifies the permissions of the corresponding file in sysfs. The permissions can be specified in the usual octal format, for example `0644` (owner can read and write, group can read, everyone else can read), or by ORing together the usual `S_Ifoo` defines, for example `S_IRUGO | S_IWUSR` (everyone can read; user can also write). A value of zero disables the sysfs entry altogether.

The macro does not declare the variable for you. You must do that *before* using the macro. Therefore, typical use might resemble

```
/* module parameter controlling the capability to allow live bait on the pole */
static int allow_live_bait = 1;            /* default to on */
module_param(allow_live_bait, bool, 0644);  /* a Boolean type */
```

This would be in the outermost scope of your module's source file. In other words, `allow_live_bait` is global to the file.

It is possible to have the internal variable named differently than the external parameter. This is accomplished via `module_param_named()`:

```
module_param_named(name, variable, type, perm);
```

Here, name is the externally viewable parameter name, and `variable` is the name of the internal global variable. For example

```
static unsigned int max_test = DEFAULT_MAX_LINE_TEST;
module_param_named(maximum_line_test, max_test, int, 0);
```

Normally, you would use a type of `charp` to define a module parameter that takes a string. The kernel copies the string provided by the user into memory and points your variable to the string. For example

```
static char *name;
module_param(name, charp, 0);
```

If so desired, it is also possible to have the kernel copy the string directly into a character array that you supply. This is done via `module_param_string()`:

```
module_param_string(name, string, len, perm);
```

Here, `name` is the external parameter name, `string` is the internal variable name, `len` is the size of the buffer named by `string` (or some smaller size, but that does not make much sense), and `perm` is the sysfs permissions (or zero to disable a sysfs entry altogether). For example

```
static char species[BUF_LEN];
module_param_string(specifies, species, BUF_LEN, 0);
```

You can accept a comma-separated list of parameters stored in a C array via `module_param_array()`:

```
module_param_array(name, type, nump, perm);
```

Here, `name` is again the external parameter and internal variable name, `type` is the data type, and `perm` is the sysfs permissions. The new argument, `nump`, is a pointer to an integer in which the kernel stores the number of entries stored into the array. Note that the array pointed to by `name` must be statically allocated. The kernel determines the array's size at compile-time and ensures that it does not cause an overrun. Use is simple. For example

```
static int fish[MAX_FISH];
static int nr_fish;
module_param_array(fish, int, &nr_fish, 0444);
```

You can name the internal array something different than the external parameter with `module_param_array_named()`:

```
module_param_array_named(name, array, type, nump, perm);
```

The parameters are identical to the other macros.

Finally, you can document your parameters by using `MODULE_PARM_DESC()`:

```
static unsigned short size = 1;
module_param(size, ushort, 0644);
MODULE_PARM_DESC(size, "The size in inches of the fishing pole.");
```

All these macros require the inclusion of `<linux/module.h>`.

Exported Symbols

When modules are loaded, they are dynamically linked into the kernel. As with user-space, dynamically linked binaries can call only into external functions explicitly *exported* for use. In the kernel, this is handled via special directives called EXPORT_SYMBOL() and EXPORT_SYMBOL_GPL().

Exported functions are available for use by modules. Functions not exported cannot be invoked from modules. The linking and invoking rules are much more stringent for modules than code in the core kernel image. Core code can call any nonstatic interface in the kernel because all core source files are linked into a single base image. Exported symbols, of course, must be nonstatic, too. The set of exported kernel symbols are known as the *exported kernel interfaces*.

Exporting a symbol is easy. After the function is declared, it is usually followed by an EXPORT_SYMBOL(). For example

```
/*
 * get_pirate_beard_color - return the color of the current pirate's beard.
 * @pirate is a pointer to a pirate structure
 * the color is defined in <linux/beard_colors.h>.
 */
int get_pirate_beard_color(struct pirate *p)
{
        return p->beard.color;
}
EXPORT_SYMBOL(get_pirate_beard_color);
```

Presuming that get_pirate_beard_color() is also declared in an accessible header file, any module can now access it.

Some developers want their interfaces accessible to only GPL-compliant modules. The kernel linker enforces this restriction through use of the MODULE_LICENSE() directive. If you want the previous function accessible to only modules that labeled themselves as GPL-licensed, use instead

```
EXPORT_SYMBOL_GPL(get_pirate_beard_color);
```

If your code is configurable as a module, you must ensure that when compiled as a module all interfaces that it uses are exported. Otherwise linking errors (and a broken module) result.

The Device Model

A significant new feature in the 2.6 Linux kernel is the addition of a unified *device model*. The device model provides a single mechanism for representing devices and describing their topology in the system. Such a system provides several benefits:

- Minimization of code duplication
- A mechanism for providing common facilities, such as reference counting

- The capability to enumerate all the devices in the system, view their status, and see to what bus they attach
- The capability to generate a complete and valid tree of the entire device structure of the system, including all buses and interconnections
- The capability to link devices to their drivers and vice versa
- The capability to categorize devices by their class, such as input device, without the need to understand the physical device topology
- The capability to walk the tree of devices from the leaves up to the root, powering down devices in the correct order

The initial motivation for the device model was this final point: providing an accurate device tree to facilitate power management. To implement device-level power management in the kernel, you need to build a tree representing the device topology in the system: for example, what drive connects to what controller, and what device connects to what bus. When powering down, the kernel must power down the lower (leaf) nodes of the tree before the higher nodes. For example, the kernel needs to turn off a USB mouse before it turns off the USB controller, and the kernel must power down the USB controller before the PCI bus. To do this accurately and efficiently for the entire system, the kernel needs a tree of devices.

Kobjects

At the heart of the device model is the *kobject*, short for *kernel object*, which is represented by struct kobject and defined in <linux/kobject.h>. The kobject is similar to the Object class in object-oriented languages such as C# or Java. It provides basic facilities, such as reference counting, a name, and a parent pointer, enabling the creation of a hierarchy of objects.

Without further ado:

```
struct kobject {
        const char              *name;
        struct list_head        entry;
        struct kobject          *parent;
        struct kset             *kset;
        struct kobj_type        *ktype;
        struct sysfs_dirent     *sd;
        struct kref             kref;
        unsigned int            state_initialized:1;
        unsigned int            state_in_sysfs:1;
        unsigned int            state_add_uevent_sent:1;
        unsigned int            state_remove_uevent_sent:1;
        unsigned int            uevent_suppress:1;
};
```

The name pointer points to the name of this kobject.

The `parent` pointer points to this kobject's parent. In this manner, kobjects build an object hierarchy in the kernel and enable the expression of the relationship between multiple objects. As you shall see, this is actually all that sysfs is: a user-space filesystem representation of the kobject object hierarchy inside the kernel.

The `sd` pointer points to a `sysfs_dirent` structure that represents this kobject in sysfs. Inside this structure is an `inode` structure representing the kobject in the sysfs filesystem.

The `kref` structure provides reference counting. The `ktype` and `kset` structures describe and group kobjects. We look at them in the next two subsections.

Kobjects are usually embedded in other structures and are generally not interesting on their own. Instead, a more important structure, such as `struct cdev`, defined in `<linux/cdev.h>`, has a `kobj` member:

```
/* cdev structure - object representing a character device */
struct cdev {
        struct kobject                  kobj;
        struct module                   *owner;
        const struct file_operations    *ops;
        struct list_head                list;
        dev_t                           dev;
        unsigned int                    count;
};
```

When kobjects are embedded inside other structures, the structures receive the standardized functions that a kobject provides. Most important, the structure's embedded kobject now enables the structure to become part of an object hierarchy. For example, the cdev structure is presentable in an object hierarchy via the parent pointer `cdev->kobj.parent` and the list `cdev->kobj.entry`.

Ktypes

Kobjects are associated with a specific type, called a *ktype*, short for *kernel object type*. Ktypes are represented by `struct kobj_type` and defined in `<linux/kobject.h>`:

```
struct kobj_type {
        void (*release)(struct kobject *);
        const struct sysfs_ops  *sysfs_ops;
        struct attribute        **default_attrs;
};
```

Ktypes have the simple job of describing default behavior for a family of kobjects. Instead of each kobject defining its own behavior, the behavior is stored in a ktype, and kobjects of the same "type" point at the same `ktype` structure, thus sharing the same behavior.

The `release` pointer points to the deconstructor called when a kobject's reference count reaches zero. This function is responsible for freeing any memory associated with this kobject and otherwise cleaning up.

The `sysfs_ops` variable points to a `sysfs_ops` structure. This structure describes the behavior of sysfs files on read and write. It's covered in more detail in the section "Adding Files to sysfs."

Finally, `default_attrs` points to an array of `attribute` structures. These structures define the default *attributes* associated with this kobject. Attributes represent properties related to a given object. If this kobject is exported to sysfs, the attributes are exported as files. The last entry in the array must be `NULL`.

Ksets

Ksets, short for *kernel object sets*, are aggregate collections of kobjects. Ksets work as the base container class for a set of kernel objects, collecting related kobjects, such as "all block devices," together in a single place. Ksets might sound similar to ktypes and prompt the question, "Why have both?" Ksets group related kernel objects together, whereas ktypes enable kernel objects (functionally related or not) to share common operations. The distinction is kept to allow kobjects of identical ktypes to be grouped into different ksets. That is, there are only a handful of ktypes, but many ksets, in the Linux kernel.

The `kset` pointer points at a kobject's associated kset. ksets are represented by the `kset` structure, which is declared in `<linux/kobject.h>`:

```
struct kset {
        struct list_head        list;
        spinlock_t              list_lock;
        struct kobject          kobj;
        struct kset_uevent_ops  *uevent_ops;
};
```

In this structure, `list` is a linked list of all kobjects in this kset, `list_lock` is a spinlock protecting this entry in the list (see Chapter 10, "Kernel Synchronization Methods," for a discussion on spinlocks), `kobj` is a kobject representing the base class for this set, and `uevent_ops` points to a structure that describes the hotplug behavior of kobjects in this kset. *Uevent*, short for *user events*, is a mechanism for communicating with user-space information about the hotplugging and hot removal of devices from a system.

Interrelation of Kobjects, Ktypes, and Ksets

The handful of structures thus far discussed is confusing not because of their number (there are only three) or their complexity (they are all fairly simple), but because they are all interrelated. In the world of kobjects, it is hard to discuss one structure without discussing the others. With the basics of each structure covered, however, you can develop a firm understanding of their relationships.

The important key object is the kobject, represented by `struct kobject`. The kobject introduces basic object properties—such as reference counting, parent-child relationship, and naming—to kernel data structures. The `kobject` structure provides these features in a standard unified way. Kobjects, in and of themselves, are not particularly useful. Instead, kobjects are typically embedded in other data structures, giving those containing structures the features of the kobject.

Kobjects are associated with a specific ktype, which is represented by struct kobj_type and pointed at by the ktype variable inside of the kobject. ktypes define some default properties of related kobjects: destruction behavior, sysfs behavior, and default attributes. The ktype structure is not well named; think of ktypes not as a grouping but as a set of shared operations.

Kobjects are then grouped into sets, called ksets, which are represented by struct kset. Ksets provide two functions. First, their embedded kobject acts as a base class for a group of kobjects. Second, ksets aggregate together related kobjects. In sysfs, kobjects are the individual directories in the filesystem. Related directories—say, perhaps all subdirectories of a given directory—might be in the same kset.

Figure 17.1 depicts the relationship between these data structures.

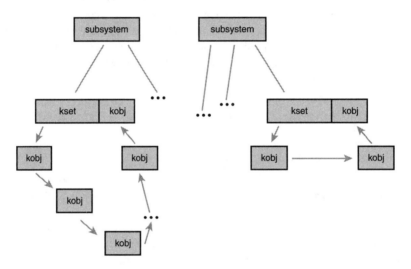

Figure 17.1   Relationship between kobjects, ksets, and subsystems.

Managing and Manipulating Kobjects

With the basic internals of kobjects and friends behind you, it's time to look at the exported interfaces used for managing and manipulating kobjects. Most of the time, driver writers do not have to deal with kobjects directly. Instead, kobjects are embedded in some class-specific structure (as you saw with the character device structure) and managed "behind the scenes" by the associated driver subsystem. Nonetheless, kobjects are not intended to remain hidden and can seep through into driver code or you might be hacking on the driver subsystem itself.

The first step in using a kobject is declaring and initializing it. kobjects are initialized via the function kobject_init, which is declared in <linux/kobject.h>:

```
void kobject_init(struct kobject *kobj, struct kobj_type *ktype);
```

The function's first parameter is the kobject to initialize. Before calling this function, the kobject must be zeroed. This might normally happen during the initialization of the larger function in which the kobject is embedded. If not, a simple call to `memset()` does the trick:

```
memset(kobj, 0, sizeof (*kobj));
```

It is safe to initialize `parent` and `kset` after the zeroing. For example

```
struct kobject *kobj;

kobj = kmalloc(sizeof (*kobj), GFP_KERNEL);
if (!kobj)
        return -ENOMEM;
memset(kobj, 0, sizeof (*kobj));
kobj->kset = my_kset;
kobject_init(kobj, my_ktype);
```

This multistep effort is handled automatically by `kobject_create()`, which returns a newly allocated kobject:

```
struct kobject * kobject_create(void);
```

Usage is simple:

```
struct kobject *kobj;

kobj = kobject_create();
if (!kobj)
        return -ENOMEM;
```

Most uses of kobjects should favor `kobject_create()` or a related helper function rather than directly manipulate the structure.

Reference Counts

One of the primary features provided by kobjects is a unified reference counting system. After initialization, the kobject's reference count is set to one. So long as the reference count is nonzero, the object continues to exist in memory and is said to be *pinned*. Any code that holds a reference to the object first elevates the reference count. When the code is finished with the object, the reference count is decremented. Bumping the reference count is called *getting* a reference to the object, and decrementing the reference count is called *putting* a reference to the object. When the reference count reaches zero, the object can be destroyed and any associated memory freed.

Incrementing and Decrementing Reference Counts

Incrementing the reference count is done via `kobject_get()`, declared in
`<linux/kobject.h>`:

```
struct kobject * kobject_get(struct kobject *kobj);
```

This function returns a pointer to the kobject or `NULL` on failure.

Decrementing the reference count is done via `kobject_put()`, also declared in
`<linux/kobject.h>`:

```
void kobject_put(struct kobject *kobj);
```

If the provided kobject's reference count reaches zero, the release function pointed at
by the ktype associated with the kobject is invoked, any associated memory is freed, and
the object is no longer valid.

Krefs

Internally, the kobject reference counting is provided by the `kref` structure, which is
defined in `<linux/kref.h>`:

```
struct kref {
        atomic_t refcount;
};
```

The lone member is an atomic variable used to hold the reference count. A structure is
used simply to provide type checking. Before using a kref, you must initialize it via
`kref_init()`:

```
void kref_init(struct kref *kref)
{
        atomic_set(&kref->refcount, 1);
}
```

As you can see, this function simply initializes the internal `atomic_t` to one. Consequently, krefs are pinned with a reference count of one as soon as they are initialized; this
is the same behavior as kobjects.

To obtain a reference to a kref, use `kref_get()`, declared in `<linux/kref.h>`:

```
void kref_get(struct kref *kref)
{
        WARN_ON(!atomic_read(&kref->refcount));
        atomic_inc(&kref->refcount);
}
```

This function bumps the reference count. It has no return value. To drop a reference to
a kref, use `kref_put()`, declared in `<linux/kref.h>`:

```
int kref_put(struct kref *kref, void (*release) (struct kref *kref))
{
        WARN_ON(release == NULL);
```

```
        WARN_ON(release == (void (*)(struct kref *))kfree);

        if (atomic_dec_and_test(&kref->refcount)) {
                release(kref);
                return 1;
        }
        return 0;
}
```

This function drops the reference count by one and calls the provided `release()` function if the count is now zero. As noted by the ominous `WARN_ON()` statement, the provided `release()` function cannot simply be `kfree()` but must be a specialized function that accepts `struct kref` as its lone argument and has no return value. The function returns zero, unless the put reference was the last reference to the object, in which case it returns one. Normally, callers of `kref_put()` are unconcerned with the return value.

Rather than having kernel code implement its own reference counting via `atomic_t` types and simple "get" and "put" wrapper functions, developers are encouraged to use the kref type and its helpers to provide a common and known-correct reference counting mechanism in the kernel.

All these functions are defined in `lib/kref.c` and declared in `<linux/kref.h>`.

sysfs

The *sysfs filesystem* is an in-memory virtual filesystem that provides a view of the kobject hierarchy. It enables users to view the device topology of their system as a simple filesystem. Using attributes, kobjects can export files that enable kernel variables to be read from and optionally written to.

Although the intended purpose of the device model was initially to provide a device topology for power management reasons, an offshoot was sysfs. To facilitate debugging, the device model's developer decided to export the tree as a filesystem. This quickly proved quite useful, at first as a replacement for device-related files that previously found themselves in /proc, and later as a powerful view into the system's object hierarchy. Indeed, sysfs, originally called driverfs, predated kobjects. Eventually sysfs made it clear that a new object model would be quite beneficial, and kobject was born. Today, every system with a 2.6 kernel has sysfs. Most systems mount it at /sys.

The magic behind sysfs is simply tying kobjects to directory entries via the `dentry` member inside each kobject. Recall from Chapter 12 that the `dentry` structure represents directory entries. By linking kobjects to dentries, kobjects trivially map to directories. Exporting the kobjects as a filesystem is now as easy as building a tree of the dentries in memory. But wait! kobjects already form a tree, our beloved device model. With kobjects mapping to dentries and the object hierarchy already forming an in-memory tree, sysfs became trivial.

Figure 17.2 is a partial view of the sysfs filesystem as mounted at /sys.

```
|-- block
|   |-- loop0 -> ../devices/virtual/block/loop0
|   |-- md0 -> ../devices/virtual/block/md0
|   |-- nbd0 -> ../devices/virtual/block/nbd0
|   |-- ram0 -> ../devices/virtual/block/ram0
|   `-- xvda -> ../devices/vbd-51712/block/xvda
|-- bus
|   |-- platform
|   |-- serio
|-- class
|   |-- bdi
|   |-- block
|   |-- input
|   |-- mem
|   |-- misc
|   |-- net
|   |-- ppp
|   |-- rtc
|   |-- tty
|   |-- vc
|   `-- vtconsole
|-- dev
|   |-- block
|   `-- char
|-- devices
|   |-- console-0
|   |-- platform
|   |-- system
|   |-- vbd-51712
|   |-- vbd-51728
|   |-- vif-0
|   `-- virtual
|-- firmware
|-- fs
|   |-- ecryptfs
|   |-- ext4
|   |-- fuse
|   `-- gfs2
|-- kernel
|   |-- config
|   |-- dlm
|   |-- mm
|   |-- notes
|   |-- uevent_helper
|   |-- uevent_seqnum
|   `-- uids
`-- module
    |-- ext4
    |-- i8042
    |-- kernel
    |-- keyboard
    |-- mousedev
    |-- nbd
    |-- printk
    |-- psmouse
    |-- sch_htb
    |-- tcp_cubic
    |-- vt
    `-- xt_recent
```

Figure 17.2 A partial view of the **/sys** tree.

The root of the sysfs contains at least 10 directories: `block`, `bus`, `class`, `dev`, `devices`, `firmware`, `fs`, `kernel`, `module`, and `power`. The `block` directory contains one directory for each of the registered block devices on the system. Each of those directories, in turn, contains any partitions on the block device. The `bus` directory provides a view of the system buses. The `class` directory contains a view of the devices on the system organized by high-level function. The `dev` directory is a view of registered device nodes. The `devices` directory is a view of the device topology of the system. It maps directly to the hierarchy of device structures inside the kernel. The `firmware` directory contains a system-specific tree of low-level subsystems such as ACPI, EDD, EFI, and so on. The `fs` directory contains a view of registered filesystems. The `kernel` directory contains kernel configuration options and status information while the `modules` directory contains a view of the system's loaded modules. The `power` directory contains systemwide power management data. Not all systems have all directories and yet other systems have directories not mentioned here.

The most important directory is `devices`, which exports the device model to the world. The directory structure is the actual device topology of the system. Much of the data in other directories is simply alternative organizations of the data in the `devices` directory. For example, `/sys/class/net/` organizes devices by the high-level concept of registered network interfaces. Inside this directory might be the subdirectory `eth0`, which contains the symlink `device` back to the actual device directory in `devices`.

Take a look at `/sys` on a Linux system that you have access to. Such an accurate view into the system's device is neat, and seeing the interconnection between the high-level concepts in `class` versus the low-level physical devices in `devices` and the actual drivers in `bus` is informative. The whole experience is even more rewarding when you realize that this data is provided *free*, as a side effect of the kernel maintaining a device hierarchy, and that this is the representation of the system as maintained inside the kernel.[1]

Adding and Removing kobjects from sysfs

Initialized kobjects are not automatically exported to sysfs. To represent a kobject to sysfs, you use `kobject_add()`:

```
int kobject_add(struct kobject *kobj, struct kobject *parent, const char *fmt, ...);
```

A given kobject's location in sysfs depends on the kobject's location in the object hierarchy. If the kobject's `parent` pointer is set, the kobject maps to a subdirectory in sysfs inside its parent. If the `parent` pointer is not set, the kobject maps to a subdirectory inside

---

[1] *If you find sysfs interesting, you might be interested in HAL, a hardware abstraction layer, which can be found at http://www.freedesktop.org/wiki/Software/hal. HAL builds an in-memory database based on the data in sysfs, linking together the concepts of class, device, and driver. On top of this data, HAL provides a rich API enabling for smarter, more hardware-aware applications.*

`kset->kobj`. If neither the `parent` nor the `kset` fields are set in the given kobject, the kobject is assumed to have no parent and maps to a root-level directory in sysfs. In most use cases, one or both of `parent` and `kset` should be set appropriately before `kobject_add()` is called. Regardless, the name of the directory representing the kobject in sysfs is given by `fmt`, which accepts a `printf()`-style format string.

The helper function `kobject_create_and_add()` combines the work of `kobject_create()` and `kobject_add()` into one function:

```
struct kobject * kobject_create_and_add(const char *name, struct kobject *parent);
```

Note that `kobject_create_and_add()` receives the name of the kobject's directory as a direct pointer, `name`, while `kobject_add()` uses `printf()`-style formatting.

Removing a kobject's sysfs representation is done via `kobject_del()`:

```
void kobject_del(struct kobject *kobj);
```

All of these functions are defined in `lib/kobject.c` and declared in `<linux/kobject.h>`.

Adding Files to sysfs

Kobjects map to directories, and the complete object hierarchy maps nicely to the complete sysfs directory structure, but what about files? Sysfs is nothing but a pretty tree without files to provide actual data.

Default Attributes

A default set of files is provided via the `ktype` field in kobjects and ksets. Consequently, all kobjects of the same type have the same default set of files populating their sysfs directories. The `kobj_type` structure contains a member, `default_attrs`, that is an array of `attribute` structures. Attributes map kernel data to files in sysfs.

The `attribute` structure is defined in `<linux/sysfs.h>`:

```
/* attribute structure - attributes map kernel data to a sysfs file */
struct attribute {
        const char      *name;    /* attribute's name */
        struct module   *owner;   /* owning module, if any */
        mode_t          mode;     /* permissions */
};
```

The `name` member provides the name of this attribute. This will be the filename of the resulting file in sysfs. The `owner` member points to a `module` structure representing the owning module, if any. If a module does not own this attribute, this field is `NULL`. The `mode` member is a `mode_t` type that specifies the permissions for the file in sysfs. Read-only attributes probably want to set this to `S_IRUGO` if they are world-readable and `S_IRUSR` if they are only owner-readable. Writable attributes probably want to set `mode` to `S_IRUGO | S_IWUSR`. All files and directories in sysfs are owned by uid zero and gid zero.

Although `default_attrs` lists the default attributes, `sysfs_ops` describes how to use them. The `sysfs_ops` member is a pointer to a structure of the same name, which is defined in `<linux/sysfs.h>`:

```
struct sysfs_ops {
        /* method invoked on read of a sysfs file */
        ssize_t (*show) (struct kobject *kobj,
                         struct attribute *attr,
                         char *buffer);

        /* method invoked on write of a sysfs file */
        ssize_t (*store) (struct kobject *kobj,
                          struct attribute *attr,
                          const char *buffer,
                          size_t size);
};
```

The `show()` method is invoked when the sysfs entry is read from user-space. It must copy the value of the attribute given by `attr` into the buffer provided by `buffer`. The buffer is `PAGE_SIZE` bytes in length; on x86, `PAGE_SIZE` is 4096 bytes. The function should return the size in bytes of data actually written into `buffer` on success or a negative error code on failure.

The `store()` method is invoked on write. It must read the `size` bytes from `buffer` into the variable represented by the attribute `attr`. The size of the buffer is always `PAGE_SIZE` or smaller. The function should return the size in bytes of data read from `buffer` on success or a negative error code on failure.

Because this single set of functions must handle file I/O requests on *all* attributes, they typically need to maintain some sort of generic mapping to invoke a handler specific to each attribute.

Creating New Attributes

Generally, the default attributes provided by the ktype associated with a kobject are sufficient. Indeed, the purpose of ktype is to provide common operations to kobjects. Sharing ktypes between kobjects not only simplifies programming, but also provides code consolidation and a uniform look and feel to sysfs directories of related objects.

Nonetheless, often some specific instance of a kobject is somehow special. It wants or even needs its own attributes—perhaps to provide data or functionality not shared by the more general ktype. To this end, the kernel provides the `sysfs_create_file()` interface for adding new attributes on top of the default set:

```
int sysfs_create_file(struct kobject *kobj, const struct attribute *attr);
```

This function associates the `attribute` structure pointed at by `attr` with the kobject pointed at by `kobj`. Before it is invoked, the given attribute should be filled out. This function returns zero on success and a negative error code otherwise.

Note that the `sysfs_ops` specified in the kobject's ktype is invoked to handle this new attribute. The existing default `show()` and `store()` methods must be capable of handling the newly created attribute.

In addition to creating actual files, it is possible to create symbolic links. Creating a symlink in sysfs is easy:

```
int sysfs_create_link(struct kobject *kobj, struct kobject *target, char *name);
```

This function creates a link named `name` in the directory mapped from `kobj` to the directory mapped from `target`. This function returns zero on success and a negative error code otherwise.

Destroying Attributes

Removing an attribute is handled via `sysfs_remove_file()`:

```
void sysfs_remove_file(struct kobject *kobj, const struct attribute *attr);
```

Upon call return, the given attribute no longer appears in the given kobject's directory. Symbolic links created with `sysfs_create_link()` can be removed with `sysfs_remove_link()`:

```
void sysfs_remove_link(struct kobject *kobj, char *name);
```

Upon return, the symbolic link `name` in the directory mapped from `kobj` is removed.

All four of these functions are declared in `<linux/kobject.h>`. The `sysfs_create_file()` and `sysfs_remove_file()` functions are defined in `fs/sysfs/file.c`. The `sysfs_create_link()` and `sysfs_remove_link()` functions are defined in `fs/sysfs/symlink.c`.

sysfs Conventions

The sysfs filesystem is currently *the place* for implementing functionality previously reserved for `ioctl()` calls on device nodes or the procfs filesystem. Instead of these deprecated kernel interfaces, today kernel developers implement such functionality as sysfs attributes in the appropriate directory. For example, instead of a new `ioctl()` on a device node, add a sysfs attribute in the driver's sysfs directory. Such an approach avoids the type-unsafe use of obscure `ioctl()` arguments and the haphazard mess of /proc.

To keep sysfs clean and intuitive, however, developers must follow certain conventions. First, sysfs attributes should export one value per file. Values should be text-based and map to simple C types. The goal is to avoid the highly structured or highly messy representation of data we have today in /proc. Providing one value per file makes reading and writing trivial from the command line and enables C programs to easily slurp the kernel's data from sysfs into their own variables. In situations in which the one-value-per-file rule results in an inefficient representation of data, it is acceptable to place multiple values of the same type in one file. Delineate them as appropriate; a simple space probably makes the most sense. Ultimately, think of sysfs attributes as mapping to individual kernel variables (as they usually do), and keep in mind ease of manipulation from user-space, particularly from the shell.

Second, organize data in sysfs in a clean hierarchy. Correctly parent kobjects so that they map intuitively into the sysfs tree. Associate attributes with the correct kobject and keep in mind that the kobject hierarchy exists not only in the kernel, but also as an exported tree to user-space. Keep the sysfs tree organized and hierarchical.

Finally, remember that sysfs provides a kernel-to-user service and is thus a sort of user-space ABI. User programs can rely on the existence, location, value, and behavior of sysfs directories and files. Changing existing files in any way is discouraged, and modifying the *behavior* of a given attribute but keeping its name and location is surely begging for trouble.

These simple conventions should enable sysfs to provide a rich and intuitive interface to user-space. Use sysfs correctly and user-space developers can have a simple and clean, yet powerful and intuitive, interface to the kernel.

The Kernel Events Layer

The Kernel Event Layer implements a kernel-to-user notification system on top of kobjects. After the release of 2.6.0, it became clear that a mechanism for pushing events out of the kernel and up into user-space was needed, particularly for desktop systems that needed a more integrated and asynchronous system. The idea was to have the kernel push events up the stack: Hard drive full! Processor is overheating! Partition mounted!

Early revisions of the event layer came and went, and it was not long before the whole thing was tied intimately to kobjects and sysfs. The result, it turns out, is pretty neat. The Kernel Event Layer models events as *signals* emitting from objects—specifically, kobjects. Because kobjects map to sysfs paths, the *source* of each event is a sysfs path. If the event in question has to do with your first hard drive, /sys/block/hda is the source address. Internally, inside the kernel, we model the event as originating from the backing kobject.

Each event is given a *verb* or *action* string representing the signal. The strings are terms such as *modified* or *unmounted* that describe *what* happened.

Finally, each event has an optional payload. Rather than pass an arbitrary string to user-space that provides the payload, the kernel event layer represents payloads as sysfs attributes.

Internally, the kernel events go from kernel-space out to user-space via netlink. Netlink is a high-speed multicast socket that transmits networking information. Using netlink means that obtaining kernel events from user-space is as simple as blocking on a socket. The intention is for user-space to implement a system daemon that listens on the socket, processes any read events, and transmits the events up the system stack. One possible proposal for such a user-space daemon is to tie the events into D-BUS,[2] which

---

[2] *More information on D-BUS is available at http://dbus.freedesktop.org/.*

already implements a systemwide messaging bus. In this manner, the kernel can emit signals just as any other component in the system.

To send events out to user-space from your kernel code, use `kobject_uevent()`:

```
int kobject_uevent(struct kobject *kobj, enum kobject_action action);
```

The first parameter specifies the kobject emitting this signal. The actual kernel event contains the sysfs path to which this kobject maps.

The second parameter specifies the *action* or *verb* describing this signal. The actual kernel event contains a string that maps to the provided enum `kobject_action` value. Rather than directly provide the string, the function uses an enumeration to encourage value reuse, provide type safety, and prevent typos and other mistakes. The enumerations are defined in `<linux/kobject.h>` and have the form KOBJ_*foo*. Current values include KOBJ_MOVE, KOBJ_ONLINE, KOBJ_OFFLINE, KOBJ_ADD, KOBJ_REMOVE, and KOBJ_CHANGE. These values map to the strings "move," "online," "offline," "add," "remove," and "change," respectively. Adding new action values is acceptable, so long as an existing value is insufficient.

Using kobjects and attributes not only encourages events that fit nicely in a sysfs-based world, but also encourages the creation of new kobjects and attributes to represent objects and data not yet exposed through sysfs.

This and related functions are defined in `lib/kobject_uevent.c` and declared in `<linux/kobject.h>`.

Conclusion

In this chapter, we looked at the kernel functionality used to implement device drivers and manage the device tree, including modules, kobjects (and the related ksets and ktypes), and sysfs. This functionality is important to device driver authors because it enables them to write modular, advanced drivers.

In the final three chapters, we switch the discussion from specific Linux kernel subsystems to general kernel issues, starting in the next chapter with a treatment on debugging the Linux kernel.

18

Debugging

One factor that differentiates kernel development from user-space development is the hardship associated with debugging. It is difficult, relative to user-space, to debug the kernel. To complicate the matter, the stakes are much higher. A fault in the kernel can bring down the whole system.

Success in debugging the kernel—and ultimately, success in kernel development as a whole—is largely a function of your experience and understanding of the operating system. Sure, looks and charm help, too, but to successfully debug kernel issues, you need to understand the kernel. This chapter looks at approaches to debugging the kernel.

Getting Started

Kernel debugging is often a long, head-scratching endeavor. Some bugs have perplexed the entire kernel development community for months. Fortunately, for every one of these laborious issues, there are many simple bugs with an equally simple fix. With luck, all your bugs will remain simple and trivial. You will not know that, however, until you start investigating. For that, you need

- A bug. It might sound silly, but you need a well-defined and specific bug. It helps if it is reliably reproducible (at least for someone), but unfortunately bugs are not always well behaved or well defined.

- A kernel version on which the bug exists. Knowing where the bug *first* appeared is even better. If you do not yet know that, this chapter can teach you a trick for quickly determining it.

- Knowledge of the associated kernel code or luck. Debugging the kernel is tricky, and the more you understand the surrounding code, the better.

Most of this chapter's techniques presume that you can reliably reproduce the bug. Your success in debugging relies on your ability to duplicate the problem. If you cannot, fixing the bug is limited to conceptualizing the problem and finding a flaw in the code. This does often happen, but chances of success are obviously much larger if you can reproduce the problem.

It might seem strange that there are bugs that someone cannot reproduce. In user-space programs, bugs are quite often a straightforward affair. For example, *doing* foo *makes my application dump core*. Bugs in the kernel are often much less clear. The interactions between the kernel, user-space, and hardware are often quite delicate. Race conditions might rear their ugly heads only once in a million iterations of an algorithm. Poorly designed or even miscompiled code can result in acceptable performances on some systems but terrible performances on others. It is common for some specific configuration, on some random machine, under some odd workload, to trigger a bug otherwise unseen. The more information you have when tackling a bug, the better. Many times, if you can reliably reproduce the bug, you are more than halfway home.

Bugs in the Kernel

Bugs in the kernel vary widely. They occur for myriad reasons and manifest themselves in just as many forms. Bugs range from clearly incorrect code (for example, not storing the correct value in the proper place) to synchronization errors (not properly locking a shared variable) to incorrectly managing hardware (sending the wrong operation to the wrong control register). They manifest themselves as everything from poor performance to incorrect behavior to corrupt data to a deadlocked system.

Often, it is a long chain of events that leads from the error in the code to the error witnessed by the user. For example, a shared structure without a reference count might cause a race condition. Without proper accounting, one process might free the structure whereas another process still wants to use it. Later on, the second process may attempt to use the no longer existent structure through a now invalid pointer. This might result in a NULL pointer dereference, reading of garbage data, or nothing bad at all (if the data was not yet overwritten). The NULL pointer dereference causes an oops, whereas the garbage data leads to corruption (and then bad behavior or an oops). The user reports the oops or incorrect behavior. The kernel developer must then work backward from the error and see that the data was accessed after it was freed, there was a race, and the fix is to add proper reference counting on the shared structure.

Debugging the kernel might sound difficult, but in reality, the kernel is not unlike any other large software project. The kernel does have unique issues, such as timing constraints and race conditions, which are a consequence of allowing multiple threads of execution inside the kernel.

Debugging by Printing

The kernel print function printk() behaves almost identically to the C library printf() function. Indeed, throughout this book we have made use of few real differences. For most intentions, this is fine; printk() is simply the name of the kernel's formatted print function. It does have some special features, however.

Robustness

One property of `printk()` easily taken for granted is its robustness. The `printk()` function is callable from just about *anywhere* in the kernel at *any time*. It can be called from interrupt or process context. It can be called while any lock is held. It can be called simultaneously on multiple processors, yet it does not require the caller to hold a lock.

It is a resilient function. This is important because the usefulness of `printk()` rests on the fact that it is always there and always works.

A chink in the armor of `printk()`'s robustness does exist. It is unusable before a certain point in the kernel boot process, prior to console initialization. Indeed, if the console is not initialized, where is the output supposed to go? This is normally not an issue, unless you debug issues early in the boot process (for example, in `setup_arch()`, which performs architecture-specific initialization). Such debugging is a challenge to begin with, and the absence of any sort of print method only compounds the problem.

There is some hope, but not a lot. Hardcore architecture hackers use the hardware that does work (say, a serial port) to communicate with the outside world. This is not fun for most people. The solution is a `printk()` variant that can output to the console early in the boot process: `early_printk()`. The behavior is the same as `printk()`, only the name and its capability to work earlier are changed. This is not a portable solution, however, because not all supported architectures have such a method implemented. It might be your best hope, however, if the architecture you use does implement it—most, including x86, do.

Unless you need to write to the console early in the boot process, you can rely on `printk()` to always work.

Loglevels

The major difference in usage between `printk()` and `printf()` is the capability of the former to specify a *loglevel*. The kernel uses the loglevel to decide whether to print the message to the console. The kernel displays all messages with a loglevel below a specified value on the console.

You specify a loglevel like this:

```
printk(KERN_WARNING "This is a warning!\n");
printk(KERN_DEBUG "This is a debug notice!\n");
printk("I did not specify a loglevel!\n");
```

The `KERN_WARNING` and `KERN_DEBUG` strings are simple defines found in `<linux/kernel.h>`. They expand to a string such as "<4>" or "<7>" that is concatenated onto the front of the `printk()` message. The kernel then decides which messages to print on the console based on this specified loglevel and the current console loglevel, `console_loglevel`. Table 18.1 is a full listing of the available loglevels.

Table 18.1   **Available Loglevels**

Loglevel	Description
KERN_EMERG	An emergency condition; the system is probably dead.
KERN_ALERT	A problem that requires immediate attention.
KERN_CRIT	A critical condition.
KERN_ERR	An error.
KERN_WARNING	A warning.
KERN_NOTICE	A normal, but perhaps noteworthy, condition.
KERN_INFO	An informational message.
KERN_DEBUG	A debug message—typically superfluous.

If you do not specify a loglevel, it defaults to DEFAULT_MESSAGE_LOGLEVEL, which is currently KERN_WARNING. Because this value might change, you should always specify a loglevel for your messages.

The kernel defines the most important loglevel, KERN_EMERG, as <0>, and it defines KERN_DEBUG, the least critical loglevel, as <7>. For example, after the preprocessor is done, the previous examples resemble the following:

```
printk("<4>This is a warning!\n");
printk("<7>This is a debug notice!\n");
printk("<4>did not specify a loglevel!\n");
```

The avenue that you take with your printk() loglevels is up to you. Of course, normal messages that you intend to keep around should have the appropriate loglevel. But the debugging messages you sprinkle everywhere when trying to get a handle on a problem—admit it, we all do it and it works—can have any loglevel you want. One option is to leave your default console loglevel where it is and make all your debugging messages KERN_CRIT or so. Conversely, you can make the debugging messages KERN_DEBUG and change your console loglevel. Each has pros and cons; you decide.

The Log Buffer

Kernel messages are stored in a circular buffer of size LOG_BUF_LEN. This size is configurable at compile time via the CONFIG_LOG_BUF_SHIFT option. The default for a uniprocessor machine is 16KB. In other words, the kernel can simultaneously store 16KB of kernel messages. If the message queue is at this maximum and another call to printk() is made, the new message overwrites the oldest one. The log buffer is called *circular* because the reading and writing occur in a circular pattern.

Using a circular buffer has multiple advantages. Because it is easy to simultaneously write to and read from a circular buffer, even interrupt context can easily use printk().

Furthermore, it makes log maintenance easy. If there are too many messages, new messages simply overwrite the older ones. If there is a problem that results in the generation of many messages, the log simply overwrites itself in lieu of uncontrollably consuming memory. The lone disadvantage of a circular buffer—the possibility of losing messages—is a small price to pay for the simplicity and robustness it affords.

syslogd and klogd

On a standard Linux system, the user-space klogd daemon retrieves the kernel messages from the log buffer and feeds them into the system log file via the syslogd daemon. To read the log, the klogd program can either read the /proc/kmsg file or call the syslog() system call. By default, it uses the /proc approach. In either case, klogd blocks until there are new kernel messages to read. It then wakes up, reads any new messages, and processes them. By default, it sends the messages to the syslogd daemon.

The syslogd daemon appends all the messages it receives to a file, which is by default /var/log/messages. It is configurable via /etc/syslog.conf.

You can have klogd change the console loglevel when it loads by specifying the -c flag when you start it.

Transposing printf() and printk()

When you first start developing kernel code, you most likely will often transpose printf() for printk(). This transposition is only natural, as you cannot deny years of repetition using printf() in user-space development. With luck, this mistake will not last long because the repeated linker errors will eventually grow rather annoying.

Someday, you might find yourself accidentally using printk() instead of printf() in your user-space code. When that day comes, you can say you are a true kernel hacker.

Oops

An *oops* is the usual way a kernel communicates to the user that something bad happened. Because the kernel is the supervisor of the entire system, it cannot simply fix itself or kill itself as it can when user-space goes awry. Instead, the kernel issues an oops. This involves printing an error message to the console, dumping the contents of the registers, and providing a back trace. A failure in the kernel is hard to manage, so the kernel must jump through many hoops to issue the oops and clean up after itself. Often, after an oops the kernel is in an inconsistent state. For example, the kernel could have been in the middle of processing important data when the oops occurred. It might have held a lock or been in the middle of talking to hardware. The kernel must gracefully back out of its current context and try to resume control of the system. In many cases, this is not possible. If the oops occurred in interrupt context, the kernel cannot continue and it panics. A panic results in an instant halt of the system. If the oops occurred in the idle task (pid zero) or the init task (pid one), the result is also a panic because the kernel cannot continue without these important processes. If the oops occurs in any other process, however, the kernel kills the process and tries to continue executing.

An oops might occur for multiple reasons, including a memory access violation or an illegal instruction. As a kernel developer, you will often deal with (and undoubtedly cause) oopses.

What follows is an oops example from a PPC machine, in the timer handler of the tulip network interface card:

```
Oops: Exception in kernel mode, sig: 4
Unable to handle kernel NULL pointer dereference at virtual address 00000001

NIP: C013A7F0 LR: C013A7F0 SP: C0685E00 REGS: c0905d10 TRAP: 0700
Not tainted
MSR: 00089037 EE: 1 PR: 0 FP: 0 ME: 1 IR/DR: 11
TASK = c0712530[0] 'swapper' Last syscall: 120
GPR00: C013A7C0 C0295E00 C0231530 0000002F 00000001 C0380CB8 C0291B80 C02D0000
GPR08: 000012A0 00000000 00000000 C0292AA0 4020A088 00000000 00000000 00000000
GPR16: 00000000 00000000 00000000 00000000 00000000 00000000 00000000 00000000
GPR24: 00000000 00000005 00000000 00001032 C3F7C000 00000032 FFFFFFFF C3F7C1C0
Call trace:
[c013ab30] tulip_timer+0x128/0x1c4
[c0020744] run_timer_softirq+0x10c/0x164
[c001b864] do_softirq+0x88/0x104
[c0007e80] timer_interrupt+0x284/0x298
[c00033c4] ret_from_except+0x0/0x34
[c0007b84] default_idle+0x20/0x60
[c0007bf8] cpu_idle+0x34/0x38
[c0003ae8] rest_init+0x24/0x34
```

PC users might marvel at the number of registers (a whopping 32!). An oops on x86-32, which you might be more familiar with, is a little simpler. The important information, however, is identical for all the architectures: the contents of the registers and the back trace.

The back trace shows the exact function call chain leading up to the problem. In this case, you can see exactly what happened: The machine was idle and executing the idle loop, cpu_idle(), which calls default_idle() in a loop. The timer interrupt occurred, which resulted in the processing of timers. A timer handler, the tulip_timer() function, was executed, which performed a NULL pointer dereference. You can even use the offsets (those numbers such as *0x128/0x1c4* to the right of the functions) to find exactly the offending line.

The register contents can be equally useful, although less commonly so. With a decoded copy of the function in assembly, the register values help you re-create the exact events leading to the problem. Seeing an unexpected value in a register might shine some light on the root of the issue. In this case, you can see which registers held NULL (a value of all zeros) and discover which variable in the function had the unexpected value. In situations such as this, the problem is often a race—in this case, between the timer and some other part of this network card. Debugging a race condition is always a challenge.

ksymoops

The previous oops is said to be *decoded* because the memory addresses are translated into the functions they represent. An undecoded version of the previous oops is shown here:

```
NIP: C013A7F0 LR: C013A7F0 SP: C0685E00 REGS: c0905d10 TRAP: 0700
Not tainted
MSR: 00089037 EE: 1 PR: 0 FP: 0 ME: 1 IR/DR: 11
TASK = c0712530[0] 'swapper' Last syscall: 120
GPR00: C013A7C0 C0295E00 C0231530 0000002F 00000001 C0380CB8 C0291B80 C02D0000
GPR08: 000012A0 00000000 00000000 C0292AA0 4020A088 00000000 00000000 00000000
GPR16: 00000000 00000000 00000000 00000000 00000000 00000000 00000000 00000000
GPR24: 00000000 00000005 00000000 00001032 C3F7C000 00000032 FFFFFFFF C3F7C1C0
Call trace: [c013ab30] [c0020744] [c001b864] [c0007e80] [c00061c4]
[c0007b84] [c0007bf8] [c0003ae8]
```

The addresses in the back trace need to be converted into symbolic names. This is done via the `ksymoops` command in conjunction with the `System.map` generated during kernel compile. If you use modules, you also need some module information. `ksymoops` tries to figure out most of this information, so you can usually invoke it via

```
ksymoops saved_oops.txt
```

The program then spits out a decoded version of the oops. If the default information `ksymoops` uses is unacceptable, or you want to provide alternative locations for the information, the program understands various options. `ksymoops`' manual page has a lot of information that you should read before using it. The `ksymoops` program most likely came with your distribution.

kallsyms

Thankfully, dealing with `ksymoops` is no longer a requirement. This is a big deal, because although developers might have had little problem using it, end users often mismatched `System.map` files or failed to decode oopses altogether.

The 2.5 development kernel introduced the `kallsyms` feature, which is enabled via the `CONFIG_KALLSYMS` configuration option. This option stores in the kernel the symbolic name of function addresses mapped into the kernel image so that the kernel can print decoded back traces. Consequently, decoding oopses no longer requires `System.map` or `ksymoops`. On the downside, the size of the kernel increases a bit because the address-to-symbol mappings must reside in permanently mapped kernel memory. It is worth the memory use, however, during not only development but also deployment. The configuration option `CONFIG_KALLSYMS_ALL` additionally stores the symbolic name of all symbols, not only functions. This is generally needed only by specialized debuggers.

The `CONFIG_KALLSYMS_EXTRA_PASS` option causes the kernel build process to make a second pass over the kernel's object code. It is useful only when debugging `kallsyms` itself.

Kernel Debugging Options

Multiple configure options that you can set during compile to aid in debugging and testing kernel code are available. These options are in the Kernel Hacking menu of the Kernel Configuration Editor. They all depend on `CONFIG_DEBUG_KERNEL`. When hacking on the kernel, consider enabling as many of these options as practical.

Some of the options are rather useful, enabling slab layer debugging, high-memory debugging, I/O mapping debugging, spin-lock debugging, and stack-overflow checking. One of the most useful settings, however, is sleep-inside-spinlock checking, which actually does much more.

Starting with 2.5, the kernel has an excellent infrastructure for detecting all sorts of atomicity violations. Recall from Chapter 9, "An Introduction to Kernel Synchronization," that *atomic* refers to something's capability to execute without division; the code completes without interruption or it does not complete at all. Code that holds a spin lock or has disabled kernel preemption is atomic. Code cannot sleep while atomic—sleeping while holding a lock is a recipe for deadlock.

Thanks to kernel preemption, the kernel has a central atomicity counter. The kernel can be set such that if a task sleeps while atomic, or even does something that *might* sleep, the kernel prints a warning and provides a back trace. Potential bugs that are detectable include calling `schedule()` while holding a lock, issuing a blocking memory allocation while holding a lock, or sleeping while holding a reference to per-CPU data. This debugging infrastructure catches a lot of bugs and is highly recommended.

The following options make the best use of this feature:

```
CONFIG_PREEMPT=y
CONFIG_DEBUG_KERNEL=y
CONFIG_KALLSYMS=y
CONFIG_DEBUG_SPINLOCK_SLEEP=y
```

Asserting Bugs and Dumping Information

A number of kernel routines make it easy to flag bugs, provide assertions, and dump information. Two of the most common are `BUG()` and `BUG_ON()`. When called, they cause an oops, which results in a stack trace and an error message dumped to the kernel. Why these statements cause an oops is architecture-dependent. Most architectures define `BUG()` and `BUG_ON()` as illegal instructions, which result in the desired oops. You normally use these routines as assertions, to flag situations that should not happen:

```
if (bad_thing)
        BUG();
```

Or even better

```
BUG_ON(bad_thing);
```

Most kernel developers believe that BUG_ON() is easier to read and more self-documenting compared to BUG(). Also, BUG_ON() wraps its assertion in an unlikely() statement. Do note that some developers have discussed the idea of having an option to compile BUG_ON() statements away, saving space in embedded kernels. This means that your assertion inside a BUG_ON() should not have any side effects. The macro BUILD_BUG_ON() performs the same purpose, but at compile time. If the provided statement evaluates to true at compile time, the compilation aborts with an error.

A more critical error is signaled via panic(). A call to panic() prints an error message and then halts the kernel. Obviously, you want to use it only in the worst of situations:

```
if (terrible_thing)
        panic("terrible_thing is %ld!\n", terrible_thing);
```

Sometimes, you just want a simple stack trace issued on the console to help you in debugging. In those cases, dump_stack() is used. It simply dumps the contents of the registers and a function back trace to the console:

```
if (!debug_check) {
        printk(KERN_DEBUG "provide some information...\n");
        dump_stack();
}
```

Magic SysRq Key

A possible lifesaver is the Magic SysRq key, which is enabled via the CONFIG_MAGIC_SYSRQ configure option. The SysRq (system request) key is a standard key on most keyboards. On the i386 and PPC, it is accessible via Alt+PrintScreen. When this configure option is enabled, special combinations of keys enable you to communicate with the kernel regardless of what else it is doing. This enables you to perform some useful tasks in the face of a dying system.

In addition to the configure option, there is a sysctl to toggle this feature on and off. To turn it on:

```
echo 1 > /proc/sys/kernel/sysrq
```

From the console, you can hit SysRq-h for a list of available options. SysRq-s syncs dirty buffers to disk, SysRq-u unmounts all filesystems, and SysRq-b reboots the machine. Issuing these three key combinations in a row is a safer way to reboot a dying machine than simply hitting the machine reset switch.

If the machine is badly locked, it might not respond to any Magic SysRq combinations, or it might fail to complete a given command. With luck, however, these options might save your data or aid in debugging. Table 18.2 is a listing of the supported SysRq commands.

Table 18.2 **Supporting SysRq Commands**

Key Command	Description
SysRq-b	Reboots the machine
SysRq-e	Sends a SIGTERM to all processes except init
SysRq-h	Displays SysRq help on the console
SysRq-i	Sends a SIGKILL to all processes except init
SysRq-k	Secures Access Key: kills all programs on this console
SysRq-l	Sends a SIGKILL to all processes including init
SysRq-m	Dumps memory information to console
SysRq-o	Shuts down the machine
SysRq-p	Dumps registers to console
SysRq-r	Turns off keyboard raw mode
SysRq-s	Syncs all mounted filesystems to disk
SysRq-t	Dumps task information to console
SysRq-u	Unmounts all mounted filesystems

The file `Documentation/sysrq.txt` in the kernel source tree has more information. The actual implementation is in `drivers/char/sysrq.c`. The Magic SysRq Key is a vital tool for aiding in debugging or saving a dying system. Because it provides powerful capabilities to any user on the console, however, you should exercise caution on important machines. For your development machine, however, it is a great help.

The Saga of a Kernel Debugger

Many kernel developers have long demanded an in-kernel debugger. Unfortunately, Linus does not want a debugger in his tree. He believes that debuggers lead to bad fixes by misinformed developers. No one can argue with his logic—a fix derived from real understanding of the code is certainly more likely to be correct. Nonetheless, plenty of kernel developers want an official in-kernel debugger. Because it is unlikely to happen anytime soon, a number of patches have arisen that add kernel-debugging support to the standard Linux kernel. Despite being external unofficial patches, these tools are quite well featured and powerful. Before you delve into these solutions, however, it's a good idea to look at how much help the standard Linux debugger, gdb, can give you.

gdb

You can use the standard GNU debugger to glimpse inside a running kernel. Starting the debugger on the kernel is about the same as debugging a running process:

```
gdb vmlinux /proc/kcore
```

The `vmlinux` file is the uncompressed kernel image stored in the root of the build directory, not the compressed `zImage` or `bzImage`.

The optional `/proc/kcore` parameter acts as a core file, to let `gdb` actually peek into the memory of the running kernel. You need to be root to read it.

You can issue just about any of the `gdb` commands for reading information. For example, to print the value of a variable:

```
p global_variable
```

To disassemble a function:

```
disassemble function
```

If you compile the kernel with the `-g` flag (add `-g` to the `CFLAGS` variable in the kernel `Makefile`), `gdb` can provide much more information. For example, you can dump the contents of structures and follow pointers. You also get a much larger kernel, so do not routinely compile with debugging information included.

Unfortunately, this is about the limit of what `gdb` can do. It cannot modify kernel data in any way. It is unable to single-step through kernel code or set breakpoints. The inability to modify kernel data structures is a large downside. Although it is undoubtedly useful for it to disassemble functions on occasion, it would be much more useful if it could modify data, too.

kgdb

`kgdb` is a patch that enables `gdb` to fully debug the kernel remotely over a serial line. It requires two computers. The first runs a kernel patched with `kgdb`. The second debugs the first over the serial line (a null modem cable connecting the two machines) using `gdb`. With `kgdb`, the entire feature set of `gdb` is accessible: reading and writing any variables, settings breakpoints, setting watch points, single stepping, and so on! Special versions of `kgdb` even enable function execution.

Setting up `kgdb` and the serial line is a little tricky, but when complete, debugging is simple. The patch installs plenty of documentation in `Documentation/`—check it out.

Different people maintain the `kgdb` patch for various architectures and kernel releases. Searching online is your best bet for finding a patch for a given kernel.

Poking and Probing the System

As you gain experience in kernel debugging, you gain little tricks to help you poke and probe the kernel for answers. Because kernel debugging can prove rather challenging, every little tip and trick helps. Let's look at a couple.

Using UID as a Conditional

If the code you are developing is process-related, sometimes you can develop alternative implementations without breaking the existing code. This is helpful if you are rewriting an important system call and would like a fully functional system with which to debug it.

For example, assume you are rewriting the `fork()` algorithm to take advantage of an exciting new feature. Unless you get everything right on the first try, it would not be easy to debug the system: A nonfunctioning `fork()` system call is certain to result in a nonfunctioning system. As always, there is hope.

Often, it is safe to keep the remaining algorithm in place and construct your replacement on the side. You can achieve this by using the user id (UID) as a conditional with which to decide which algorithm to use:

```
if (current->uid != 7777) {
    /* old algorithm .. */
} else {
    /* new algorithm .. */
}
```

All users except UID 7777 will use the old algorithm. You can create a special user, with UID 7777, for testing the new algorithm. This makes it much easier to test critical process-related code.

Using Condition Variables

If the code in question is not in process context, or if you want a more global method of controlling the feature, you can use a condition variable. This approach is even simpler than using the UID. Simply create a global variable and use it as a conditional check in your code. If the variable is zero, you follow one code path. If it is nonzero, you follow another. The variable can be set via an interface you export or a poke from the debugger.

Using Statistics

Sometimes you want to get a feel for how often a specific event occurs. Sometimes you want to compare multiple events and generate some ratios for comparison. You can do this easily by creating statistics and a mechanism to export their values.

For instance, say you want to look at the occurrence of *foo* and the occurrence of *bar*. In a file, ideally the one where these events occur, declare two global variables:

```
unsigned long foo_stat = 0;
unsigned long bar_stat = 0;
```

For each occurrence of these events, increment the appropriate variable. Then export the data however you feel fit. For example, you can create a file in `/proc` with the values or write a system call. Alternatively, simply read them via a debugger.

Note that this approach is not particularly SMP-safe. Ideally, you would use atomic operations. For a trivial one-time debugging statistic, however, you normally do not need such protection.

Rate and Occurrence Limiting Your Debugging

Often, you want to stick some debugging checks (with some corresponding print statements) in an area to sniff out a problem. In the kernel, however, some functions are called many times per second. If you stick a call to `printk()` in such a function, the system is overwhelmed with debugging output and quickly grows unusable.

Two relatively simple tricks exist to prevent this problem. The first is *rate limiting*, which is useful when you want to watch the progression of an event, but the event occurs rather often. To prevent a deluge of debugging output, you print your debug message (or do whatever you are doing) only every few seconds. For example

```
static unsigned long prev_jiffy = jiffies;    /* rate limiting */


if (time_after(jiffies, prev_jiffy + 2*HZ)) {
    prev_jiffy = jiffies;
    printk(KERN_ERR "blah blah blah\n");
}
```

In this example, the debug message is printed at most every 2 seconds. This prevents any flood of information on the console, and the computer remains usable. You might need the rate limiting to be larger or smaller, depending on your needs.

If you are *only* using `printk()`, you can use a special function to rate limit your `printk()` calls:

```
if (error && printk_ratelimit())
        printk(KERN_DEBUG "error=%d\n", error);
```

The `printk_ratelimit()` function returns zero if rate limiting is in effect and nonzero otherwise. By default, the function allows only one message every 5 seconds but allows an initial burst of up to ten messages before that cap is enforced. These parameters are tunable via the `printk_ratelimit` and `printk_ratelimit_burst` sysctl, respectively.

Another sticky situation arises if you try to determine if a codepath is exercised in a particular way. Unlike the previous example, you do not want real-time notification. This is an especially sticky situation if it is of the sort where if it is triggered once, it is triggered a lot. The solution here is not to rate limit the debugging, but *occurrence limit* it:

```
static unsigned long limit = 0;


if (limit < 5) {
    limit++;
    printk(KERN_ERR "blah blah blah\n");
}
```

This example caps the debugging output to five. After five such messages, the conditional is always false.

In both examples, the variables should be `static` and local to the function, as shown. This enables the variable's values to persist across function calls.

Neither of these examples are SMP- or preempt-safe, although a quick switch to atomic operators makes them safe. For temporary debugging checks, you often need not be so fastidious.

Binary Searching to Find the Culprit Change

It is usually useful to know when a bug was introduced into the kernel source. If you know that a bug occurred in version 2.6.33, but not 2.4.29, you have a clear picture of the changes that occurred to cause the bug. The bug fix is often as simple as reverting or otherwise fixing the bad change.

Many times, however, you do not know what kernel version introduced the bug. You know that the bug is in the *current* kernel, but it seemed to have always been in the current kernel! With a little effort, you can find the offending change. With the change in hand, the bug fix is usually near.

To start, you need a reliably reproducible problem—preferably, a bug that you can verify immediately after boot. Next, you need a known-good kernel. You might already know this. For example, if you know a couple months back the kernel worked, grab a kernel from that period. If you are wrong, try an earlier release. It shouldn't be too hard to find a kernel without the bug.

Next, you need a known-bad kernel. To make things easier, start with the earliest kernel you know to have the bug.

Now, you begin a binary search from the known-bad kernel down to the known-good kernel. Let's look at an example. Assume the latest known-good kernel is 2.6.11 and the earliest known-bad is 2.6.20. Start by picking a kernel in the middle, such as 2.6.15. Test 2.6.15 for the bug. If 2.6.15 works, you know the problem began in a later kernel, so try a kernel in between 2.6.15 and 2.6.20—say, 2.6.17. On the other hand, if 2.6.15 does not work, you know the problem is in an earlier kernel, so you might try 2.6.13. Rinse and repeat.

Eventually you should narrow the problem down to two subsequently released kernels—one of which has the bug and one of which does not. You then have a clear picture of the changes that caused the bug. This approach beats looking at every kernel!

Binary Searching with Git

The git source management tool provides a useful mechanism for performing binary searches. If you use git to control your copy of the Linux source tree, it can automate the binary search process. Moreover, the git tool performs the binary search at the *revision level*, actually pinpointing the specific commit that introduced the bug. Unlike many git-related tasks, binary searching with git is not hard. To start, you tell git you want to begin a binary search:

```
$ git bisect start
```

You then provide git with the earliest broken revision:

```
$ git bisect bad <revision>
```

If the latest version of the kernel is your known-earliest offender, you do not need to provide a revision:

```
$ git bisect bad
```

You then provide git with the latest working revision:

```
$ git bisect good v2.6.28
```

Git then automatically checks out the Linux source tree bisecting the provided bad and good revisions. You then compile, run, and test that revision. If it works, you run:

```
$ git bisect good
```

If it does not work—that is, if the given kernel revision demonstrates the bug—you run

```
$ git bisect bad
```

On each command, git again bisects the tree on a per-revision basis, returning the next bisection as needed. You repeat the process until there are no more bisections possible. Git then prints the offending revision number.

This can be a long process, but git does make it easy. If you think you know the source of the bug—say, it is clear in x86-specific boot code—you can instruct git to only bisect among commits touching a specified list of directories:

```
$ git bisect start – arch/x86
```

When All Else Fails: The Community

Perhaps you have tried everything that you can think of. You have slaved over the keyboard for countless hours—indeed, perhaps countless days—and the solution still escapes you. If the bug is in the mainstream Linux kernel, you can always elicit the help of the other developers in the kernel community.

A brief, but complete, email sent to the kernel mailing list describing the bug and your findings might help aid in discovery of a solution. After all, no one likes bugs.

Chapter 20, "Patches, Hacking, and the Community," specifically addresses the community and its primary forum, the Linux Kernel Mailing List (LKML).

Conclusion

This chapter covered debugging the kernel, the process of determining *why* implementation diverges from intention. We looked at several techniques, from built-in kernel debug infrastructure to debuggers, from logging to binary searching with git. Because debugging the Linux kernel can be a significantly more difficult task than debugging a user-space application, the material in this chapter is crucial to anyone intending to actually write kernel code.

In the next chapter, we cover another general topic: portability in the Linux kernel. Onward!

19

Portability

Linux is a *portable* operating system that supports a wide range of computer architectures. *Portability* refers to how easily—if at all—code can move from one system architecture to another. We know that Linux is portable because it has already been *ported* to various systems. But this portability did not occur overnight—it requires diligence and a constant eye toward writing portable code. Consequently, it is now easy, relatively speaking, to bring Linux up on a new system. This chapter discusses how to write portable code—the issues you need to keep in mind when writing both core kernel code and device drivers.

Portable Operating Systems

Some operating systems are designed with portability as a primary feature. As little code as possible is machine-specific. Assembly is kept to a minimum, and interfaces and features are sufficiently general and abstract so that they work on a wide range of architectures. The obvious benefit is the relative ease with which a new architecture can be supported. In some cases, highly portable and simple operating systems can be moved to a new architecture with just a few hundred lines of unique code. The downside is that architecture-specific features are not supported, and code cannot be hand-tuned for a specific machine. With this design choice, optimal code is traded for portable code. Some examples of highly portable operating systems are Minix, NetBSD, and many academic systems.

On the opposite side are operating systems that trade all portability for highly customized, optimal code. As much as possible, code is written in assembly or otherwise designed for a specific architecture. Kernel features are designed around specific architectural features. Consequently, moving the operating system to a new architecture is tantamount to rewriting the kernel from scratch and, even if possible, the operating system might be ill-suited for use on other architectures. With this design decision, portable code is traded for optimal code. Such systems are often harder to maintain than more portable systems. Of course, these systems need not be more efficient than a more portable system; their willingness to disregard portability, however, allows for a no-compromise design. Microsoft DOS and Windows 95 are two examples of this design decision.

Linux takes the middle road toward portability. As much as practical, interfaces and core code are architecture-independent C code. Where performance is critical, however, kernel features are tuned for each architecture. For example, much fast-path and low-level code is architecture-dependent and often written in assembly. This approach enables Linux to remain portable without foregoing optimizations. Where portability would hinder performance, performance generally wins. Otherwise, code is kept portable.

Generally, exported kernel interfaces are architecture-independent. If any parts of the function need to be unique for each supported architecture (either for performance reasons or as a necessity), that code is implemented in separate functions and called as needed. Each supported architecture then implements its architecture-specific functions and links them into the kernel image.

A good example is the scheduler. The large majority of the scheduler is written in architecture-independent C and lives in `kernel/sched.c`. A few jobs of the scheduler, such as switching processor state or swapping out the address space, are architecture-dependent. Consequently, the C method `context_switch()`, which switches from one process to another, calls the methods `switch_to()` and `switch_mm()`, to switch processor state and switch address space, respectively.

The code for `switch_to()` and `switch_mm()` is independently implemented by each architecture that Linux supports. When Linux is ported to a new architecture, the new architecture must provide an implementation for these functions.

Architecture-specific files are located in `arch/`*`architecture`*`/`, where *architecture* is a short name representing each architecture in Linux. As an example, the Intel x86 architecture is given the short name x86. (This architecture supports both x86-32 and x86-64.) Architecture-specific files for these machines live in `arch/x86`. The supported architectures in the 2.6 kernel series are `alpha`, `arm`, `avr32`, `blackfin`, `cris`, `frv`, `h8300`, `ia64`, `m32r`, `m68k`, `m68knommu`, `mips`, `mn10300`, `parisc`, `powerpc`, `s390`, `sh`, `sparc`, `um`, `x86`, and `xtensa`. A more complete listing of these architectures is in Table 19.1, later in this chapter.

History of Portability in Linux

When Linus first unleashed Linux on the unsuspecting world, it ran only on Intel i386 machines. Although the operating system was rather generalized and well written, portability was not a major concern. In fact, Linus even once suggested Linux would never run on anything but the i386 architecture! In 1993, however, work began on porting Linux to the Digital Alpha architecture. The Digital Alpha was a modern high-performance RISC-based architecture with 64-bit memory addressing. This is a stark contrast to Linus's original 386. Nonetheless, the initial port of Linux to the Alpha took about a year, and the Alpha became the first officially supported architecture after x86. This port was perhaps rather difficult because it had the unwelcome challenge of being the first. Instead of simply grafting support for the Alpha onto the kernel, pieces of the kernel were rewritten as needed with portability in mind.[1] Although this made for more work overall, the result was much cleaner and future porting was made much easier.

Although the first releases of Linux supported only the Intel i386 architecture, the 1.2 kernel series added support for Digital Alpha, MIPS, and SPARC—although support was somewhat experimental.

With the release of the 2.0 kernel, Linux officially added support for the Motorola 68k and PowerPC. Additionally, the architectures previously supported in 1.2 were labeled official and stable.

The 2.2 kernel series brought even more architecture support with the addition of ARM, IBM S/390, and UltraSPARC. A few years later, 2.4 nearly doubled the number of supported architectures to 15, as support was added for the CRIS, IA-64, 64-bit MIPS, HP PA-RISC, 64-bit IBM S/390, and Hitachi SH.

The current kernel, 2.6, brought the number of supported architectures to 21 with the addition of AVR, FR-V, Motorola 68k without MMU, M32xxx, H8/300, IBM POWER, Xtensa, and a version of the kernel that runs in a virtual machine under Linux, known as Usermode Linux.

Each of these architectures supports various chip and machine types. Some supported architectures, such as ARM and PowerPC, each support many different chips and machine types. Others, such as x86 and SPARC, support both 32-bit and 64-bit variants of their processors. Therefore, although Linux runs under 21 broad architectures, it runs on many more machines!

Word Size and Data Types

A *word* is the amount of data that a machine can process at one time. This fits into the document analogy that includes *characters* (usually 8 bits) and *pages* (many words, often 4KB or 8KB worth) as other measurements of data. A word is an integer number of bytes—for example, one, two, four, or eight. When someone talks about the "n-bits" of a machine, they are generally talking about the machine's *word size*. For example, when people say that the Intel i7 is a 64-bit chip, they are referring to its word size, which is 64 bits, or eight bytes.

The size of a processor's general-purpose registers (GPRs) is equal to its word size. The widths of the components in a given architecture—for example, the memory bus—are usually at least as wide as the word size. Typically, at least in the architectures that Linux supports, the virtual memory address space is equal to the word size, although the physical address space is sometimes less. Consequently, the size of a pointer is equal to the word size. Additionally, the size of the C type `long` is equal to the word size, whereas the size of

---

[1] *This is a common occurrence in Linux kernel development. If something is going to be done at all, it must be done right. Kernel developers are not averse to rewriting large amounts of code in the name of perfection.*

the int type is sometimes less than that of the word size. For example, the Alpha has a 64–bit word size. Consequently, registers, pointers, and the long type are 64 bits in length. The int type, however, is 32-bits long. The Alpha can access and manipulate 64 bits—one word—at a time.

Words, Doublewords, and Confusion

Some operating systems and processors do not call the standard data size a *word*. Instead, a word is some fixed size based on history or arbitrary naming decisions. For example, some operating systems might partition data sizes into bytes (8 bits), words (16 bits), double words (32 bits), and quad words (64 bits), despite the fact that the system in question may be 32 bits. Windows NT-based systems, such as Windows 7, employ this naming scheme. In this book—and Linux in general—a word is the standard data size of the processor, as previously discussed.

Each supported architecture under Linux defines BITS_PER_LONG in <asm/types.h> to the length of the C long type, which is the system word size. A full listing of all supported architectures and their word size is in Table 19.1.

Table 19.1   **Supported Linux Architectures**

Architecture	Description	Word Size
alpha	Digital Alpha	64 bits
arm	ARM and StrongARM	32 bits
avr	AVR	32 bits
blackfin	Blackfin	32 bits
cris	CRIS	32 bits
frv	FR-V	32 bits
h8300	H8/300	32 bits
ia64	IA-64	64 bits
m32r	M32xxx	32 bits
m68k	Motorola 68k	32 bits
m68knommu	m68k without MMU	32 bits
mips	MIPS	32 and 64 bits
parisc	HP PA-RISC	32 and 64 bits
powerpc	PowerPC	32 and 64 bits
s390	IBM S/390	32 and 64 bits
Sh	Hitachi SH	32 bits
Sparc	SPARC	32 and 64 bits
Um	Usermode Linux	32 and 64 bits
x86	x86-32 and x86-64	32 and 64 bits

Table 19.1 **Supported Linux Architectures**

Architecture	Description	Word Size
xtensa	Xtensa	32 bits

Traditionally, Linux implemented 32- and 64-bit variants of a given architecture separately. For example, early in the 2.6 kernel series there existed both i386 & x86-64, mips & mips64, and ppc & ppc64 architectures. An effort, now complete, has unified these architectures under a single directory in arch/, capable of supporting both 32 and 64-bits from a single codebase.

The C standard explicitly leaves the size of the standard variable types up to implementations.[2] The uncertainty in the standard C types across architectures is both a pro and a con. On the plus side, the standard types can take advantage of the word size of various architectures, and types need not explicitly specify a size. The size of the C long type is guaranteed to be the machine's word size. On the downside, however, code cannot assume that the standard C types have any specific size. Furthermore, there is no guarantee that an int is the same size as a long.[3]

The situation grows even more confusing because there doesn't need to be a relation between the types in user-space and kernel-space. The sparc64 architecture provides a 32-bit user-space; therefore, pointers and both the int and long types are 32-bit. In kernel-space, however, sparc64 has a 32-bit int type and 64-bit pointers and long types. This is not the norm, however.

Some rules to keep in mind:

- As dictated by the ANSI C standard, a char is always 1 byte.
- Although there is no rule that the int type be 32 bits, it is in Linux on all currently supported architectures.
- The same goes for the short type, which is 16 bits on all current architectures, although no rule explicitly decrees that.
- Never assume the size of a pointer or a long, which can be either 32 bits or 64 bits on the currently supported machines in Linux.
- Because the size of a long varies on different architectures, *never* assume that sizeof(int) is equal to sizeof(long).
- Likewise, do not assume that a pointer and an int are the same size.

Operating systems use a simple mnemonic to describe what sizes their types are. For example, 64-bit Windows is said to be *LLP64*, which means that long and pointer types

---

[2] *With the exception of char, which is always 1 byte.*

[3] *On the 64-bit architectures supported in Linux, in fact, an int and a long are not the same size; an int is 32 bits and a long is 64 bits. Linux's supported 32-bit architectures define both int and long to 32 bits.*

are 64 bits. 64-bit Linux systems are *LP64*: `long` and pointer types are 64-bit. 32-bit Linux systems are ILP32: `int`, `long`, and pointer types are all 32-bit. The mnemonic is useful for showing at a glance what type of operating system implements its word size, because that choice involves a trade off.

Consider ILP64, LP64, and LLP64. In ILP64, the `int`, `long`, and pointer types are all 64 bits in size. This makes programming easier because the main C types are the same size (size mismatch between integers and pointers is a frequent source of programming error), but it has the downside that the common integer type is much larger than often needed. In LP64, programmers can use differently sized integer types, but must be mindful that the size of an `int` type is smaller than that of a pointer. With LLP64, programmers are stuck with both `int` and `long` types of the same size and also have to worry about a size mismatch between all integers and pointers. Most programmers greatly prefer LP64, the model Linux employs.

Opaque Types

Opaque data types do not reveal their internal format or structure. They are about as "black box" as you can get in C. There is not a lot of language support for them. Instead, developers declare a `typedef`, call it an opaque type, and hope no one typecasts it back to a standard C type. All use is generally through a special set of interfaces that the developer creates. An example is the `pid_t` type, which stores a process identification number. The actual size of this type is not revealed—although anyone can cheat and take a peak and see that it is an `int`. If no code makes explicit use of this type's size, it can be changed without too much hassle. Indeed, this was once the case: In older Unix systems, `pid_t` was declared as a `short`.

Another example of an opaque type is `atomic_t`. As discussed in Chapter 10, "Kernel Synchronization Methods," this type holds an integer value that can be manipulated atomically. Although this type is an `int`, using the opaque type helps ensure that the data is used only in the special atomic operation functions. The opaque type also helps hide the usable size of `atomic_t`, which was not always the full 32 bits because of architectural limitations on 32-bit SPARC.

Other examples of opaque types in the kernel include `dev_t`, `gid_t`, and `uid_t`.

Keep the following rules in mind when dealing with opaque types:

- Do not assume the size of the type. It might be 32-bit on some systems and 64-bit on others. Moreover, kernel developers are free to change its size over time.
- Do not convert the type back to a standard C type.
- Be size agnostic. Write your code so that the actual storage and format of the type can change.

Special Types

Some data in the kernel, despite not being represented by an opaque type, requires a specific data type. One example is the `flags` parameter used in interrupt control, which should always be stored in an unsigned `long`.

When storing and manipulating specific data, always pay careful attention to the data type that represents the type and use it. It is a common mistake to store one of these values in another type, such as unsigned int. Although this will not result in a problem on 32-bit architectures, 64-bit machines will have trouble.

Explicitly Sized Types

Often, as a programmer, you need explicitly sized data in your code. This is usually to match external requirements, such as those imposed by hardware, networking, or binary files. For example, a sound card might have a 32-bit register, a networking packet might have a 16-bit field, or an executable file might have an 8-bit cookie. In these cases, the data type that represents the data needs to be *exactly* the right size.

The kernel defines these explicitly sized data types in <asm/types.h>, which is included by <linux/types.h>. Table 19.2 is a complete listing.

Table 19.2 **Explicitly Sized Data Types**

Type	Description
s8	Signed byte
u8	Unsigned byte
s16	Signed 16-bit integer
u16	Unsigned 16-bit integer
s32	Signed 32-bit integer
u32	Unsigned 32-bit integer
s64	Signed 64-bit integer
u64	Unsigned 64-bit integer

The signed variants are rarely used.

These explicit types are merely typedefs to standard C types. On a 64-bit machine, they may look like this:

```
typedef signed char s8;
typedef unsigned char u8;
typedef signed short s16;
typedef unsigned short u16;
typedef signed int s32;
typedef unsigned int u32;
typedef signed long s64;
typedef unsigned long u64;
```

On a 32-bit machine, however, they are likely defined as follows:

```
typedef signed char s8;
typedef unsigned char u8;
```

```
typedef signed short s16;
typedef unsigned short u16;
typedef signed int s32;
typedef unsigned int u32;
typedef signed long long s64;
typedef unsigned long long u64;
```

These types can be used only inside the kernel, in code that is never revealed to user-space (say, inside a user-visible structure in a header file). This is for reasons of namespace. The kernel also defines user-visible variants of these types, which are simply the same type prefixed by two underscores. For example, the unsigned 32-bit integer type that is safe to export to user-space is __u32. This type is the same as u32; the only difference is the name. You can use either name inside the kernel, but if the type is user-visible, you must use the underscored prefixed version to prevent polluting user-space's namespace.

Signedness of Chars

The C standard says that the char data type can be either signed or unsigned. It is the responsibility of the compiler, the processor, or both to decide what the suitable default for the char type is.

On most architectures, char is signed by default and thus has a range from −128 to 127. On a few other architectures, such as ARM, char is unsigned by default and has a range from 0 to 255.

For example, on systems where a char is by default unsigned, this code ends up storing 255 instead of −1 in i:

```
char i = -1;
```

On other machines, where char is by default signed, this code correctly stores −1 in i. If the programmer's intention is to store −1, the previous code should be

```
signed char i = -1;
```

And if the programmer really intends to store 255, the code should read

```
unsigned char = 255;
```

If you use char in your code, assume it can be *either* a signed char or an unsigned char. If you need it to be explicitly one or the other, declare it as such.

Data Alignment

Alignment refers to a piece of data's location in memory. A variable is *naturally aligned* if it exists at a memory address that is a multiple of its size. For example, a 32-bit type is naturally aligned if it is located in memory at an address that is a multiple of 4 (that is, its lowest 2 bits are zero). Thus, a data type with size 2^n bytes must have an address with the n least significant bits set to zero.

Some architectures have stringent requirements on the alignment of data. On some systems, usually RISC-based ones, a load of unaligned data results in a processor trap (a handled error). On other systems, accessing unaligned data works but results in a degradation of performance. When writing portable code, alignment issues must be avoided, and all types should be naturally aligned.

Avoiding Alignment Issues

The compiler generally prevents alignment issues by naturally aligning all data types. In fact, alignment issues are normally not major concerns of the kernel developers—the gcc developers worry about them so other programmers need not. Issues arise, however, when a programmer plays too closely with pointers and accesses data outside the environment anticipated by the compiler.

Accessing an aligned address with a recast pointer of a larger-aligned address causes an alignment issue (whatever that might mean for a particular architecture). That is, this is bad news:

```
char wolf[] = "Like a wolf";
char *p = &wolf[1];
unsigned long l = *(unsigned long *)p;
```

This example treats the pointer to a char as a pointer to an unsigned long, which might result in the 32- or 64-bit unsigned long value being loaded from an address that is not a multiple of 4 or 8, respectively.

This sort of convoluted access might look obscure, and it usually is. Nevertheless, it comes up; so be careful. The real-world examples are generally not so obvious or convoluted.

Alignment of Nonstandard Types

As mentioned, the aligned address of a standard data type is a multiple of the size of that data type. Nonstandard (complex) C types have the following alignment rules:

- The alignment of an array is the alignment of the base type; thus, each element is further aligned correctly.
- The alignment of a union is the alignment of the largest included type.
- The alignment of a structure is such that an array of the structure will have each element of the array properly aligned.

Structures also introduce padding, which introduces other issues.

Structure Padding

Structures are padded so that each element of the structure is naturally aligned. This ensures that when the processor accesses a given element in the structure, that element is aligned. For example, consider this structure on a 32-bit machine:

```
struct animal_struct {
        char dog;               /* 1 byte */
        unsigned long cat;      /* 4 bytes */
```

```
        unsigned short pig;    /* 2 bytes */
        char fox;              /* 1 byte */
};
```

The structure is not laid out exactly like this in memory because the natural alignment of the structure's members is insufficient. Instead, the compiler creates the structure such that in memory, the struct resembles the following:

```
struct animal_struct {
        char dog;              /* 1 byte */
        u8 __pad0[3];          /* 3 bytes */
        unsigned long cat;     /* 4 bytes */
        unsigned short pig;    /* 2 bytes */
        char fox;              /* 1 byte */
        u8 __pad1;             /* 1 byte */
};
```

The padding variables exist to ensure proper natural alignment. The first padding provides a 3-byte waste-of-space to place cat on a 4-byte boundary. This automatically aligns the remaining types because they are all smaller than cat. The second and final padding is to pad the size of the struct. The extra byte ensures the structure is a multiple of 4, and thus each member of an array of this structure is naturally aligned.

Note that sizeof(animal_struct) returns 12 for *either* of these structures on most 32-bit machines. The C compiler automatically adds this padding to ensure proper alignment.

You can often rearrange the order of members in a structure to obviate the need for padding. This gives you properly aligned data without the need for padding and therefore a smaller structure:

```
struct animal_struct {
        unsigned long cat;     /* 4 bytes */
        unsigned short pig;    /* 2 bytes */
        char dog;              /* 1 byte */
        char fox;              /* 1 byte */
};
```

This structure is only 8 bytes in size. It might not always be possible to rearrange structure definitions, however. For example, if this structure were specified as part of a standard or already used in existing code, its order is set in stone, although such requirements are less common in the kernel (which lacks a formal ABI) than user-space. Often, you might want to use a specific order for other reasons—for example, to best lay out variables to optimize cache behavior. Note that ANSI C specifies that the compiler must never change the order of members in a structure[4]—it is always up to you, the programmer. The

---

[4] If the compiler could arbitrarily change the order of items in a structure, any existing code using the structure would break. In C, functions calculate the location of variables in a structure simply by adding offsets to the base address of the structure.

compiler can help you out, however: The -Wpadded flag instructs gcc to generate a warning whenever padding is added to a structure.

Kernel developers need to be aware of structure padding when using structures whole-sale—that is, when sending them out over the network or when saving a structure directly to disk, because the required padding might differ among various architectures. This is one reason C does not have a native structure comparison operator. The padding in a structure might contain gibberish, and it is not possible to do a byte-by-byte comparison of one structure to another. The C designers (correctly) felt it is best for the programmer to write a comparison function unique to each situation, taking advantage of the structure's layout.

Byte Order

Byte ordering is the order of bytes within a word. Processors can number the bytes in a word such that the least significant bit is either the first (left-most) or last (right-most) value in the word. The byte ordering is called *big-endian* if the most significant byte is encoded first, with the remaining bytes decreasing in significance. The byte ordering is called *little-endian* if the least significant byte is encoded first, with the remaining bytes growing in significance.

Never assume any given byte ordering when writing kernel code (unless you are writing code for a specific architecture, of course). The Linux kernel supports machines of both byte orders—including machines that can select from either ordering upon boot—and generic code must be compatible with either.

Figure 19.1 is an example of a big-endian byte ordering. Figure 19.2 is an example of a little-endian byte ordering.

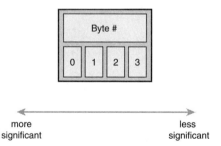

Figure 19.1   Big-endian byte ordering.

The x86 architecture, in both 32- and 64-bit variants, is little-endian. Most other architectures are big-endian.

Let's look at what this encoding means in practice. Consider the number 1027, stored as a four-byte integer in binary:

```
00000000 00000000 00000100 00000011
```

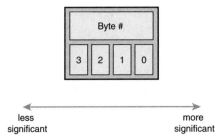

Figure 19.2   Little-endian byte ordering.

The internal storage in memory is different on big- versus little-endian, as shown in Table 19.3.

Table 19.3   **Big Versus Little Endian**

Address	Big Endian	Little Endian
0	00000000	00000011
1	00000000	00000100
2	00000100	00000000
3	00000011	00000000

Notice how the big-endian architecture stores the most significant bytes in its smallest address. This is the exact inverse of little-endian.

As a final example, here is a simple code snippet to test whether a given architecture is big- or little-endian:

```
int x = 1;

if (*(char *)&x == 1)
    /* little endian */
else
    /* big endian */
```

This works either in user-space or inside the kernel.

History of Big- and Little-Endian

The terms *big-endian* and *little-endian* derive from Jonathan Swift's 1726 satirical novel, *Gulliver's Travels*. In the novel, the fictional Lilliputians' major political issue is whether eggs should be cracked open on the big end or the little end. Those who favor the big end are big-endians, whereas those who favor the small are little-endians.

The similarity between the Lilliputians and our big-endian versus little-endian debate is that the argument is rooted deeper in politics than technical merits.

Each supported architecture in Linux defines one of __BIG_ENDIAN or __LITTLE_ENDIAN in <asm/byteorder.h> in correspondence to the machine's byte order. This header file also includes a family of macros from include/linux/byteorder/, which help with conversions to and from the various orderings. The most commonly needed macros are

```
u23 __cpu_to_be32(u32);    /* convert cpu's byte order to big-endian */
u32 __cpu_to_le32(u32);    /* convert cpu's byte order to little-endian */
u32 __be32_to_cpu(u32);    /* convert big-endian to cpu's byte order */
u32 __le32_to_cpus(u32);   /* convert little-endian to cpu's byte order */
```

These convert from one byte order to another. In the case that the orders are the same (for example, if converting from native ordering to big-endian, and the processor is big-endian), the macros do nothing. Otherwise, they return the converted value.

Time

The measurement of time is another kernel concept that can differ between architectures or even kernel revisions. Never assume the frequency of the timer interrupt or the number of jiffies per second. Instead, always use HZ to scale your units of time correctly. This is important because not only can the timer frequency differ among the various architectures, but it can also change on a given architecture from one kernel release to the next.

For example, HZ is 100 on the x86 platforms. That is, the timer interrupt occurs 100 times per second, or every 10 milliseconds. Earlier in the 2.6 kernel series, however, HZ was 1000 on x86. On other architectures, the value differs: Alpha has HZ equal to 1024 and ARM has it equal to 100.

Never simply compare jiffies to a number such as 100 and assume that always means the same thing. To scale time appropriately, multiply or divide by HZ. For example

```
HZ            /* one second */
(2*HZ)        /* two seconds */
(HZ/2)        /* half a second */
(HZ/100)      /* 10 ms */
(2*HZ/100)    /* 20 ms */
```

HZ is defined in <asm/param.h>. The subject is discussed further in Chapter 10.

Page Size

When working with pages of memory, never assume the page size. It is a common mistake for x86-32 programmers to assume that the page size is 4KB. Although this is true on x86-32 machines, other architectures have different sizes. Some architectures support multiple page sizes, in fact! Table 19.4 lists each support architecture's valid page size(s).

Table 19.4   **Architecture Page Size(s)**

Architecture	PAGE_SHIFT	PAGE_SIZE
alpha	13	8KB
arm	12, 14, 15	4KB, 16KB, 32KB
avr	12	4KB
cris	13	8KB
blackfin	12	4KB
frv	14	16KB
h8300	12	4KB
	12, 13, 14, 16	4KB, 8KB, 16KB, 64KB
m32r	12	4KB
m68k	12, 13	4KB, 8KB
m68knommu	12	4KB
mips	12	4KB
mn10300	12	4KB
parisc	12	4KB
powerpc	12	4KB
s390	12	4KB
sh	12	4KB
sparc	12, 13	4KB, 8KB
um	12	4KB
x86	12	4KB
xtensa	12	4KB

When working with pages of memory, use PAGE_SIZE as the size of a page, in bytes. The value PAGE_SHIFT is the number of bits to left-shift an address to derive its page number. For example, on x86-32 with 4KB pages, PAGE_SIZE is 4096 and PAGE_SHIFT is 12. These values are defined in <asm/page.h>.

Processor Ordering

Recall from Chapter 9, "An Introduction to Kernel Synchronization," and Chapter 10 that architectures have varying degrees of processor ordering. Some have strict ordering constraints in which all loads and stores occur in the order prescribed by the code. Other chips have weak ordering, and loads and stores are reordered as the processor sees fit.

In your code, if you depend on data ordering, ensure that even the weakest ordered processor commits your load and stores in the right order by using the appropriate barriers, such as `rmb()` and `wmb()`. Chapter 10 has more information.

SMP, Kernel Preemption, and High Memory

It might seem somewhat incorrect to include symmetrical multiprocessing, kernel preemption, and high memory in a discussion of portability. After all, these are not machine characteristics that affect an operating system, but instead they are features of the Linux kernel that are indeed somewhat architecture-agnostic. They represent, however, important configuration options that you should always assume are available in your code. That is, always program for an SMP/preempt/highmem system and you will always be safe, in any configuration. In addition to the previous portability rules, you need to follow these as well:

- Always assume your code will run on an SMP system and use appropriate locking.
- Always assume your code will run with kernel preemption enabled and use appropriate locking and kernel preemption statements.
- Always assume your code will run on a system with high memory (memory not permanently mapped) and use `kmap()` as needed.

Conclusion

Writing portable, clean, proper code for the Linux kernel has two major implications:

- Always code for the greatest common factor: Assume anything can happen and any potential constraint is in place.
- Always assume that only the lowest common denominator is available: Do not assume any given kernel feature is available and require only the minimum architectural features.

Writing portable code requires awareness of many issues, including wordsize, data type size, alignment, padding, byte order, signedness, endianness, page size, and processor load/store ordering. In the majority of kernel programming, the primary concern is in ensuring that data types are used correctly. Nonetheless, one day an archaic architecture issue will arise, so it is important to understand portability issues and always write clean, portable code inside the kernel.

Patches, Hacking, and the Community

One of the greatest benefits of Linux is the large community of users and developers that surround it. The community provides eyes to check your code, experts to provide advice, and users to test and report issues. Most important, the community is the final arbiter of what code is accepted into Linus' official kernel tree. Understanding how the system works is extremely important.

The Community

If the Linux kernel community had to call somewhere home, it would be the *Linux Kernel Mailing List*. The Linux Kernel Mailing List (or as the regulars abbreviate it, just *lkml*) is the location of the majority of the announcements, discussions, debates, and flame wars over the kernel. New features are discussed, and most code is posted to the list before any action is taken. The list sees upward of 300 messages a day, so it is not for the faint of heart. Subscribing (or at least reading a digest or the archives) is recommended for anyone interested in serious kernel development. You can learn a lot simply by watching the wizards at work.

You can subscribe by sending the following message in plain text to `majordomo@vger.kernel.org`:

```
subscribe linux-kernel <your@email.address>
```

You can get more information at http://vger.kernel.org/ and a FAQ is available at http://www.tux.org/lkml/.

Numerous websites and other mailing lists pertain to the kernel specifically and Linux in general. An excellent resource for beginning kernel hackers is http://kernel-newbies.org/—a website that, of all things, caters to those cutting their teeth on the kernel. Two other excellent sources of kernel information are http://www.lwn.net/, Linux Weekly News, which has a great kernel news section, and http://www.kerneltrap.org/, Kernel Trap, which provides insightful commentary on kernel development.

Linux Coding Style

The Linux Kernel, like any large software project, has a defined coding style that stipulates the formatting, style, and layout of your code. This is done not because the Linux kernel style is superior (although it might be) or because your style is illegible, but because *consistency* of coding style is crucial to *productivity* in coding. Yet it is often argued that coding style is irrelevant because it does not affect the compiled object code. In a large project, such as the kernel, in which many developers are involved, consistency of coding style is crucial. Consistency implies familiarity, which leads to ease of reading, lack of confusion, and further expectations that code will continue to follow a given style. This increases the number of developers who can read your code, and the amount of code in which you can read. In an open-source project, the more eyes the better.

It is not so important *what* style is chosen as long as one is indeed selected and used exclusively. Fortunately, Linus long ago laid out the style we should use and most code sticks to it. The majority of the style is covered in Linus's usual humor in the file `Documentation/CodingStyle` in the kernel source tree.

Indention

The stylistic convention for indention is to use tabs that are eight characters in length. This does not mean it is okay to use eight spaces for indention. Each level of indention is a tab over from the previous, and a tab is eight characters in length. For example:

```
static void get_new_ship(const char *name)
{
        if (!name)
                name = DEFAULT_SHIP_NAME;
        get_new_ship_with_name(name);
}
```

For unclear reasons, this rule is one of the most commonly broken, despite its high impact on readability. Eight-character tabs make clearly identifying indention of different code blocks orders of magnitude easier after hours of hacking. The downside, of course, of eight character tabs is that after several levels of indention, not much usable space is left on the line. This is compounded by 80-character line length limits (see subsequent section). Linus' rejoinder to this is that your code should not be so complex and convoluted as to require more than two or three levels of indention. Need you go that deep, he argues, you should refactor your code to pull out layers of complexity (and thus levels of indention) into separate functions.

Switch Statements

Subordinate `case` labels should be indented to the same level as the parent `switch` statement, which helps alleviate the impact of eight character tabs. For example:

```
switch (animal) {
```

```
case ANIMAL_CAT:
        handle_cats();
        break;
case ANIMAL_WOLF:
        handle_wolves();
        /* fall through */
case ANIMAL_DOG:
        handle_dogs();
        break;
default:
        printk(KERN_WARNING "Unknown animal %d!\n", animal);
}
```

It is common (and good) practice to comment when deliberately falling through from one case statement to another, as shown in this example.

Spacing

This section covers the spacing around symbols and keywords, not the spacing used in indention, which we covered in the last two sections. Generally speaking, Linux coding style dictates spaces around most keywords and no spaces between functions and their parentheses. For example:

```
if (foo)
while (foo)
for (i = 0; i < NR_CPUS; i++)
switch (foo)
```

Conversely, functions, macros, and keywords that look like functions—such as sizeof, typeof, and alignof—similarly have no space between the keyword and the parenthesis.

```
wake_up_process(task);
size_t nlongs = BITS_TO_LONG(nbits);
int len = sizeof(struct task_struct);
typeof(*p)
__alignof__(struct sockaddr *)
__attribute__((packed))
```

Within parentheses, there is no space proceeding or preceding the argument, as previously shown. For example, this is verboten:

```
int prio = task_prio( task );  /* BAD STYLE! */
```

Around most binary and tertiary operators, put a space on either side of the operator. For example:

```
int sum = a + b;
int product = a * b;
int mod = a % b;
int ret = (bar) ? bar : 0;
```

```
return (ret ? 0 : size);
int nr = nr ? : 1; /* allowed shortcut, same as "nr ? nr : 1" */
if (x < y)
if (tsk->flags & PF_SUPERPRIV)
mask = POLLIN | POLLRDNORM;
```

Conversely, around most unary operators, put no space between the operator and the operand:

```
if (!foo)
int len = foo.len;
struct work_struct *work = &dwork->work;
foo++;
–bar;
unsigned long inverted = ~mask;
```

Getting the spacing right around the dereference operator is particularly important. The correct style is

```
char *strcpy(char *dest, const char *src)
```

Placing a space on either side of the dereference operator is incorrect style:

```
char * strcpy(char * dest, const char * src)  /* BAD STYLE */
```

Also incorrect is the C++ style of placing the dereference operator next to the type:

```
char* strcpy(char* dest, const char* src)  /* BAD STYLE */
```

Braces

Brace placement is personal, and few technical reasons exist for one convention over the other, but we have to agree on something. The accepted kernel style is to put the opening brace on the first line, at the end of the statement. The closing brace goes on a new line as the first character. Following is an example:

```
if (strncmp(buf, "NO_", 3) == 0) {
        neg = 1;
        cmp += 3;
}
```

If the following token is a continuation of the same statement, the closing brace is not on a line by itself, but on a line shared with that token. For example:

```
if (ret) {
        sysctl_sched_rt_period = old_period;
        sysctl_sched_rt_runtime = old_runtime;
} else {
        def_rt_bandwidth.rt_runtime = global_rt_runtime();
        def_rt_bandwidth.rt_period = ns_to_ktime(global_rt_period());
}
```

And this example:

```
do {
        percpu_counter_add(&ca->cpustat[idx], val);
        ca = ca->parent;
} while (ca);
```

This rule is broken for functions, because functions cannot nest inside functions:

```
unsigned long func(void)
{
  /* ... */
}
```

Finally, statements that do not *need* braces can omit them. For example, the following is encouraged but not required:

```
if (cnt > 63)
      cnt = 63;
```

The logic behind all this is *K&R*.[1] Most of Linux coding style follows *K&R Style*, which is the C coding style used in that famous book.

Line Length

Lines of source code should be kept to fewer than 80 characters in length. This allows code to fit lengthwise on a standard 80×24 terminal.

There is no accepted standard on what to do in cases where code absolutely must wrap 80 characters. Some developers just allow the line to wrap, letting their editor handle the chore of displaying the code in a readable fashion. Other developers break up the lines, manually inserting line breaks where appropriate, perhaps starting each new line a tab stop over from the original.

Similarly, some developers line up function parameters that wrap lines with the open parenthesis. For example:

```
static void get_new_parrot(const char *name,
                           unsigned long disposition,
                           unsigned long feather_quality)
```

Other developers break up the lines but do not line the parameters up, instead use a standard two tabs:

```
int find_pirate_flag_by_color(const char *color,
            const char *name, int len)
```

---

[1] The C Programming Language, *by Brian Kernighan and Dennis Ritchie (Prentice Hall, ISBN# 0-13-11-362-8), nicknamed K&R, is the bible of C, written by C's author and his colleague.*

As there is no definitive rule in this case, the choice is left up to you, the developer. Many kernel contributors, including myself, prefer the former example: Manually break up lines greater than 80 characters in length, trying to align the resulting new lines cleanly with the previous line.

Naming

No name should employ *CamelCase*, *Studly Caps*, or other mixed case schemes. Calling a local variable `idx` or even just `i` is perfectly fine if it is clear what it does. A cute name such as `theLoopIndex` is unacceptable. Hungarian notation (encoding the variable type in the variable name) is unnecessary and should never be used. This is C, not Java; Unix, not Windows.

Nonetheless, global variables and functions should have descriptive names, in lowercase and delimited via an underscore as needed. Calling a global function `atty()` is confusing; a name such as `get_active_tty()` is much more acceptable. This is Linux, not BSD.

Functions

As a rule of thumb, functions should not exceed one or two screens of text and should have fewer than ten local variables. A function should do one thing and do it well. There is no harm in breaking a function into a series of smaller functions. If you are worried about function call overhead, employ *inline functions* via the `inline` keyword.

Comments

Commenting your code is important, but the commenting must be done correctly. Generally, you want to describe *what* and *why* your code is doing what it is doing, not *how* it is doing it. The *how* should be apparent from the code itself. If not, you might need to rethink and refactor what you wrote. Additionally, comments should not include who wrote a function, the modification date, or other trivial nonsense. Such information is generally acceptable at the top of the source file, however.

The kernel uses C-style comments, even though `gcc` supports C++-style comments, too. The general style of a comment in the kernel resembles:

```
/*
 * get_ship_speed() - return the current speed of the pirate ship
 * We need this to calculate the ship coordinates. As this function can sleep,
 * do not call while holding a spinlock.
 */
```

In comments, important notes are often prefixed with "XXX:", and bugs are often prefixed with "FIXME:" like so:

```
/*
```

```
 * FIXME: We assume dog == cat which may not be true in the future
 */
```

The kernel has a facility for self-generating documentation. It is based on GNOME-doc, but slightly modified and renamed Kernel-doc. To create the standalone documentation in HTML format, run

```
make htmldocs
```

Or for postscript

```
make psdocs
```

You can use the system to document your functions by following a special format for your comments:

```
/**
 * find_treasure - find 'X marks the spot'
 * @map - treasure map
 * @time - time the treasure was hidden
 *
 * Must call while holding the pirate_ship_lock.
 */
void find_treasure(int map, struct timeval *time)
{
  /* ... */
}
```

For more information, see `Documentation/kernel-doc-nano-HOWTO.txt`.

Typedefs

The Linux kernel developer community employs a strong dislike of the `typedef` operator. Their rationale is

- `typedef` hides the real type of data structures.
- Because the type is hidden, code is more prone to do bad things, such as pass a structure by value on the stack.
- `typedef` is just being lazy.

Therefore, to avoid ridicule, avoid `typedef`.

Of course, there are a few good uses of `typedefs`: hiding an architecture-specific implementation of a variable or providing forward compatibility when a type may change. Decide carefully whether the `typedef` is truly needed or exists just to reduce the number of characters you need to type.

Use Existing Routines

Do not reinvent the wheel. The kernel provides string manipulation functions, compression routines, and a linked list interface, so use them.

Do not wrap existing interfaces in generic interfaces. Often you see code that was obviously ported from one operating system to Linux, and various kernel interfaces are wrapped in some gross glue function. No one likes this, so just use the provided interfaces directly.

Minimize `ifdefs` in the Source

Putting `ifdef` preprocessor directives directly in the C source is frowned upon. You should never do something like the following in your functions:

```
        . . .
#ifdef CONFIG_FOO
        foo();
#endif
        . . .
```

Instead, define `foo()` to nothing if `CONFIG_FOO` is not set:

```
#ifdef CONFIG_FOO
static int foo(void)
{
        /* .. */
}
#else
static inline int foo(void) { }
#endif /* CONFIG_FOO */
```

Then, you can unconditionally call `foo()`. Let the compiler do the work for you.

Structure Initializers

Labeled identifiers need to be used to initialize structures. This is good because it prevents structure changes from resulting in incorrect initialization. It also enables values to be omitted. Unfortunately, C99 adopted quite an ugly format for labeled identifiers, and gcc is deprecating usage of the previous GNU-style labeled identifier, which was rather handsome. Consequently, kernel code needs to use the new C99 labeled identifier format, however ugly it is:

```
struct foo my_foo = {
    .a    = INITIAL_A,
    .b    = INITIAL_B,
};
```

In this code, a and b are members of `struct foo` and INITIAL_A and INITIAL_B are their initialized values, respectively. If a field is not set, it is set to its default value per ANSI C (for example, pointers are NULL, integers are zero, and floats are 0.0). For example, if `struct foo` also has `int c` as a member, the previous statement would initialize c to zero.

Fixing Up Code Ex Post Facto

If a pile of code falls into your lap that fails to even mildly resemble the Linux kernel coding style, do not fret. A little elbow grease and the `indent` utility can make everything perfect. `indent`, an excellent GNU utility found on most Linux systems, formats source according to given rules. The default settings are for the GNU coding style, which is not too pretty. To get the utility to follow the Linux kernel style, execute the following:

```
indent -kr -i8 -ts8 -sob -l80 -ss -bs -psl <file>
```

This instructs the utility to format the code according to the kernel coding style. Alternatively, the script `scripts/Lindent` automatically invokes `indent` with the desired options.

Chain of Command

Kernel hackers are the developers who work on the kernel. Some do it for pay, some as a hobby, but nearly all for fun. Kernel hackers with significant contributions are listed in the CREDITS file in the root of the kernel source tree.

Most parts of the kernel have an associated *maintainer*. The maintainer is the individual (or individuals) who is in charge of specific parts of the kernel. For example, each individual driver has an associated maintainer. Each kernel subsystem—for example, networking—also has an associated maintainer. The maintainer for a specific driver or subsystem is usually listed in the file MAINTAINERS, which is also located in the root of the kernel source tree.

There is a special type of maintainer, known as the kernel maintainer. This individual actually maintains the kernel tree. Historically, Linus maintains the development kernel (where the real fun is) and the stable kernel for some period after development ends. Shortly after a development kernel becomes a stable kernel, Linus passes the torch to one of the top kernel developers. That developer continues to maintain the tree while Linus begins work on the new development tree. Given the "new world order" in which development on 2.6 continues in perpetuity, Linus remains the maintainer of the 2.6 kernel series. Another developer maintains the 2.4 series, which is in a strict bug-fix-only mode.

Submitting Bug Reports

If you encounter a bug, the best course of action is to write a fix, create a patch, test it, and submit it as discussed in the following sections. Of course, you can also report the problem and get someone to fix it for you.

The most important part of submitting a bug report is fully describing the problem. Describe the symptoms, any system output, and a fully decoded oops (if there is an oops). More important, if you can, provide steps to reliably reproduce the problem and a brief description of your hardware.

Deciding to whom to send the bug report is the next step. The file MAINTAINERS, in the root of the kernel source tree, lists the individuals associated with each driver and subsystem—they should receive any issues related to the code they maintain. If you cannot find an interested party, send the report to the Linux Kernel Mailing List at linux-kernel@vger.kernel.org. Even if you do find a maintainer, CC the kernel mailing list.

The files REPORTING-BUGS and Documentation/oops-tracing.txt provide more information.

Patches

All changes to the Linux kernel are distributed in the form of patches, which are the output of the GNU diff(1) program in a form that is readable by the patch(1) program.

Generating Patches

The simplest way to generate a patch is to have two source trees, one that is the vanilla stock kernel and another that is the stock tree with your modifications. A common scheme is to name the stock tree linux-x.y.z (which is what the source tarball extracts to, initially) and to name your modified tree simply linux. Then, to generate a patch of the two trees, issue the following command from one directory below your trees:

```
diff -urN linux-x.y.z/ linux/ > my-patch
```

This is typically done somewhere in your home, and not /usr/src/linux so that you do not need to be root. The -u flag specifies that the unified diff format should be used. Without this, the patch is ugly and not readable by humans. The -r flag instructs diff to recursively diff all directories, and the -N flag specifies that new files in the modified tree should be included in the diff. Alternatively, if you need to diff only a single file, you can do

```
diff -u linux-x.y.z/some/file linux/some/file > my-patch
```

You need to always diff the trees from one directory below your source trees. This creates a patch that is usable by others, even if their directory names differ. To apply a patch made in this format, do the following from the root of your source tree:

```
patch -p1 < ../my-patch
```

In this example, the patch is named my-patch and is created one directory below the current. The -p1 flag instructs diff to strip the first directory from the patch. This enables you to apply a patch regardless of the directory-naming convention used by the patch maker.

A useful utility is `diffstat`, which generates a histogram of a patch's changes (line additions and removals). To generate the output on one of your patches, do

```
diffstat -p1 my-patch
```

It is often useful to include this output when you post a patch to lkml. Because the `patch(1)` program ignores all lines until a diff is detected, you can even include a short description at the top of the patch.

Generating Patches with Git

If you use Git to manage your source tree, you need to use Git to likewise generate your patches—there is no point going through all the aforementioned manual steps *and* bear the complexity of Git. Generating patches with Git is an easy two-part process. First, you need to author and then locally *commit* your changes. Making changes to a Git tree is the same as a standard source tree. You do not need to do anything special to edit a file stored in Git. After you make your changes, you need to commit them to your Git repository:

```
git commit -a
```

The `-a` flag instructs Git to commit *all* your changes. If you only want to commit changes to a specific file, you can do that, too:

```
git commit some/file.c
```

Even with the `-a` flag, however, Git will not commit new files until they are explicitly added to the repository. To add a file and then commit it (and all other changes), issue the following two commands:

```
git add some/other/file.c
git commit -a
```

When you run *git commit*, Git enables you to enter a change log. Make this entry verbose and complete, fully explaining the commit. (We cover exactly what to include in the next section.) You can create multiple commits against your repository. Thanks to Git's design, subsequent commits can even be against the same file, building off of each other. When you have a commit (or two) in your tree, you can generate a patch for each commit, which you can treat as you do the patches described in the previous section:

```
git format-patch origin
```

This generates patches for all commits in your repository and not in the original tree. Git creates the patches in the root of your kernel source tree. To generate patches for only the last N commits, you can execute the following:

```
git format-patch -N
```

For example, this command generates a patch for only the last commit:

```
git format-patch -1
```

Submitting Patches

Patches should be generated as described in the previous section. If the patch touches a specific driver or subsystem, the patch should be sent to the maintainer listed in MAINTAINER. Either way, the Linux Kernel Mailing List at linux-kernel@vger.kernel.org should be carbon copied. The patch should be sent to the kernel maintainer (for example, Linus) only after extensive discussion, or if the patch is trivial and clearly correct.

Typically, the subject line of the email containing the patch is of the form "*[PATCH] brief description.*" The body of the email describes in technical detail the changes your patch makes and the rationale behind them. Be as specific as possible. Somewhere in the email, note the kernel version against which the patch was created.

Most kernel developers want to read your patch inline with your email and optionally save the whole thing to a single file. Consequently, it is best to insert the patch directly inline in the email, at the end of your message. Be aware that some email clients might wrap lines or otherwise change formatting; this breaks the patch and annoys developers. If your email client does this, see whether it has an "Insert Inline," "Preformat," or similar feature. Otherwise, attaching the patch as plain text without encoding works, too.

If your patch is large or contains several logical changes, you should break the patch into chunks, with each chunk representing a logical change. For example, if you both introduce a new API and change a handful of drivers to use it, you can break the changes into two patches (the new API and then the driver changeover) and two emails. If any chunk requires a previous patch, explicitly state that.

After posting, remain patient and wait for a reply. Do not be discouraged by any negative response—at least you got a response! Discuss the issues and provide updated patches as needed. If you fail to receive *any* response, try to discover what was wrong and resolve the issues. Solicit additional comments from the mailing list and maintainer. With luck, you might see your changes in a future kernel release—congratulations!

Conclusion

The most important quality of any hacker is desire and drive—an itch to scratch, and the determination to scratch it. This book provided a tour of key parts of the kernel, discussing interfaces, data structures, algorithms, and rationale. It provided an insider's view of the kernel, in a practical fashion, to satisfy your curiosity or get you off the ground running in your kernel endeavors.

As I have said before, however, the only way to start is by *reading* and *writing* code. Linux provides a community that not only enables but also *encourages* both activities—so start reading and coding! Happy hacking!

Bibliography

This bibliography lists works complementary to this book. Note that the absolute best "additional reading" to complement this book is the kernel source. Working on Linux, we are all gifted with full and unrestricted access to the source code for an entire modern operating system. Do not take that for granted. Dive in! Read and write code!

Books on Operating System Design

These books cover OS Design as discussed in an undergraduate course. They all tackle the concepts, algorithms, problems, and solutions involved in designing a functional operating system. I recommend them all, but if I had to pick only one, the Deitel book is both comprehensive and enjoyably readable.

Deitel, H., P. Deitel, and D. Choffnes. *Operating Systems*. Prentice Hall, 2003. An awesome *tour de force* on the theory of operating systems, with some excellent case studies putting the theory to practice.

Tanenbaum, Andrew. *Modern Operating Systems*. Prentice Hall, 2007. A strong overview of the standard operating system design issues, plus discussion on many of the concepts used in today's modern operating systems, such as UNIX and Windows.

Tanenbaum, Andrew. *Operating Systems: Design and Implementation*. Prentice Hall, 2006. A great introductory work on both the design and implementation of a Unix-like system, Minix.

Silberschatz, A., P. Galvin, and G. Gagne. *Operating System Concepts*. John Wiley and Sons, 2008. Also known as "the dinosaur book," for the seemingly irrelevant dinosaurs on the cover. A great introduction to OS design. The book has frequent revisions; any of them should do fine.

Books on Unix Kernels

These books tackle the design and implementation of Unix kernels. The first five discuss a specific flavor of Unix, and the later two focus on issues common to all Unix variants. If you were only going to buy two of these books, I'd insist on these last two.

Bach, Maurice. *The Design of the Unix Operating System*. Prentice Hall, 1986. A good discussion on the design of Unix System V Release 2.

McKusick, M., K. Bostic, M. Karels, and J. Quarterman. *The Design and Implementation of the 4.4BSD Operating System.* Addison-Wesley, 1996. A good discussion on the design of the 4.4BSD system by the system designers.

McKusick, M. and G. Neville-Neil. *The Design and Implementation of the FreeBSD Operating System.* Addison-Wesley, 2004. A good discussion on the design and implementation of FreeBSD 5.2.

McDougall, R. and J. Mauro. *Solaris Internals: Solaris and OpenSolaris Kernel Architecture.* Prentice Hall, 2006. An interesting discussion on the core subsystems and algorithms in the Solaris kernel.

Cooper, C., and C. Moore. *HP-UX 11i Internals.* Prentice Hall, 2004. A look at the internals of HP-UX and the PA-RISC architecture.

Vahalia, Uresh. *Unix Internals: The New Frontiers.* Prentice Hall, 1995. A superb book on modern Unix features, such as thread management and kernel preemption.

Schimmel, Curt. *UNIX Systems for Modern Architectures: Symmetric Multiprocessing and Caching for Kernel Programmers.* Addison-Wesley, 1994. A superb book on the perils of supporting a modern Unix on a modern architecture. Highly recommended.

Books on Linux Kernels

These books, as with this one, discuss the Linux kernel. There are not too many good books in this category. These two, however, I recommend.

Benvenuti, Christian. *Understanding Linux Network Internals.* O'Reilly and Associates, 2005. A deep dive into Linux networking.

Corbet, J., A. Rubini, and G. Kroah-Hartman. *Linux Device Drivers.* O'Reilly and Associates, 2005. An excellent discussion on how to write device drivers for the 2.6 kernel, with a focus on the programming interfaces supporting various types of devices.

Books on Other Kernels

Understanding your competitors never hurts. These books discuss the design and implementation of operating systems other than Linux. See what they got right and what they got wrong.

Kogan, M. and H. Deitel. *The Design of OS/2.* Addison-Wesley, 1996. An interesting look at OS/2 2.0.

Singh, Amit. *Mac OS X Internals: A Systems Approach.* Addison-Wesley Professional, 2006. A treatise on the entire Mac OS X system that is as deep as it is wide.

Solomon, D., and M. Russinovich. *Windows Internals: Covering Windows Server 2008 and Windows Vista.* Microsoft Press, 2009. An interesting look at a rather non-Unix operating system.

Books on the Unix API

In-depth discussions of the Unix system and its API are important not only for writing powerful user-space programs, but for also understanding the responsibilities of the kernel.

Love, Robert. *Linux System Programming*. O'Reilly and Associates, 2007. My own work on system-level Linux programming, covering the Linux system call and libc API and attention to Linux-specific tricks and tips.

Stevens, W.R. and S. Rago. *Advanced Programming in the UNIX Environment*. Addison-Wesley, 2008. An excellent if not definitive discussion on the Unix system call interface.

Stevens, W. Richard. *UNIX Network Programming, Volume 1*. Prentice Hall, 2004. A classic text on the sockets API used by Unix systems.

Books on the C Programming Language

The Linux kernel, along with much of the Linux system, is written in C. These two books own that subject.

Kernighan, B. and D. Ritchie. *The C Programming Language*. Prentice Hall, 1988. The definitive book on C programming language, written by the author of C and his coworker.

van der Linden, Peter. *Expert C Programming*. Prentice Hall, 1994. A great discussion on some of the less understood details in C. The author has a wonderful sense of humor.

Other Works

This is a collection of other books not strictly related to operating systems, but discussing topics that undoubtedly affect them.

Hofstadter, Douglas. *Gödel, Escher, Bach: An Eternal Golden Braid*. Basic Books, 1999. A profound and indispensable look at human thought that delves wildly into multiple subjects, including computer science.

Knuth, Donald. *The Art of Computer Programming, Volume 1*. Addison-Wesley, 1997. An invaluable tome on the fundamental algorithms of computer science, including best- and worst-fit algorithms used in memory management.

Websites

Kernel.org. The official repository of the kernel source. It is also home to a large number of the core kernel hacker's patches. www.kernel.org.

Linux Weekly News. An excellent news site with smart, accurate commentary on the week's Linux news, including kernel happenings. Highly recommended. www.lwn.net.

OS News. Operating System News, along with original articles, interviews, and reviews. www.osnews.com.

Index

B

N

O

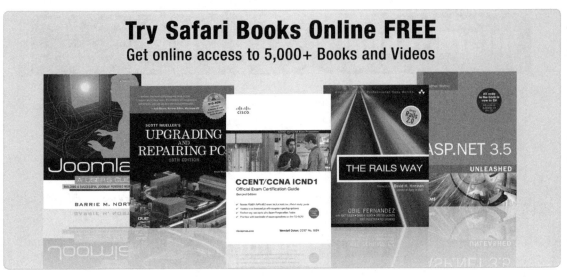

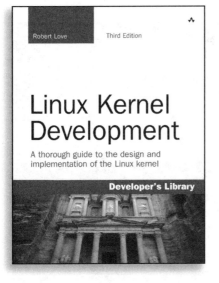

FREE Online Edition

Your purchase of **Linux Kernel Development** includes access to a free online edition for 45 days through the Safari Books Online subscription service. Nearly every Addison-Wesley Professional book is available online through Safari Books Online, along with more than 5,000 other technical books and videos from publishers such as Cisco Press, Exam Cram, IBM Press, O'Reilly, Prentice Hall, Que, and Sams.

SAFARI BOOKS ONLINE allows you to search for a specific answer, cut and paste code, download chapters, and stay current with emerging technologies.

Activate your FREE Online Edition at
www.informit.com/safarifree

> **STEP 1:** Enter the coupon code: IPAFGDB.

> **STEP 2:** New Safari users, complete the brief registration form.
> Safari subscribers, just log in.

Safari
Books Online